P9-CEF-406

"The Cuisinart Cooking Club is dedicated to the advancement of home cooking in America. Some of the recipes in this book have appeared in *The Pleasures of Cooking*, the club's bi-monthly magazine for cooking enthusiasts."

CUISINE of the AMERICAN SOUTHWEST

CUISINE
of the
AMERICAN SOUTHWEST

by Anne Lindsay Greer

Cuisinart Cooking Club, Inc., Publisher
Greenwich, Connecticut

1817

HARPER & ROW, PUBLISHERS, New York

Cambridge, Philadelphia, San Francisco, London
Mexico City, São Paulo, Sydney

Copyright © 1983 by Cuisinart Cooking Club, Inc.

Second Edition

All rights reserved. Printed in the United States of America. No part of this book may be used or reproduced in any manner whatsoever without written permission except in the case of brief quotations embodied in critical articles and reviews. For information address Harper & Row, Publishers, Inc., 10 East 53rd Street, New York, N.Y. 10022. Published simultaneously in Canada by Fitzhenry & Whiteside Limited. Toronto.

Art Direction by Christine Goulet
Design by Anne M. Teters
Illustration by Leslie Szabo and Gerry O'Hearn
Photography by Jeffrey Weir

Greer, Anne Lindsay.
    Cuisine of the American Southwest.
    Includes index.
    1. Cookery, American — Southwestern States.
    I. Title.
TX715.G816   1983   641.5979   83-47650
ISBN 0-06-181320-6

Dedication:

To my many Mexican-American friends, especially Jesse and Carmen Calvillo, Mary Trevino, the Ringland-Winston family of South Texas, Dave Guarduno and the de Baca family of New Mexico, Joe and Tony Franco and Ninfa Laurenzo, who generously shared family traditions and recipes that made this book possible.

Acknowledgements:

To my editor, Melanie Barnard, to Christine Goulet whose art direction made this book as lovely as it is, and to Barbara Somers who diligently tested and tasted every recipe.

TABLE OF CONTENTS

CUISINE of the AMERICAN SOUTHWEST

Few regional styles of American cooking have as wide and diversified appeal as the Mexican food of the Southwest. The dishes may vary from state to state, even city to city, but a common style of cooking, a blend of ingredients seasoned with a festive romantic spirit, unifies all Mexican-American cuisine.

The current popularity of "Tex-Mex" food and a flood of recent articles and regional books all lead to the same question. What is Tex-Mex, Cal-Mex, Sante Fe Style, Sonora Style? A casual answer could easily lead to a national controversy. Southwesterners may not be able to define clearly regional cuisines, but they definitely can taste the difference and are quick to voice an opinion. One thing all Southwesterners have in common is a passion for preserving their traditional regional food.

To elaborate on the differences between a Santa Fe Enchilada and a Texas Taco leads to an endless discussion of cumin versus oregano, Longhorn cheddar cheese versus Monterey Jack, ground versus shredded beef and which chile is the authentic one for Chile Rellenos. Whether tacos should be crisp or soft, or Chile con Carne should or should not have beans are issues that will probably not be resolved, at least not in this book.

It is more productive to concentrate on the similarities. Mexican-American food, whether you call it "Tex-Mex" or New Mexico style, is a compromise between the cooking of the Mexican natives, Spanish settlers, and the demands

of the Anglos and Mexican-Americans who have called the Southwest their home for generations. It's the foods that they love, prepared as their mothers and grandmothers prepared them. The roots are many and varied.

In isolated parts of the Southwest, people lived on a rather plain diet until the Spaniards and their traveling commissary arrived. Chiles and spices gave personality to the food. Variety was introduced with new and unusual fresh fruits, such as peaches, cherries, apples and plums. They also brought nuts, white flour, figs, dates, and pomegranates. Other Southwestern areas that bordered on or were part of Mexico enjoyed many of Mexico's fresh fruits and vegetables. These areas have a long tradition of outdoor markets filled with lush and plentiful produce. Avocados, tomatoes, chocolate, vanilla, chiles and turkeys are all culinary gifts from Mexico that have been adopted by the entire world. These foods are as much a part of Southwest Cuisine as the many and more familiar tortilla specialties.

All this blends into a flavorful, sometimes picante blend of distinctive flavors and customs. This book is an attempt to introduce the fresh foods and recipes from the Southwest to the rest of the country.

I have loved this colorful and tasty cuisine since my college days in Arizona and California. Over the past ten years of teaching cooking classes in the Southwest, I have collected many recipes that have become favorites among my family and friends. These recipes and menus are so versatile that they will please and impress your dinner guests as well as be accepted by your children. Southwest food has a personality of its own that is distinctive, fresh, economical, romantic and often unpredictable.

Contrary to popular opinion, it's not all "hot." The amount and kind of chile and whether it is fresh, dried or ground determines the hotness. Some dishes are quite mild and intentionally so. The ever-present table salsas supply plenty of assertive flavor. Be sure to read the introductory material on chiles, and their preparation. A glossary is included to help you with names and terms. All recipes are prepared in the fastest, easiest way, therefore food processor instructions are given. If you don't have a food processor, read the section on *Hand Techniques*.

Besides the old and traditional favorites, some recipes presented here are new inspirations or variations on a classic theme. All have been lovingly gathered from knowledgeable sources, tested with enthusiasm and enjoyed by many. It is my hope that you will use them, vary them and make them a part of your repertoire.

INGREDIENTS

Southwestern cooking really doesn't require a great number of exotic or hard-to-obtain ingredients. Nevertheless, I've included shopping descriptions and usage charts for all comestibles and flavorings called for, set forward so that any mysteries or confusions can be cleared up immediately. If any ingredient is unknown to you, a glance at the entry in the appropriate chart should set you straight.

Many fresh fruits and vegetables and pantry staples are available from well-stocked supermarkets. The same holds true for poultry, meats and seafood used for most Mexican-style cooking. Even though much of the fresh produce is familiar, it is included in the charts for ease of reference, quantities, and storage information. Unfamiliar fruits and vegetables are described in detail, as are herbs and pantry staples.

You will find an extensive listing for cheeses. It is not my intention to write a glossary of Mexican cheeses; however the popularity of Mexican food has prompted some manufacturers to produce cheese labeled either "Mexican cheese" or "enchilada cheese"; even worse, certain packages carry the name of a true Mexican cheese, although the cheese inside may bear no resemblance to the real thing. In years to come I expect there will be more Mexican-style cheese made in greater variety, so some explanation of these cheeses that American cheese producers are trying to duplicate is necessary.

Those ingredients that are not readily available in local markets will often be found in Latin American markets; these include chayote (vegetable pear), tomatillos, and jicama, although jicama is fast becoming a familiar offering throughout the country. Oriental markets carry a number of foodstuffs and flavorings, including cilantro (fresh coriander) which is also known as Chinese parsley, and dried and powdered chiles.

Clockwise from top left: masa harina, jicama, cilantro, pine nuts, garbanzo beans, Mexican Sausage (Chorizo Mejicana), cinnamon (canela), achiote seeds, chiles serrano, corn husks, tomatillos, chayote. Pumpkin seeds and chiles ancho in center.

FRESH VEGETABLES

Vegetables of high quality are an important part of Southwestern cooking. Platters of marinated or crisp raw vegetables frequently accompany meals.

Chayote (Mirliton, Vegetable Pear): Pale green and pear shaped, with light green flesh. A member of the squash family and a staple of Mexican cuisine for centuries. Requires cooking and can be used cold in salad. It is also mashed and stuffed, and even sweetened as a dessert. Faint taste resemblance to cucumber. Buy those darkest in color, hard and firm. Keeps well for 2 weeks in the refrigerator. Available November to April.

Garlic: Mexican garlic heads are bluish-purple and sharper in taste than white garlic; either may be used. Store in a cool, dark place.

Green and Red Bell Peppers: Large green peppers are used in many sauces and as substitutes for fresh Chile Poblano. Red ones are used in combination with green in season. Use both raw, or roasted and peeled. Keep in a dry refrigerated place; do not store in plastic bags.

Jicama: A slightly sweet crisp tuber, eaten raw for snacks or in salad. Similar in texture to apples and water chestnuts. Also used cooked. Keeps for 2 weeks, refrigerated. Peeled Jicama does not turn brown. Available November through June.

Nopales (Cactus): Delicious and succulent, somewhat similar in taste to green beans. All "eyes" must be removed with a knife or potato peeler before preparation. Use in egg dishes, vegetable casseroles, or cold in salads. Wash, cut in squares, and cook in salted water. Choose unbruised cactus; smaller leaves are generally more tender. Refrigerate.

Onions (white, red, yellow and scallions): Second only to Chiles as a common ingredient. Red onions are used less often than white or yellow in salsas, sauces and Ceviche. Store in a cool, dry place.

Tatume or Tatum Squash

Squash: All varieties are used in Southwestern cooking. Choose firm, crisp squash and do not store in plastic bags. Wash before using.

Tomatillos (Fresadillas, green tomatoes): A small green member of the Nightshade family, known to the Aztecs. It is covered with a brown paper husk. Ranges in size from a walnut to a large lemon. Tart lemon flavor, good for sauces. Choose from specimens green to yellow-green with dry husks. Avoid shriveled or bruised ones; do not wash before storing. Wrap between paper towels. Keeps 3 to 4 weeks. Remove husks and wash prior to use.

FRESH FRUITS

Fruits of high quality are an important part of Southwestern cooking. Platters of fresh fruits frequently accompany meals. Unfortunately, restaurants claiming to serve authentic Mexican food often ignore them.

Avocado: Green, buttery fruit available year-round. Use as garnish, in salads or as an accompaniment. Avocados vary widely. The Hass (small, black skin) has fine flavor though the flesh darkens more rapidly than that of smoother varieties. Fuerte, the common green avocado, is flavorful. If you grow house plants from the pits, the leaves make an interesting seasoning. When possible buy unripe fruits and allow to ripen at home. Ripe fruit yields to gentle pressure of the fingers.

Coconut: Use in drinks, candies and baked goods. Freeze freshly grated meat.

Guava: Not widely available; buy it when you see it. Fruits may be sliced to serve with cheese and biscuits or to fill Empanadas.

Limes: Mexican limes are small, light green to yellow, and very juicy. Similar to Key limes. Substitute any lime.

Lemons, Oranges: Both are used in Sangria and Ceviche. Fresh fruit is essential.

Papayas: Ripe when they turn greenish-yellow and feel soft. The large Mexican papayas are not available. Ripen at room temperature, then refrigerate.

Pineapple: Use the fresh fruit in salads, or

slice it for dessert. The skins are used for a flavorful syrup.

Mangos: a tropical fruit, ranging in size from avocado to grapefruit; red to yellow when ripe.

Melons: Southwestern markets carry an astounding array of melons. Melon is served plain or with lime wedges; at breakfast, as an entree accompaniment, or as dessert.

FRESH
HERBS

Basil: Used fresh in soups having a tomato puree base. Combines well with other fresh herbs such as oregano, and dried spices like cumin. Shake or rinse dirt from leaves and dry thoroughly. Store refrigerated in sealed plastic bags.

Cilantro: The leaf of fresh coriander, sometimes called Chinese parsley. Use fresh, as dried cilantro loses much of the distinct flavor. The taste com-

plements and tempers hot chiles. Wash, remove lower stems and dry thoroughly. Store refrigerated in sealed plastic bags.

Epazote: A green sometimes called "lamb's quarters" that escapes easily from cultivation. American plants are milder than Mexican ones, and are used in several ways. Young Epazote is cooked much like spinach, and older leaves are used for seasoning, especially beans. Easy to grow, though difficult to find fresh in markets. Epazote is supposed to reduce the bloating caused by beans, and is therefore often an addition. Store refrigerated in plastic bags.

Mint: Wild mint is commonly used for flavoring soups, sauces and for garnish. Any fresh mint can be used.

Oregano: Fresh oregano is relatively easy to grow and there are many varieties. Although fresh is preferred, you can use dried oregano for any of the recipes in this book. Use in sauces, salads and soups.

Parsley: Not commonly used in Southwest cooking since cilantro is preferred. Parsley, however, seems an acceptable substitute from an aesthetic point of view.

DRIED
HERBS
AND
SPICES

All herbs and spices should be stored in a cool, dry place. Keep spices in tightly closed jars.

Achiote: Deep orange seeds prized for the yellow color they impart to foods. Shown in paste form. See page 2 for achiote seeds.

Anise: Pleasantly scented seeds or oil used for pastries or syrup.

Azafrán (Saffron): The Mexican is not the same as the very expensive true saffron, but either may be used to flavor rice.

Canela (Cinnamon, both ground and stick): The bark of Mexican cinnamon is slightly different in both

taste and appearance. Use in meat fillings, sauces and desserts.

New Mexico Chile Powder

Gebhardt's Chile Powder

Ancho or California Pasilla Chile Powder

Chile Powders: (See Chile section) Keep on hand a good selection of mild and hot chile powders, as well as a good commercial product such as Gebhardt's. New Mexico chile powder is pure ground chile from Ristra Chiles, bright red in color and less so when mixed with other spices. When Ristra chiles are less hot, supplement with chile de Arbol or cayenne powder.

Cumin (Comino): Ground cumin is used extensively in soups, sauces and meat dishes.

Paprika: Powder from a sweet chile. Use it in combination with other chile powders, or for garnish.

Manzanilla: Dried flowers used to make a flavorful tea.

5

Shrimp, dried or powdered (Camaron Seca): Powdered shrimp is used to season and flavor egg dishes. Both whole and powdered shrimp may be found in Oriental markets. Should be toasted before use.

NUTS AND SEEDS

Nuts are widely used in Mexican-American cooking. Be sure to refrigerate them, or if you wish to keep them for a month or longer, freeze them.

Pecans: Native to Mexico and used extensively in pralines and desserts. Often added to make a caramel-nut sauce for crepes.

Pine Nuts (Piñon, Pignolas): Seeds of large pine cones from trees grown throughout Arizona and New Mexico.

Unshelled Pumpkin Seeds

Shelled Pumpkin Seeds

Pumpkin Seeds (Pepitas): Used, ground, for sauces or whole as a snack. Available shelled, either unsalted or lightly salted.

Sesame Seeds: Used whole as garnish; ground, used in sauces.

MEATS POULTRY AND SEAFOOD

Beef (Skirt Steaks; Shoulder; Chuck; Bottom Round; Rib-eye; Tenderloin (See Food Processor Techniques): Beef may be used ground, or boiled and then shredded, for many Tortilla Specialties. This is a matter of custom and personal preference. You may substitute shredded, cooked meat wherever ground meat is specified. The ever-present garlic and onion in a recipe must first be cooked, and 1 to 2 tablespoons additional fat per pound is needed when substituting shredded meat for ground. Skirt steaks are the usual cut used for outdoor grilling. Tenderloin is as common, though quite expensive. When grilling, use any good steak cut. Quite often prime cuts are used for Chile con Carne. Less tender cuts, like Shoulder, Chuck or Bottom Round, are used for Guisado (stew) or other preparations where meat is boiled.

Chorizo: Spanish Chorizo is a firm smoked sausage often used in Paella. The Mexican Chorizo is quite different. It is sold in casings or in bulk. I prefer bulk Chorizo, coarsely ground; use it in all recipes in this book, except Paella. If you cannot find it, make your own, or buy a seasoned pork sausage. Add 2 to 3 teaspoons of pure ground Chile Powder, 2 tablespoons of vinegar and several sprigs of finely chopped cilantro per pound.

Poultry: Chicken and turkey are used in hundreds of preparations. Most commonly, hens or whole chickens are poached in a flavorful stock. The meat is shredded for Tortilla Specialties, and the stock reserved for soups or Red and Green Chile Sauces. Leftover chicken and turkey may be used in many recipes.

Salt Water Fish, Fresh: Many of the fish from the warm Gulf of Mexico are available locally only. Red Snapper (frozen as well as fresh) is most commonly used in cooking. Salt water fish suitable for Ceviche are redfish, flounder, turbot and shark. Almost any fish is enhanced by a Southwestern-style sauce, which can be mild or picante, depending on the chiles used.

Shellfish: Shellfish, particularly shrimp, crab and scallops, is used a great deal in Tortilla Specialties, Ceviche and salads. Use fresh when available. Frozen shellfish is quite suitable for many recipes.

CHEESES

When the Spaniards brought cattle to Mexico and to the American Southwest, they taught the native peoples how to make cheese. The techniques were typically European but soils and climate were so different that the cheeses had their own distinctive tastes.

The combination of rich flavor and good melting quality is the prized characteristic of some cheeses. Others have a lightly salted flavor and crumble easily. Because it is difficult to obtain Mexican cheeses, Southwesterners have come up with their own substitutes. Cheesemakers in Texas and California are producing white cheeses labeled Pañela, Asadero, Queso Fresco, and Enchilada.

The following is a guide to both Mexican cheeses produced in the United States and to American or imported cheeses commonly used in Mexican-American cooking. There are many regional favorites and I suggest you try those readily available in supermarkets. Experiment with different combinations of cheeses, letting your personal preference be your guide.

Anejo (Mexican): A very strong, salty, white cheese not readily available in the U.S. usually used grated or shredded. It is similar to Feta. To substitute, combine 3 parts of Feta to 1 part of dry cottage cheese, or Gruyère and dry cottage cheese, or use Parmesan. Use as a filling for Enchiladas.

Asadero, Chihuahua, or Mennonite Cheese: Also referred to as Oaxaca. A creamy white Mexican cheese with a tangy, salty taste. Available imported in some large cities. Melts and forms strings; has a high fat content. Substitute Longhorn Cheddar, Swiss, or a combination of Monterey Jack and Mozzarella. Use for grilled cheese or melted atop Enchiladas.

Cojack (Wisconsin): A combination of Colby Cheddar and Monterey Jack that is seen frequently in Southwestern markets. Use for Enchiladas, Nachos, Sandwiches and Southwestern Specialties.

Farmer's Cheese: A dry cottage cheese, often called "baker's cheese." Some cheese sold under this label is actually more like Monterey Jack and will be somewhat yellow in color with a rubbery texture. Substitute dry cottage cheese or ricotta cheese. Use as an accompaniment to fruit; for Sweet Empanada filling, or as Enchilada filling or topping.

Havarti (Danish): A soft, mild, creamy cheese that is an excel-lent accompaniment to Mexican dishes. Good combined with Mozzarella in Enchiladas or substituted for other cheeses in sweet combinations such as Cheese and Raisin fillings. Use chilled with fruit, in Enchiladas, Chile with Cheese, and Nachos.

Jalapeño Cheese: Usually Asadero cheese mixed with chopped Jalapeño chiles.

Longhorn Cheddar: A mild Cheddar, less sharp than Wisconsin Cheddar. Used extensively in Southwestern cooking. Often combined with Monterey Jack. I prefer it to the American processed cheeses more commonly used in Chile con Queso. Use for Nachos; Enchiladas; Chiles with Cheese; melted on Chalupas; and in Southwestern Specialties.

Monterey Jack: A white cheese widely available throughout the U.S. Similar to white Mexican cheeses, though less salty. In combination with Mozzarella, it is similar to Asadero and used as such. Can also be combined with Swiss or Muenster. Use for or with Enchiladas, Nachos, Soups, Chalupas, and Grilled Cheese.

Mozzarella: Whole milk Mozzarella has good melting qualities and forms strings. It combines well with Monterey Jack as a substitute for Asadero or Oaxaca cheese. The skim milk variety, grated, is a fine white garnish cheese. Use melted atop Enchiladas; for Grilled Cheese; Chiles Rellenos; grated atop Chalupas; and in soups.

Pañela (Mexican): A mild, white, non-salty cheese. Some California cheeses are labeled Pañela. True Pañela is more acid and spongy than cream cheese. Substitute Monterey Jack. Serve cold as a garnish or with fruit.

Queso Fresco (Mexican): A perishable white cheese made with rennet. Not soft like cream cheese; more closely resembles dry cottage cheese or Farmer's Cheese, though saltier. There are, however, some cheeses labeled "Farmer's Cheese" that are more like Monterey Jack, so be warned. Jimenez and Jalisco both make a good Queso Fresco. This cheese is still made on ranches throughout Texas and New Mexico and is sometimes called "Ranchero Seca." Substitute a good quality white Cheddar, crumbled; a combination of dry cottage and Feta cheeses; or so-called "Enchilada" cheese. Use, crumbled, to top or fill Enchiladas, salads, and Vegetables. Also often served with fresh fruits or avocado.

CANNED VEGETABLES

Capers: Those capers labeled "Mexican" are large; use if available. Otherwise substitute any capers.

Chiles (See Chile Section): Keep a good selection — 3 to 4 cans — of garnish chiles (Jalapeño and Serrano) and whole and diced green chiles, both mild and picante.

Corn (canned or frozen): Use as a vegetable, or combine with Masa for Tamale Pies and Cornbread.

Garbanzo Beans: Use in soups or salads.

White Hominy

Yellow Hominy

Hominy: Both white and yellow are available. Use for Tamale dough, as a vegetable or in soup.

Hearts of Palm: Tender portion of a palm tree. Not available fresh. Use in soups and salads.

Italian Style Plum Tomatoes: The best substitute when fresh red tomatoes are unavailable.

Nopalitos: Tender cactus strips or chunks used in egg dishes, salads and omelettes. Must be washed several times before use.

Pimientos: Used in many sauces and dressings, and as a garnish. May be substituted for red bell peppers.

Tomatillos (Fresadillas, green tomatoes): Substitutes for fresh tomatillos. Liquid should be drained. You may combine with a few fresh, unripe green tomatoes for a fresher taste.

DRIED AND CANNED FRUITS

Dried Fruits (Raisins, Apricots, etc.): Use in fillings for Empanadas, Tamales and pastries, often in combination with meat.

Guava Paste

Membrillo Paste

Fruit Paste: (Guava, Mango, Membrillo Quince, Payaya): Serve with cheese and biscuits for desserts; use in Empanadas. Refrigerate after opening.

Mangos: Usually packed in large cans; suitable to use wherever mangos are specified.

MISCELLANEOUS PANTRY ITEMS

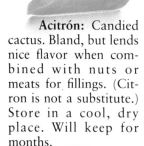

Acitrón: Candied cactus. Bland, but lends nice flavor when combined with nuts or meats for fillings. (Citron is not a substitute.) Store in a cool, dry place. Will keep for months.

Caramel Cajeta

Cajeta: a thick fruit paste or, more commonly, a heavy caramel sauce.

Dried Black Beans

Dried Pinto Beans

Dried Garbanzo Beans

Dried Beans: Dried beans are best bought fresh, in bulk. Best quality is usually found at the health food stores. Fresh dried beans are consistently more tender and delicious than older ones. Store in closed glass containers. Do not soak before using; refrigerate after cooking.

Candied Pumpkin

Candied Orange

Candied Sweet Potato

Candied Fruits & Vegetables (Pumpkin, Orange and Sweet Potatoes): Available both dried and canned. Softer and sweeter than domestic products. Delicious additions to meat fillings, Empanadas and fruit pastries. Perishable. Refrigerate or freeze.

Chicharrónes: Fried pork rinds used in egg dishes or as soup garnish. Store in airtight containers.

Coconut Milk (Cream of Coconut): A thick coconut "cream" used for drinks or fruit ices.

Corn Husks (Hojas): Essential for making Tamales. Available in most Mexican markets, or by mail order. You may also use dried fresh corn husks.

Corn Tortilla: a soft flat pancake made from fresh ground corn flour (masa) and used as a bread. Thickness will vary. See 'How to use Corn and Flour Tortillas' on page 23.

Cuban Biscuits: Mildly sweet biscuits served with white cheese and fruits. Bremner wafers are a good substitute. Made in

Florida, and sold in Latin markets.

Flour Tortilla: a soft flat pancake made from white flour, water, salt and shortening and used as a bread. See 'How to Use Corn and Flour Tortillas' on p. 23 for uses, and p. 240 for recipe.

Grenadine Syrup: Made from the juice of pomegranates and used to flavor drinks.

Instant Grits: Ground white Posole (hominy) useful for making Tamales.

Kahlua: Coffee-flavored liqueur.

Lard (Manteca): Good lard is difficult to find, but for Tamales and some baked products lard produces the best results. Substitute solid shortening if desired.

Masa Harina: Dehydrated ground corn flour for Tamales or other Tortilla Specialties. Substitute for fresh masa.

Mexican chocolate: block chocolate made with cinnamon. It

is sweeter and grainier than American or European chocolate.

Oil: Use your favorite vegetable or olive oil for vinagrette dressings and marinades. Peanut oil is recommended for deep frying in place of traditional lard. Food thus may be fried at a higher temperature and will absorb less fat.

Orange Liqueur: Use in Sangria.

Piloncillo: Unrefined sugar in cone shapes, similar to dark brown sugar, used in syrups and sauces. Sometimes called panocha. Substitute dark brown sugar.

Posole: If available, usually found in the meat section. *Posole* is dried corn which must be soaked in pickling lime to make *nixtamal*, which is ground into fresh masa dough for Tortillas and Tamales.

Rice (long grain): Whole-grain rice is essential; pre-cooked or quick-cooking rice is not suitable.

Tamarind: the brown pods, classified

as a fruit, from the tamarind tree. Filled with 4 to 5 pulp-filled seeds, eaten as a candy or soaked and used in various drinks.

Vermicelli: thin spaghetti used in Sopa de Fideo.

CHILES

The Aztec "chilli" or the Spanish "chile" is known to have existed as early as 700 B.C., but its birthplace remains a mystery. To understand, appreciate or cook Mexican-American food, one must first come to grips with the chile or, as it is often called the "chile-pepper."

More chiles are produced and consumed than any other seasoning in the world. No other ingredient resists standardization with such persistence. All chiles retain an element of unpredictability. While it is true that they are an integral part of all Mexican-American cooking it is not true that all Mexican food or all chiles are hot. The hundreds of varieties with similar or inconsistent names add to the confusion. Some problems stem from the differences in climatic conditions and soil; others from the nature of the plant itself.

Early South and Central American cultures used chiles for me-

dicinal purposes, currency, and as a discipline for disobedient children. It has been thought to be an aid to digestion, to give protection from colds and to cure everything from a toothache to colic to an indifference towards romance.

Separating fact from folklore eliminates some of the mystique from chiles, but these statements remain undisputed:

1. Chiles are high in vitamins A and C. One ounce of dried chile has 2 times the daily requirement of vitamin A.
2. Chiles serve as a natural meat preservative by retarding the oxidation of fats.
3. Chile added flavor and personality to an otherwise bland diet of early Southwesterners.
4. Once you include chile in your cooking, you will quite possibly become addicted.

After Columbus discovered chiles in the West Indies (though he called them peppers), they were enthusiastically adopted by the rest of the world. Indian food, Szechuan sauces, Cajun cooking Indonesian and South African cuisines all depend on chiles for their assertive flavors.

Chiles are named for their color (chile colorado), their use (chile de ristra), their shape (chile Ancho), their place or origin (chile Anaheim, Chimaya) or their hotness (Numero

6). Confusion stems not only from the wide variety of chiles but also from the custom of changing the name of the chiles as they turn red and are dried. For example, chile Ancho is a dried Poblano chile. What's more confusing is the fact that this same chile (Ancho) is called Pasilla in California!

Rather than attempt to categorize all chiles, I will concentrate on those most likely to be found in American markets. The Glossary includes identification of the most common chiles, both Mexican and American. If chiles, fresh, dried or powdered are not available in your supermarket, try a small specialty market, an Oriental market or check the Latin community in your area. Supermarkets operate on supply and demand and frequent requests usually produce results. In any event, mail order sources are given.

FRESH LARGE
COOKING
CHILES

Chiles and peppers come in easily identified varieties like the bell pepper, or may be so specialized and varied that the University of New Mexico has them categorized on a scale from 1-10. In order to simplify a complicated subject I have limited my descriptions to the most common chiles likely to be found in American supermarkets.

All green chiles and peppers should be stored in the refrigerator, in a dry space lined with paper towels. Do not store in plastic bags.

California Green Chile: Also called Anaheim. Widely available. Bright green in color, ranging from 6-8 inches long to 1½ inches wide, usually with a rounded tip. Firm and thick-fleshed. Seldom hot, though the same chile (also called Anaheim) is hotter when grown in New Mexico. SUBSTITUTE canned, mild green chiles. USE for Stuffed Chiles, Chiles with Cheese, sauces, casseroles, egg dishes.

Green Bell Pepper: Available year round in all areas. USE in sauces, stews, soups, meat fillings, and as a substitute for fresh chiles. Roasted, peeled and pureed, green peppers may be combined with canned hot green chiles to make a substitute for mild green chile puree. This would be used for Guacamole, fillings or pureed sauces.

New Mexico Green Chile: Also called Chile Verde, Anaheim, Big Jim and a variety of regional names. Bright green, similar in shape to the California Ana-

heim though ranging in length from 4 to 8 inches, often with more pointed tip. Medium hot to hot. Available August through November. SUBSTITUTE fresh California green chiles (though milder); canned, medium hot to hot green chiles; or a combination of mild green chiles and Jalapeño chiles. USE for Stuffed Chiles, Chiles with Cheese, relishes, sauces, stews.

Poblano: Sometimes called Mulato or misnamed Pasilla. Not widely available. Large and dark green chile. Ranges from mild to medium hot with full, distinct, pleasant flavor. Will be referred to as Poblano in this book. Use within 3-4 days or roast and freeze in plastic bags without peeling. SUBSTITUTE California Anaheim, fresh or mild canned, or, green bell or Italian peppers, roasted and peeled. USE for Stuffed Chiles, Chile Strips, and Chiles with Cheese.

Red Bell Pepper: Available in many areas for 6-9 months of the year. Combines well with Poblano chiles or Green Bell Peppers. SUBSTITUTE canned red peppers or bottled pimientos: use slightly less of a preserved product as they are sweeter and have more distinctive flavors. USE for Chile Strips, sauces, salads, casseroles.

FRESH
GARNISH & RELISH
CHILES

Fresno: Found only in California. About the size of a Jalapeño, only conical in shape. Very hot. SUBSTITUTE fresh or canned Jalapeño or Serrano chiles. USE for relishes (salsas), and sauces.

Guero: Yellow pepper about the size and shape of a Jalapeño. Similar chile varieties are yellow wax or Caribe. Very hot. SUBSTITUTE canned or pickled Jalapeños. USE for relishes (salsas) or pickled vegetables.

Jalapeño: A small chile about 2½ inches long by 1 inch wide. All are hot, but the smaller ones are hottest. Sometimes used in their red stage, freshly ground, with egg dishes. Available fresh in most areas; keeps well. SUBSTITUTE canned or pickled Jalapeños, or fresh Fresno or Serrano chiles. USE for relishes, egg dishes, sauces, marinated vegetables, garnishes, Nachos and flavored pasta.

Serrano: Smaller and lighter green than the Jalapeño. Some almost as thin as a toothpick. Very hot. SUBSTITUTE fresh Jalapeño or cayenne pepper; canned Serrano or Jalapeño chiles. USE for relishes (salsas), Green Sauce with Tomatillos, flavored pasta.

DRIED AND CANNED CHILES

Dried Chiles: To simplify preparation without sacrificing authentic flavor, I have recommended using a combination of chile pods and chile powders. Store chiles in a cool, dry place and use within 1 year.

Ancho: This is the Poblano in its dried state. In California often misnamed Pasilla in Texas, Pisado. In this book, all wrinkled skin chiles with this shape, ranging from deep red to blackish color are called Ancho. It is the "Chile con Carne" chile used in many commercial chile powders and gives a rich/mahogany color to a sauce. Wrinkled skin chiles have significant pulp which will steam off easily. Skins are usually not bitter, nor is the cooking or soaking liquid, as is the case with smooth skinned, oven dried chiles. SUBSTITUTE pure ground, brick-red chile powder, 1 tablespoon for every 2 pods; or Gebhardt's Chile Powder, 1½ tablespoons per 2 pods or California Chile Powder (often labled Pasilla), 1 tablespoon per 2 pods. USE for Chile Con Carne,

Molé, Red Chile Sauce, Enchilada Sauce, Meat in Red Chile, Tamales, soups and stews.

Arbol: Resembles Japónes, but longer and thinner. Very hot. Chile de Arbol can refer to any chile powder made from hot dried chiles. SUBSTITUTE cayenne pepper. USE as seasoning.

California Chile Pods: This is the mild California Anaheim chile in its dried state. Sometimes misnamed Pasilla or Cascabel. Brighter red in color than the Ancho and always smooth-skinned. (Sun-dried chiles will always appear brighter and more translucent than oven-dried ones). The shape is similar to its fresh counterpart. SUBSTITUTE pure ground chile powder, sometimes labled "molido," 1 tablespoon per 2 pods. This powder is a lighter red than Ancho powder. USE in combination with Chile Ancho pods in Molé or stews, Enchilada sauces, Red Chile sauces, Meat in Red Chile and Tamales.

Cascabel: A moderately hot chile with exceptional flavor. The true Cascabel is not available in the U.S. at this time. However, in the Southwest many long, red, dried chiles, resembling New Mexico or California chiles, are mislabeled Cascabel. NO SUBSTITUTE. USE in sauces and relishes.

Chile Pequin, Tepin, Petine: Very small and *very* potent red chiles, either round or oval in shape. Originally used by Indians to preserve dried meats; later used to season fresh salsas. SUBSTITUTE Cayenne or Chile Árbol. USE as a relish or in salsas.

Chipotle: Smoked, brick-red dried Jalapeño chiles, usually canned though often found fresh. Very hot with wrinkled skins. NO SUBSTITUTE. USE in egg dishes and relish salsas.

Japónes: The serrano chile, dried. Very, very hot. SUBSTITUTE cayenne pepper. USE for seasoning, particularly in oriental dishes.

Negro: This is probably the true Pasilla, though I feel on thin ice making any such positive statement about chiles. The chile is rarely seen in U.S. markets; if so, it was probably imported from Mexico. used primarily in Molé sauces. Wrinkled skin and considera-

bly longer and darker than the Ancho. Could be labled either Negro or Pasilla. (Many Mexican recipes call for a combination of these chiles and Ancho chiles.) SUBSTITUTE (if you must) 1 tablespoon of dark Chile Ancho powder for every 2 pods of Negro called for in a recipe. USE for Molé sauce.

New Mexico Red Chile: Also called Chile de Ristra. Both New Mexican and California Red Chiles are strung in wreaths and chains. Both are smooth-skinned though the New Mexican chile is often more twisted and smaller. Almost always very hot: mild ones are picked for commercial canneries. Sun-dried chiles are sweet in addition to being hot, and their skins or soaking liquid is not bitter. For a milder chile powder, mix pure ground New Mexico chile powder with California chile powder using equal amounts. SUBSTITUTE 1-2 teaspoons hot chile powder per chile pod. USE for Posole, stews, Meat fillings and sauces.

Canned Red Bell Pepper: a better substitute for fresh red bell peppers than pimentos in jars. Found in Italian markets.

Chiles

Chile Identification

The chart divides chiles into 5 categories:

1. Fresh Large Cooking Chiles:
Used primarily for sauces and special dishes (i.e.: Stuffed Chiles) and tortilla specialties. Sometimes, particularly in New Mexico, they will be used roasted and peeled in relishes.

2. Garnish and Relish Chiles:
Almost always used in their natural state, though sometimes seeds and veins are removed to decrease hotness. Often pickled and canned, but with skins on and unroasted. Used in garnishes and salsas (relishes). Garnish in this way: to finish a sauce, as in Red Snapper Veracruz, or where pickled chiles are added to a sauce, or strips placed atop an appetizer as in Nachos. (Not usually just "decorative.")

3. Dried Chiles, Small to Large:
Used primarily for sauces or to season other dishes. Some of the small ones are sometimes used in very hot salsas, others roughly chopped and added to eggs, though this is an exception.

4. Chile Powders, Pure and Commercial:
Used as substitutes for dried chiles.

5. Canned Chiles:
Used as substitutes for fresh green chiles, both in cooking and as a relish.

How to Buy Chiles and Peppers

These are general rules. Chiles are a bit unpredictable and any rule has numerous exceptions.

Fresh Green Chiles:
Avoid mis-shaped or severely twisted chiles. Among other problems, they are most difficult to roast evenly for peeling. Choose chiles with a bright color, smooth and unbruised skins and free of mold. Fresh chiles should feel firm to the touch

Larger chiles of the same variety are usually milder. Chiles with pointed tips are said to be hotter than round-tipped chiles. Most green chiles, particularly the Anaheim or New Mexican Green varieties, keep 3-4 weeks if loosely wrapped in paper towels and refrigerated in moisture free space. Do not store in plastic bags or they will quickly spoil. All varieties freeze well after roasting and peeling (see p.14 for instructions).

Canned Green Chiles:
Many good canned chiles, such as Ortega, Clementes Jacques, Tia Mia and El Paso, are available. Buy only those that are marked "fire roasted and peeled" and avoid those that are pressure-cooked for they will be stringy. Whole or chopped "Green Chiles" are usually the mild California or hotter New Mexican varieties. Those canned in their own liquid instead of in a brine solution are preferable since less flavor is lost and the liquid can be used in cooking. Chiles canned in their own liquid need not be rinsed. If they are canned in brine, be sure to discard the packing solution.

If using canned chiles for Chile Rellenos (Stuffed Chiles), use thick-fleshed, whole chiles. Ortega makes a consistently reliable product. So does Tia Mia, but these are slightly hotter and more expensive.

All chiles marked "jalapeño" or "serrano" are garnish chiles. They are not roasted and peeled and are usually packed in brine or vinegar and are often pickled with seasonings and pieces of onion or carrot. Though all of these chiles are hot, canned ones are milder than fresh. Most products are acceptable and these hot chiles are useful to combine with mild green chiles to increase their "personality." "Chipotles" are canned in a red sauce and are relatively uncommon and extremely hot.

Red Chiles, Fresh and Dried:
A red chile is a mature green chile left to ripen on the plant. They are as hot as when they are green, but their increased sweetness masks this

hotness. Although most fresh red chiles are picked and then dried, in limited areas sauces are made with the pulp of these fresh chiles. Fresh red chiles and bell peppers should be fully ripe, but firm and unblemished and free of mold spots. Bell peppers may be used alone or in conjunction with other chiles. Both fresh red bell peppers and red chiles freeze well after roasting and peeling (see p. 14 for instructions.)

Dried red chiles seem less hot than when they are fresh and are available in pods or as powder. Although there are some commercially canned red chile and enchilada sauces, I've yet to find one I liked.

The best dried chiles are sun-dried and are transparent, glossy and bright red. Outside the Southwest, it is difficult to determine if this drying method was used. Most commercially available dried chiles are oven-dried which can cause the skins to have a bitter taste. Consequently, I recommend that dried chiles be toasted, soaked and then the skins removed (see p.15 for instructions).

Dried chile pods are usually marketed in plastic packages. Good quality pods will have an even red color free of black or yellow spots. They should also be unbroken and free of insects (a common problem). Fresh dried chiles with a crisp, firm texture peel more easily; ask the grocer how long they have been on the shelf.

Store chile pods in a dry place and use within one year.

Dried Chile Powder:

All chile powders have more "bite" than fresh ground chile or chile pods. Consequently, dried chile powder cannot be substituted in equal amounts for dried chile pulp.

Chile powder made from New Mexican and California chiles will be marked Mild, Medium-hot or Hot on the container and are becoming more widely available. Many commercial chile powders contain spices and seasonings such as cumin, oregano, onion, garlic or salt. Although some people find this objectionable, I see no reason not to use these blends if they are of good quality and fresh. Most of these spices are commonly added to the dish anyway. Gebhardt's is a good quality chile powder with added spices.

All chile powders should have good bright color; if it is yellowish it has probably been ground with the seeds or is old and will result in poor taste and an unpleasantly hot flavor. Since there are many new brands appearing in the market, I suggest that you try them alone or in combination until you find one that suits your taste.

Dark red chile powder is made from the wrinkled skin chile Ancho. The chart on p.11 will help you become familiar with the color differences since names of chiles are often completely reversed or changed from one area to another.

All chile powder should be stored in a cool dry place or in the refrigerator. I often freeze pure ground fresh chile powder to ensure freshness and full flavor.

Chiles

Chile Preparation and Canned Substitutions

Precautions on Handling Hot Chiles:

First and foremost, take care when handling all chiles. The oils found in the seeds and veins can cause skin irritation or severe burning — often delayed in its action. When handling fresh chiles (especially the hot ones such as Jalapeño and Serrano), either wear gloves or generously oil your hands. If, by chance, you are exposed to the hot veins or oils, rub the area with sugar to neutralize. Soap and water are useless at this point.

Roasting and Peeling Fresh Chiles:

Fresh chiles are roasted and peeled to enhance flavor and remove tough outer skins. (The small chile Serrano and chile Jalapeño are exceptions and are roasted and peeled only if added to a cooked sauce.) Removing seeds and veins from chiles is optional and will tone down the "hotness."

To roast fresh chiles, red or green bell peppers, first make a slit in the chile to avoid impromptu "explosions" during the roasting process. Then proceed using one of the following methods:

1. Spear with a long-handled fork and place over the flame of a gas or electric stove.
2. Set, 3 or 4 at a time, on a cake rack over an electric burner on medium to medium-high heat.
3. Place on a cookie sheet and set under a pre-heated broiler 4-6 inches from the heat source.

Chiles are roasted when the skins are blistered and charred — even blackened in some places. Take care, however, not to deeply burn the skin or you may damage the flesh and make the chile bitter. Watch closely and turn until all sides are roasted.

Immediately place the roasted chiles in plastic bags and set in the freezer for about 10 minutes to stop the cooking process and "steam" off the skins. Remove from the freezer and use a sharp knife to peel off the skins. For most uses, the stems should also be removed by pulling outward. This removes some of the seeds in the process. Scrape away any remaining seeds and veins if desired. For Chile Rellenos or Stuffed Chiles, leave stems intact and use a scissors to increase the original slit to allow for the filling. Remove as many seeds as possible taking special care not to tear the flesh. Some chiles tear easily, so it is sometimes easier to leave the seeds in close to the stem, advising guests of their presence.

Roasted and peeled chiles may be used immediately or frozen quite successfully. If planning to freeze, do not remove the skins or the flesh will deteriorate; the skins will easily slip off after thawing. If you plan to use the chiles within a few days, peel and seed them, then immerse in a mixture of 1 part vinegar to 4 parts water with a few tablespoons of oil and 1 teaspoon each of salt and sugar. Store in the refrigerator. As they soak, they will become less picante.

Canned Chile Preparation:

Canned chiles are good substitutes in most recipes. Exceptions are Chile Strips (p. 50), some Stuffed Chiles (p. 202) and some Relish Salsas that lose their character with canned products. I have notes in each recipe in the book if canned chiles can be substituted for fresh. Chile Poblanos, used for the classic Chile Rellenos (stuffed chiles) are seldom found in cans — I've never seen them.

Canned green chiles are packed either in their own liquid or in vinegar or in brine. If packed in their own liquid, include the liquid in the sauce or the chiles may be bland or flavorless. If packed in brine or vinegar, discard the liquid but don't be too zealous in washing the chiles themselves or you also lose flavor. You may discard the seeds from canned chiles, but do not scrape the veins.

When preparing whole chiles for the Stuffed Chile dishes that can use them, select whole, thick-fleshed brands such as Ortega. Handle them carefully so the flesh does not tear.

Canned garnish chiles such as Jalapeño and Serrano need only be drained before using. Transfer to glass containers and they will keep for 3-4 weeks in the refrigerator.

Dried Chile Preparation:

Dried chiles are almost always in shades of red or black, though in some areas of New Mexico it is still customary to dry green chiles for winter use. These are soaked in water and used in place of canned chiles or when fresh are not available.

Dried red or brownish-red chile pods come in infinite varieties, many looking quite similar. However, the skins will be either wrinkled or smooth. The skin of the wrinkled-skin varieties or the larger California Anaheim is easier to remove and will be less bitter. Since only sun-dried chiles have skins that are consistently not bitter, I recommend toasting, soaking and then removing the skins for most recipes. Most of the recorded methods for chile preparation include using the soaking liquid and then blending the chile and liquid to obtain the pulp as a red chile base for a sauce. (This method works well with smooth-skinned chiles, using a blender to liquify the skins.) However, again, since the skins and liquid may often be bitter, I recommend the following method which discards the liquid and separates the pulp from the skin.

Since chile pulp spoils easily, unless you make copious sauces or have a lot of chile pods to use up, it seems more practical to prepare the finished sauce which freezes quite well (see Red Chile Sauces on pp. 46-47).

The wrinkled skins loosen easily by boiling the chiles in water to cover for 10 minutes, then covering and letting them steep in the water for about 45 minutes. (Longer simmering is required for the smooth-skinned chiles and less pulp is obtained.) Scrape the pulp from the skins and discard the cooking liquid. Or, drain off and discard the cooking liquid and process the chiles and some of the chicken or beef stock from the sauce recipe using the metal blade. Press the pulp and stock through a strainer and reserve. Discard any pieces of unprocessed skin.

The resulting paste is often referred to as a Chile Caribe. This pulp is combined with enough stock (and often tomato paste) to make a sauce the consistency of thin catsup and seasoned with garlic, oregano, salt and other spices. The sauce is simple and, in its traditional form, without flour or other thickeners.

Dried chiles are also used for meat stews, classic dishes such as Chicken in Chile Sauce (Molé), Chile con Carne and Meat in Red Chile (Carne Adobada). Each recipe gives preparation instructions and some suggest chile powder as a matter of convenience. If dried chiles are available, however, use them instead.

Well washed, whole dried pods are often added to soups or stews. As they cook or simmer, the skins loosen easily after 30-40 minutes. There is rarely a problem with bitter skins due to the small amount of chile used (2-3) and the presence of many other flavors in the dish. If you use dried chiles in this manner, wash them first and remove the seeds and stems. You may find that many of your favorite soups and stews are enhanced when several dried pods are added. Pureed or whole chile pods, used in place of cayenne pepper, also add a delicate picante flavor to many sauteed or stir-fry dishes.

To Make Chile Powder from Dried Pods:

Roast the chiles, leaving seeds and stems intact, by spreading on a cookie sheet and placing in a 250° oven for 8-10 minutes. Turn frequently and watch closely because they burn easily. Let cool, then break open and discard the seeds. For best results, use a coffee grinder to make the powder.

Commercial Chile Powder Preparation:

Commercial chile powder often should be toasted to remove the raw taste of the chile (each individual recipe specifies if this is necessary). This "toasting" is usually done in a skillet using a small amount of oil. Cook over medium heat, stirring constantly, for 2-3 minutes. Watch carefully because the powder burns easily. A quality commercial powder is a perfectly good substitute for home ground chile, but avoid those familiar brands sold from spice racks.

Chiles

Tempering Chiles and Chile Sauces:

1. To temper dried chile sauces, reduce the amount of chile powder or combine the powder with paprika. You may also increase the amount of tomato sauce, using either fresh tomato pulp or canned sauce.
2. Toasted flour or a beaten egg whisked into the final sauce is another old technique for thickening and tempering the fire of dried chile sauces.
3. Cooked, ground tomatillos temper sauces very effectively, but using more than 4 per sauce recipe will add a slightly tart flavor. (Most people like this addition, but it is a matter of personal preference.) You can use tomatillos to tone down fresh Relish Salsas. For fresh Green Chile Sauces, try cooked tomatillos and strain the seeds if desired.
4. Fresh red bell pepper or Italian red pepper pulp (roasted and peeled, see p.14) also tempers and adds flavor to sauces.
5. Remove veins and seeds from fresh chiles and/or soak them in a combination of 4 parts water to 1 part vinegar to reduce hotness.
6. Reduce the amount of hot green chile pulp and replace with roasted bell pepper pulp to tone down the taste.

Checkpoints for Chile and Pepper Substitutions:

1. When substituting bell peppers for fresh chiles, keep in mind that chiles have a more subtle flavor, so use a lesser volume of roasted and peeled bell peppers. Combining bell pepper with canned green chiles to reduce the hotness is customary.
2. Since some canned (and even fresh) green chiles may be quite bland, you can increase the flavor lost in the canning by avoiding washing the chiles and discarding the packing liquid (only if it is vinegar or a brine solution). You may also wish to add 1 seeded, pickled Jalapeño chile or a small minced hot green chile to increase the flavor. The best advice, however, is to avoid canned brands that consistently give bland results to your recipes.
3. Chile pods produce a lighter and more delicate flavor than powder. Some dried chiles have more pulp than others and, as a general rule, $\frac{1}{2}$ tablespoon chile powder equals 1 pod. But hard and fast rules are difficult to apply, so some experimentation is needed.
4. When using chile powder with added spices, omit or adjust those that are duplicated in a particular recipe.
5. In most sauces and dishes, you can use bell peppers, Italian peppers or combinations of these with canned chiles. (See individual recipes.)
6. Paprika may be used to improve the color of a sauce. Use about $1\frac{1}{2}$ tablespoons to replace 4 tablespoons mild chile powder. Do not use Hungarian Sweet Paprika unless it is to be combined with hot pure ground chile powder.

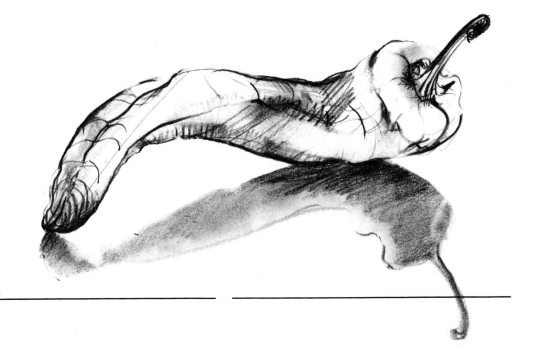

EQUIPMENT & TECHNIQUES

Before the days of current modern equipment, preparing Mexican food was a tedious, all-day affair. It is no wonder that the preparation of dishes such as Tamales, Posole or Molé were reserved for special occasions and needed many helpers in the kitchen. The great amounts of fresh herbs, spices, chiles, fruits and vegetables used required endless grinding, chopping, dicing and pulping. The mortar and pestle (molcajete and tejolote) were essential pieces of equipment for any number of uses.

Today, blenders, food processors, spice grinders and corn grinders have modernized even the most traditional Mexican kitchen. Traditional tools, among them bean mashers, chocolate beaters and molcajetes are now often used for decoration or as serving dishes. Modern equipment purees the sauces, foams the chocolate and grates the onions.

Contrary to popular opinion, Mexican food is not "fast food." There is little room for short cuts, canned sauces or so-called convenience products. Many steps in a recipe may be done ahead and then completed in an assembly line process, but the success of a finished dish depends upon quality ingredients, freshly prepared.

A minimum of special equipment is required to produce good results, and the items are described in this section. All the recipes in this book may be prepared by traditional hand methods, but I would strongly recommend the use of a food processor for the enormous amount of chopping and slicing called for. Any brand will do most jobs nicely, but for some of the breads and the fruit ices, you must have a processor that has a heavy duty motor. Some cooks prefer to liquify red and green chile sauces in a blender, though this is a matter of choice. You will find a processor more useful than a blender, since it will chop and slice as well as blend.

Salsas and guacamole, both used a great deal in Southwestern cooking, have traditionally been prepared with the molcajete and tejolote, the mortar and pestle dating from time immemorial. Before the food processor came along, no other equipment produced good results.

Clockwise from top left: flour tortillas, tortilla press, onions, corn tortilla croutons, shredded cheese, sliced chicken, sliced jicama.

*Equipment
Chart*

EQUIPMENT

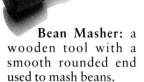

Bean Masher: a wooden tool with a smooth rounded end used to mash beans.

Comal (Cast iron griddle): A comal is a flat griddle available in several different materials and used primarily for making tortillas. It needs to be well seasoned before using and cared for in the same manner as any seasoned pan. It is also useful for reheating tortillas, and roasting garlic and peppers.

Deep Fryer: Many Tortilla Specialties require deep frying and a fryer with a basket is essential.

Food Processor: (see Food Processor Techniques on p. 21) A food processor is useful to puree salsas, sauces and guacamole; slice and chop vegetables; pulp and peel tomatoes; shred poultry and beef; dice, slice and chop onions; slice lettuce or cabbage; mince garlic; shred cheese; mash beans; beat eggs into chocolate; and process frozen drinks into ices.

Lime Squeezer: This is an amazingly efficient though crude looking contraption that squeezes juice from a lime or small lemon. Handy, as a squirt of lime or lemon is often used with salsas.

Molcajete and Tejolote: a three legged mortar and pestle made from volcanic rock, used as a grinding tool.

Molinillo: a carved wooden tool used for mixing and beating chocolate, to foam the chocolate and prevent it from scorching.

Rolling Pin: A short, thin rolling pin is important if you attempt to prepare and roll your own flour tortillas.

Skillet and Tongs: An 8-10 inch skillet is used to soften and seal tortillas. When making enchiladas, it is handy to have two skillets, one for oil, one for sauce.

Spice Grinder: If you wish to grind your own spices or make chile powder from toasted chiles, a spice grinder is essential. Some cooks like the small electric coffee mill.

Strainer: Used to strain raw onions for salsas and garnish.

Tortilla Press: Both iron and wood ones are made. These are not much help with flour tortillas, though indispensable for corn tortillas and recipes using Masa Harina.

Food Processor Techniques

Several food processor techniques are used repeatedly in this book. Rather than explain them in every recipe, I have described them in this section.

Slicing, Shredding Lettuce or Cabbage:

Iceburg lettuce, so often used for garnish and with tortilla specialties is sliced with the 2mm disc (or a disc thinner than standard equipment). If Romaine lettuce is used for garnish, use the 3 or 4mm disc (or one that is standard equipment). The thinner the disc, the finer the lettuce. Thin shreds of cabbage, which are used interchangeably with lettuce, are made with a thin slicing disc.

Pulping and Peeling Tomatoes:

Tomatoes are peeled and the pulp used in a sauce or soup. If preliminary roasting is not called for, you can accomplish this in one easy step using the shredding disc. This technique always uses ripe tomatoes.

1. Core tomatoes and, one at a time, compress them to fit the feed tube placing cut side against the shredding disc.
2. Use firm pressure and process one tomato at a time. After each time, remove the skin that remains atop the disc or the pieces that fall into the bowl.

Double Slicing:

Many vegetables are attractive and cook uniformly when cut in matchstick strips. This is a very useful technique for jicama which is commonly cut into strips for an appetizer. Use either a standard (3 or 4mm) slicing disc or a thicker slicing disc (5 or 6mm). The thicker one produces a cut about the size of a French fried potato.

1. Precut the vegetable to fit horizontally into the feed tube in order to obtain a longer strip.
2. Remove the slices, fitting them back together, to simulate the uncut piece. Load them again in the feed tube, cut pieces upright. Slice again.

Shredding Cheese:

Soft cheeses shred better when chilled. It is important to use light pressure, almost allowing the cheese to "self-feed." Use the shredding disc and use the pusher as a guide, with a "push and release" action.

Cut harder cheeses, like Parmesan or Romano into 1/2 to 3/4 inch pieces. These harder cheeses are always grated with the metal blade. If extremely hard, place room temperature pieces directly into the bowl. Process with the pulse to break the chunks into small pieces, then run the machine until finely grated.

Peeling Garlic:

Generous amounts of garlic are used in Southwestern cooking. You can use the metal blade to knock off the peel as well as mince cloves. Put 1-2 cloves directly in the bowl and turn the machine on and off several times. In most cases the peel separates in several pieces from the cloves. If not, pulse again. Remove and continue processing to mince.

Shredding Meat:

Ground beef is used alternately with the more traditional shredded meat. Both preparations may be done in a food processor. Shredded, cooked beef may be substituted for any recipe using ground beef. Always cook onions and garlic first over low heat until tender. You may have to add 1-2 tablespoons fat if using cooked, shredded beef.

To shred cooked poultry, use a thin slicing disc and have chicken at room temperature or warmed. Arrange long pieces vertically in the feed tube.

To shred beef, have the meat at room temperature. Use the metal blade, turning the machine on and off rapidly until finely chopped.

Raw beef or pork is ground with the metal blade doing from 3/4 to 2 pounds at one time, depending on the capacity of the machine.

Dicing, Chopping and Mincing Onions:

Peel and quarter the onion.

Coarsely: Use the French fry disc with light pressure. Discard any whole pieces of skin that fall into the bowl. If using onions raw, rinse them in a strainer under cool water.

Finely chopped or minced: Use the metal blade. If you are not cooking onions, rinse briefly under cool water, using a strainer.

Chopping Chiles:

If you are using 1-2 chiles only, process them with another ingredient (onions, cilantro or parsley) to aid even chopping. Otherwise, use the metal blade turning the machine on and off rapidly.

Hand Techniques

There are several techniques, some which may be done more efficiently in a food processor, that are repeated throughout the book. These are described below:

Chile Preparation:

(See Chile section, this must be done by hand)

Peeling Tomatoes:

Plunge tomatoes in boiling water (being sure they are covered) for about 20 seconds. Remove and plunge into ice water to stop cooking. Peel and core using as directed in the recipe.

Roasting Tomatoes:

Tomatoes are often roasted to enhance their flavor for use in salsas or soups. They may be cored though this is not really necessary. (The juices are less likely to bleed out if the core is left in.) The easiest method is to use a large, lightly oiled, cookie sheet. Place tomatoes 4-6 inches from the broiling element and roast on both sides until browned and quite soft, about 15-20 minutes total. Cool, then remove the blackened peel and puree as directed in the recipe. (Many cooks do not peel them, which adds color to the sauce.)

Roasting Garlic:

Garlic may be roasted, in the peel, to minimize its strength. The flavor is exceptional. You could use 4 to 5 times the garlic the recipe called for if desired. Place cloves on a cookie sheet and roast 6 inches from the broiling element, turning to roast both sides. They should be lightly browned and soft. Peel and puree as directed in the recipe.

If you have a comal or heavy, well-seasoned cast iron griddle, garlic may be roasted on the comal. The comal may be used as an alternate method for toasting chiles.

Toasting Chile Powder:

Chile powder needs preliminary toasting before using. See the section on Chiles for more information about chile powders.

Combine the powder with the oil or 3-4 tablespoons liquid in the recipe and simmer, stirring constantly for several minutes, over medium low heat. Watch carefully as chile burns quite easily. Chile powder may be toasted in a 250° oven 8-10 minutes but requires careful watching.

Sauces:

All the sauces may be made using the same method as directed in recipes, using a blender instead of a food processor. In some cases, they will be somewhat thinner.

Hand Method For Egg Breads (Pan de Huevos) and Pumpkin Rolls or Bread:

To prepare the dough by hand, use a portable electric hand mixer. The ingredients remain the same, however the shortening should be melted in the milk.

Proof the yeast by dissolving in warm water and sugar. Let it stand 5-8 minutes until a thick layer of foam coats the top.

Beat eggs, sugar and melted shortening with a hand mixer. Add the yeast mixture and 2 cups flour, beating constantly. Beat the remaining flour in by hand with a wooden spoon. It is not necessary to "knead" the dough, however it must be thoroughly mixed and elastic.

Butter your working surface and your hands, proceeding as in the master recipe to prepare the dough for rising, baking and shaping.

Hand Method for Standard Bread Doughs:

This method is for French Bread, Bolillos or Zuni Bread:

Mixing the Dough: Proof the yeast by dissolving it in warm water and sugar.

In a mixing bowl, combine 2 cups flour and salt. Stir in the yeast mixture and 1 cup water, beating until you have a smooth dough. This much may be done with a hand mixer. Continue adding additional flour until you can no longer stir it in. Transfer the dough to a lightly floured surface and knead the remaining flour in by hand until you have a soft, pliable dough.

Kneading by Hand: With lightly floured hands, flatten the dough. Pick up the farthest edge and fold it toward you. Push the dough away from you, using the heels of your hands.

Turn the dough one-quarter turn and repeat. Continue kneading *without adding flour* until the dough is smooth and elastic.

Cover with oiled plastic wrap and let it rise as directed in master recipe.

Proceed as directed to shape and bake bread or rolls.

How to Use
Corn and Flour Tortillas

Corn and flour tortillas are the "bread" of Southwest cooking as well as the base or garnish for many tortilla specialties. The basic recipe for Flour Tortillas appears on pp. 240-42.

When used as a bread, tortillas are served warm and loosely wrapped in a napkin.

Other uses and preparations are described in this section with a step-by-step illustration.

1. To Heat or Soften Corn or Flour Tortillas to use for Bread, Burritos or Soft Tacos:

If tortillas feel somewhat dry, dampen your hand and pat each side lightly. Heat, turning frequently, on a hot comal or griddle until soft and hot, about 30-40 seconds. Alternate methods are:

A) Wrap the tortillas in a tea towel and set them in a collander over simmering water for about 5 minutes. Do not allow the water to touch the tortillas.

B) Microwave tortillas on high power for 30 seconds. Do not heat more than 6 at a time as they will dry out rather quickly upon standing.

For best results, serve warm tortillas immediately.

If making Burritos, Chimichangas, or Soft Tacos, fill tortillas while they are still soft and pliable.

See Illustration (p.26) for Chimichanga method and for two Flauta methods

2. Oil Method to Soften Corn Tortillas for Enchiladas or Huevos Rancheros:

Use about ⅓ cup vegetable oil or equal amounts of butter and oil. In a 10-12 inch skillet, heat oil to about 275-300°. Using tongs, dip the tortillas into the oil, one at a time, just long enough to soften, about 30-60 seconds. Remove and press between paper towels to remove the excess oil. This both softens and seals the tortillas and is the common method when preparing Enchiladas (p.195-201) or Huevos Rancheros (p.64).

3. To Toast Flour Tortillas:

To make Cheese Crisps (p.86), Chalupas (p.126) or Tostados: Brush the tortilla on both sides with melted butter and place on a cookie sheet. Bake in preheated oven 5-8 minutes or until crisp and lightly browned. Reduce the temperature to 300° for larger "Sonora" style tortillas (16-18 inches in diameter), which may be placed directly on the rack. Bake until crisp and golden brown, about 5 minutes.

*How To Use
Corn & Flour
Tortillas*

To make Decorative Shapes and Containers:

Round Bowl: Use a 7 or 10-12 inch tortilla and brush both sides with butter. Press into a buttered pyrex bowl and bake at 375° for 5-8 minutes or until firm. When the tortilla will hold its shape, set it directly on the oven rack and toast 1-2 minutes or until crisp. Use for individual salads, or dips to hold various fillings.

1 Brushing sun-shaped 7" or 10" tortilla on both sides with butter

2 Pressing into a round bowl to bake in a round shell, and finished baked shell

"Tostado del Rey": Use a 10-12 inch flour tortilla and brush both sides with butter. Press into a buttered 4-cup pyrex measure and bake at 375° for 5-8 minutes or until firm. When the tortilla will hold its shape, remove it from the cup and place directly on the oven rack and toast 1-2 minutes or until crisp and lightly browned.

1 Brushing large 10" or 12" (Burrito size) tortilla on both sides with butter

2 Pressing into a buttered 4-cup measure to bake in a decorative shape, and finished baked shell

Sun Shape: Using scissors, cut any size flour tortilla into a sun shape and brush both sides with butter. Press into a bowl and bake at 375° for 5-8 minutes until firm. Remove from the mold and place directly on the oven rack until crisp and toasted, about 1-2 minutes.

1 Cutting the tortilla in a sun shape

2 Brushing sun-shaped 7" or 10" tortilla on both sides with butter

3 Pressing into buttered pyrex bowl and make a round sun-shaped shell

4. To Fry Corn or Flour Tortillas:

For Flat Quesadillas (Cheese Crisps) or Chalupas: Using a skillet large enough to accommodate the tortilla, deep fry in at least ½ inch hot oil until puffed and crisp, about 30-60 seconds. Top immediately with grated cheese. Uncooked flour tortillas may also be fried flat using this method. The result is the same as Navaho Fry Bread (p.236).

For Sun Baskets to Hold Ices, Granitas, or Ice Cream: Using scissors, cut a flour tortilla in a sun shape. In a medium saucepan 1-1½ inches smaller than the diameter of the tortilla, bring enough oil for deep frying to 375°. Using tongs, press the tortilla into the oil. Press the tortilla down in the center, and it will naturally assume a cup shape. Turn to brown both sides. These cook quickly in about 45-60 seconds. Drain and dredge each one in cinnamon sugar. These may be made 24 hours in advance.

For Fried Empanadas: Prepare the dough as for Flour Tortillas (p.240) and then roll each one in a circle as illustrated below. Fill the tortillas and then turn over to enclose the filling, pressing the edges together to seal. Crimp the edges (see illustration below) for a decorative border and then deep fry the Empanadas at 375° until crisp and golden brown, about 60-90 seconds.

1 Cutting the tortilla in a sun shape to fry

2 Dredging fried shell in cinnamon sugar to coat completely

1 Rolling in a circle

2 Enclosing cheese and fruit filling

3 Turning over and pressing edges together to seal

4 Crimping edges

How To Use Corn & Flour Tortillas

For Flautas (p. 152) and Chimichangas (p. 145): Using tongs, deep fry prepared Flautas or Chimichangas at 375° until crisp and golden brown. Drain on paper towels and serve immediately with desired garnishes (grated cheese, guacamole, sauces or relishes).

1 For appetizer Flautas: Placing filling in soft, halved corn tortillas

2 Rolling and securing with a toothpick

1 For Entree for Flautas: Placing filling in softened tortilla

2 Rolling and securing with a toothpick

1 For Chimichangas: Spooning filling in 10″-12″ flour tortrilla

2 Rolling tortilla, folding edges inward

3 Rolling tortilla, folding edges inward

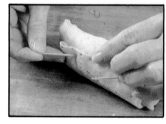

4 Securing with toothpicks

For Decorative Shells: Using the same method and technique as in flour tortillas (p.241 illustration), cut the corn tortilla in a sun shape and using tongs, fry crisp in deep fat heated to 375° and shape as desired. Use as containers for salads, dips, guacamole or as fancy chalupa shells.

Taco Shells: Using tongs, deep fry corn tortillas shaping them as they fry. Fry until they are crisp and hold their shape, about 90 seconds.

Corn Chips or Tostaditos: Quarter corn tortillas and fry 4-5 at a time until crisp, about 60 seconds. Drain on paper towel and sprinkle with salt, if desired. Use with dips, salsa or as a garnish for guacamole.

Soup and Salad Garnishes: Corn tortillas may be used as croutons for soups or salads and are shaped in several ways.
  A) Cut tortillas into thin julienne strips about 1/8-1/4 inch wide and then fry in small batches.
  B) Cut tortillas into 1/2 inch strips and then into crouton size diamonds or squares and fry in small batches until crisp. Drain on paper towels.

5. To Shape and Fry Fresh Masa:

To make Masa Shells, or Chalupas: Press prepared masa into tartlet or miniature quiche shells. Trim the edges with a sharp knife and then push the masa over the lip of the shell. Using tongs, deep fry the shell in oil heated to 375° until crisp and golden brown, about 60 seconds. The dough will separate from the form and is easily turned to brown both sides. Drain on paper towel to remove excess fat.

These shells may be filled with assorted fillings and toppings or used in place of tostados (fried tortilla chips) for Nachos.

1 Pressing prepared masa into tartlet shell and trimming with a sharp knife

2 Pushing masa over the lip of the tartlet shell

3 Frying the shell in hot oil

4 Removing puffed portion with a sharp knife

How To Use Corn & Flour Tortillas

To Make Corn Tortilla Turnovers (Quesadillas): fresh masa turnovers require careful handling as the dough tears easily. The procedure is quite simple, however, it is essential to always peel the plastic wrap from the dough rather than attempt to remove the dough from the wrap.

First form a round of masa dough about the size of a golf ball. Use either a tortilla press or 2 saucers about 6-7 inches in diameter. Have ready 2 pieces of plastic wrap 2-3 inches larger than the saucers. Place one piece of wrap over a saucer. Put the dough in the center with the second piece of plastic on top. Firmly press the second saucer over the dough on top of the plastic to make a round tortilla shape.

Leaving the tortilla enclosed in plastic, remove it from the saucers and place on a flat surface. Roll over the wrap several times in one direction to make an oval and then give the dough a quarter turn and roll in the opposite direction to make a thin tortilla. Place the desired filling in the center and then holding onto the wrap, fold and press the edges together to encase the filling. Trim and crimp ragged edges. Carefully peel the wrap from the tortilla and deep fry 1½-2 minutes at 375° or until golden brown.

1 Forming round of masa dough

2 Placing second piece of plastic wrap over round of dough

3 Placing saucer on top of plastic

4 Shaped tortilla made from pressing down on saucer

5 Rolling tortilla between plastic wrap

6 Folding top portion of plastic covered tortilla over filling

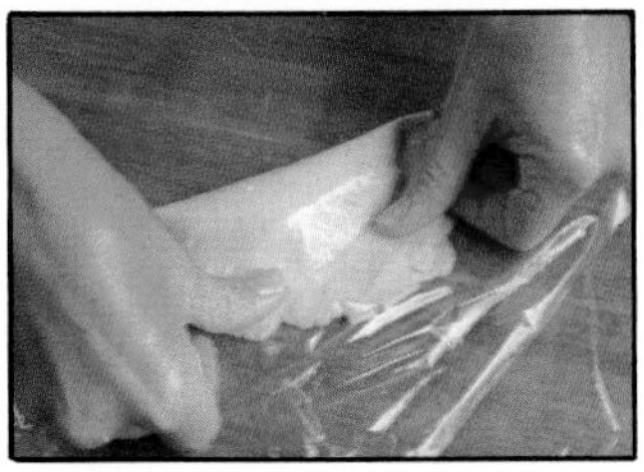

7 Pressing edges together to seal

8 Trimming ragged edges

9 Crimping finished edge

To Make "Little Fat Cakes" (Gorditas): Gorditas are made from freshly prepared masa. Additional fat is usually worked into the masa and then the dough is patted into thick tortillas, about 1/2-3/4 inch by 5 inches in diameter. The tortillas are then deep fried and split across the top to hold shredded meat.

To Make Puff Tacos: Traditional taco shells are formed by shaping corn prepared tortillas into an open half circle as they fry.

Puff tacos are made from fresh masa dough and also shaped as they fry. The fresh masa is fragile and more difficult to handle, but makes a very tender and light taco shell.

Prepare and shape the tortilla as for turnovers (Quesadillas). When you have completed rolling out the dough and have a moderately thin tortilla (see p.28), carefully peel the wrap from the tortilla and transfer to 375° oil in a medium saucepan or deep fat fryer. In several seconds, as soon as the tortilla begins to hold its shape, use tongs to fold it into a half circle. The dough will puff, so take care to leave enough of an opening to hold the fillings. When crisp, drain on paper towel and fill as desired while still hot.

MENU & PARTY SUGGESTIONS

It seems to me that Southwestern cooking came into being with parties in mind. No food could be more appropriate for a convivial occasion, be it lavish buffet, a gathering for the teen-age set, or a family get-together. Whatever the event, there are many, many delectable dishes that will suit it to a tee.

Nevertheless, I feel it is helpful — especially for those to whom our Mexican-inspired cooking is new — to suggest menus for parties and family meals as well. Even to the old hand at Southwestern cuisine, serving suggestions might be welcome; a chance to try novel combinations and pairings of dishes that may not have occurred to you. I know that I am always open to suggestions for arranging pleasing menus — I think all good cooks are.

So here they are — menus for every sort of occasion I can think of. There are Barbecues, both indoor and outdoor, and not one but *two* Christmas menus. I give you Brunch, Luncheon, a Cocktail Party and Dinners; menus fashioned around every time of the day when hungry and congenial people meet to partake of food.

I hope you will take these menus in the spirit in which I suggest them — as guides and inspirations to your own creativity. Southwestern cooking is made for hospitality and good times.

Clockwise from top left: Piña Colada Ice, Guacamole, Marinated Fish (Ceviche), Chile Strips (Rajas), Meat Strips (Carnitas), Broccoli Saute with Pine Nuts.

Brunch

Tequila Sunrise

Fresh Tropical Fruits

Baked Eggs in Tortilla Cups
or Pinto Beans
with Mexican Sausage

Spanish Fritters

Luncheon

White Wine Lemonade

Chicken Chalupas with White Cheese

Almond Dessert

Chile Con Carne Party

Roasted Pepper and Zucchini Salad

Chile con Carne with Garnishes

Fresh Tortillas or Southwest Cornbread

Assorted Mexican Cookies and
Frozen Ices

Cocktail Party

Savory Turnovers (Empanadas)

Tender Beef on a Stick

Chicken Flutes

Nachos

Cheese and Chile Paté

Marinated Fish, Acapulco Style
with Tostados

Margaritas

Mexican Fiesta Buffet

Cheese and Chiles with Tostaditos

Fresh hot Flour and Corn Tortillas
with assorted fillings and toppings:
Guacamole
Avocado slices
Beef Stew
Spicy Meat Hash
Texas Hot Salsa
Fresh Salsa
Sliced lettuce or cabbage
Shredded cheese
Diced tomatoes
Ranch Style Beans

Jicama with Fresh Lime

Fresh Fruit Platter
with Assorted Cheeses

Mexican Nut Cookies

Técate Mexican Beer
with Lime

Teen-Age Party

Piñata with Assorted Candies
and Pennies

Frozen Fruit Punch

Nachos or Cheese Crisps

"Make Your Own Burrito"
with Assorted Fillings:
Refried Beans
Seasoned Meat
Shredded cheese
Fresh Salsa
Chopped tomatoes
Avocado slices

Buñuelo Crisps for Garnishing
Assorted Fresh Fruit Ices

Dinner Party

Papaya-Shrimp Salad
Meat in Red Chile
Wild Spinach with Pinto Beans
Southwest Cornbread
Mexican Chocolate Roll

Dinner Party

Chile Pesto Oysters
Chicken Tortilla Soup
Orange Salad
Pina Colada Freeze
Powder Cakes

Dinner Party
for "Aficionados"

Marinated Fish
Chicken in Chile Sauce (Molé)
White Rice
Zucchini Salad
Caramel Custard

New Mexican Dinner

Stuffed Chiles (appetizer)
New Mexican Grilled Meat
Guacamole Salad
Sopaipillas with Apple Filling
Vanilla Ice

Family Favorites

King Ranch Casserole
Beef and Tortilla Casserole
Enchiladas
Chile con Carne with Nachos
Chicken and Rice
Baked Chicken, Mexican Style
Tacos and Chalupas
Monterrey Chicken and Rice

Festive Indoor Barbeque

Jicama with Fresh Lime

Grilled Meat (deep-fry method)
with Accompaniments
Guacamole served from a Moljacete
Texas Hot Salsa
Chile Strips

Northern Style Cheese
with Chiles

Fresh hot Flour Tortillas

Ranch Style Beans

Caramel Custard

Have guests fill hot tortillas
with bits of meat and
accompaniments of their choice.

Mexican Barbeque

Grilled Cheese

Grilled Meat with Variations

Cheese Enchiladas

Roasting Corn

Cauliflower Salad

Texas Hot Salsa or Ranch-Style Salsa

Mango Ice garnished
with Fresh Mango Slices

Assorted Mexican Candies

New Mexican Christmas

Sopaipillas with Honey

Pork and Hominy Soup

Meat with Red Chile

Tomato and Pine Nut Salad

Buñuelos and Ice Cream

Christmas Party

Tamales (Sweet and Savory)

Salsa of choice

Red and Green Chile Sauces

Avocado Halves

Buñuelos and Vanilla Ice

Anise Syrup

Mexican Chocolate

Mexican Coffee

RELISHES, SAUCES & FILLINGS

Salsas are the salt and pepper of the Southwest. The English translation of "sauce" can be misleading because traditional Mexican-American table salsas are more like relishes. The Red and Green Chile Sauces and special sauces served with enchiladas are more typical of what we usually think of as sauces. These are all tomato or chile based, whether the chiles are green, red, dried or fresh. Relish-type salsas are based on chile and tomato pulp for thickening; true sauces rely on dried chile pulp, tomato paste and in some cases flour for thickening. In this book, relishes are also called "salsas."

Every region, town and even household has its own unique combinations and preparations of the basic tomato, chile and onion ingredients. Most salsas contain chives, though some in California are simply tomatoes, onions and cilantro — to list all variations is impossible. Contrary to popular opinion, not all salsas are "hot" — just the ones the tourists seem to get!

The following recipes are taken from all regions of the Southwest and constitute a sampling of useful and delicious relish salsas, sauces and fillings used in many dishes.

Because the Southwest has a seemingly endless supply of fresh and flavorful tomatoes, excellent salsas are easy to produce. If these are not available in your area, substitute fine quality Italian-style canned plum tomatoes — do not attempt to make a good salsa from tasteless "hot house" tomatoes. Fresh salsas should be used shortly after preparation, but leftovers can be simmered to become a cooked salsa which can be refrigerated for 3 to 4 days and, in most cases, frozen for longer storage. If they become watery, it is customary to stir in a little tomato paste or sauce to correct the problem.

Salsas are used in countless ways as accompaniments to egg dishes, grilled meats, cold seafood and chicken, tacos and other tortilla specialties. You will, I'm sure, find even more ways to use these important "seasonings" in Southwest cooking.

A food processor speeds up and simplifies the preparation of salsas. But the mincing and chopping can always be done by hand; it just takes longer.

Clockwise from top left: Pinto Bean Dip (Frijoles Salsa), Pickled Chiles, Mexican Sausage (Chorizo Mejicano), Green Chile Sauce, Red Chile Sauce, Red Chile Sauce with Meat.

Raw Tomato Salsa

Salsa Cruda

Prepare this when tomatoes are fresh and flavorful. It is one of my favorite recipes and most popular in Arizona. Because I like it quite picante, I use Jalapeño or Serrano chiles. If you prefer a milder salsa, use chile Poblanos or mild chile Verdes (usually the long and bright green Anaheim), roasted and peeled, or you can even use mild canned green chiles in combination with fresh Jalapeños. The addition of tomatillos will also tone down the salsa.

> 3 fresh Jalapeño or Serrano chiles (see p.14 for precautions on handling hot chiles)
> 1 small yellow onion, peeled and quartered
> 4-5 sprigs fresh cilantro or parsley
> 5 very ripe fresh tomatoes, cored or 1 (14½ ounce) can Italian plum tomatoes including juices
> 1-2 fresh tomatillos, optional
> ½-1 teaspoon salt
> ½ cup tomato sauce, optional

Remove stems from chiles and, if desired, scrape seeds and veins. Using the metal blade, pulse to mince together the chiles and onions. Place in a strainer and rinse under cool water to remove bitter milky liquid.

Using the metal blade, pulse to chop together the cilantro and tomatoes. (If using the tomatillos, remove husks and chop with the cilantro and tomatoes.)

By hand, stir together the onion and tomato mixtures and add salt to taste. If the sauce lacks good color, stir in the tomato sauce.

Use the salsa within a few hours of preparation. Yield: 3 cups.

Fresh Salsa

Salsa Fresca

This is similar to the Raw Tomato Salsa except that the tomatoes are oven-roasted. The quality of the tomatoes will determine the taste of the sauce. If you have never roasted fresh tomatoes, I urge you to try it because the taste is delicious.

If you wish a less picante sauce, substitute a 4 ounce can of mild green chiles or 1 green bell pepper for the Serrano or Jalapeño chiles. You could also substitute fresh roasted and peeled green or Anaheim chiles or a combination of two of each for the hot chiles. Personal taste will be your guide.

Some Mexican cooks do not remove the charred tomato peel and feel that it gives the sauce a better color. Feel free to suit yourself.

> 5 ripe tomatoes, cored or 1 (14½ ounce) can Italian plum tomatoes including juices
> 2-3 fresh Jalapeño or Serrano chiles (see p.14 for precautions on handling hot chiles) or 4 fresh green chiles, roasted and peeled (p.14)
> 1 small yellow onion, peeled and quartered
> 4-5 sprigs fresh cilantro or parsley
> ½ teaspoon salt or to taste
> ½-1 cup tomato sauce, optional

If using fresh tomatoes, place them on a cookie sheet and set under a preheated broiler about 6 inches from the heat source. Broil, turning until charred on all sides. Set aside to cool.

Remove stems and cut chiles in half. (If desired, remove seeds and veins.) Jalapeño or Serrano chiles should be placed with the onion in the workbowl using the metal blade. Pulse to mince, then place in a strainer and rinse under cool water to remove bitter, milky liquid. (Green chiles should be minced separately from the onions and only the onions need to be rinsed.)

Remove the peel from the tomatoes, if desired. Place the tomatoes and cilantro in the workbowl using the metal blade and process to puree. By hand, stir in the onions, chiles and salt to taste. If the salsa lacks a good color, add the tomato sauce.

This salsa keeps several days in the refrigerator but does not freeze well. You can, however, simmer any leftovers for 5-8 minutes to make a cooked salsa that can be frozen. Yield: 3 cups.

Texas Hot Salsa
Pico de Gallo Salsa

I'm not sure how this salsa inherited its name because Pico de Gallo is also a traditional Latin American appetizer made with jicama, oranges and red chile powder (see p.107). Literally, the name means "rooster's beak," referring to the way roosters have of chopping up their food. Nonetheless, this is the salsa that gave Texas the reputation for fiery hot sauces. Some old Texas cookbooks have name it "Salsa Brava" (Brave Sauce). The hotness can be toned down by substituting roasted, peeled and chopped mild green chiles for the Jalapeño or Serrano chiles. Fresh cilantro or two fresh minced tomatillos will also tame the salsa and help bring out the flavor. It is interesting that in California this familiar relish omits chiles completely and uses only onion, tomato and lemon.

    **3-4 fresh chile Serranos or 1-2 chile
      Jalapeños (see p.14 for precautions on
      handling hot chiles)
    6 sprigs fresh cilantro
    1 small yellow onion, peeled and quartered
    4 firm ripe tomatoes, unpeeled
      salt to taste**

Remove stems, seeds and veins from chiles. Using the metal blade, drop the chiles through the feed tube with the motor running to mince. (Do not breathe deeply if close to the feed tube opening . . . the fumes are strong.) Add the cilantro and pulse to chop. Remove from workbowl and set aside.

Place the onion in the same workbowl and pulse to coarsely chop. Rinse in a strainer under cool water to remove bitter milky liquid.

By hand, cut the tomatoes into "thumb-nail" size pieces. (If you have a 6mm (thick) slicing disc, you can first slice the tomatoes, then finish the procedure by hand.)

Combine all of the ingredients and add salt to taste. The salsa can be prepared 3-4 hours in advance, but you will need to drain off the liquid before serving. It will keep 24 hours, but some of the picante flavor will be lost.

Texas Hot Salsa is a lively relish for Cheese Crisps, Nachos, eggs or omelettes, hamburgers and tortilla specialty dishes. It can also be used as a base for Chile con Queso or Quick Ranch Style Salsa. Yield: 2²/₃ cups.

Green Tomato Salsa
Tomatillo Salsa

This uncooked green salsa has a distinct flavor of fresh cilantro and tomatillos. You may substitute parsley, but do use only fresh tomatillos or unripe green tomatoes.

Use this salsa with Tostaditos (Corn Chips) or with dishes using white cheeses. Sour cream and avocados compliment the salsa and you might try this combination with cold pork, chicken or fish.

    **1 clove garlic, peeled, optional
    ¹/₃-¹/₂ yellow onion, peeled
    3 chile Serranos or 1 Jalapeño chile, stems
      removed (see p.14 for precautions on
      handling hot chiles)
    12-16 fresh tomatillos (2¹/₂ pounds)
    pinch sugar
    salt to taste
    3-4 sprigs fresh cilantro or parsley
    few drops water, if needed**

Using the metal blade, drop the garlic through the feed tube with the motor running to mince. Add the onion to the workbowl and pulse to chop. Place in a strainer and rinse under cool water to remove bitter taste.

Remove husks from the tomatillos, then rinse and quarter them. Place the tomatillos and chiles in the workbowl using the metal blade. Pulse to finely mince. Add the cilantro and pulse to combine.

Stir together the onions, tomatillos and add sugar and salt to taste.

The salsa should be made on the day of serving. If made 6-8 hours ahead, you may need to add a little cold water as it tends to congeal upon standing. Yield: 2¹/₂ to 3 cups.

Green Salsa

Salsa Verde

During the chile harvest in New Mexico, fresh salsas made with local green chiles are found on every table. The aroma of carefully chosen, fresh roasted chiles fills the air as cooks prepare them for freezing. Chiles that are left to redden on the vine will be picked and strung in Ristras to dry. Restaurant owners make trips to the chile fields for their yearly supply and natives seek out the best sun-dried pods to make traditional Red Chile sauces. It is a colorful sight unique to this area.

The basic salsa of garlic, salt and green chile is used on eggs, with cheese sandwiches, Chile con Queso or over meats. It is nearly always combined with one or more of the options given to make a green chile relish. Since chiles vary in their hotness from season to season, a few minced Jalapeño chiles can be added to make the salsas more picante.

> 2 cloves garlic, peeled
> 5-6 sprigs fresh cilantro or parsley
> 15-16 fresh green chiles, roasted and peeled
>   (p.14)
> 3/4-1 teaspoon salt
> pepper to taste

Using the metal blade, drop the garlic and cilantro through the feed tube with the motor running to mince. Remove stems from chiles and, if desired, remove seeds and veins. Add the chiles to the workbowl and pulse to coarsely chop. Season to taste with salt and pepper. Yield: 2½ to 3 cups.

Here are two variations on this sauce:

1. Pulse ⅛ teaspoon black pepper, 1 tablespoon vinegar, ½ teaspoon sugar and 2 tablespoons roasted and salted pine nuts or pumpkin seeds into the finished salsa.

2. Use the metal blade to mince 1 small onion, then saute in 2 tablespoons vegetable oil until the onion is translucent. Finely chop 3 red tomatoes or 1 (10½ ounce) can tomatoes or 3 fresh tomatillos. (The tomatillos can be chopped with the garlic, but the onions and tomatoes should be stirred into the finished salsa by hand.)

Green Salsa with Meat

Salsa Verde con Carne

This New Mexican relish is surprisingly good served cold as a table salsa and becomes a delicious sauce with some added stock or broth.

I like to serve three salsas with Tostaditos (Corn Chips). These are Raw Sauce with tomato puree from Arizona, Texas Hot Sauce and this one from New Mexico.

> 2 cloves garlic, peeled
> 1 small onion, peeled
> ½ pound ground beef
> 2 teaspoons vinegar
> 1-1½ teaspoons salt
> 15-16 (1 pound) fresh green chiles,
>   roasted and peeled (p.14) or 5 (4 ounce)
>   cans green chiles

Using the metal blade, drop the garlic through the feed tube with the motor running to mince. Add the onion to the workbowl and pulse to chop. Saute the beef with the onion, garlic, vinegar and salt until the meat is browned.

Stem and seed the fresh chiles, then chop fresh or canned chiles using the metal blade. Remove the beef mixture from the skillet with a slotted spoon and stir into the chiles. Adjust seasonings to taste.

Chill the salsa, then remove and discard hardened fat. Serve chilled or at room temperature. Yield: 2-3 cups.

Variation: Omit the ground beef. Peel and slice 1 small eggplant making 6-8 slices. Sprinkle with 1 teaspoon salt and let stand 30 minutes. Drain well, pressing out the bitter juices, then coarsely chop using the metal blade. Saute the eggplant with the onion and garlic in 2 tablespoons vegetable oil. Pulp and Peel (p.21) 1 ripe tomato and stir into the eggplant mixture. Cook a few minutes until soft and tender. Season with an additional ½ teaspoon salt and ⅛ teaspoon pepper to taste. Combine with the chiles as directed.

Red Salsa

Salsa Roja

This is a smooth, picante table salsa that uses pure ground chile powder as a base. It is good hot or cold with Tostados (Corn Chips) or any meat dish. It may also be thinned with additional tomato sauce and heated for use as an enchilada sauce.

This very tangy salsa keeps well about 4 days, but will become less picante as time passes.

    1 clove garlic, peeled
    3 ounces pork back fat or any piece of fatty
      pork
    4 cups chicken stock
    ¼ cup pure ground chile, see note
    6 ounces tomato paste
    pinch sugar
    1 teaspoon salt or to taste
    ½ teaspoon oregano
    6 sprigs fresh snipped cilantro

Using the metal blade, drop the garlic through the feed tube with the motor running to mince. Set aside.

In a large skillet or 2 quart saucepan, fry the pork fat for about 5 minutes until rendered. Discard solid pieces and leave up to 1½ tablespoons fat in the pan. Add 3-4 tablespoons of the chicken stock, the ground chile and garlic. Stir constantly over medium heat for 3-4 minutes to cook the chile and remove raw taste. Watch carefully for the chile burns easily.

Stir in the tomato paste, remaining chicken stock, sugar, salt and oregano. Simmer about 15 minutes, then stir in the cilantro. Serve hot or cold. The sauce may be refrigerated up to 4 days. Yield: 4 cups.

Note: You may wish to double the chile powder if using a mild or commercial variety. As with all sauces, dried pods (see p.15 for preparation) may be substituted for some of the powder. Use 2 pods per 1 tablespoon powder.

Quick Ranch Style Salsa

Rápido Salsa Ranchero

This is a good way to convert leftover Texas Hot Salsa into a cooked Ranch Style Salsa that can be refrigerated for at least a week. It is excellent on eggs, omelettes, spaghetti squash or fish.

    1 cup (approximately) Texas Hot Salsa
      (p.39)
    1 cup tomato sauce
    1 tablespoon minced fresh cilantro or
      parsley
    2 tablespoons tomato paste
    1 teaspoon sugar
    ¼ teaspoon oregano
    ¼ teaspoon black pepper
    1 tablespoon safflower oil
    1 teaspoon vinegar
    tomato juice or water if necessary

Use the metal blade to process all the ingredients except tomato juice until well blended. Simmer 10-15 minutes over medium heat. If necessary, thin with a small amount tomato juice or water. Taste and adjust salt. Yield: about 2½ cups.

Relish
Salsas

Ninfa's Ranch Style Salsa
Ninfa's Salsa Ranchero

Salsa Ranchero is usually a combination of bell peppers or green chile strips, onion and tomatoes that is sauteed in oil. Sometimes tomato sauce is added. The salsa is served hot with grilled meats or eggs.

2 strips bacon
1 tablespoon corn oil
1 clove garlic, peeled
1 large yellow onion, peeled and cut to fit the feed tube
1 large bell pepper, stemmed and seeded
2 ripe fresh tomatoes or 1 cup canned tomato wedges including juices
1-3 mild Jalapeño chiles, see note
salt and pepper to taste

Fry the bacon in a 10-12 inch skillet until browned. Remove with a slotted spoon and add the corn oil to the skillet. Set aside off heat.

Using the metal blade, drop the garlic through the feed tube with the motor running to mince. Change to 3 or 4mm (standard) slicing disc and process the onion. Saute garlic and onion in reserved skillet over medium-low heat for 5 minutes.

Cut the bell pepper into about 6 sections to fit horizontally in the feed tube. Use the 3 or 4mm (standard) slicing disc to process the pepper into long strips. Add to the skillet and simmer about 5 minutes more until the onions are translucent.

Meanwhile, prepare the fresh tomatoes. Place on a cookie sheet and set under a preheated broiler about 4-6 inches from the heat source. Roast, turning until all sides are charred. Watch carefully to prevent burning. Let cool, then remove and discard skin. Cut the tomatoes into wedges and reserve any juices. (Canned tomatoes do not need to be roasted.) Add wedges and juices to the skillet.

Remove stems, seeds and veins from the chiles and slice into thin strips. Add to the skillet and simmer 5 minutes. Add salt and pepper to taste. Use immediately or refrigerate until ready to use. The salsa is served hot. Yield: 2-2½ cups.

Note: Before handling hot chiles, see p. 14 for precautions. The degree of hotness in the salsa is determined by the amount of chiles used. One chile will not overpower the sauce, but adds a nice tangy taste. If you want a mild taste with no chile strips, omit the fresh Jalapeños and add 4 canned whole Jalapeño chiles to the sauce during the last few minutes of cooking. Allow them to sit in the salsa for 15-20 minutes, then remove and discard.

Ninfa's Green Salsa
Ninfa's Salsa Verde

This is the salsa for which Ninfa's Restaurant in San Antonio is famous. When I asked her how it was developed, she answered simply, "necessity." The story is familiar to anyone who has ever researched the origin of a distinctive recipe. A favorite customer wanted a green salsa for the table, but a few key ingredients were missing. Fortunately, the chief cook (Ninfa) was in the kitchen; the salsa was such a success that, until now, the recipe has been kept under lock and key.

This salsa may be made a day ahead since the acid in the tomatillos keeps it from darkening. It will need to be stirred or processed briefly to restore the texture because it tends to congeal upon standing.

Serve it as a table salsa with Tostados (Corn Chips), raw vegetables or grilled meats.

1-3 chile Jalapeños, roasted but not peeled (p.14), see note
6 tomatillos
2 large or 4 small green tomatoes
1 clove garlic, peeled
1 large ripe avocado, peeled and cut in 3-4 pieces
4 tablespoons sour cream
½-¾ teaspoons salt or to taste
white pepper to taste

Remove stems and seeds from chiles and set aside.

Remove husks from tomatillos, rinse and cut in half. Core and quarter the green tomatoes. Using the metal blade, drop the garlic through the feed tube with the motor running to mince. Add tomatillos and tomatoes to the workbowl and pulse to chop. Transfer to a saucepan and simmer 1 minute over medium heat.

In the same workbowl using the metal blade, drop the chile through the feed tube to mince. Add the tomatillo mixture to the workbowl and process to puree. With the machine running, drop the avocado pieces through the feed tube. Add the sour cream and process to combine. Add salt and white pepper to taste.

This is good warm or at room temperature. Yield: about 4 cups.

Note: See p.14 for precautions on handling hot chiles. Use the greater amount of chiles and do not remove seeds and veins to make a hotter sauce.

Spanish Style Sauce

Seasoned Tomato Sauce

This is a mild salsa that is an excellent multi-purpose sauce for eggs, vegetables, chicken or fish. Southwesterners make these types of salsas weekly to keep on hand to make dishes like Ranch Style Eggs and Spanish Omelettes quick and simple to prepare. The sauce keeps well for at least a week in the refrigerator and freezes successfully although all sauces will lose some of their "hotness" within 24 hours. You can easily make it more picante by adding one or two minced canned Jalapeño chiles.

2 chile Poblanos, roasted and peeled (p.14), see note
2 cloves garlic, peeled
1 large red onion, peeled and quartered
2 tablespoons safflower oil
4-5 ripe tomatoes or 1 (14½ ounce) can Italian Plum tomatoes with their juices
½ teaspoon oregano
1 cup tomato sauce
1 scant teaspoon sugar
1 teaspoon vinegar
½-1 teaspoon salt or to taste
¼ teaspoon black pepper
1-2 canned Jalapeño chiles, optional

Remove stems and seeds from chile Poblanos and set aside.

Using the metal blade, drop the garlic through the feed tube with the motor running to mince. Add onion and chiles to workbowl and pulse to mince. Heat the oil in a medium saucepan and add the onion mixture. Saute lightly about 3 minutes until the onions are translucent.

Meanwhile, use the shredding disc to Pulp and Peel (p.21) the fresh tomatoes. (Use the metal blade to mash canned tomatoes.)

Add the tomato pulp, chiles, oregano, tomato sauce, sugar, vinegar, salt and pepper to the saucepan. Taste and adjust seasoning. If you wish a hotter sauce, mince the Jalapeño chiles with the metal blade and add. Simmer the sauce over medium heat for about 20-25 minutes. Use immediately or chill or freeze for later use. Yield: 4 cups.

Note: You may substitute 1 bell pepper or 1 (4 ounce) can green chiles for the chile Poblanos. If using a bell pepper, chop with the onion and saute in the oil. If using canned chiles, drain only if packed in brine. Otherwise, add the liquid to the sauce for added flavor. Chop the canned chiles using the metal blade and add as you would the chile Poblanos.

This is usually served as a sauce for poultry or beef enchiladas, but is excellent for any rolled enchilada.

Mexican tomatoes are deep bright red in color with a sweet, distinctive taste. Only homegrown fresh tomatoes come close. Canned Italian plum tomatoes are acceptable, but the fresh taste is not as evident.

Sauces like this are usually processed in a blender after cooking. This results in a finer salsa with less texture or body. Restaurants use blenders for many Mexican and Spanish sauces.

½ small yellow onion, peeled
8 homegrown ripe tomatoes, cored or 2½ cups Italian plum tomatoes
3-4 leaves fresh basil or ½ teaspoon dried basil
2-3 sprigs fresh parsley or ½ teaspoon dried parsley
1 teaspoon minced pimiento
1 tablespoon vegetable oil
1 tablespoon vinegar
1 teaspoon sugar
½ teaspoon salt or to taste
fresh ground black pepper to taste
¼ teaspoon ground cumin
1¼-1½ cups beef stock

Use a 2 or 3mm (thin or standard) slicing disc to process the onion. Remove from workbowl and set aside.

If using fresh tomatoes, place on a cookie sheet and set under a preheated broiler about 8 inches from the heat source. Roast, turning to brown and char all sides — about 10-15 minutes. Let cool, then slip off the skins and halve the tomatoes. (Canned tomatoes do not need to be roasted.) Using the metal blade, process the tomatoes in two batches with the fresh herbs and pimiento until pureed.

Heat the oil in a skillet, then stir in the tomato puree, dried herbs if using, vinegar, sugar, salt, pepper and cumin. Simmer 5-10 minutes, skimming off foam that rises to the surface. Adjust seasonings to taste, then thin with as much beef stock as necessary to make a medium-thick sauce. Serve warm. Yield: about 4 cups.

Variation: Add an additional ½ cup sliced onions along with 1 cup roasted and peeled green chile strips (p.14) to make a well-seasoned Ranch Style Sauce.

Enchilada Sauce

I find many of the heavy Tex-Mex sauces too thick for my taste and some of the New Mexican sauces too hot. Since I am not always able to obtain pure ground chile powder, I have come up with a lighter sauce using the more readily available Gebhardt's Chile Powder. It may be used with beef or cheese enchiladas or as a substitute for the sauce in Tex-Mex Enchiladas on p.196.

> 2 cloves garlic, peeled
> 1/4 stick (1 ounce) butter
> 6 tablespoons Gebhardt's Chile Powder, see note
> 5 fresh ripe tomatoes or 1 (14 1/2 ounce) can Italian plum tomatoes
> 2 tablespoons tomato paste
> 1 cup chicken stock
> 1 cup water
> 1/4 teaspoon salt or to taste
> 1/8 teaspoon pepper or to taste
> 1/2 cup fresh cilantro or parsley sprigs

Using the metal blade, drop the garlic through the feed tube with the motor running to mince. In a 1 1/2-2 quart saucepan, saute the garlic in the butter over medium heat for 1-2 minutes. Reduce heat to low and stir in the chile powder. Cook, stirring constantly, for 2-3 minutes to remove the raw chile taste. Watch carefully because the chile burns easily. Set aside off heat.

If using fresh tomatoes, use the shredding disc to Pulp and Peel (p.21). If using canned tomatoes, mash with a fork. Stir the tomato plup, tomato paste, chicken stock, water, salt and pepper into the chile powder in the saucepan. Set over medium heat and simmer, stirring frequently, for 10 minutes. Taste and adjust seasonings.

Meanwhile, use the metal blade to mince the cilantro or parsley and stir into the sauce after cooking. The sauce may be used immediately, refrigerated for 3-4 days or frozen for longer storage. Yield: 3 1/2 cups.

Note: If you can easily obtain pure ground chile powder, use 4 tablespoons "hot" or 6 tablespoons "mild" in place of the Gebhardt's Powder. (See Chile Preparation on p.14 for more information.) Increase the salt to 3/4-1 teaspoon and, if desired, add 1/4 teaspoon ground cumin. The sauce is also improved by using dried chile pods (Ancho, California or New Mexican Hot) to replace 2-2 1/2 tablespoons of the chile powder. (See p.15 for preparation of dried chiles.)

Red and Green Chile Sauces

In New Mexico there are two basic sauces, commonly called "Red" and "Green." The Red Sauces are made from dried red chiles or pure ground chile powder and range from mild to hot depending upon the chile used. Dried chiles are soaked or cooked in water to "cook off" the skins and the resulting blend of chile pulp and soaking liquid is called "Chile Caribe." Many Red Sauces are made by combining the Caribe with stock, seasonings, garlic and tomato puree. The specific ingredients and amounts depend upon regional and personal taste.

New Mexico produces more fresh green chile varieties than any other state. The simple basic Green Sauce is made from roasted and peeled chiles (p.14), water, garlic, salt and pepper and are either blended smooth or have the chiles added in strips or diced. Green chile sauces are often added to ground beef to make a thick, stew-like consistency and the sauce is usually folded into hot flour tortillas and served "burrito" style.

There are many methods for making Red Chile Sauce. They can be made from dried chile pods (which make a more delicate sauce), or commercially ground chile powders (usually with added spices) and pure ground chile powders. Another, less common, method is to grind dried pods into powder to make the sauce. This was very confusing to me at first, since some cooks liquify the skins with the pulp and others strain the pulp claiming the skins are too bitter. I subsequently learned that only sun-dried chiles can be liquified with skins. I have found that with most commercially available dried chiles, the soaking liquid is bitter and I prefer to strain the skins and discard the liquid.

Green Chile Sauce

New Mexican Green Sauce

Many cooks still use a blender for all chile sauces, since it is the only way to completely liquify the skins of red chiles and make a smooth sauce. The food processor produces a good textured sauce, especially since the unprocessed pieces of skin can be strained and discarded.

Another point of confusion is the ratio of chile pulp to powder if substituting. Some chiles, particularly the wrinkled-skin varieties, have more pulp per chile than smooth-skin types. This, as well as the amount of tomato or flour added, is a determining factor in the thickness of the sauce.

In view of these variables, I have given one method using chile pods and one using powder with thickening and tempering options for both. For the best taste, I recommend combining fresh pods with powder when dried chile pods are scarce.

Begin with the basic sauce in either recipe, then work with the options to taste. The finished sauce should be the consistency of thin catsup or thick tomato sauce.

This is a standard green chile sauce and comes from Rancho Chimaya, one of the finest restaurants in the Sante Fe area.

> 1 pound (15-16) fresh green chiles, roasted
>   and peeled (p.14) or 5 (4 ounce) cans
>   green chiles
> 1 clove garlic, peeled
> ¼ small onion
> 1 tablespoon vegetable oil
> 2 teaspoons salt
> 1 teaspoon Worcestershire sauce
> 1 tablespoon cornstarch
> 2 cups water
> 2 cups beef broth

Remove stems and seeds from chiles and cut into strips about ¼ inch wide and 1½-2 inches long. Set aside.

Using the metal blade, drop the garlic through the feed tube with the motor running to mince. Add the onion to the workbowl and pulse to coarsely chop. In a large skillet or 2 quart saucepan, cook the onion and garlic in the oil until the onions are limp. Stir in the chiles, salt and Worcestershire sauce. Cook, stirring, over medium heat for 5 minutes. Dissolve the cornstarch in the water and add, along with the broth, to the pan. Simmer 10 minutes, stirring occasionally. Adjust seasonings to taste. Yield: 5-6 cups.

Here are two variations on this sauce:

1. Saute ½ pound coarsely ground beef and 1 small sliced onion with the garlic. Complete the sauce as directed.

2. Pulp and Peel (p.21) 4 or 5 fresh tomatoes or mash a 14½ ounce can of tomatoes including the juices. Stir into the simmering sauce and complete the recipe as desired. If desired, you can also saute 1 small sliced onion with the garlic.

Red Chile Sauce I

This is a recipe for pure chile sauce using pods. Often, tomato sauce is added when making this for an enchilada sauce, but is a matter of personal preference. Both egg and toasted flour are traditional ways to thicken and temper hotness. While bell pepper is not traditional, it does enhance the sauce. This sauce is frequently used in Northern Mexico and Texas in tamale doughs.

You may refrigerate Red Chile Sauce for 4-5 days or freeze for longer storage.

> **14-18 dried chile pods, see note**
> **3-4 cups boiling water**
> **2 cloves garlic, peeled**
> **1½ teaspoons salt or to taste**
> **¼-½ teaspoon leaf oregano**
> **¼-½ teaspoon cumin**
> **⅛ teaspoon ground cloves**
> **⅛ teaspoon ground cinnamon (preferably ground canela)**
> **3½ cups chicken or beef broth**
> **3 tablespoons pork lard, bacon fat or oil**

Options to reduce hotness and thicken (use one):

> **1 egg, beaten**
> **2 tablespoons flour, toasted on a cookie sheet for 30 minutes at 350°**
> **1 fresh red bell pepper, roasted, peeled, stemmed and seeded (p.14)**
> **1-1½ cups tomato sauce**

Wash chiles thoroughly and pat dry. Place on a cookie sheet and toast for 10-12 minutes in a preheated 350° oven. (They should be softened, but not browned.) Cool until you can handle them, then remove and discard stems and seeds. Scrape the veins for a less picante sauce.

Place the chiles in a saucepan and cover with the boiling water. Simmer, covered, for 5 minutes, then let steep, off the heat, for 45 minutes to 1 hour. The skins should be relatively easy to separate from the pulp. (If the skin does not come off easily, see the note at the end of the recipe for alternate instructions.)

Drain the chiles and discard the liquid. Scrape the pulp from the skin and place in the workbowl using the metal blade. Process to puree. Add the garlic, salt, oregano, cumin, cloves and cinnamon to the workbowl and process smooth. (This may take 60-90 seconds and you may need to add some of the broth.) Leave in workbowl.

Meanwhile, bring the broth and oil to a boil. With the machine running, pour 1½ cups of the mixture through the feed tube and process until very smooth. Return to the remaining stock mixture in the saucepan and bring to a boil, stirring to combine the ingredients. Simmer about 5 minutes and adjust seasonings to taste. Yield: 4 cups.

Optional Additions:

If using the eggs to thicken, process using the metal blade along with 1 cup of the finished sauce. Then whisk into the remaining finished sauce. Skim foam from the sauce.

If using toasted flour to thicken or red bell pepper to enhance, puree using the metal blade along with 1 cup of the finished sauce. Then stir into the remaining finished sauce.

If adding tomato sauce, stir in the desired amount during the final 2-3 minutes of cooking time.

Note: The wrinkled-skin Ancho pods usually have more pulp than the California or New Mexican chile and the lesser amount is needed. You can combine them using 7 of each or you may replace 7 pods with 3½ tablespoons pure ground chile powder.

If you have difficulty scraping the pulp from the skin, use the metal blade to process the chiles with 3 cups of the broth. (Heat remaining broth with the oil.) Press the processed mixture through a strainer, reserving the pulp and discarding the skins. Place the chile pulp in the broth in the workbowl, add the seasonings and proceed to add the remaining broth and oil through the feed tube with the motor running. Note that if you are using this procedure, you will need to increase the broth to a total of 4 cups.

Red Chile Sauce II

Chile powder alone is used for this sauce. You may use a commercial brand of chile powder in combination with pure ground chile or Gebhardt's Chile Powder alone or a combination of mild and hot chile powders. Experimentation and personal taste will be your guide. Note that if you toast and grind fresh pods to a powder, a greater amount will be needed.

You may refrigerate the sauce for 3-4 days and freeze it for longer storage.

> 3¹/₂ cups beef or chicken broth
> 2 cloves garlic, peeled
> ¹/₂-²/₃ cup chile powder, see note
> 3 tablespoons lard, bacon fat or oil
> 1-1¹/₂ teaspoons salt or to taste
> ¹/₄-¹/₂ teaspoon leaf oregano
> ¹/₄-¹/₂ teaspoon ground cumin
> ¹/₈ teaspoon ground cloves
> ¹/₈ teaspoon ground cinnamon

Options to reduce hotness and thicken (use one):

> 1 egg, beaten
> 1 fresh red bell pepper, roasted and peeled, stemmed and seeded (p.14)
> 2 tablespoons flour, toasted on a cookie sheet for 30 minutes at 350°
> 1 cup tomato sauce

Bring the broth to a boil in a medium saucepan.

Meanwhile, using the metal blade, drop the garlic through the feed tube with the motor running to mince. Add the chile powder, ¹/₂ cup of the broth and the lard. Process to combine. Transfer to a skillet set over medium heat and cook, stirring constantly, for 2-3 minutes to remove raw taste from the chile. (Watch closely because the chile burns easily.) Return the mixture to the workbowl and add the salt, oregano, cumin, cloves and cinamon. With the machine running, pour 1¹/₂ cups of the hot broth through the feed tube. Return to the remaining broth in the pan and bring to a boil. Reduce heat and cook 5 minutes. Adjust seasonings to taste. Yield: 4-4¹/₂ cups.

Optional Additions:

If using the egg to thicken, process using the metal blade along with 1 cup of the finished sauce. Then whisk into the remaining finished sauce. Skim foam from top.

If using the bell pepper to enhance the sauce or the toasted flour to thicken, puree using the metal blade along with 1 cup of the finished sauce. Then stir into the remaining sauce. The tomato sauce should be added to the sauce during the final 2-3 minutes of cooking time.

Note: You may use ¹/₄ cup ground Pasilla, Molido (bright red chile powder) and ¹/₄ cup ground Ancho (deep reddish brown chile powder) in place of the commercial chile powder. In all cases, color and flavor are best if using the freshest chile powder available. This is a pungent sauce. Begin by using the lesser amount of chile powder.

Sauces

Red Chile Sauce with Meat

Red Chile Sauce is often prepared by baking or simmering pork ribs in the sauce to give added flavor. The meat is either then removed and used to fill tortilla specialties or used with the sauce. Use the greater amount of stock for a sauce and the lesser for use as a filling.

This savory pork or beef filling has an infinite variety of uses. It can be served plain like an American stew, with Mexican Rice or Pork and Hominy Soup or as a filling for Empanadas, Navaho Fry Bread or Soft Tacos made with flour tortillas. It can also be used in Tortas which is the Mexican-American version of a hot submarine sandwich on Bolillos or French Bread.

My favorite presentation of Red Chile Sauce is a filling for homemade flour tortillas or in a fried Empanada made with masa dough. Served with Ninfa's Green Salsa, this is delicious!

    6 meaty pork or beef "country style" ribs
    1 tablespoon oil or bacon fat
    2 cloves garlic, peeled
    1/2 cup pure ground mild chile powder or
        Gebhardt's Chile Powder, see note
    2-3 1/2 cups chicken stock
    1 teaspoon oregano
    1 cup water
    1/2 cup tomato sauce
    1/2-1 teaspoon salt or to taste
    pepper to taste

In a skillet, sauté the beef or pork in the oil or fat until browned on all sides. Remove meat and reserve drippings in skillet. Trim as much fat from the meat as possible and set aside.

Using the metal blade, drop the garlic through the feed tube with the motor running to mince. Place the garlic, chile powder and 1/2 cup of the stock in the reserved skillet. Set over medium-low heat and cook, stirring constantly, for 2-3 minutes to "roast" the chile powder and remove raw taste. Watch carefully to prevent burning. Take off heat and stir in the remaining stock, oregano and water. Place the meat in this mixture to marinate at least 2 hours or overnight.

After the marinating time, bring the meat and sauce to a boil, then lower heat and simmer covered for 30 minutes until the meat is tender. Remove meat, cool and cut from the bones into chunks. Set aside.

Add the tomato sauce, salt and pepper to the sauce. (Gebhardt's Chile Powder contains some salt and pepper.) Add the meat chunks and keep warm until ready to use.

Use as a filling or add additional liquid to use as a meat sauce. Yield: 4-6 cups.

Note: Chile pods give a more delicate and rich flavor, but are not available everywhere. If you can find them, use 10-14 pods in place of the chile powder. (See p.14 for instructions on preparing chile pods and the chart on p.11 for substituting commercial chile powder for pure ground chile.)

Guacamole

The original Guacamole or "Indian Butter" was prepared using only avocados, garlic, lemon and salt. However, since gaining almost universal popularity, the ingredients have been expanded to include tomatoes, onion, bell pepper and fresh cilantro. In some parts of Mexico tomatillos are added, perhaps because they aid in preserving the fresh green color. Unripe, hard green tomatoes have a high enough acid content to nearly accomplish the same thing, but lack the fresh and lemony taste of tomatillos.

This recipe is a basic and somewhat plain guacamole suitable to use as a garnish or a spread in various sandwich-type preparations. The optional additions will make a more assertive guacamole suitable for salads or to serve as a dip with Tostados. It is always easy to make guacamole more picante with the addition of a few minced Jalapeño chiles.

Basic Guacamole:

2 cloves garlic, peeled
2-3 tablespoons fresh lemon juice
3-4 avocados, peeled, pitted and quartered
1 teaspoon salt or to taste
pinch chile powder or to taste

Using the metal blade, drop the garlic through the feed tube with the motor running to mince. Add avocados and lemon juice to the workbowl and pulse to combine well. Then process until smooth if desired. Season to taste with salt and chile powder. Yield: 2½-4 cups.

Optional Additions:
(use one or a combination as desired)
1. Mince 1 canned *or* fresh (roasted and peeled – p.14) chile with the garlic and proceed as above.
2. Mince 2-3 fresh tomatillos, cut up *or* 1 unripe green tomato, cored and quartered with the garlic and proceed as above.
3. Mince 3-4 sprigs fresh cilantro with the garlic and proceed as above.
4. Mince 1 small yellow onion *and/or* 1 small bell pepper, stemmed and seeded. Saute in about 1 tablespoon vegetable oil until softened, then pulse into the finished guacamole.
5. Thinly slice 3-4 scallions and pulse into the finished guacamole.
6. Core and quarter 1 small ripe tomato and pulse into the finished guacamole.
7. To make a salad dressing or sauce, add sour cream as desired to the finished guacamole. Amount added depends upon the consistency desired. Serve warm as a sauce or cold as a salad dressing. You may further thin the sauce with cream or evaporated milk.

Optional Presentations:
1. Serve as a salad over lettuce and garnish with a few Tostados or chopped tomatoes.
2. Serve as a dip with Tostados.
3. Serve as a filling for sandwich-type dishes.
4. Serve as a topping for Chalupas or Tostados.
5. Serve as an accompaniment to grilled meat or egg dishes.
6. Serve cold as a salad dressing.
7. Serve warmed as a sauce for vegetables, fish or Burritos.

Pickled Chiles
Chile Polcas

Red and green chile or pepper strips are an integral part of Southwestern cooking. They are often pickled in vinegar and used to accompany meat dishes. Even when well-drained, they have a definite "sweet-sour" flavor. Although both red bell peppers and chile Poblanos freeze well after roasting (do not peel them if freezing), they become slightly watery and mushy when thawed. Pickled Chiles, however, can be kept in the refrigerator for several weeks or home-canned and stored much longer. These may be used as a substitute for fresh roasted and peeled chiles in several dishes in this book such as Chicken and Chiles (p.170), Roasted Pepper Salad (p.106), and Cold Rice Salad (p.113).

When red bell peppers are in season, take an afternoon to "put up" this colorful combination. Note that using all bell peppers makes a sweeter mixture.

> 6 chile Poblanos or green bell peppers, roasted and peeled (p.14)
> 8 fresh red bell peppers, roasted and peeled (p.14)
> 1 large white onion, peeled
> 1 cup water, see note
> 1/2 cup vegetable oil
> 2 cups cider vinegar, see note
> 1/4 cup sugar
> 1 teaspoon salt
> 1 bay leaf, broken
> 1 teaspoon black peppercorns

Remove stems and seeds from roasted chiles and peppers. By hand cut them into 2 1/2 x 1/4 inch strips. Use the 3 or 4mm (standard) slicing disc to process the onion, then rinse it under cool water to remove bitter taste.

In a saucepan large enough to accommodate the vegetables, bring the water, oil, vinegar, sugar, salt, bay leaf and peppercorns to a boil. Add the onions, then remove the mixture from the heat. Add the chiles and peppers.

Pour into sterilized jars and refrigerate several weeks, or seal according to manufacturers directions and store 10-12 months. Take the same canning precautions with chiles as you would with tomatoes. Yield: 3 cups.

Note: The liquid should completely cover the chiles and onions. If it does not, add equal amounts water and vinegar to cover.

Pinto Bean Dip
Frijoles Salsa

Pinto beans are an integral part of the entire Southwest cuisine and are prepared in a variety of ways. This is my version of a popular appetizer dip usually served with Tostados (Corn Chips).

An especially nice presentation is to serve a bowl of Bean Dip accompanied by sour cream, Raw Salsa and Guacamole. I usually set out baskets of Tostados or warmed fresh flour tortillas or quartered pita breads.

> 2 strips bacon
> 1 clove garlic, peeled
> 1 small onion, peeled
> 1 tablespoon butter
> 3 ounces soft cream cheese
> 1 tablespoon (mild or hot) chopped canned green chiles
> 1 1/2 cups cooked Pinto Beans (p.215) including 2-3 tablespoons liquid, see note
> 1/2 cup sour cream or 1/4 cup sour cream and 1/4 cup plain yogurt
> 1/2 teaspoon salt
> 1/4-1/2 teaspoon ground cumin
> 2 tablespoons toasted pumpkin seeds, optional garnish
> 2 tablespoons chopped chives or parsley, optional garnish

In a small skillet, fry the bacon crisp. Drain and reserve. Discard fat in skillet, but do not wash. Using the metal blade, drop the garlic through the feed tube with the motor running to mince. Add the onion to the workbowl and process to chop. Rinse in a strainer under cool water to remove bitter liquid.

Using the reserved skillet, saute the garlic and onion in the butter for about 3 minutes until the onion is soft. Take off heat.

Break the bacon into several pieces and place in the workbowl using the metal blade. Pulse to chop, then add the cheese, chiles, beans and sour cream through the feed tube with the motor running. Process until well combined. Add the onion mixture, salt and cumin. Pulse until just combined. (Do not overprocess or the dip may become bitter.) Taste and adjust the seasonings.

Serve garnished with pumpkin seeds and chopped chives or parsley, if desired. Yield: 3 cups.

Note: Do not use canned beans. You may use half cooked Pinto Beans and half garbanzo beans.

Harlequin Dip

Having taught many classes in Albuquerque, New Mexico over the past ten years, I have made many friends who have taught me "New Mexico" style cooking. I have adapted the following recipe from *Simply Simpático,* the Junior League of Albuquerque cookbook. It is a wonderful table salsa with Tostados (Corn Chips).

Fresh chiles are essential in this recipe.

8 fresh green chiles, roasted and peeled
   (p.14)
1-1$^{1}/_{2}$ cups pitted black olives, drained
4 scallions, both green and white part, sliced
3 fresh tomatoes, cored
$^{2}/_{3}$ cup pine nuts or salted pumpkin seeds
1 clove garlic, peeled
$^{1}/_{2}$ cup fresh parsley sprigs
2 tablespoons white wine vinegar
2 tablespoons olive oil
$^{1}/_{2}$ teaspoon salt
$^{1}/_{4}$ teaspoon black pepper

Remove stems and seeds from chiles. Place chiles, olives and scallions in the workbowl using the metal blade and pulse to chop. Remove the mixture to a mixing bowl. Do not wash workbowl.

Insert the French fry disc, cut the tomato to fit the feed tube and process, using firm pressure, into small strips. Stir the tomatoes and pine nuts or pumpkin seeds into the chile mixture.

Using the metal blade, drop the garlic and parsley through the feed tube with the motor running to mince. Add the vinegar, oil, salt and pepper and process to combine. Toss with the vegetables. Adjust salt and pepper to taste. Yield: 3-4 cups.

Apple and Green Chile Relish

This recipe is neither traditional nor authentic to the Southwest. However, I am quite fond of combining apples and chiles (both abundant in the area) as an accompaniment to roast pork or turkey.

$^{1}/_{3}$ cup raisins
1$^{1}/_{2}$ cups hot water
1 clove garlic, peeled
4 apples, peeled, cored and halved
1 large onion, halved
2 tablespoons vegetable oil
$^{1}/_{2}$ pound fresh green chiles, roasted and
   peeled (p.14) or 6-8 canned green chiles
4 tablespoons white wine vinegar
1 tablespoon brown sugar
$^{1}/_{2}$ teaspoon salt
$^{1}/_{8}$ teaspoon white pepper

Soak the raisins in the water for 30-45 minutes. Drain and reserve water. Reserve raisins for other uses.

Using the metal blade, drop the garlic through the feed tube with the motor running to mince. Change to a 3 or 4mm (standard) slicing disc and process the apples and onion.

Saute the mixture in the oil for 5-8 minutes until the onions are translucent. Meanwhile, seed the chiles and cut into strips. Stir the chiles, vinegar, brown sugar and raisin water into the apple mixture and simmer about 20 minutes until thickened. Season with salt and pepper. Add additional water as necessary to make a moderately thick sauce similar to applesauce. Yield: 4-4$^{1}/_{2}$ cups.

Relishes

Jalapeño Jelly

This very different jelly is both sweet and mildly hot. It is delicious spooned atop a block of cream cheese and served with crackers or crisp tortillas. Also try it with roasted or cold meats. A jar of Jalapeño Jelly is a wonderful gift and a classic Tex-Mex favorite.

> 6 fresh Jalapeño chiles, trimmed, seeded and veins removed (see p.14 for precautions on handling hot chiles)
> 2 green bell peppers, seeded
> 1½ cups cider vinegar
> 5½ cups sugar
> 6 ounces (2 pouch package) liquid pectin
> few drops green food coloring

Cut each chile and pepper into 3-4 pieces. (Some cooks like to leave in a few seeds.) Using the metal blade, drop the chile and pepper pieces through the feed tube with the motor running. Process to finely mince. (Do not lean over and breathe deeply during processing — the fumes are quite strong.)

Place the chiles, peppers, vinegar and sugar in a 3 quart saucepan and bring to a boil, stirring to dissolve sugar. Lower heat and simmer 10 minutes, skimming foam from the top. Stir in the pectin and food coloring and boil 1 minute. Remove from heat and let stand 15 minutes, then pour into sterilized jars and seal with paraffin according to manufacturer's directions. Yield: 6 cups.

Variation: Make a Red Pepper Jelly by substituting red bell peppers for the green peppers and red Jalapeños or another fresh red chile for the green Jalapeños. Prepare as directed.

Green Chile Pesto
Chile Verde Pesto

The "heat" of this pesto depends on the kind of chile used – from mild canned green chiles to fresh Anaheim or Poblanos. Although both are usually mild, all chiles are somewhat unpredictable. Fresh chiles make the best pesto and, in general, small and thin-skinned varieties are usually hotter. You might want to taste the chile before using to be certain. For very mild and sensitive palates, use bell peppers. I can't imagine anyone using Jalapeño chiles for this!

Use this Pesto interchangeably with the Cilantro Pesto recipe that follows or in the many vegetable or pasta dishes in this book.

> 2 cloves garlic, peeled
> 4 ounces Parmesan cheese, room temperature and cut in 5 pieces
> 6 green chiles or 3 bell peppers, roasted and peeled (p.14) or 2 (4 ounce) cans mild green chiles, drained
> ¾ cup hulled and salted pumpkin seeds or pine nuts
> ½ cup fresh parsley sprigs
> 2-3 tablespoons safflower oil
> ¼-1 teaspoon salt (use lesser amount if pumpkin seeds are salted)

Using the metal blade, drop the garlic and cheese through the feed tube with the motor running. Process until the cheese is finely grated.

Remove stems and seeds from chiles or peppers and add to the workbowl. Add the seed or nuts, parsley and oil. Process to make a smooth paste. Add salt to taste.

The pesto can be refrigerated for a week or frozen for several months. Yield: 2 cups.

Cilantro Pesto

Southwestern Vinaigrette

Make this when you have fresh cilantro. You could use 1½ cups fresh parsley and 2 tablespoons dried cilantro, but the fresh and distinctive taste will be diminished.

Cilantro Pesto can be refrigerated for 3-4 days or frozen for several months. It is wonderful to keep on hand for it has a variety of uses. Try it as a dip for raw vegetables by simply mixing with an equal amount of mayonnaise, sour cream or yogurt. For another easy appetizer, spread the Pesto on canapes and toast. It makes a great salad dressing by adding lemon juice or vinegar and oil to taste. You might also want to stir 2-3 tablespoons of the Pesto into sauteed vegetables or scrambled eggs for an exciting taste difference.

 2 cloves garlic, peeled
 4 ounces Parmesan cheese, room
   temperature and cut in 5 pieces
 2 cups fresh cilantro sprigs
 ⅓ cup pine nuts or pumpkin seeds
 2-3 tablespoons safflower oil
 ¼-½ teaspoon salt or to taste

Using the metal blade, drop the garlic and then the cheese pieces through the feed tube with the motor running. Process until the cheese is finely grated. Add the nuts or pumpkin seeds, the cilantro and the oil. Process until the mixture is well combined into a pasty mixture. Add salt to taste and refrigerate or freeze the Pesto until ready to use. Yield: 1-1½ cups.

A common practice throughout the Southwest is to add fresh ground chile powder to a classic vinaigrette and call it "French Dressing." More optional additions such as oregano, orange juice and sugar vary according to the region and creativity of individual cooks. Chile is botanically a fruit and treated commercially as a vegetable. If you use a hot chile powder, the orange juice or sugar will tame some of the "bite" without masking the flavor.

 1 clove garlic, peeled
 3 tablespoons red or white wine vinegar
 ½ cups vegetable or safflower oil
 ½ teaspoon salt
 ⅛ teaspoon dry mustard
 ¼-½ teaspoon pure ground chile

Using the metal blade, drop the garlic through the feed tube with motor running to mince. Stop machine and add remaining ingredients. Process about 5-10 seconds to blend well.

The dressing may be made 24 hours in advance. Yield: about ¾ cup.

Variations:

Lemon-Parsley: Mince 3-4 sprigs parsley with the garlic and add 1 tablespoon fresh lemon juice to the remaining ingredients. This is good on fruit or vegetable salads.

Creamy Vinaigrette: Blend 1 whole egg or egg white into the finished dressing. The dressing can be thinned with the addition of 1 tablespoon water or lemon juice. If the dressing is to be used on salads containing fresh chiles, substitute ¼ teaspoon pepper for the chile powder in the dressing recipe. This is good with potato or other vegetable salads.

Orange-Parsley: Mince 3-4 sprigs fresh parsley with the garlic and add 1 tablespoon fresh orange juice with the remaining ingredients. This is good with fruit salads or cooked fish or chicken.

Cilantro: Mince 3-4 sprigs fresh cilantro with the garlic and prepare the dressing as above. This is good with tomato salads and vegetables.

Mixed Vinaigrette: Mince 3-4 sprigs fresh parsley with the garlic. Add ¼ teaspoon ground cumin, ⅛ teaspoon ground oregano and if desired 1 tablespoon lemon juice and 1 egg white. This is especially good on cold cooked beef or pork.

*Sweet
Sauces*

Guava Sauce

Guava has such a definite perfume and delicious taste that it is practically impossible to bring it across the border unnoticed. One sniff identifies its presence no matter how carefully it is concealed.

This sauce is delicious over ice cream, crepes, sweet Tamales, Coconut Almond Dessert or fresh papayas.

> 1 (10 ounce) package frozen raspberries, thawed
> 1/4 cup canned guavas with their juice or 2 tablespoons guava paste
> 2 large oranges
> 2 tablespoons butter
> 2 ounces raspberry or strawberry liquer

Place the guavas and berries in the workbowl using the metal blade. Process until smooth and pureed.

Remove 4-5 strips of orange peel (colored portion only) and place in a saucepan with the butter. Saute about 2 minutes over low heat. Add the juice from the oranges and simmer about 5 minutes. Add the guava and berry puree and simmer, stirring constantly, for 3-5 minutes. Stir in enough water to make a thin sauce consistency. Add the liquer and simmer 2-3 minutes more.

Let cool and store in refrigerator. Yield: about 1 cup.

Caramel Sauce

Cajeta

I feel quite certain that Caramel was Mexico's gift to candy makers! "Leche Quemada" candies and sauces made from boiling milk and sugar together for 3-5 hours are quite common, though often impractical. Instead of resorting to condensed milk or brown sugar to simulate rich caramel flavor and color, try this recipe taught to me by a Mexican-American friend.

This thin sauce keeps for weeks in the refrigerator and can be used in any recipe calling for Caramel sauce such as the Caramel Crepes (p.267). The sauce can also be served as a fruit fondue dipping sauce with bananas, apples, pears, strawberries and pound cake squares and makes a simple, delicious treat.

Bottled Caramel Cajeta sauce is available and is quite thick. If using, thin it with some evaporated or whole milk to the consistency of crepe batter.

- 8 cups whole milk
- 1/2 teaspoon baking soda
- 1/2 teaspoon cornstarch
- 2 cups sugar, divided
- 2 tablespoons water

In a 4 quart saucepan, bring the milk to a boil. Remove about 1/2 cup and dissolve baking soda and cornstarch in it. Then return to the pan and stir in 1 1/2 cups of the sugar. Keep the mixture at a gentle boil.

Meanwhile, combine the remaining 1/2 cup sugar and the water in a small saucepan and caramelize over high heat. Do not stir, but watch carefully because the sugar burns easily. As soon as it turns amber, stir and remove from heat. Take the boiling milk off the heat and gradually pour the caramelized sugar into the milk. (The mixture will foam up quite vigorously.) Return to medium-high heat and cook at a gentle boil for 45-60 minutes until somewhat thickened and creamy. Let cool, then refrigerate until needed. Yield: 3-4 cups.

Note: This is a relatively thin sauce. It can be made thicker by simply cooking for a longer time.

Lemon-Orange Sauce

This is a wonderful sauce for Sweet Tamales. Garnish each tamale with the strips of citrus peel from the sauce.

- 2 1/2 fresh lemons, peel and juice
- 1 fresh orange, peel and juice
- 1/2 stick (2 ounces) butter
- 3/4 cup sugar
- 1/2 teaspoon vanilla

Use a citrus stripper to remove 2 inch strips of peel from lemons and orange. Squeeze juices to make 3/4 cup total. Melt the butter in a saucepan, then add the sugar, juice, peel and vanilla. Simmer 6 minutes, then let cool and refrigerate until needed. Yield: about 1 cup.

Sweet Sauces

Fillings

Chicken Stew
Pollo Guisado

This "stew" is rarely served alone as a main course, but rather is frequently used as a filling for Tortas, Tacos or Chalupas.

> 2 pounds boneless raw chicken, skinned and cut into bite-size pieces, see note
> 1 tablespoon flour
> 1/4 teaspoon pepper
> 2 tablespoons vegetable oil
> 1-2 tablespoons butter
> 1 medium yellow onion, peeled and quartered
> 1 small bell pepper, seeded and quartered
> 1 (14 1/2 ounce) can Italian plum tomatoes with the juices
> 1 teaspoon ground cumin
> chicken broth, if needed to thin, see note
> salt and pepper to taste

Place the flour, salt and pepper in a paper bag. Add the chicken in several batches and shake vigorously to coat very lightly with the seasoned flour. In a large skillet, saute the chicken in the oil and butter until all sides are lightly browned. Add additional butter if necessary. Remove the chicken and reserve the skillet off the heat.

Use the metal blade to mince the onion and bell pepper together. Saute 1-2 minutes in the remaining fat in the skillet. Stir in the tomatoes and the juices, breaking up the tomatoes with a fork. Stir in the cumin and simmer, uncovered for 20 minutes. Add the chicken and some stock if the mixture seems too thick. Simmer, stirring occasionally, for 8-10 minutes. Add salt and pepper to taste.

Serve as a filling for Tortas, Tacos or Chalupas. Yield: filling for 12 Tacos or 6 Tortas.

Note: Because this is a "filling," the amounts of chicken and liquid are variable depending upon how you plan to use it.

Mexican Sausage
Chorizo Mejicano

Since commercial Mexican-Style "Chorizo" sausage is difficult to obtain in many areas, this is an excellent recipe to make at home. "Chorizo" is usually sold as bulk sausage rather than link and is not smoked or cooked like Spanish Chorizo and thus tastes quite different. It is often used in breakfast dishes with eggs or as a filling for Tacos, Chalupas or Stuffed Chiles. The "hotness" of the sausage is determined by the kind and amount of chile powder used.

Spanish Chorizo may not be substituted for bulk Mexican Sausage or Chorizo in most dishes because it alters taste and texture. The only exception and use for Spanish Chorizo in this book is in Paella.

> 3 cloves garlic, peeled
> 5-6 sprigs fresh cilantro
> 2 pounds fresh lean pork, partially frozen and cut in 1 inch chunks
> 1/4-1/2 pound fresh pork fat, chilled and cut in 1 inch chunks
> 2 tablespoons ground red chile powder or to taste
> 2 tablespoons sweet paprika
> 1/4-1 teaspoon ground cumin (use greater amount if using pure ground chile powder without added cumin)
> 1/4 teaspoon ground coriander
> 1 teaspoon salt
> 1/4 teaspoon pepper
> 1 teaspoon oregano
> 1 teaspoon ground cloves
> 1/3 cup cider vinegar

Using the metal blade, drop the garlic and cilantro through the feed tube with the motor running to mince. Stop machine and place half of the pork and pork fat in the workbowl. Pulse to process to a texture slightly more coarse than commercial ground meat. Remove to a large mixing bowl. Process remaining pork, pork fat and remaining ingredients except vinegar in the same manner. Add to mixing bowl. Add vinegar and use your hands or a blending fork to combine the ingredients.

The sausage may be refrigerated for a day or two or may be frozen for longer storage. It makes an excellent breakfast sausage or can be used in any recipe calling for Chorizo Sausage. Yield: 2 1/4-2 1/2 pounds.

Spicy Meat Hash

Picadillo

This delightful mixture can be used to fill warmed tortillas, as a filling for Empanadas, Stuffed Chiles, Tacos, omelettes or Tamales. Not only is it versatile, the Picadillo can be made a day or two ahead and reheated — making it a real time saver as well.

It is not necessary to peel potatoes, apples or tomatoes because the skins will be incorporated, undetected, into the meat mixture.

If you spoon the Picadillo into torillas or pita breads, it is especially good to offer a Salsa, sliced avocado and a mixture of 1 cup sour cream combined with ½ cup heavy cream as garnishes.

This is one of those recipes that may not look good, but it is always deemed a winner by my Northern and Eastern cooking classes!

    1 clove garlic, peeled
    1 pound boneless pork, trimmed of fat and
        connective tissue and cut into 1 inch
        pieces
    1 pound boneless beef round or chuck,
        trimmed of fat and connective tissue and
        cut in 1 inch pieces
    1 large yellow onion, peeled and quartered
    1 fresh green Anaheim chile or bell pepper,
        roasted, peeled and seeded (p.14)
    3 tablespoons vegetable oil
    1 large potato, scrubbed and quartered
    1 large apple, cored and quartered
    ¼-½ cup beef stock
    2 tablespoons cider vinegar
    4 tomatoes, quartered
    1 tablespoon commercial or pure ground
        chile powder
    2 teaspoons salt
    1½ teaspoons ground cinnamon
    1½ teaspoons ground cumin
    ½ teaspoon ground cloves
    ¾ cup raisins
    ¾ cup whole pine nuts or slivered blanched
        almonds

Using the metal blade, drop the garlic through the feed tube with the motor running to mince. Stop machine and add ⅓ of the beef and ⅓ of the pork to the workbowl. Pulse until the meat is chopped to a medium-fine texture. Remove and set aside. Repeat the procedure in 2 more batches to chop all the meat. Wipe workbowl.

Place the onion and chile or pepper in the workbowl using the metal blade. Process to mince.

Heat the oil in a 12 inch skillet and saute the onion over medium heat for 5 minutes. Add the meat and saute, stirring constantly, until browned — about 5 minutes.

Place the potato and apple in workbowl using the metal blade and pulse to finely chop. Add to the skillet along with the stock and vinegar. Reduce heat to medium-low and simmer 15 minutes, stirring occasionally.

Pack the tomatoes vertically into the feed tube using the French fry disc and process to dice. Discard any unprocessed pieces of skin and add tomatoes, chile powder, salt, cinnamon, cumin and cloves to the skillet. Simmer, uncovered, for 20 minutes until thick. (If the mixture seems too thick, add additional beef stock.) Stir in raisins and nuts.

Use immediately or let cool and then refrigerate. Serve re-heated. Yield: about 7 cups (enough to generously fill 12 tortillas).

Fillings

Seasoned Meat

This is an easy all-purpose beef filling that can be used to fill 12-16 Tacos, Enchiladas or Burros. It is also delicious for use in main dish salads.

2 medium size red potatoes, optional
½-1 tablespoon butter
½-1 tablespoon oil
1 clove garlic, peeled
1 large yellow onion, peeled and quartered
2 pounds ground beef or cooked and
    shredded meat, see note
2 teaspoons salt
⅛-¼ teaspoon black pepper
¼ teaspoon oregano
½ teaspoon ground cumin, optional
1 teaspoon chile powder or to taste
3 tablespoons fresh Salsa of choice or
    tomato sauce

Peel and halve the optional potato and parboil until just tender. Drain, cool and cut into small bite-sized pieces. Saute in the butter and oil until golden brown, adding additional butter and oil as necessary. Set aside.

Using the metal blade, drop the garlic through the feed tube with the motor running to mince. Add the onion to the workbowl and pulse to chop. Saute the garlic and onion with the beef for about 15 minutes until the onions are soft and the meat is cooked. As the mixture cooks, add the remaining ingredients except the potatoes. (If necessary, stir in a little water to prevent sticking.)

Stir in the fried potatoes and use the filling as desired. Yield: 2-3 cups.

Note: You may grind your own beef using the metal blade. Process 2 pounds of cubed, chilled beef chuck in two batches until ground.

Mincemeat

Homemade mincemeat is wonderful in pies, cakes, as a filling for sweet rolls or crepes or served with ice cream. It is also a traditional filling for baked or fried Turnovers (Empanadas). You may omit the beef and suet and add an additional cup of fresh or dried fruit. Mincemeat can be refrigerated for about a week and also freezes well.

2 ounces fresh suet, chilled and cut in pieces
½ pound lean beef, chilled and cut in cubes
outer peel from 1 orange
outer peel from 1 lemon
¼ cup sugar
1 apple, cored and quartered
1 pear, cored and quartered (do not use
    canned pears)
½ cup firmly packed dates
½ cup pecans or pine nuts
½ cup seedless raisins
½ teaspoon mace
½ teaspoon cinnamon
½ teaspoon allspice
½ teaspoon nutmeg
2 tablespoons molasses or honey
¼ teaspoon salt
1 cup apple juice (approximately)
applesauce, if needed
2 ounces brandy

Place meat and suet in the workbowl fitted with the metal blade. Process using the pulse to grind. Remove and saute in a 12 inch skillet. Reserve.

Use a sharp knife to remove the outer peel from the orange and lemon. Avoid the bitter tasting white membrane. Wipe out workbowl and place peels and about half of the sugar. Process using the pulse to mince. Add the apple and pear and pulse to chop. Add to the skillet.

Use the metal blade to process the dates and nuts with the remaining sugar. Pulse several times, then run the machine for several seconds to finely chop. Add to the skillet. Bring to a simmer. Add the raisins, spices, molasses, salt and apple juice. Simmer, uncovered, for 30-40 minutes adding more juice if necessary. If, at the end of the cooking time, liquid is needed, stir in some applesauce. The consistency should be like thick, chunky applesauce. Stir in the brandy and simmer 5 minutes more.

Refrigerate the mincemeat in glass containers or pack into sterilized jars and seal according to manufacturers directions. Yield: 1 quart.

MORNING MEALS

In Southwestern living, breakfast is often a special occasion. Various combinations of eggs, cheese, tortillas and salsas are first-rate eye-openers.

Our brunches are justly famous. The dish called Huevos Rancheros, eggs prepared with fresh salsa, has become a classic in American cooking. Another contender that could star at any brunch buffet is Heuvos con Chile Verde. Teamed with fresh fruit this makes an easy, tasty morning buffet.

This section contains not only recipes for parties, occasions and for families indulging in leisurely weekend or holiday breakfasts, but plenty of dishes for those on the run, as well.

What's more, all are nutritionally sound. The Potato Omelette — found throughout the Southwest — is a case in point. In one easily-prepared dish are cheese, potatoes, onions, chiles, spinach and eggs; a delicious way to set yourself and your family up for the day.

Thanks to the food processor, no one need rise at dawn to prepare the ingredients necessary for most of these dishes. In most cases, also, you can prepare certain sections of a recipe ahead of time.

The many delicious sweet breads (pan dulce), rolls, and Cuernos (croissants) are delightful treats in the morning, although Mexicans tend to eat them later in the day. You will find a number of them in the Breads & Pastries section.

Clockwise from top left: Fresh Fruit Platter, Tequila Sunrise, Eggs with Avocado Sauce, Shrimp with Eggs, Fresh Salsa.

Potato Omelette

Torta de Huevos

This is the original Spanish "tortilla" and appears in some form, served with or without a salsa, in every region of the Southwest. Traditionally, it is fried on both sides and contains some filling. This quick and easy breakfast or lunch dish is as typical of the area as is American "hash-browns."

2 ounces Monterey Jack or Mozzarella cheese, chilled, optional
2 small potatoes, peeled and quartered
1 yellow onion, peeled and quartered
2 green chiles, roasted and peeled (p.14)
1/2 pound cooked spinach, squeezed of all moisture, optional
1/4 stick (1 ounce) butter
2 tablespoons vegetable oil
6 eggs
1/3 cup water
1/2 teaspoon salt
1/2 teaspoon red chile powder or paprika
salsa of choice or sour cream and chives for garnish

Use the shredding disc to process the optional cheese and set aside.

Place the potatoes and onion in the workbowl fitted with the metal blade. Pulse to coarsely dice. Remove and reserve. Process the chiles and optional spinach together in the same way.

Heat the butter and oil in a 12 inch ovenproof skillet. Saute the potatoes and onions for 8-10 minutes over medium-low heat until the onions are translucent and the potatoes are tender. Stir occasionally and add more butter or oil if necessary to prevent sticking and browning. Add the chiles and cook, covered, over low heat for 1 minute.

Place the eggs, water and salt in the work bowl using the metal blade. Process about 5 seconds to blend. Pour the eggs over the potato mixture in the skillet. Cook over low heat, tilting pan and lifting the cooked edges to allow uncooked portion to run underneath, until the eggs begin to set. When the eggs are still a bit runny, sprinkle with the shredded cheese and chile powder or paprika. Set under a preheated broiler about 5 inches from the heat source. Broil about 1 minute or until the eggs are set and the cheese is melted. Watch carefully to prevent burning.

To serve the omelette, cut into 4 sections and serve directly from the skillet. Serve with a table salsa and/or sour cream and chives as a garnish. Serves 4.

Variation: If available, a dried chile Cascabel can be substituted for the green chile to make a more picante omelette. Seed and coarsely chop the dried chile. Saute in the butter and oil for 2 minutes before adding the potatoes and onions.

Eggs with Green Chile
Huevos con Chile Verde

This classic Mexican-American combination of chiles, eggs and cheese is a cousin of the familiar cheese "strata." It is a good example of the similarities of cooking techniques the world over. Huevos con Chile Verde can be assembled a day ahead and simply baked at serving time. Teamed with fresh fruit, this makes an easy and tasty brunch buffet.

6 ounces Monterey Jack or Longhorn
    cheddar cheese
12 slices stale white or French bread
1 stick (4 ounces) butter, softened
4 fresh green Anaheim chiles, roasted and
    peeled (p.14) or 2 (7 ounce) cans green
    chiles
6 eggs
1½ cups milk
½ teaspoon salt
¼ teaspoon pepper

Use the shredding disc to process the cheese. Set aside.

Butter both sides of the bread and then butter a 9 x 12 casserole. Place half of the bread in the dish in a single layer. Cut the chiles so they lay flat and place over the bread in a single layer. Cover the chiles with the grated cheese and top with the remaining bread in a single layer.

Place the eggs, milk, salt and pepper in workbowl fitted with the metal blade. Process about 5 seconds until blended. Pour over the bread to cover evenly. (If the bread is very dry an additional egg along with an additional ¼ cup milk may be needed.) The bread should be thoroughly soaked but not soupy. Cover the casserole and refrigerate overnight.

Bake the casserole uncovered in a preheated 375° oven for 40-45 minutes until the top is puffed and browned. Cut in squares to serve. This is good either hot or at room temperature. Serves 8.

Variation: Saute ½-¾ pound crumbled bulk Mexican Sausage (p.56) in a skillet. Drain off fat and add the sausage between the bread layers. Bake and serve as above.

Eggs with Avocado Sauce
Huevos con Salsa Aguacate

This unusual presentation of scrambled eggs is especially good served with fresh seasonal fruit and sauteed Mexican Sausage.

½ small yellow onion, peeled
¼ stick (1 ounce) unsalted butter
2 ripe avocados, peeled, pitted and cut in
    small chunks
1½ teaspoons lemon juice
½ teaspoon salt or to taste
2-3 tablespoons evaporated milk
½-1 teaspoon coarsely chopped dried red
    peppers or to taste, see note
8 eggs
¼ teaspoon salt
2 tablespoons water
1½ tablespoons butter
fresh salsa of choice or bottled salsa for
    garnish

Use the metal blade to chop the onion, then saute in a medium skillet in the butter for 3-4 minutes until the onion is translucent. Gently stir in the chopped avocado, then the lemon juice, salt, milk and peppers. Simmer, stirring gently, until some of the avocado melts into a sauce leaving only small chunks. Keep warm while scrambling the eggs.

Beat the eggs, salt and water with a fork, then scramble softly in the butter. Spoon the avocado sauce over each serving of eggs and garnish with the salsa. Serve immediately. Serves 4.

Note: Some pepper flakes are hotter than others. If you are not sure, use the lesser amount. If smooth-skinned, dried red chiles are available, use in place of the dried red peppers. Remove stems and seeds, then using the metal blade or a blender, coarsely chop the chiles. Add to the sauce as directed.

Ranch or Country Style Eggs
Huevos Rancheros

Today, the eggs for Huevos Rancheros are usually fried or scrambled and served atop a corn tortilla which has been passed through hot oil. In many areas, however, the ancient custom of poaching eggs in salsa is still practiced. Before the Spaniards brought pigs to the Southwest and central Mexico, native cooking techniques were limited to boiling, steam or roasting over an open fire. When cooks learned to render lard from pork, an important dimension was added to food preparation and many cooking techniques changed.

Whether the eggs are poached in the salsa or fried separately, the choice of salsa is flexible. The Spanish Sauce or Quick Ranch Style Salsa would be suitable for poaching, and any uncooked salsa or Red or Green Chile sauce could be used for eggs that have been cooked separately. I have given both cooking methods in this recipe and have used a sauce suitable for either.

Huevos Rancheros are usually served with Refried Beans or Refried Beans with Mexican Sausage.

The Sauce:
- 1 clove garlic, peeled
- 1 small onion, peeled and quartered
- 3 tablespoons vegetable or olive oil
- 6 fresh green chiles, roasted and peeled (p.14) or 1 (7 ounce) can green chiles
- 1 (14½ ounces) can Italian plum tomatoes including juices
- ⅛ teaspoon dried mint or one sprig fresh mint
- 2 springs fresh basil or ¼ teaspoon dried basil
- ¼ teaspoon leaf oregano
- several sprigs fresh cilantro
- ½-1 teaspoon salt or to taste

To Finish the Dish:
- 4 corn tortillas
- ½ stick (2 ounces) butter
- 3 tablespoons vegetable oil
- 4 eggs
- 1 avocado, sliced for garnish

First, prepare the sauce. Using the metal blade, drop the garlic through the feed tube with the motor running to mince. Add the onion to the workbowl and pulse to mince. In a skillet large enough to finish the sauce, saute the garlic and onion in the oil until the onion is limp.

Meanwhile, use the metal blade to chop together the tomatoes and chiles. Add to the skillet (along with tomato juices). Add the remaining sauce ingredients and simmer for 10-12 minutes. Keep warm.

Prepare the tortillas. In a skillet, heat the butter and oil to about 350°. Pass the tortillas, one at a time, through the hot butter and oil just long enough to soften. (Some cooks prefer them slightly crisp.) Drain on paper towels.

Prepare the eggs by either poaching them in the simmering sauce until the whites are cooked or by frying or scrambling them separately. Serve the eggs atop the tortillas with sauce spooned over. Garnish with the avocado. Serve immediately. Serves 4.

Eggs Baked in Sauce
Huevos al Horno

Since eggs are supposed to tame hot chile sauces, I have often wondered if Huevos Rancheros evolved from an effort to neutralize a sauce, or was just one of those happy combinations.

This is the way I usually make eggs, with tortillas, for a crowd. The eggs are tender and the tortillas both soft and crisp. Any salsa may be used to accompany the dish. Refried Beans, Mexican Sausage or fresh fruit is usually served alongside.

> 2 cups Salsa of choice or Red Chile Sauce
>   (p.46)
> 8 corn tortillas
> 1/4 stick (1 ounce) butter
> 2 tablespoons oil
> 8 eggs

The Garnish:
> 2 ounces Feta cheese
> 1/2 cup dry cottage cheese
> paprika or chile powder

Prepare the salsa and reserve. Have ready 8 well-buttered muffin tins or 8 one ounce souffle dishes.

In a small skillet, heat the butter and oil. Pass each tortilla through the hot oil to soften and seal, then press between paper towels to remove excess oil. (Do not fry the tortillas until crisp.) Press the softened tortillas into the prepared tins or dishes to form a cup.

Spoon about 1 tablespoon salsa into each tortilla "cup." Crack an egg into each and bake 15-20 minutes in a preheated 375° oven until the egg white is nearly set, but still appears loose. (The eggs will continue to cook after removal from the oven.) While the eggs are baking, crumble the Feta cheese and drain the cottage cheese. Toss together to combine and reserve for garnish.

Run a knife around the edge of each tortilla and transfer the egg filled "cup" to a dessert size plate. Crumble the cheese mixture over the top and sprinkle with a dash of paprika or chile powder.

Serve the eggs with the salsa. Serves 8.

Variation: Use the metal blade to combine together 1 (10 ounce) package frozen spinach that has been thawed and squeezed dry, 1 egg, 5-6 tablespoons sour cream, 1/2 teaspoon salt and 1/8 teaspoon cayenne pepper. Spoon about 1 tablespoon of this mixture into the tortilla "cups" in place of the salsa and proceed as above. Serve a salsa of choice with the baked eggs.

Spicy Scrambled Eggs
Huevos Revueltos

This perfect brunch or luncheon dish is sometimes served atop crisply fried corn tortillas. It is equally good accompanied by Guacamole (p.49) or Texas Hot Salsa (p.39) or simply surrounded with a garnish of seasonal fresh fruits.

> 4 ounces Monterey Jack cheese, chilled
> 8 eggs
> 2 tablespoons water
> salt and fresh ground black pepper to taste
> 1 large tomato, quartered and seeded
> 1 fresh green Anaheim chile, roasted and
>   peeled and seeded (p.14) or 1 (4 ounce)
>   can green chiles, minced
> 1 tablespoon butter
> 1 tablespoon vegetable oil
> cayenne pepper to taste
> sliced avocado for garnish, optional

Use the shredding disc to process the cheese. Set aside to come to room temperature.

Place the eggs, water, salt and pepper in workbowl fitted with the metal blade. Process 10 seconds to mix. Remove and set aside.

Dice the tomato with a sharp knife and place in a strainer to drain off excess juices. Set aside.

Stem and seed the fresh chiles. Using the metal blade, drop the fresh chile pieces through the feed tube with the motor running to mince.

In a 12 inch skillet, heat the butter and oil. Add the tomato and chile and simmer 1-2 minutes, stirring constantly. Add the eggs and gently stir over low heat until they are softly scrambled — about 2 minutes.

Turn off the heat and sprinkle the cheese over the eggs. Cover the skillet for 30 seconds to melt the cheese. Dust lightly with cayenne pepper and serve immediately accompanied by sliced avocados, if desired. Serves 4-6.

Scrambled Eggs with Tostados
Migas

This is a simple, yet unusual way to serve scrambled eggs. A good friend who grew up in Texas gave me the recipe from his mother's cookbook and it has become a favorite at our house. When my boys invite friends for a slumber party, everyone wants homemade flour tortillas and Migas. (The word "Migas" literally means "crumbs" – a perfect use for small broken Tostados or corn chips.)

Some people like to add Mexican Sausage to the eggs, but I prefer to cook the sausage separately. I may even combine the cooked sausage with Refried Beans to serve with the eggs for a super breakfast.

1 small onion, peeled and quartered
1 bell pepper, stemmed, seeded and cut in
   5-6 pieces or 2-3 mild green chiles,
   canned or fresh roasted and peeled (p.14)
2 small tomatoes, cored and quartered
5 large eggs
1/2 teaspoon salt
1/8 teaspoon black pepper, optional
1 teaspoon chile powder
2-3 tablespoons oil
4 corn tortillas, cut into 1/2 inch squares
1/4 stick (1 ounce) butter
fresh parsley or cilantro for garnish
sliced ripe avocado for garnish

Use the metal blade to coarsely chop the onion with the pepper or chiles. Use the French fry disc to process the tomatoes into thin strips. (If you do not have this disc, cut into small chunks by hand.) Drain the tomatoes and set aside.

Beat the eggs with the salt, pepper and chile powder.

Heat the oil in a 10-12 inch skillet until very hot. Fry the tortilla pieces, in several batches, stirring and turning until crisp. Drain on paper towels.

Drain off all but 1 tablespoon oil from the skillet and add the butter. Saute the onions and pepper or chiles until the onions are transluscent – about 3 minutes. Add the tomatoes, eggs and fried tostados (tortilla pieces). Stir gently or agitate pan until the eggs are softly scrambled.

Serve immediately garnished with the cilantro and avocado. Serves 6-8.

Eggs Baked with Tortilla Chips
Huevos Chilaquiles

This is one of the ways that broken tortilla chips (those not in perfect quarters) can be used. The result is a dish similar to a quiche and is wonderful for breakfast or brunch.

1 small onion, peeled and quartered
1 clove garlic, peeled
1/4 stick (1 ounce) butter
2 (14 1/2 ounce) cans Italian plum tomatoes
1 (7 ounce) can mild or hot green chiles,
   drained
1/2 teaspoon oregano
1/2 teaspoon ground cumin
1/4 teaspoon salt or to taste
10 corn tortillas, quartered or 40 leftover
   tostados (p.242)
oil for frying tortillas
1 pound Monterey Jack cheese, chilled
9 eggs, beaten
2 cups sour cream
3 scallions (green and white part),
   sliced thin

Use the metal blade to chop the onion. In a large skillet or medium saucepan, saute the onion and whole garlic in the butter for about 3 minutes until the onion is translucent. Discard garlic.

Use the metal blade and pulse to chop the tomatoes and chiles together. Add to the onions in the pan along with the oregano, cumin and salt. Simmer about 30 minutes over low heat.

Meanwhile, if using tortillas, fry crisp in oil heated to 360°. Drain on paper towels and reserve.

Use the shredding disc to process the cheese.

Butter a 9 x 12 baking dish and layer the ingredients. Make a layer using half of the tostados or tortillas, covering with half of the sauce, the half of the eggs and half of the cheese. Make a second layer ending with the cheese.

Bake 35 minutes in a preheated 350° oven until the eggs are set, but still soft like a quiche. Spread sour cream over top and return to the oven for 1 minute.

Cut into squares and serve garnished with the sliced scallions. Serves 6-8.

Shrimp with Eggs
Camarónes con Huevos

Shrimp and egg Tacos, either soft or crisp, are a popular breakfast and brunch dish. This version is served in a fresh fried masa tartlet shell. The same filling may be served in prepared crispy taco shells, soft flour tortillas or on a crisp chalupa shell. You will need metal tartlet shells.

Masa Shell:
    1 cup packaged Masa Harina
    water
    1 tablespoon shortening
    2 teaspoons sugar
    1/4 teaspoon baking soda
    oil for frying

Filling:
    1 potato (about 4 ounces), peeled and cut in
       several pieces
    1 tablespoon minced onion
    1 1/2 tablespoons butter
    1/2 tablespoon oil
    2 tablespoons diced green chile
    1/2 pound fresh shrimp (small to medium
       size), peeled and deveined
    1/2 teaspoon salt
    pepper to taste
    6 eggs, beaten
    red tomato Salsa of choice

Prepare the Masa Harina and water according to package directions adding the shortening, sugar and baking soda. Let rest about 20 minutes. Begin to heat oil for deep-frying to 360° while preparing the filling.

Boil the potato for about 8 minutes until just tender. Drain and chop into bite-size pieces. In a medium skillet, saute the potato and onion in 1/2 tablespoon of the butter and the oil until lightly browned. Remove from skillet and stir together with the chile.

Use 6 metal tartlet shells in the shape of your choice. Press some of the masa into each shell to cover completely with as thin a layer as possible. Using tongs, immerse the entire shell into the hot oil and fry until the dough is crisp and golden brown. (As the masa fries, the dough will begin to separate from the mold. Use the tongs to completely separate in order to brown the dough on both sides.) The masa shell may puff, but you can deflate by puncturing after frying. Drain the shells on paper towels.

Add the remaining 1 tablespoon butter to the skillet and saute the shrimp for a few minutes until they turn pink. Season with salt and pepper, then add the eggs and scramble until softly set but still a bit runny. Stir in the potato mixture and keep warm.

Fill each shell with some of the egg mixture and serve topped with the Salsa of choice. Serves 6.

Chile Egg Omelette
Chile con Torta

I have been given many recipes for this New Mexican breakfast specialty — primarily from first generation cooks who have prepared it at home for years. This particular variation comes from the Guarduno family who operate a restaurant called Guarduno's of Mexico in Albuquerque. Although I have recommended the Spanish sauce, feel free to use any other of your favorite Salsas. The sweet variation is an unusual treat.

Spanish Sauce (p.43)
3 eggs, separated
2 tablespoons flour
1 1/2 teaspoons cornstarch
1/4 teaspoon salt
1/4 teaspoon baking powder
1 tablespoon dried shrimp powder
oil or melted shortening

Have ready the Sauce of choice. Beat the egg yolks, flour, cornstarch, salt, baking powder and shrimp powder until thick. In a separate bowl, beat the egg whites to stiff peaks, then fold into the yolks.

Lightly coat a griddle with oil or shortening and heat. Drop the batter by spoonfuls onto the hot griddle or electric skillet and fry as you would pancakes, turning to brown both sides. Serve immediately with the Sauce or Salsa. Serves 3-4.

Here are three variations on this omelette;

1. Fold 3/4 cup rinsed, dried canned Nopalitas (chopped cactus) into the batter. Fry and serve as directed.

2. Fold 2 tablespoons grated Parmesan cheese into batter. Serve as directed.

3. For a sweet version, add 1 teaspoon powdered sugar and 1 tablespoon Cointreau or Grand Marnier to the batter. Fry as directed and serve with orange sauce (p.55) and a dusting of powdered sugar.

French Toast
Torrejas

Although I have never been fond of the Mexican bread pudding called Capirotada, I was served this absolutely delightful variation in New Mexico. I would present it like French Toast at breakfast or brunch and accompany with fruits.

The Sauce:
1 cup water
2 cups piloncillo or dark brown sugar
1 stick cinnamon, broken
3-4 strips orange peel, colored part only

The French Toast and Assembly:
1/4 cup chopped acitron plus 1-2 tablespoons sugar or 1/4 cup raisins or candied pineapple, optional
4 cups cubed French bread or leftover sweet bread
1/2 cup pine nuts or sliced almonds
oil for deep-frying
2 eggs, separated
1/2 cup powdered sugar for garnish

To make the sauce, bring the water, piloncillo or brown sugar, cinnamon stick and orange peel to a boil, stirring to dissolve the sugar. Let boil, undisturbed, for 10-12 minutes to a thick, syrupy consistency. Discard cinnamon and orange peel. Keep warm or make ahead and reheat at serving time.

If using acitron, place in workbowl with the sugar using the metal blade. Process to finely mince and set aside for garnish.

Spread the bread cubes and nuts in a single layer on two separate baking sheets. Place in a preheated 450° oven and toast the nuts for 2-3 minutes and the bread for 3-4 minutes. Watch so they don't burn. Remove from oven and reserve.

Heat about 3 inches of oil in a deep saucepan or deep fryer to 375-400°.

Beat the egg yolks until thick. In a clean bowl, beat the egg whites to stiff peaks. Fold the whites into the yolks. Using tongs, dip the bread cubes into the egg batter, then fry in the hot oil for about 20 seconds until golden brown. Drain on paper towels; keep warm while frying remaining bread.

Mound the fried bread cubes on individual serving plates. Top with the acitron or raisins and the nuts. Sprinkle with powdered sugar and pass the hot sauce. Serves 4-5.

Variation: Omit the acitron and nuts. Mound the fried bread cubes on chunks of fresh pineapple, banana or papaya and pour hot sauce over all.

BEVERAGES

Many Southwestern beverages are sweet — intentionally so. This is because sweetness balances spiciness. If a food seems to be too picante, a sip of a soothing sweetened drink neutralizes the sting. Or, to put it another way, a spicy dish needs a beverage with enough "punch" to stand up to it. At any rate, the combination is just right. And speaking of punches, Sangria, both red wine and white wine versions, not only make wonderful aperitifs but are excellent accompaniments throughout a meal.

The fame of Mexican-style cocktails has spread just about everywhere. Margaritas and Piña Coladas are, I think, at their best when frozen, and those are the recipes I have developed. They, along with the colorful Tequila Sunrise, are truly festive drinks.

Of course not all Southwestern drinks contain alcohol. Refreshing Fruit Punch and Mexican Pineapple Drink are always welcome. The punch would be perfect for a children's party, an afternoon meeting, or a bridge get-together.

Coffee in the Southwest is really special, and often flavored with both cinnamon and Mexican vanilla. You can make drinks with it that can more than adequately take the place of dessert *and* after-dinner drinks.

Hot chocolate is significantly sweeter than the standard American cocoa drink, and is traditionally served with sugar-topped Buñuelos.

Clockwise from top center: Red Wine Punch (Sangría), Mexican Coffee, Frozen Fruit Punch, White Wine Lemonade (Sangría Blanco), Frozen Margarita.

White Wine Lemonade

Sangría Blanco

Sangría is a wonderful accompaniment to Southwest food, especially the more picante dishes. The sweetness neutralizes spicy appetizers, leaving a clean palate for dinner!

> 1 lemon
> 2 limes
> 2 oranges
> 1/2 cup water
> 1/2 cup sugar
> cracked ice
> 1 quart Chablis
> 1 cup sparkling mineral water
> 2 ounces orange liquer (preferably
>   Triple-sec)

Cut a slice from the ends of the fruits to make them stand flat. Reserve fruit and place the end slices in a small saucepan with the water and sugar. Bring to a boil over medium-high heat, stirring to dissolve sugar. Lower heat and simmer, undisturbed, for 3 minutes to make a simple syrup. Remove from heat and let cool to room temperature. Strain the syrup squeezing juices from the fruit. Discard the fruit end slices. Chill the syrup, covered, up to 1 week.

On day of serving, use a 2mm (thin) slicing disc to process the lemon and limes. Use a 3 or 4mm (standard) slicing disc to process the oranges. (Halve the oranges to fit the feed tube if necessary.) Discard seeds from fruit slices. Chill the slices, covered, until ready to use — up to 8 hours.

To serve the Sangría, pour the syrup into a bowl or large pitcher filled with cracked ice. Add the reserved fruit slices and stir in the wine, mineral water and liquer. Serve immediately. Serves about 6.

Variation: Replace simple syrup with 3/4 cup pineapple syrup from Mexican Pineapple Drink (p.73).

Red Wine Punch

Sangría

Little is known about the origin of Sangría except that it is Spanish. It is intentionally quite sweet to make a perfect accompaniment to spicy food. You may, however, decrease the sugar if you wish. See the note at the end of the recipe for ways to use up leftover Sangría and fruits.

> 2 cups water
> 1/3-1/2 cup sugar
> 4-5 lemons, ends removed and reserved
> 2 apples, cores reserved
> 2-3 oranges, ends removed and reserved
> cracked ice
> 5 ounces Triple-sec
> 5 ounces brandy
> 2 bottles red wine
> 12 ounces club soda

Place the water, sugar and cores and ends of the fruit in a saucepan. Bring to a boil, stirring constantly to dissolve sugar. Let boil 2 minutes. Take off heat and let cool. Strain the syrup, squeezing all the juices from the fruit pieces. Discard the solids. The syrup can be chilled up to a week.

At serving time, slice the fruits using the standard or thin slicing disc. Pour the syrup and sliced fruits over cracked ice in a large pitcher. Stir in the liquers, wine and club soda. Serves 8.

Note: Leftover Sangría can be frozen in ice cube trays for a terrific fruit ice (see Ices and Granitas on p. 246).

Variation: During the holidays, you can substitute 3 cups of cranapple juice for the sugar syrup.

Frozen Margaritas

Mexican Pineapple Drink
Jugo de Piña

This could be called the national drink of Mexico, though it is also claimed to be a border invention. The most popular of the many stories about the origin is that it was invented by Francisco Morales in Juarez, Mexico (twin city to El Paso, Texas) for his wife, Margarita.

The frozen and slushy version was devised by a colorful restauranteur in Dallas. He terminated his search for the perfect frozen Margarita at a "convenience" store by using the "Frozen Icy Machine." Now his "Margarita Machine" idea has spread nationwide, although his formula is a well-kept secret.

With a bit of advance planning and a food processor, you can duplicate the consistency without the bother of crushed ice. Mix the ingredients a day ahead and freeze for 24 hours. (The alcohol will keep the drink from ever freezing solid.) Process to a slush just prior to serving or a few hours ahead and refreeze.

> 1 large egg white, at room temperature
> 1-1½ tablespoons powdered sugar
> 1 cup fresh lime juice (12-14 key limes or
>   about 8 regular limes)
> 1 cup Tequila
> 4 ounces Triple-sec
> ⅓ cup cold water
> coarse salt
> lime slices for garnish

Prepare the Margarita mixture 24 hours before serving. In a medium bowl, beat the egg white with a fork until frothy. Beat in the powdered sugar, then stir in the lime juice, Tequila, Triple-sec and water. Pour into 2 divided ice cube trays and freeze until nearly solid.

Moisten the rims of stemmed glasses and dip in coarse salt. Place the glasses in the freezer.

When ready to serve or a few hours ahead, remove one of the ice cube trays from the freezer. Loosen the "cubes" with a knife and place in the workbowl using the metal blade. Pulse to chop, then run the machine continuously to obtain a slushy texture. Spoon into chilled glasses if serving immediately. Otherwise refreeze the slush. Repeat to process the remaining "cubes." (If you have a large capacity food processor, both trays may be processed at once.)

Serve in the chilled glasses garnished with a half slice of fresh lime. Serves 6.

Note: If the drink is refrozen, you may need to stir before serving to restore the slushy texture.

This is a favorite drink of the Mexican-Americans in Southwestern Texas. Their technique is to allow the pineapple liquid to ferment for several days. I think it's highly unlikely that people today will take the time to ferment pineapple skins. This modern technique is a great way to utilize the part of the pineapple meat that is otherwise wasted. The syrup makes a lovely "lemonade" or unusual base for Sangría or the Frozen Fruit Punch on p.75. This recipe utilizes the skins assuming that you have other plans for the fruit. Make it whenever you use fresh pineapples.

> 2 large pineapples, skin and core
> 3 lemons
> 1½ cups sugar
> 8 cups water
> ice cubes
> additional water, club soda or mineral
>   water to taste
> fresh lemon or pineapple slices for garnish

Scrub the outside of the pineapple with a vegetable brush. Remove the green top, then the skin and core.

Use the 2mm (thin) slicing disc to process the lemon.

Place the cores, skins and lemon slices in a 3 quart saucepan. Add water and sugar and bring to a boil. Simmer over medium heat for 30 minutes, then let cool with the skins and lemon in the liquid. When cool, squeeze the juice from the fruit solids, then discard solids. Strain the syrup into a glass container and chill until ready to use.

To prepare the drink, pour syrup over cracked ice adding about 1 cup additional water or club soda. Add additional sugar if desired and garnish with a fresh lemon or pineapple slice. Serves 8-10.

Sangrita

This spicy Southwest version of a Bloody Mary is served with tequila as a "chaser" and lime slices as a "refresher." You can control the hotness by the number of Jalapeños you use. You may use 1-2 tablespoons of the juice from canned Jalapeños, if desired.

> 1-3 fresh Jalapeño chiles, stemmed and seeded
> 1 small onion, peeled
> 1 teaspoon sugar
> 3 very ripe home-grown tomatoes (or) 1 (14 1/2-ounce) can Italian style tomatoes, undrained
> 3 cups tomato juice
> juice from 2 fresh oranges, about 1 cup
> juice from 3 fresh limes, about 1/3 cup
> juice from 1 fresh lemon, about 2 tablespoons
> 3-5 drops Tabasco
> 1-2 teaspoon Worcestershire sauce, optional
> tequila
> lime slices

Using the metal blade process to mince the Jalapeño and onion with the sugar. Leave in workbowl.

Core and quarter fresh tomatoes and then add to the bowl. Process 15-20 seconds to finely chop the tomatoes. Combine the tomato-onion mixture with tomato juice, citrus juices and seasonings. Strain and then chill for several hours before serving.

The drink congeals slightly upon standing and needs to be stirred prior to serving. Add Tequila to taste and garnish each drink with a lime slice. Yield: about 1 1/2 quarts.

Tequila Sunrise

This colorful and sweet Southwest drink is especially good for lunch or brunch. It is best made in a blender.

> 1 fresh orange
> 1 fresh lime
> 1 1/2 cups fresh squeezed orange juice (about 4 oranges)
> 1/2 cup fresh lime juice (about 2 limes)
> 1/2 cup grenadine syrup
> 1-1 1/2 cups tequila
> 1 cup crushed ice (about 10 cubes)
> 1 egg white

Cut off the ends of the orange and lime and insert into the feed tube, cut side down, using the 2 or 3mm (thin or standard) slicing disc. (It may be necessary to cut fruit in half to fit the feed tube.) Process to slice, then set the fruit aside for the garnish.

Place the remaining ingredients in a blender and process to combine well. Pour into glasses and serve immediately garnished with the fruit slices. Serves 6.

Piña Colada Ice

This is a popular and sweet Southwestern drink. Since the sugar tends to neutralize the "hotness" in chiles, Pina Coladas are great to serve with spicy appetizers. The standard preparation is to mix the ingredients and serve over crushed ice. The following method eliminates the need for the ice and produces a texture much like a Frozen Margarita. Be sure to begin at least a day in advance of serving.

> $^2/_3$ cup coconut milk or coconut cream, see note
> 1$^1/_2$ cups unsweetened pineapple juice
> $^1/_3$ cup fresh squeezed orange juice
> $^1/_2$ cup water
> 8 ounces light rum
> 4-5 slices fresh pineapple for garnish
> 4-5 maraschino cherries for garnish

Stir together the coconut milk, pineapple juice, orange juice, water and rum until well combined. Pour into 2 divided ice cube trays and freeze for at least 24 hours. Because of the alcohol content, the mixture will not freeze solid.

When ready to serve, loosen the "cubes" in one of the trays with a knife and place in the workbowl using the metal blade. Pulse until finely chopped, then run machine continuously to obtain a slushy texture. Spoon into chilled glasses. Repeat to process the remaining "cubes." (If you have a large capacity machine, both trays can be processed at once.)

Serve immediately or refreeze up to 2 hours. Garnish with a small slice of pineapple and a cherry. Serves 4-5.

Note: If you use homemade coconut milk, which is thinner and less sweet than the canned variety, add 3 tablespoons powdered sugar to the mixture.

Frozen Fruit Punch
Helados

This is a delicious tropical fruit punch. The pineapple syrup base can be made ahead. Children, especially, love this non-alcoholic drink.

> 1 cup fresh orange juice
> $^1/_4$ cup fresh lemon juice
> 3 cups pineapple syrup (see Mexican Pineapple Drink on p.73)
> 1 cup mineral water or club soda
> 4 scoops pineapple sherbet

Use a glass bowl that will hold 2 quarts. Combine the fruit juices with the pineapple syrup in the bowl. Just before serving, stir in the mineral water. Float the sherbet in the punch and stir several times before serving. Serves 6-8.

Mexican Coffee
Café Mejicano

Mexican Coffee is to the Southwest as Cappuccino is to Italy. If Mexican vanilla is not available, use a double amount of standard vanilla. Many of the custards, candies, cookies and cream toppings of Mexico are colored with green, red, yellow or white to resemble the native flag. As shown in this recipe, the Southwest has adopted the same colorful and festive spirit.

> ground coffee beans to make 8 cups coffee
> (use recommended amount for your
> coffeemaker)
> 1 teaspoon Mexican vanilla (or 2 teaspoons
> pure vanilla extract)
> 8 ounces Kahlua
> 2 ounces Tequila
> 1½ cups heavy cream, chilled
> 3 tablespoons powdered sugar
> red and green food color for garnish
> 8 sticks cinnamon for garnish

If using a drip coffeemaker add the vanilla to the water to brew the coffee. If using an electric percolater, add the vanilla after the coffee has finished perking.

Place one ounce of Kahlua and ½ ounce of Tequila into each of 8 large coffee mugs or cups.

Using the metal blade, pour the chilled cream through the feed tube with the motor running. Add the sugar and process to incorporate. This method emulsifies the cream into a thick mass that pipes out and holds its shape well.

Fill the coffee mugs or cups ¾ full with hot coffee. Pipe or spoon whipped cream atop each. Use a few drops each of red and green food color to make 2 stripes over the whipped cream.

Serve immediately with a cinnamon stick "stirrer." Serves 8.

Sweet Mexican Coffee
Café Mejicana Dulce

Southwesterners have their own versions of "after dinner coffee." The most simple is to add 1 teaspoon of Mexican vanilla to the coffee grounds for each 9 cups of coffee. I often add ½ inch of canela as well to make an unusual flavor, but personal taste determines the amount and kind of additions.

I have given some of my favorite variations in this book, but since there are no hard and fast rules, feel free to substitute, add, or delete ingredients as you please.

> 1 ounce Mexican chocolate or 1 ounce
> semi-sweet chocolate and ⅛ teaspoon
> cinnamon
> 1 cone piloncillo or 1 cup loosely packed
> brown sugar, see note
> 10-12 cups medium-strong hot coffee
> whipped cream or Vanilla Ice (p.246)
> kahlua

Using the metal blade, drop the chocolate through the feed tube with the motor running and process until finely ground. Add the sugar and process to combine. Place in a small bowl.

Serve the coffee with separate bowls of whipped cream or Ice, chocolate mixture and Kahlua. Allow each guest to flavor their coffee as desired. Serves 10-12.

Note: If using piloncillo, melt with ⅓ cup hot water and then stir in the ground chocolate.

Mexican Chocolate
Chocolaté

Chocolate is one of Mexico's most treasured gifts to the culinary world. For centuries it has been used as a measure of value . . . for currency or romance.

Steaming mugs of hot chocolate were present at ancient Mayan tables and are still traditional in Mexico as well as the American Southwest. Cortez was so taken with the beverage that he stopped on his flight from Mexico to take home some of the chocolate beans and one of the secret ingredients, "thitxochitl" (vanilla beans). Today, hot chocolate and Buñuelos is a tradition at Christmas and New Year's. It is a sweet drink and the sugar quantity can be reduced to personal preference.

The proper chocolate is the Mexican, cinnamon flavored, variety. A slightly lesser amount of commercial, semi-sweet chocolate and cinnamon flavor is acceptable. The original method of preparation used a "molinillo" to beat the mixture to a froth. Somewhere along the way, eggs found their way into the drink. Coupled with a modern food processor technique, an excellent froth is produced!

4 ounces Mexican chocolate or 3½ ounces semi-sweet chocolate plus 1 teaspoon cinnamon
4 tablespoons sugar
4 cups whole milk, scalded
pinch salt
1 teaspoon vanilla, preferably Mexican
2 eggs

Break the chocolate into pieces. Place in the workbowl using the metal blade. Pulse several times to break up the pieces, then run machine continuously until finely chopped. Add the sugar through the feed tube with the motor running. Then, still with the motor running, pour 1 cup of the scalding hot milk through the feed tube. Add the vanilla, salt and eggs in the same manner. Process until you have a good froth. Transfer to the remaining scalded milk in the saucepan, stirring constantly over low heat. Serve immediately. Serves 4.

APPETIZERS & SNACKS

The Spanish word for appetizer is "antijito," which means — literally — "little whim," or "fancy." It has come to mean "snack," which is appropriate, I think, because that's just what a snack does — it satisfies a whim.

Interestingly, many of the tortilla specialities so often served on combination plates in Mexican-style restaurants in the United States fall into this category. Examples are the small Taco (taquito), Burrito, Tamale, Flauta, (flaquito), and Sweet Stuffed Chile. To fashion them as Antijitos, consult the recipe index for these dishes and simply make them in smaller versions.

Americans freely adopt, adapt and modify Mexican appetizer and snack foods, and the repertory includes the variety of light-to-substantial Antijitos presented here. A number of them are ideal for stand-up cocktail parties; among these are Jicama with Fresh Limes (very low-calorie as well!) Cream Cheese with Jalapeño Jelly, and Cheese and Chile Paté. To begin an elegant meal, serve Marinated Fish (Ceviche) in your prettiest stemmed glass serving dishes. You will find that the large array of tortilla specialties, Empanadas and other Mexican-American snacks and appetizers are naturals for casual get-togethers or buffet suppers.

Clockwise from top center: White Wine Lemonade (Sangría Blanco), Oysters in Chile Pesto, Marinated Fish (Ceviche), Flautas, Fresh Salsa.

Jicama with Fresh Limes

Jicama is an ugly, tuberous root widely available in the Southwest from November through July. Despite its appearance, the crisp and delicious white meat inside the brown speckled skin tastes like a cross between an apple and a water chestnut. Both the con leche (milk) and con agua (water) varieties of jicama can be used for this popular, light and low-calorie appetizer.

> 1 medium-small jicama, see note
> 4 limes, Mexican or Key preferred if
>   available
> 1/2 teaspoon fresh ground chile powder or
>   paprika or cayenne pepper
> salt, optional

Use a sharp knife to remove the thick outer peel of the jicama. Then remove the inner fibrous material to expose the white "meat." Rinse under cool water, then cut into 3-4 pieces that will fit snugly into the feed tube. Use the 5-6mm (thick) slicing disc and the Double Slicing Technique (p.21) to make matchstick strips. (If you do not have this disc, slice using the 3-4mm (standard) slicing disc and then cut into strips by hand.)

Arrange the jicama strips on a serving platter and squeeze the juice of the limes over all. Sprinkle with chile powder, paprika or cayenne pepper. (Paprika gives the mildest flavor.)

If desired, place a small salt cellar near the platter for dipping. This is a finger food. Serves 8.

Note: Jicama can be quite large. For best texture, select the smaller ones.

Cream Cheese with Jalapeño Jelly

This is a quick and delicious appetizer. Jalapeño Jelly is a Tex-Mex staple often served on crackers with cream cheese or as a favorite accompaniment to cold meats.

Homemade Jalapeño Jelly is essential for this appetizer.

> 12 ounces softened cream cheese
> 6 ounces Jalapeño Jelly (p.52)
> Cuban biscuits or quartered, buttered and
>   toasted flour tortillas

Use the metal blade to process the cheese until light and fluffy. Mold into a block on a serving platter and top with Jalapeño Jelly. Serves 6-8.

Variation: Add 3 chunks canned pineapple, 1 tablespoon minced toasted onion and 3 tablespoons shredded Monterey Jack cheese to the processed cream cheese.

Marinated Fish
Ceviche

Ceviche may be made with any firm-fleshed *fresh* salt water fish. Some fish that is labeled "fresh" may have been previously frozen. Therefore, unless you are sure, the partial cooking is recommended. Since many shrimp and scallops in this country are frozen, too, this seems the best bet in all cases.

Ceviche should be made at least 4 hours in advance, but eaten within 24 hours of preparation. You may substitute any salt water fish such as cod, flounder, shark or turbot for the shellfish or use a combination of your favorites.

The recipe given is often called "Acapulco Style," but note the interesting variation using a vinaigrette dressing, onion rings, chile strips and capers.

1/2 pound fresh shrimp (medium size)
1 pound medium-large scallops
water to cover
1 tablespoon black peppercorns
1 tablespoon mustard seed
1 lemon, sliced
1 bay leaf, broken
3/4 cup fresh lemon juice (about 6 lemons)
3/4 cup fresh lime juice (about 8 limes)
1 recipe Texas Hot Salsa (p.39), see note
salt and pepper to taste
tablespoon fresh minced cilantro, optional
2 ripe avocados
2 tablespoons fresh orange juice, optional
Boston lettuce leaves
6 sprigs fresh cilantro, optional garnish
Tostados (p.242), optional garnish

Place the shrimp and scallops in a saucepan or skillet with cold water to cover. Tie the peppercorns and mustard seed in a spice bag and add along with lemon slices and bay leaf. Bring to a full boil and boil for 30 seconds. Rinse the shellfish under cool water to stop cooking, then peel and devein the shrimp. If the scallops are large, cut into bite-size pieces.

Marinate the shellfish in the lemon and lime juices in a shallow dish, covered, for at least 4 hours and up to 8 hours.

Prepare the Texas Hot Salsa and reserve.

No more than an hour before serving, drain the shellfish and combine with the Salsa. Adjust salt and pepper to taste and add the minced cilantro. Just prior to serving, peel and halve the avocado and cut into bite-size pieces. Drain off excess liquid from the fish mixture and lightly combine the shellfish with the avocado. Sprinkle with the optional orange juice.

Line chilled stemmed glasses with lettuce leaves and spoon in the Marinated Fish. Garnish with the cilantro sprigs and a few crisp Tostados. Serves 6.

Note: You may use any number of Salsas in place of the Texas Hot Sauce and each imparts a unique flavor. Spanish Style Sauce (p.43) makes a sweeter dish and Fresh Salsa gives a similar smooth texture, but is more tart.

Variation: Make a vinaigrette dressing using 1 cup oil, 3/4 cup white vinegar, 1 tablespoon large capers, 1 teaspoon salt, 1/2 teaspoon sugar and black pepper to taste. Omit the Salsa, avocados and optional orange juice. Instead, marinate the drained shellfish in the vinaigrette and add 1 red or yellow onion (sliced in rings) and 1 small red bell pepper and 2 green chiles, both roasted, peeled and cut in strips (p.14). Chill at least 1 hour or up to 6 hours. Serve garnished with the fresh snipped cilantro. Note that you can choose red or yellow onions depending upon the availability of red peppers. Yellow onions, red peppers and green chiles make a colorful presentation.

Turnovers
Empanadas

Empanadas are pastries with sweet or savory fillings and are baked or fried depending upon regional custom in the Southwest. Baked Empanadas made with a cake-like dough and filled with a pumpkin or sweet potato mixture are favored in many bakeries, especially along the Mexican border. Others, especially popular in New Mexico, feature a flaky pastry and an almond or apricot filling. Fried Empanadas, common in Texas, are made from a Buñuelo dough much like flour tortillas and are often filled with tropical fruits, creamy almond custards or dried fruits and nuts. They are light, crispy and usually served as dessert.

All of the following Empanadas may be made small and served as finger food appetizers and the sweet ones as dessert. Or they can be shaped into larger pastries for a main dish.

I have given two recipes for a basic Empanada dough — one to be fried and the other to be baked. Also, see p.25 for further information on Empanadas. The sweet and savory fillings that follow are interchangeable with either pastry. I urge you to try the fried Empanadas because they are usually light, crispy and probably have fewer calories than the baked ones!

The baked pastries can be frozen and reheated. The fried pastries do not freeze well, but can be made several hours ahead and refrigerated.

Baked Pastry:
  2 cups all-purpose flour
  1/2 teaspoon baking powder
  1/2 teaspoon salt
  1 tablespoon sugar
  1 cup shortening (do not use butter)
  1 small egg
  1/2 tablespoon vinegar
  1/2 teaspoon anise oil, optional
  1 egg yolk combined with 1 tablespoon cream or 1 egg white combined with 1 tablespoon water
  granulated sugar or cinnamon sugar

Place the flour, baking powder, salt, sugar and shortening in the workbowl using the metal blade. Pulse to cut in the shortening. Add egg, water, vinegar and anise oil to workbowl. Pulse until the liquid is incorporated and the dough begins to form a ball. Stop processing before a ball forms.

Place the dough on a flat surface and pinch off rounds slightly larger than a golf ball for entree size and smaller for appetizer size. Using a rolling pin, roll several times in one direction, give the dough a quarter turn and roll in the opposite direction to make a 6-7 inch circle. Place 1-1 1/2 tablespoons desired filling in the center of each dough circle, fold in half and crimp the edge with a pastry tool or flute in the traditional manner (see illustration p.25).

Place on a cookie sheet and chill 45 minutes. Brush with the egg yolk or egg white mixture and sprinkle tops with granulated or cinnamon sugar if making sweet empanadas. Bake 12-15 minutes in a preheated 400° oven. Serve warm or let cool on a rack. Yield: 8-10 entree or dessert turnovers, or 16-20 appetizer empanadas.

Fried Pastry:

- 2 cups all-purpose flour
- 1 teaspoon salt
- 1 teaspoon sugar
- 2 tablespoons soft shortening (do not use butter)
- 2/3 cup hot water
- oil for deep-frying
- powdered sugar, optional

Place the flour, salt, sugar and shortening in a mixing bowl. Use a blending fork or your hands to cut in the shortening. Add hot water and mix to form a dough. Lightly flour your hands and turn dough several times to knead. Cover with plastic wrap and let rest about 20 minutes.

Pinch off rounds of dough about the size of a golf ball for entree size and smaller for appetizer size. Dip each ball in flour, then use your thumbs to make a circle about 2-2¼ inches in diameter. Using a rolling pin, roll each circle into a 6-7 inch circle. Roll several times in one direction, give the dough a quarter turn and roll several times in the opposite direction. Place 1-1½ tablespoons desired filling in the center of each dough circle, then fold in half and crimp edges to seal in the filling.

Heat about 3 inches oil to 375°. Deep fry the pastries 1 at a time, spooning hot oil over the top rather than attempting to turn, until golden brown. Drain on paper towels and dust with powdered sugar if making sweet empanadas. Yield: 12-14 entree or dessert or 20 appetizer empanadas.

Sweet Turnover Fillings

Sweet empanadas may be baked without sugar topping or glazed with egg white and sprinkled with granulated or cinnamon sugar. Fried sweet empanadas are usually dusted with powdered sugar. Either may be served plain or accompanied by sweetened sour cream or sweetened whipped cream.

Almond Cheese Filling:

- 1/2 cup almonds
- 1/2 cup powdered sugar
- 8 ounces cream cheese, cut in pieces
- 1 egg yolk
- 1 teaspoon vanilla
- 1 teaspoon almond extract

Using the metal blade, grind the almonds. Add remaining ingredients to the workbowl and process until smooth. Use to fill as directed.

Apple Filling:

- 4 apples, peeled and cored and cut into bite-sized chunks
- 3 tablespoons (1 1/2 ounces) butter
- juice of 1 lemon
- 1/3 cup sugar
- 2 teaspoons cornstarch
- pinch ground cinnamon

Saute the apples in the butter for 3-4 minutes until softened. Add the remaining ingredients and cook, stirring, until the mixture is thickened and the apples are tender. Let cool and fill as directed. These empanadas are best served with whipped cream that has been sweetened with 2 teaspoons cinnamon sugar and 1 tablespoon apple brandy per cup of heavy cream.

Apricot Filling:

- 1/2 pound dried apricots, see note
- equal amounts sherry and water to cover
- 3/4 cup sugar

Combine the ingredients in a saucepan, using enough sherry and water to cover the apricots. Bring to a simmer, stirring to dissolve the sugar. Take off heat and allow mixture to stand at least 15 minutes until the apricots are soft. Use to fill as directed.

Note: You may use other dried fruits or combinations such as pineapple, candied squash or pumpkin or citron. Prepare as above.

Banana-Nut Filling:

- 1 large or 2 small bananas, chopped into small pieces
- 1/2 cup raisins
- 1/2 cup chopped nuts
- 2 tablespoons honey, heated

Combine all ingredients and use to fill as directed. This empanada is best served with whipped cream sweetened with cinnamon sugar to taste.

Fruit and Cheese Filling:

- 8 ounces softened cream cheese, cut in strips
- 2 papayas, peeled and cut in strips, see note

Allow 4 slices or strips of fruit and 2 strips cheese per empanada. Each slice or strip should be 1 inch long and between 1/4 and 1/2 inch wide. Fill as directed.

Note: You could also use 2 canned mangoes or 6 canned guava halves, drained and cut into strips. Or, you could use strips of guava or quince paste.

Mincemeat Filling:

- 1 3/4 cups mincemeat (p.58)
- 1/4 cup chopped pecans or pine nuts

Combine mincemeat and nuts and use to fill as directed.

Pumpkin or Sweet Potato Filling:

- 1 1/4 cups mashed pumpkin or sweet potato
- 1/2 cup brown sugar
- 1/4 teaspoon anise oil
- 1/2 teaspoon allspice
- 1/2 teaspoon pumpkin pie spice
- 1 egg yolk
- 1 1/2 tablespoons raisins, optional

Combine all ingredients in a small bowl. Use to fill as directed.

Savory Turnover Fillings

Two favorite savory fillings are: 2 cups Spicy Meat Hash (p.57), and 2 cups Seasoned Meat filling (p.58). Others follow.

Chicken and Green Chile Filling:

1 cup shredded cooked chicken
2 tablespoons sour cream
2 chopped green chiles, fresh roasted and peeled (p.14) or canned
salt and pepper to taste
1 tablespoon chicken stock, approximately

Mix together all of the ingredients, using enough chicken stock to moisten. Fill as directed.

Grilled Meat Filling:

2 cups Grilled Meat (p.160)
1 ripe avocado, peeled, pitted and cut in strips

Chop the meat into small pieces, using enough of the sauce to thoroughly moisten. Fill empanadas with the meat and set one strip avocado over the filling for each empanada.

Pork and Apricot Filling:

This may sound like a peculiar combination, but it was the favorite every time I had a testing and tasting session.

$^{1}/_{2}$ cup chopped, dried apricots
chicken stock to cover, heated
$^{1}/_{3}$ cup sugar
$^{1}/_{2}$ cup raisins
$^{1}/_{2}$ cup pine nuts or chopped almonds
$^{1}/_{4}$ teaspoon ground cloves
$^{3}/_{4}$ cup shredded cooked pork
$^{1}/_{2}$ teaspoon cinnamon

Soak the apricots in heated chicken stock to cover for about 1 hour. Then combine with remaining ingredients. Use to fill as directed.

Cheese Crisp

Cheese Crisp, also called "quesadillas" or "Tucson Tostados," are a popular appetizer in Arizona. It was one of the first "American-Mexican" dishes I ever had during my freshman year at the University of Arizona and was the beginning of a lengthy love affair with this picante, delicious food. While many recipes in this book are light and low-calorie, this one is not for weight-watchers!

To be traditional, 18 inch "Sonora-style" flour tortillas are brought to the table sizzling hot on what looks like a pizza pan. Everyone breaks off a crisp section (although they are now often cut in wedges), adds salt or table salsa and washes it down with Mexican beer. Since these large tortillas are difficult to obtain, I suggest using 12 inch flour tortillas (made for Burritos or Burros) or even the 8-10 inch ones. Simply adjust the amount of cheese and accompaniments to the size of the tortillas. The preliminary toasting assures crispness.

I have taken the liberty of combining cheeses in the three variations that follow. Cheddar cheese, alone, is traditional — I hope that my Arizona friends will forgive!

The Tortilla Preparation:
   2 (12 inch) flour tortillas
   ¼ stick (1 ounce) lightly salted butter, softened
   topping and garnish of choice (recipes follow)

Spread one side of each tortilla with the butter. Place on cookie sheets and bake about 10 minutes in a preheated 400° oven until lightly browned and crisp.

Remove from oven and mound with topping of choice. Set oven to broil and place the topped tortillas under the broiler about 6 inches from the heat source. Broil until cheese is melted and bubbly, watching closely to prevent burning.

Serve immediately with garnishes of choice. Serves 4-6.

Topping and Garnishes:
One:
   4 ounces Longhorn Cheddar cheese, chilled
   4 ounces Swiss or Mozzarella cheese, chilled
   salsa of choice or sliced avocados or sour cream for garnish
   salt for garnish

Use the shredding disc to process both cheeses and toss together with a fork. Use to top the tortillas and broil as directed. Serve garnishes in separate condiment bowls.

Two:
   1 bunch scallions, trimmed
   4 ounces Longhorn Cheddar cheese, chilled
   4 ounces Swiss or Mozzarella cheese, chilled

Slice the scallions thinly, keeping green and white parts separated.

Use the shredding disc to process both cheeses and toss together with a fork. Top the tortillas with the white parts of the onion and the cheeses and broil as directed. Sprinkle with the green parts of the onion as a garnish.

Three:
   1 ounce Meunster cheese, chilled
   2 ounces Monterey Jack cheese, chilled
   2 ounces White Cheddar cheese, chilled
   ¼ cup Ricotta or cottage cheese
   1 scallion, cut in several pieces
   Green Tomato Salsa (p.39)

Use the shredding disc to process the Meunster, Monterey Jack and Cheddar cheeses. Remove from workbowl.

Use the metal blade to process the Ricotta or cottage cheese until smooth. Add the shredded cheeses and pulse to combine. Add the scallion and pulse again to combine.

Use to top the tortillas and broil as directed. Serve immediately accompanied by the Salsa.

Cheese and Chile Loaf
Torta con Queso

One of my cooking colleagues who tested many recipes for this book adapted one of her favorites to include the fresh roasted chiles and corn tortillas with which she became intimately familiar. Coupled with a mild fresh tomato vinaigrette, this loaf makes a perfect buffet appetizer. Served hot, it could be an accompaniment to chicken or beef or even a light lunch or supper main course. The loaf is equally good made with canned green chiles and pimientos instead of the green chiles and red bell peppers.

The Loaf:
    12 ounces cheddar cheese
    4 corn tortillas
    2½ cups whole milk
    1 small onion, peeled and quartered
    ½ stick (2 ounces) butter, softened
    5 sprigs fresh cilantro or parsley
    1 teaspoon salt
    ¼ teaspoon dry mustard
    3 cups cooked rice
    3 large eggs
    6 fresh green chiles, roasted and peeled
        (p.14) or 2 (4 ounce) cans green chiles
    2 large red bell peppers, roasted and peeled
        (p.14) or 2 (4 ounce) jars pimientos,
        drained

Tomato Vinaigrette:
    4 ripe tomatoes or 1 (14½ ounce) can
        Italian plum tomatoes
    2 cloves garlic, unpeeled
    ¼ cup vinegar
    ½ cup safflower oil
    1 teaspoon salt or to taste
    ¼ teaspoon fresh ground black pepper or
        to taste
    several sprigs fresh parsley or cilantro
    1-2 tablespoons tomato sauce or juice,
        optional

Use the shredding disc to process the cheese and set aside.

Soak the tortillas in 1 cup of the milk for about 45 minutes or until they are soft and falling apart. Transfer the tortillas with a slotted spoon to the workbowl using the metal blade. Reserve the soaking milk and add the remaining milk to make a total of 2 cups.

Add the onion to the workbowl and process the mixture until pureed. Add the butter, parsley, salt and dry mustard and process to combine well. Add the rice and process to combine. With the machine running, add the eggs through the feed tube. Stop machine and add half of the cheese and process to combine. Transfer half of the mixture to a large bowl. Add remaining cheese to the workbowl and pulse several times to incorporate. With the machine running, pour the milk through the feed tube.

Transfer the entire mixture to the large bowl and stir to combine all of the ingredients. (The entire mixture may be combined in the processor if you have a large capacity machine.)

Cut the chiles and peppers or pimientos into flat 2 inch strips.

Butter a 9 x 5 x 3 inch loaf pan and spread ⅓ of the cheese-rice mixture in the pan. Cover with half of the chile and pepper strips. Repeat to make 3 layers ending with the cheese-rice mixture.

Place the loaf pan in a larger pan half-filled with warm water and bake for 1¼ hours in a preheated 350° oven. The loaf should be firm. Let cool 10 minutes, then invert onto a serving platter. Serve hot or cold with the vinaigrette.

To make the vinaigrette, first roast the fresh tomatoes and garlic by placing on a cookie sheet and set under a preheated broiler about 6 inches from the heat source. Broil, turning until all sides are brown and charred. Let cool, then peel the tomatoes and garlic. (Some cooks prefer not to peel the tomato and feel it gives the dressing a better color.) Reserve any tomato juices.

Using the metal blade, drop the garlic through the feed tube with the motor running to mince. Add the tomatoes and remaining vinaigrette ingredients except tomato sauce. Process to thoroughly combine. If the tomatoes lack good flavor or color, add the tomato sauce or juice. Serves 10-12 depending on use.

Tender Beef on a Stick
Anticuchos

Anticuchos are a Texas tradition and especially popular during the Spring Food Festival Week called "Night in Old San Antonio." The festival is held annually in La Villita, a small village where the Spanish soldiers lived in the 18th century. It sports hundreds of food booths, each with a specialty unique to Mexico, New Orleans, Texas, Spain, France, Germany and Greece — sort of all inclusive!

Anticuchos are always made with beef tenderloin, and extravagance found in Mexico as well. However, you could substitute beef sirloin tip.

> 3 cloves garlic, peeled
> 1 yellow onion, peeled and quartered
> 4 chile Serranos or chile Jalapeños (canned or fresh)
> 1½ cups red wine vinegar
> 2 teaspoons salt
> ½ teaspoon black pepper
> 1 teaspoon oregano
> 1-2 teaspoons Worcestershire sauce to taste
> ½ cup ice water
> 6 (8 ounce) beef tenderloin fillets or 3 pounds sirloin tip roast

Prepare the marinade at least 12 hours in advance. Crush the garlic with the blunt end of a knife. Mince the onion in a processor with the metal blade. Combine the garlic, onion and remaining ingredients except the meat in a shallow glass dish large enough to accomodate the meat.

Cut the meat into 1 inch cubes and marinate 12 hours, turning the pieces occasionally.

Anticuchos are traditionally cooked outdoors but they can also be deep-fried.

Too cook over a grill, skewer 5-6 pieces of meat on a stick or skewer. Reserve the marinade and use to baste the meat several times as they cook over a hot fire. Total cooking time should be 3-4 minutes, although this may vary according to the fire and whether you like the meat rare or well-done.

To deep fry the meat, thoroughly drain and pat dry the beef after removing from the marinade. Heat the marinade in a saucepan. Bring at least 2-3 inches of oil in a deep saucepan or deep-fryer to about 400°. Fry the meat, 5 or 6 pieces at a time for about 1½ minutes until crisp. Thread the meat on skewers, brush with the marinade and serve immediately. Serves 5-6 generously.

Northern Style Cheese with Chiles   Chile con Queso del Norte

My friends Jesse and Carmen Calvillo from San Antonio make their Chile con Queso in this manner. Although they use Oaxaca cheese from Mexico, the combination of Mozzarella and Monterey Jack is quite good. It is best served immediately with fresh, thin flour tortillas, but Tostados are easier and very tasty. A fresh Raw Salsa (p.38) is often served on the side.

> 4 chile Poblanos or fresh green chiles, roasted and peeled (p.14)
> ½ small yellow onion, peeled
> 1 tablespoon vegetable oil
> 2 tablespoons cream or milk
> 6 ounces Mozzarella cheese, chilled
> 6 ounces Monterey Jack cheese, chilled
> 2 ounces softened cream cheese
> fresh flour tortillas or Tostados (p.27)

Seed and stem the chiles and cut into thin strips about 1½ inches long. Use a 2mm (thin) slicing disc to process the onion. In a medium skillet, saute the onion in the oil until the onion is translucent. Add the chiles and cream to the skillet. Cook, stirring, over low heat for about 2 minutes. Do not allow to boil.

Use the shredding disc to process the Mozzarella and Monterey Jack cheeses. Drop the shredded cheese in 2 batches into the skillet, allowing one to melt over low heat before adding the second. Do not allow to boil. When the cheese is melted, stir in the cream cheese and serve immediately with the tortillas or Tostados.

Variation: A bit more trouble, but an attractive presentation is to soften corn or flour tortillas, then butter and press into muffin tins. Bake until crisp and 350°, then spoon the prepared Chile con Queso into the crisp "shell." Serve as above.

Cheese with Chiles
Chile con Queso

Many variations of melted cheese and chiles exist throughout Mexico, but Chile con Queso is a very American-Mexican dish. It is a delicious hot snack or appetizer dip with Tostados (Corn Chips) as well as a good sauce for vegetables and omelettes. Sometimes only chiles and onion are used, but often tomatoes are added to the combination. Texas Hot Salsa (p.39) contains the necessary ingredients and is a fine way to use up any leftover Salsa. (This Salsa is such a Southwestern staple that many households make it every day.) Use 1/2 cup Texas Hot Salsa and omit the chiles and onions from the recipe.

Chile con Queso should be served immediately because the melted cheese loses its good texture after 15-20 minutes. Keep it warm in a fondue pot or chafing dish.

> 6 ounces Monterey Jack cheese, chilled
> 6 ounces Mozzarella or Longhorn Cheddar cheese, chilled
> 3-4 fresh green chiles, roasted and peeled (p.14) or 1/2 cup chopped mild green chiles
> 1 small yellow onion, peeled and quartered
> 1 tablespoon vegetable oil
> 1/3 cup (approximately) heavy cream or evaporated milk
> tostados (p.242), optional

Have all ingredients and serving dishes ready.

Process the cheeses using the shredding disc. Set aside. Use the metal blade to chop together the onions and chiles. Set aside.

Heat the oil in a 12-14 inch skillet and saute the onions and chiles just until the onion is transparent. (If you use the Texas Hot Salsa, saute it in the oil.) With the skillet set over medium-low heat, add the cheese by handfuls, allowing each to melt before adding another. Stir in just enough of the cream to make a thick, smooth texture. Do not allow the mixture to boil at any time.

Transfer to a heated chafing dish or fondue pot and serve at once with Tostados (Corn Chips). Stir through the mixture several times to keep the creamy texture. Serves 8.

Southwestern Appetizer

This is a colorful buffet appetizer that has many variations on the same theme. My mother, who is not particularly fond of Mexican food, remarked that she was amazed that it tasted so good "all mixed up." This festive combination truly is quite an array of textures, taste and colors.

Shred the cheese and prepare the beans early in the day, but assemble the appetizer shortly before serving.

> 3 tablespoons minced onion
> 3-4 tablespoons shortening
> 2 1/2 cups Refried Beans (p.215)
> 1/2 teaspoon chile powder
> 2 cups Guacamole (p.49)
> 1 pound bulk Mexican Sausage (p.56) or ground beef seasoned with salt, pepper, garlic, oregano and chile powder to taste
> 1/2 pound Longhorn Cheddar or Monterey Jack cheese
> 1/2 pound crumbled "Enchilada" cheese or another dry white cheese
> 2 (4 ounce) cans fire-roasted green chiles, drained
> 1/2 teaspoon salt or to taste
> 2 cups sour cream
> 1/2 cup heavy cream
> 1 large tomato, chopped and drained
> 1 cup black olives, sliced
> 2 tablespoons chopped chives or scallions (green part only)
> warm tostados (p.242)

Have ready a 12-14 inch deep platter to layer the ingredients.

Saute the onion in the shortening until softened, then stir in the beans and chile powder. Taste and adjust the seasonings, then keep warm while preparing remaining ingredients.

Prepare the guacamole and reserve.

Saute the sausage or seasoned beef, drain off excess fat and keep warm until ready to use.

Use the shredding disc to process the Cheddar or Monterey Jack cheese. Use the metal blade to chop the chiles and season with salt.

Combine the sour cream and the heavy cream.

Layer the ingredients on the platter. Begin with the beans, then layer the meat, chile, guacamole and both of the cheeses. Spoon sour cream mixture over the top and garnish with the tomatoes, sliced olives and chives or scallions. Serve with warm tostados. Serves 8-10.

Mushrooms with Cheese
Hongos con Queso

This delicious appetizer is similar to Chile con Queso and very popular in Houston restaurants. I prefer the creamy Havarti and Swiss cheese combination to traditional Mexican substitutes.

- 12 corn tortillas, quartered and fried crisp and lightly salted or 48 packaged tostados
- 8 ounces Havarti cheese, well chilled
- 6 ounces Swiss cheese, chilled
- 1/4 pound crisp, white mushrooms wiped clean with a damp cloth
- 2 cloves garlic, peeled
- 2 tablespoons oil
- 1/4-1/3 cup evaporated milk
- 1 (4 ounce) can mild or hot green chiles, drained and diced
- 2 tablespoons minced chives for garnish

Arrange the tostados in 6 individual oven-proof dishes. Heat in a pre-heated 350° oven for 5-10 minutes.

Meanwhile make the sauce. Use the shredding disc to process the cheeses. Toss with a fork to combine and set aside.

Discard stems from the mushrooms and slice thinly by hand. In a 2 quart saucepan or 10-12 inch skillet, saute the mushrooms and whole garlic in the oil until the mushrooms are soft. Discard the garlic and stir in 1/4 cup of the milk and the chiles. Then stir in the cheese by handfuls, stirring only enough to melt cheese and incorporate with the milk. If the mixture is too thick, stir in the remaining milk. Do not allow the mixture to boil.

When the cheese mixture is melted and smooth, pour over the heated tostados. Sprinkle with chives and serve immediately. Serves 6.

Pumpkin Seed Torte
Torta Pepita

One of my cooking friends who specializes in patés contributed this version — one of her favorites. It is a simple recipe, lower in fat than most patés and is one everyone seems to enjoy.

- 1 1/4 pounds raw pork and pork fat (Boston Butt or another cut with ample fat)
- 1 raw chicken breast half, boned (about 3 1/2 ounces)
- 1/4 cup brandy
- 1/4 cup dry vermouth
- 1 teaspoon salt
- 1 teaspoon pepper
- 5 scallions, white part only
- 1/2 cup parsley sprigs
- 2 eggs, beaten
- 1/3 cup pine nuts or pumpkin seeds
- 4 strips bacon
- Jalapeño Jelly (p.52)
- toast rounds or French bread

Cut the pork and fat into 1 inch cubes. (If the pork is lean, add 2 ounces pork fat.) There should be about 3 1/2 cups of cubes. Press the meat into the measuring cup for an accurate measure. Cut the chicken into 1 inch cubes. Place half of the pork and chicken in the workbowl using the metal blade. Pulse at first, then process until coarsely ground. Remove ground meat and place in a glass bowl. Repeat to grind remaining meat and chicken. Add to bowl with the brandy, vermouth, salt and pepper. Stir to combine and then refrigerate overnight.

Just before baking, use the metal blade to mince the scallions and parsley. Stir into the meat mixture along with the eggs and pine nuts or seeds.

Line a 9 x 5 loaf pan with 2 bacon strips. Pack the meat mixtrue into the pan and lay the remaining 2 strips bacon over the top. Cover with oiled wax paper and place the pan in a larger pan half filled with water. Bake 2 hours in a preheated 350° oven. Let cool, then chill 2-3 hours before slicing. The paté can also be frozen for several months.

When ready to serve, unmold and discard the bacon. Slice thin and serve as an appetizer or first course accompanied by Jalapeño Jelly and toast rounds or French Bread. Makes 18-24 slices.

Grilled Cheese
Queso Flameado

This is another border specialty very popular in Texas. Although it is not as prevalent in Arizona or New Mexico, there is a trend throughout the Southwest to blend and integrate recipes from other regions.

Oaxaca cheese is the first choice because of its distinctive acid flavor and good melting quality. Unfortunately, it is often difficult to obtain and a combination of Monterey Jack and Mozzarella cheese is a good compromise.

Be sure to use bulk Mexican Chorizo sausage or another well-seasoned bulk pork sausage meat. At the end of the recipe is a variation using cooked shrimp.

    6 ounces Monterey Jack cheese, chilled
    6 ounces Mozzarella cheese, chilled
    1/2 teaspoon salt, optional
    6 fresh flour tortillas, see note
    1/2 pound bulk Mexican Sausage (p.56) or
        well-seasoned pork sausage plus 1/4
        teaspoon chile powder
    1/2 cup (100 proof) brandy, optional

Use the shredding disc and light pressure to process both cheeses together. Add salt and set aside.

If the tortillas are not fresh and warm, reheat them by placing each on a non-stick griddle or skillet over medium heat for a few seconds on each side. Wrap in a towel to keep warm and soft.

Saute the sausage in a well-seasoned skillet until just cooked. Drain off most of the accumulated fat and add the cheese to the skillet. Set over medium heat just long enough to melt the cheese. (Do not stir or allow to boil.) When the cheese is melted, scoop into individual (6-8 ounce) ramekins.

Place each ramekin on a small serving plate with a tortilla draped over the top. The procedure is to then spoon the sausage mixture onto the tortilla, roll it up and eat like a sandwich. (Those accustomed to eating Mexican food soon learn the trick of making a small fold or elevating the end of the tortilla to prevent the filling from spilling out.)

You could make somewhat of a show with this appetizer by flambeeing the cheese mixture and serving the tortillas in a separate, covered basket. Heat the brandy and pour about one tablespoon over each ramekin, then ignite. Serves 6.

Note: If you do not make your own tortillas and cannot obtain good fresh ones, butter packaged tortillas and lightly toast in the oven. Or, use warm buttered French bread. Serve these in a separate covered basket and spoon the cheese mixture onto the tortillas or bread.

Variation: Replace the sausage with 1 pound of cooked and coarsely chopped shrimp. Saute the shrimp and 1 clove of minced garlic in 1 tablespoon each of butter and oil. Season with about 1/4 teaspoon salt and 1/8 teaspoon chile powder to taste. Add cheese to skillet and proceed as directed.

Chicken Loaf
Torta de Pollo

This mold is equally good made with cooked salmon instead of chicken. It makes a fine first course or appetizer served in thin slices and accompanied by crackers.

2 packages unflavored gelatin
1/2 cup cold water
3/4 cup well-seasoned chicken stock
1/2 medium onion, peeled
1/2 tablespoon butter
5-6 fresh green chiles, roasted and peeled
   (p.14) or 2 (4 ounce) cans green chiles
1 cup sour cream
3 tablespoons pine nuts, optional
1/2 teaspoon salt
white pepper to taste
1 cup heavy cream
1 clove garlic, peeled
1 pound cooked chicken, cut in several
   pieces
1 large avocado, peeled, pitted and cut into
   8 slices
juice of 1/2 lemon
Raw Salsa (p.38) or southwest Vinaigrette
   (p.53)
fresh cilantro sprigs for garnish

Soften the gelatin in the cold water, then heat to dissolve. Stir 2/3 of the mixtrue into the chicken stock.

Use the metal blade to chop the onion, then saute in the butter for about 3 minutes until the onion is soft and translucent. Meanwhile, remove stems and seeds from chiles and chop using the metal blade. Leave in workbowl and pulse in the sour cream, sauteed onion, pine nuts, salt, pepper and remaining 1/3 dissolved gelatin. Remove from workbowl and set aside. It is not necessary to clean the workbowl.

Use an electric mixer to whip the cream until thickened. Reserve.

Using the metal blade, drop the garlic through the feed tube with the motor running to mince. Add chicken to workbowl and process 60-90 seconds until finely ground and light in texture. Add the stock mixture and season to taste with a pinch of salt and white pepper. Fold into the thickened cream.

Sprinkle the avocado pieces with lemon juice.

To assemble the mousse, spread 1/2 of the chicken mixture in a 9 x 5 x 3 inch loaf pan. Press 4 of the avocado pieces into the loaf. Spread all of the chile mixture over the chicken, then spread with remaining chicken mixture and press in the remaining 4 avocado pieces, submerging them completely. Rap the mold several times on a counter to "settle," then chill at least 6 hours or overnight.

To serve, unmold onto a serving plate. Slice thin and serve with the Salsa or Vinaigrette. Garnish with the cilantro sprigs. Serves 10-12.

Chile Pesto Oysters

Óstiones con Chile Pesto

Oysters are as popular in the Southwestern states as they are in Mexican cities bordering the Gulf of California or Gulf of Mexico. They can be served in a picante salsa (ceviche style) or baked with green chiles. This is my own version and one that may rival Oysters Rockefeller.

If possible, buy fresh oysters in the shell. If not, use shucked oysters.

> 24 oysters, in the shell or shucked with liquer reserved
> rock salt, optional
> 1½ cups Green Chile Pesto (p.52) or Cilantro Pesto (p.53)
> 3-4 sprigs parsley
> 4 slices French bread, torn in pieces
> ¼ teaspoon salt
> ⅛ teaspoon cayenne pepper
> 5-6 tablespoons butter

If the oysters are in the shell, open them and leave on the half shell. Line a cookie sheet with rock salt and place the half shells on the bed of salt. If the oysters are already shucked, butter 4 individual ovenproof ramekins and arrange 6 oysters in each. Stir 1-2 tablespoons of the oyster liquer into the Green Chile Pesto and divide the mixture atop the oysters. Bake 5 minutes in a preheated 400° oven.

Meanwhile, using the metal blade, drop the parsley through the feed tube to mince. Add the bread, salt and pepper to the work bowl and process to make fine crumbs. Saute the crumbs in the butter until crisp and browned. Divide the mixture over the Pesto topped oysters and return to the oven for about 5 minutes until oysters are plump and edges have curled. Serve immediately. Serves 6-8.

Cheese and Chile Squares

This typical appetizer is usually baked in a rectangular pan and cut in squares. The presentation is further enhanced if accompanied by a tomato salsa of your choice. It should be served warm, but can be baked ahead and reheated.

> 2 ounces Parmesan cheese, cut in several pieces
> 2 (4-ounce) cans mild or hot green chiles
> 4 ounces Longhorn cheddar cheese, chilled
> 12 ounces Monterey Jack cheese, chilled
> 1 teaspoon salt
> several dashes tabasco sauce
> 10 eggs, divided
> ⅓ cup all-purpose flour
> 1 teaspoon baking powder
> ½ cup melted butter
> 2 cups cottage cheese

Using the metal blade, drop the Parmesan cheese pieces through the feed tube with the motor running and process until finely grated. Remove and set aside. Without washing the workbowl, use the metal blade to chop the chiles. Remove and set aside.

Use the shredding disc to process the Cheddar and Monterey Jack cheeses separately. Remove and set aside.

Using the metal blade, process to combine the salt, tabasco sauce, 2 eggs, flour, baking powder and grated Parmesan cheese. With the machine running, add the hot melted butter through the feed tube. Remove the cover and add cottage cheese and then process until smooth. With the machine running, add 3 eggs through the feed tube. Remove ⅔ of the mixture from the workbowl and combine with the Cheddar cheese and chiles. Add the remaining eggs and Monterey Jack cheese to the remaining mixture in the workbowl and process 20-30 seconds.

Combine the 2 mixtures and spread in a buttered 17 x 10 inch jelly roll pan.

Bake 15 minutes in a preheated 400° oven, then reduce temperature to 350° and bake about 35-40 minutes more until the cheese is set and firm. Cut into squares and serve warm with your favorite salsa. Makes 24 thin slices.

Note: If you have a large capacity machine, all the eggs may be added at once and both cheeses may be added and combined in the processor bowl.

Nachos

Nachos are quartered and crisply fried corn tortillas topped with a variety of ingredients, but usually including cheese. They are an inevitable combination considering the abundance of Tostados (quartered corn chips) and cheese used in Southwest cooking.

The most colorful tale of their invention comes from the El Paso-Juarez area. Apparently a humble tavern owner, Ignacio, was surprised after hours by some hungry and aggressive Texans. Unfortunately, his kitchen was quite bare, but he was able to find stale Tostados, cheese, Refried Beans and Jalapeño chiles. In a brief moment, under a hot broiler, Nachos were born. My guess is that Nachos, under different names, have been a standard in Mexican and border cooking for years.

Today, Nachos have become a "mini-pizza" and the most popular appetizer in Southwest restaurants and homes. The toppings are as varied and plentiful as the cook's imagination. No recipe is needed — just a method for preparation.

To prepare Nachos, use stale quartered corn tortillas and fry crisp in oil heated to 360°. Salt lightly and drain on paper towels. (Note that most nationally available brands of packaged Tostados or Tortilla Chips will be too thin to make satisfactory Nachos, so you should make your own.)

Arrange the fried Tostados (Tortilla Chips) on a cookie sheet, top with shredded cheese, then place under a preheated broiler about 4-6 inches from the heat source. Broil, watching carefully, until hot and the cheese is melted but not browned. Longhorn Cheddar is a traditional cheese choice, but I also like Monterey Jack and Havarti with seafood as well as a combination of Longhorn Cheddar and Mozzarella as a nice change.

Nachos should be served at once because melted cheese does not "hold" well. The first time I had these at a party, as a novice I carefully removed the hot chile strips from the top. However, I am now addicted and boast about my "cold-free" winters that are commonly attributed to the ingestion of hot chiles.

The following are some combinations of Nacho toppings for you to try. Those in italic are to be added after broiling. Use your imagination and add or delete ingredients according to preference and availability.

Toppings:
1. Refried Beans (p.215), cheese of choice, *Jalapeño chile strips*.
2. Refried Beans, cheese of choice, small pieces of grilled meat, *Guacamole (p.49), sour cream, Jalapeño chile strips*.
3. Chopped, cooked shrimp or crab, cheese of choice, *Jalapeño chile strips or fresh Salsa of choice*.
4. Refried Beans, Chicken Stew (p.56), cheese of choice, *sour cream, Guacamole*.
5. Chopped mushroom, cheese of choice, green chiles, *sour cream*.

SOUPS

For the most part, Mexican-American soups are of the hearty, stick-to-the-ribs persuasion. They are full-bodied and nourishing, and often — like Chicken Tortilla Soup (*Sopa Azteca*) — a meal in themselves. Actually, I think *Sopa Azteca* is the most beautiful soup in the world, and the most colorful. To me, it is the quintessence of San Antonio winter fare.

The word soup, or *sopa*, can be a confusing one in this cuisine. Just plain *sopa* indicates a substantial soup, like the one above. You'll sometimes see a restaurant list a course called *sopa seca* and you may know enough Spanish to figure out that the phrase means "dry soup." Now, what on earth is a dry soup? Quite simply, it is a starchy, casserole-like dish. The base may be noodles, sliced tortillas or macaroni. It could be said to correspond to the pasta course in an Italian meal. For that reason, no sopa secas appear in this section. To find a few, look in the index for Vermicelli Soup and Vermicelli Soup with Pesto; they are in the Accompaniment section in this book. Serve them either as a first course or with the meat or poultry.

Incidentally, there is another word you should know — "Caldo." It means broth.

Chicken Tortilla Soup (Sopa Azteca).

El Mirador Mexican Soup

Caldo Xochitl

This fragrant and delicious soup has brought national attention to El Mirador, a small, family-operated Mexican restaurant in San Antonio. A food processor makes short work of the many time-consuming preparation steps. I usually cook the chicken and prepare the stock a day in advance.

Accompanied by El Mirador Rice and a loaf of bread or fresh tortillas, this soup is a meal in itself.

The Stock:
    5 cloves garlic, peeled
    2½ quarts water
    1 tablespoon dried oregano
    ¼ teaspoon ground cloves
    1 tablespoon salt
    1 tablespoon ground cumin
    1 teaspoon fresh ground pepper
    3 bay leaves, broken
    1-2 sprigs fresh basil (omit if fresh is not
        available)
    3 chicken bouillon cubes
    1 (3 pound) frying chicken, cut up

The Vegetables:
    1 medium zucchini (to make 2 cups sliced)
    1 yellow onion, peeled
    2 stalks celery (to make 1 cup chopped)
    3 carrots, scraped and cut in 1-2 inch
        chunks
    1 green bell pepper, seeded and quartered
    1 (17 ounce) can garbanzo beans, drained

The Garnish:
    1 bunch scallions
    ½ bunch fresh cilantro
    2 ripe tomatoes, cored
    2 fresh green chiles
    2 avocados, peeled and pitted
    El Mirador Rice (p.218) or White Rice
        (p.217)

Prepare the chicken and stock a day ahead.

Using the metal blade, drop the garlic through the feed tube with the motor running to mince.

Bring the water to a boil in a 4-5 quart kettle. Add the garlic and remaining stock ingredients including chicken. Bring back to a boil, then lower heat and simmer, covered, for 1 hour until the chicken is tender. Skim foam from the top as it accumulates. With a slotted spoon, remove the chicken from the stock and let cool. Remove the chicken from the bones. Discard skin and return bones to stockpot and simmer for 20 minutes. Strain stock and discard bones. Chill the stock and chicken, separately, overnight.

Prepare the vegetables and garnish on serving day. Use a 3mm (standard) slicing disc to shred the chicken. Use the same disc to slice the zucchini and onion. Set aside. Cut the celery in chunks and use the metal blade to coarsely chop the celery and carrots. Add the green pepper to the workbowl with the carrot and celery and pulse until chopped. Set the vegetables and chicken aside.

Skim fat from stock and bring to a boil. Add the vegetables and simmer about 20 minutes until tender. Add the chicken and garbanzo beans. Heat through, but do not cook the soup much longer or the vegetables will be mushy.

Use the metal blade to separately chop all of the garnishes except rice and place in separate condiment dishes.

The rice may be served separately or with the soup ladled over. The garnishes should be served separately. Serves 8.

Chicken Tortilla Soup
Sopa Axteca

This is Mary Trevino's variation on Tortilla Soup. In addition to the unusually attractive presentation, Mary tells me that she serves the soup this way to keep the vegetables tender-crisp and the tortilla strips from becoming soggy. Texans have driven six hours to sample Mary's soup at her San Antonio restaurant, El Mirador.

A colorful dish for winter entertaining, the stock and vegetables may be prepared in advance and then simply combined just before serving. This hearty and filling soup is a complete meal in itself and need only be complimented by cornbread, tortillas or French rolls.

The Stock:

10 cups water
2 (14½ ounce) cans beef broth
1 tablespoon vegetable oil
4 large ripe tomatoes, cored and quartered
1 large yellow onion, peeled and quartered
4 cloves garlic, peeled
1 (2½-3 pound) chicken, quartered
3 tablespoons fresh basil leaves or 1 teaspoon dried basil
3-4 teaspoons cumin or to taste
1-2 teaspoons chile powder or to taste
1½ teaspoons coarse ground black pepper
3 teaspoons salt or to taste
1 teaspoon crushed leaf oregano

The Vegetables:

2 red potatoes
1½ tablespoons vegetable oil
20 leaves fresh spinach, washed and dried
2 medium zucchini
3 carrots, scraped
3 ribs celery, cut in pieces to fit feed tube
6 ounces Mozzarella or Monterey Jack cheese
8 corn tortillas, cut into ¼ inch strips
oil for frying tortillas
6 ounces tomato sauce
2 avocados, peeled, pitted and sliced into thin strips for garnish

Bring the water and beef stock to a boil in a stockpot large enough to accomodate the chicken. Meanwhile, coat a heavy cookie sheet with the vegetable oil and place the tomatoes and onion quarters on the sheet in a single layer. Roast under a pre-heated broiler, about 8 inches from the heat source, for about 20 minutes turning several times.

Let cool. Place the unpeeled roasted tomatoes and onion along with the garlic in a blender jar and process until pureed.

Add the chicken to the boiling stock and return to a boil. Skim the foam that rises to the top, then add the pureed tomato mixture and the remaining stock ingredients. Simmer 1½-2 hours, skimming foam from top occasionally. When the chicken is very tender and begins to fall from the bone, remove with a slotted spoon. Let cool, then remove and discard the skin and bones. Shred the chicken and set aside until ready to finish the soup. Keep the stock hot.

Prepare the vegetables. Cook the potatoes in boiling salted water until just tender. Drain, peel and cut into bite-sized pieces. Saute in the vegetable oil for 1-2 minutes, then set aside. (The sauteeing will prevent the potatoes from falling apart when added to the soup.)

Use scissors to snip the spinach into strips.

Use the 3-4mm (standard) slicing disc and the Double Slicing Technique (p.21) to process the zucchini and carrots into matchstick strips. Use the standard slicing disc to slice the celery, loading it vertically into the feed tube.

Cook the carrots and celery in the simmering stock for about 2 minutes. Add the zucchini and cook about 1 minute more. The vegetables should be crisp-tender. Remove all vegetables with a slotted spoon and set aside until ready to finish the soup. If not serving immediately, cool the stock and set aside until ready to finish the soup.

Cut the cheese into 2½ x ¼ inch strips and reserve. Fry the tortilla strips, in 5-6 batches, in oil heated to 375° until crisp. Drain on paper towels and set aside.

Shortly before serving, bring the stock to a simmer and stir in the tomato sauce. Bring remaining ingredients to room temperature.

Divide the vegetables, chicken, cheese and tortilla strips among 10 deep soup bowls. Ladle simmering stock and chicken into the bowls and serve immediately topped with several strips of avocado. Serves 10.

Tortilla Soup
Sopa de Tortilla

This is similar to Onion Soup in that it is served with tortilla strips (Mexican "bread") and an ample amount of stringy cheese. The recipe is classic, but I have somewhat changed the presentation. Instead of simmering the tortilla strips in the broth, they are fried crisp and added at the end so that they keep their shape.

The soup can be made more picante, as is usually done in Texas, by adding canned or fresh Jalapeño chiles either diced or in thin strips. Fresh roasted chile Poblanos, if available, make this soup distinctive.

2 cloves garlic, peeled
1 large yellow onion, peeled
1 tablespoon butter
2 tablespoons oil
4 mild green chiles (Poblano preferred),
    roasted and peeled (p.14) or 1 (4 ounce)
    can mild green chiles
2 Jalapeño chiles, seeds and veins removed,
    optional (see p.14 for instructions on
    handling hot chiles)
1 (14½ ounce) can Italian plum tomatoes
1 cup tomato sauce
3½ cups chicken stock
1 teaspoon ground chile powder
1 teaspoon ground cumin
¼ teaspoon leaf oregano
1 teaspoon salt or to taste
½ cup fresh parsley or several cilantro
    sprigs
12 ounces Monterey Jack or Mozzarella
    cheese, chilled
6 corn tortillas
oil for frying

Using the metal blade, drop the garlic through the feed tube with the motor running to mince. Leave in workbowl and change to a 2 or 3mm (thin) slicing disc. Cut the onions to fit the feed tube and slice. Heat the butter and oil in a 3 quart saucepan and lightly saute the onions and garlic.

Remove seeds and stems from chiles and slice into narrow strips. Add the chiles, tomatoes, tomato sauce, chicken stock, chile powder, oregano, cumin and salt to the saucepan. Stir to break up the whole tomatoes and bring to a boil. Reduce heat and simmer 15-20 minutes.

Mince the parsley or cilantro using the metal blade and stir into the soup. Use the shredding disc to process the cheese and set aside.

Cut the tortillas into ½ x 2 inch strips and fry crisp, in 5-6 batches, in 2 inches of oil heated to 375°. Drain on paper towels.

The soup may be prepared early in the day to this point. To assemble at serving time, bring the soup to a boil. Place a handful of crisp tortilla strips into each of 6 ovenproof serving bowls or a single large bowl. Pour the soup into the bowls and top with a generous amount of the cheese.

Place the bowls on a large cookie sheet and immediately place under a preheated broiler about 4 inches from the heat source just long enough to melt and lightly brown the cheese. Serve immediately. Serves 6.

Chicken Soup

Sopa de Pollo

This simple and delicious soup is from La Fogota, a restaurant honored by critics as "the best Mexican food in Texas." It is a wonderful way to use leftover Arroz Mexicana (Mexican Rice) and if the chicken and stock are prepared ahead, the Sopa can be assembled in just a few minutes at serving time. For a most attractive presentation, be sure to use only white chicken or turkey meat.

For a marvelous light lunch, serve Sopa de Pollo with hot flour tortillas or rolls. For a more substantial meal, accompany the soup with a cheese Enchilada or one of the Chile Rellenos in the book.

Chicken and Stock:

2-3 pounds raw chicken breasts or white turkey meat
2 (14½ ounce) cans chicken broth
8 cups water, approximately
2 cloves garlic, peeled
1 carrot, scraped and cut in 3 pieces
1 medium onion, peeled and stuck with 3 whole cloves
1 bay leaf, broken
5 (3 inch) pieces celery
4-5 sprigs parsley
½ teaspoon salt
4-5 whole peppercorns
½ teaspoon oregano
½ teaspoon thyme

To Finish the Soup:

additional salt to taste
½-1 teaspoon ground cumin to taste
2 cups cooked Mexican Rice (p.217), preferably without peas
2-3 ripe avocados
juice of ½ lime
4-5 Mexican or all purpose limes, quartered for garnish

The chicken and stock can be prepared a day ahead. Place the chicken in a 4-5 quart pot. Add the remaining stock ingredients and bring to a boil. Lower heat and simmer, partially covered, for about 45 minutes until the chicken is tender. Remove chicken and reserve the stock. When chicken is cool enough to handle, remove from bones and cut into bite-size chunks. Return bones to pot and boil, covered, for 2 hours to obtain a rich and flavorful stock. Strain and skim the stock and discard the vegetables. (If the stock is now to be refrigerated, the fat will solidify and can easily be removed. Otherwise, skim off the fat.) You should have 6½-7 cups stock. Refrigerate both chicken and stock separately until ready to use.

To finish the soup, bring the stock to a simmer adding the chicken chunks, salt and cumin to taste. In a separate saucepan, reheat the rice over medium heat with ½-1 cup of the hot stock stirred in to moisten the rice.

Peel, pit and cut the avocados into bite-size chunks. Sprinkle with lime juice.

To serve the soup, place about ¼ cup of the rice in each of 8 soup bowls. Add some of the avocado pieces and ladle soup into each bowl. Serve with lime wedges. Serves 8.

Pork and Hominy Soup
Posole

One of my New Mexican friends, Yvonne Beckley, told me that the first time she prepared Posole for her Northern friends, they were polite but reserved in their comments. However, Posole was their single food request on all return visits. Perhaps that is one reason that the rumor of Mexican food being addictive has credibility!

I have sometimes served Posole with small bowls of sliced radishes, crisp fried pork rinds or bacon bits, lime wedges and Raw Salsa (p.38). I suggest that you try whatever appeals to you. You may omit the pigs feet or pork rinds from the finished recipe without losing significant flavor, though including them adds authenticity to the dish. The Red Chile Sauce, however, is a must to compliment this relatively bland soup.

> 2 pounds pork shanks or pigs feet
> ½ pound pork rinds (skins)
> 2 pounds boneless pork roast, trimmed and cut into chunks
> 4 quarts water, approximately
> 1 tablespoon salt
> ¼-½ teaspoons black pepper
> 2 cups Posole, see note
> 2 cloves garlic, peeled
> 1 medium onion, peeled and quartered
> 1 teaspoon oregano
> 5 red chile pods, stemmed and seeded or 1½ tablespoons pure ground red chile powder
> Red Chile Sauce (p.46)

Optional Garnishes:
> thinly sliced radishes or lettuce or green cabbage
> avocado pieces
> crisp pork rinds
> lime wedges or chopped scallions

Have the butcher cut the pork shanks for you. In a large stockpot, place the shanks or pigs feet, the pork rinds, pork roast and enough water to cover. Add the salt and pepper and bring to a boil. Lower heat and simmer, covered, for about 1¼ hours, skimming foam from top as necessary. Remove the meat from the stock and reserve. Chill the stock for easy removal of the accumulated fat.

If using fresh Posole, rinse carefully, then place in a saucepan with enough water to cover. Boil until the posole "pops," then drain and reserve.

Using the metal blade, drop the garlic through the feed tube with the motor running to mince. Add the onion to the workbowl and pulse to chop. Skim fat from the broth, then add the garlic, onion, oregano, Posole and chile pods or powder. Bring to a boil, then lower heat and simmer about 30 minutes until the onions are soft and the skin separates from the chile pods. Remove and discard chile pod skins. Cut the meat into bite-size pieces and add to the broth. Keep hot.

Have ready the Red Chile Sauce. You may use or omit the pork in the recipe as desired. Serve the garnishes in individual bowls.

Serve the soup with the Red Chile Sauce or bowls of optional garnishes. It is traditional to leave the pigs feet in the soup for serving, but you may wish to discard them. Serves 12.

Note: Fresh Posole is found in the meat section of the grocery store. You could also use canned drained hominy or substitute 2 cups fresh white corn scraped from the cob. Place the corn in a pot with 1 quart water and 1 tablespoon lime juice. Boil until the hull is loose. Rinse 3 times, then use as directed for Posole.

Gazpacho

Southwestern Gazpacho is often made from a fresh Salsa base adding spicy tomato juice, bell peppers and cucumbers. You may substitute 3 cups of Raw Salsa (p.38), Texas Hot Salsa (p.39) or Fresh Salsa (p.38) for the tomato, onion, cilantro and chiles.

> 1 red onion, peeled and quartered
> 2-3 fresh Jalapeño chiles or 2 medium-hot canned green chiles
> 2 cloves garlic, peeled
> 6 tomatillos, husks removed and halved
> 4 large ripe fresh tomatoes, cored and quartered or 1 (1 pound 14 ounce) can Italian plum tomatoes
> 1 large green bell pepper, seeded and quartered
> 1 cucumber, peeled and cut in 5-6 pieces
> 4-8 sprigs fresh cilantro or to taste
> 2 tablespoons vegetable oil
> 3 tablespoons red wine vinegar
> 1-1½ teaspoons salt
> 1 teaspoon sugar
> ½ teaspoon leaf oregano
> 1 cup tomato sauce
> 2 cups spicy tomato juice
> 1 avocado, peeled and cut in chunks, for garnish
> lime wedges, for garnish
> crisp tostado strips or chips (p.242), for garnish

Using the metal blade, process the onions and chiles together until minced. Rinse briefly under cold water. Place in a 6 cup bowl and set aside.

Using the metal blade, drop the garlic through the feed tube with the motor running to mince. Add the tomatillos to the workbowl and process to mince finely. Add the tomatoes, bell pepper, cucumber, cilantro and oil. Process to mince and combine the ingredients. Stir into the chile and onion mixture. Stir in the vinegar, salt, sugar, oregano, tomato sauce and tomato juice. Taste and adjust seasonings. Garnish with the avocado, lime wedges and crisply fried tostados. Serves 6.

Variation: Prepare the soup as directed and dissolve 4 envelopes unflavored gelatin according to the package directions. Combine the soup and the dissolved gelatin. Pour into a 2 quart mold that has been rinsed in cold water. Refrigerate at least 8 hours or until firm. Unmold and serve with Guacamole dressing (p.49).

Arizona Cheese Soup
Sopa de Queso

Cheese and chiles combine to make a delicious and picante soup popular throughout the Southwest. This recipe comes from a marvelous Arizona cook.

> 2 red potatoes, peeled
> 6-7 cups chicken stock
> 2 cloves garlic, peeled, optional
> 1 medium onion, peeled and quartered
> 1½ tablespoons butter
> 1 (7 ounce) can chopped mild green chiles, drained, see note
> ¼-½ teaspoon chile powder or cayenne pepper
> ¼ teaspoon salt or to taste
> 8 ounces Longhorn Cheddar or Monterey Jack cheese, chilled
> 1 (16 ounce) can cream-style corn or 1½ cups peeled, chopped tomatoes including juices, optional

Use the French fry disc to process the potatoes into strips. (If you don't have this disc, use a standard slicing disc to process the potatoes and cut by hand into bite-size strips.) Place the potatoes and stock in a 3 quart saucepan and bring to a boil. Reduce heat and simmer about 20 minutes until the potatoes are tender.

Using the metal blade, drop the garlic through the feed tube with the motor running to mince. Add onion to workbowl and process to chop. In a small skillet, saute the garlic and onion in the butter about 3 minutes until the onion is translucent. Stir into the hot stock along with the chiles, chile powder and salt. Keep hot.

Use the shredding disc to process the cheese and leave in workbowl. Add 2 tablespoons of the cooked potatoes and process to make a smooth paste. With the motor running, pour 1½ cups of the hot stock through the feed tube stopping to scrape sides of workbowl as necessary to make a smooth mixture. Stir the cheese mixture into the remaining stock in the pan. Stir in the optional corn or tomatoes and heat through, but do not boil. Serve immediately. Serves 6-8.

Note: You can use any kind of chile or bell peppers. A combination of red and green bell peppers is most attractive. Fresh chiles should be roasted and peeled (p.14) and then chopped. Bell peppers need not be roasted, but should be chopped and then sauteed with the garlic and onion.

SALADS

Salads are a very important part of Southwestern cuisine. All sorts of fresh fruits and vegetables grow in abundance throughout the region, and appear in salads both raw and cooked.

Light salads are a natural accompaniment to spicy and sturdy main dishes, and provide a colorful, healthful addition to any meal. Southwesterners are fond of lettuce, of course, but they certainly don't limit their salads to greens alone! Vegetables, rice, beans and peppers — all sorts of peppers — are liberally used, and so are jicama, squashes and melons. Avocado, tomatoes and citrus fruits appear frequently.

Hearty salads have always been popular main courses in warm climates, but the people of the Southwest have embraced that tradition with a flourish, and taken the main course salad to inventive, delightful heights. I think all the versions here are wonderful, but if you are planning a luncheon party, I urge you to try The Mexican Chef's Salad, or perhaps the Composed Chicken Salad. They are both so pretty that any gathering is guaranteed a successful start!

Be sure to consult the Soup Section for Gazpacho presented as a molded salad, and the Tortilla Specialties for Chalupa variations.

Clockwise from top left: Mexican Chef's Salad, Paella Salad, Red Chile Pasta Salad, Papaya-Shrimp Salad.

Roasted Pepper Salad

This salad features a sour cream dressing combined with chiles, bell peppers and hard-cooked eggs – a super combination.

The Sour Cream Vinaigrette:
- 1 clove garlic, peeled
- 4-5 sprigs fresh parsley
- 2 tablespoons white wine vinegar
- 1 tablespoon lemon juice
- 1/2 teaspoon salt or to taste
- 1/4 teaspoon white pepper
- 1/2 teaspoon dry mustard
- 1/4 teaspoon paprika
- 1/3 cup vegetable oil
- 1/4 cup sour cream

The Salad:
- 1 head Boston lettuce, washed and dried
- 1/3 cup pumpkin seeds or pine nuts
- 10 hard-cooked eggs
- 1 red bell pepper, roasted and peeled
- 2 chile Poblanos, roasted and peeled
- 3-4 ounces crumbled Queso Fresco cheese, optional garnish

Prepare the dressing. Using the metal blade, drop the garlic and parsley through the feed tube with the motor running to mince. Add the vinegar, lemon juice, salt, pepper, mustard and paprika to workbowl. With the motor running add the oil and sour cream through the feed tube processing until combined. Taste and adjust seasonings.

Separate the lettuce into leaves and use to line 6 salad plates with 4-5 leaves on each. Toast the pumpkin seeds or pine nuts on a cookie sheet for 5-8 minutes at 350° until lightly browned. Let cool.

Halve the eggs and cut 6 of the whites into long strips. Use the French fry disc to "dice" the remaining egg whites and all of the yolks. Reserve the diced eggs for garnish.

Slice the bell pepper and chiles into thin strips. Toss lightly with the egg white strips and arrange on the lettuce leaves. Drizzle dressing over the top and garnish with the diced eggs, toasted pine nuts or seeds and the optional cheese. Serves 6.

Variation: Two cups crisp white mushrooms, sliced with the 3 or 4mm (standard) slicing disc, are a good addition to this salad.

Roasted Pepper and Zucchini Salad

This wonderful combination of bell peppers, chiles and zucchini with Feta cheese is one of my favorite salads. You could add water-packed tuna or cooked shrimp to make a light entree. In this case, you will need additional dressing.

The Salad:
- 3 red bell peppers, roasted and peeled (p.14)
- 3 chile Poblanos or green bell peppers, roasted and peeled (p.14)
- 3 medium size zucchini squash
- 8 ounces Feta cheese, drained and crumbled
- 3-4 ounces crumbled Queso Fresco cheese, optional garnish

The Vinaigrette Dressing:
- 1 clove garlic, peeled
- 3-4 sprigs fresh parsley
- 1/3 cup wine vinegar
- 1/2 cup safflower oil
- 1 teaspoon salt
- 1/2 teaspoon dry mustard
- fresh ground black pepper to taste
- pinch sugar

Stem and seed the peppers and/or chiles and cut into strips about 2 1/2-3 inches long and 1/4 inch wide. Place in a large bowl.

Cut the zucchini into pieces that fit horizontally in the feed tube. Use the shredding disc to process. Add the zucchini and Feta cheese to the peppers. Toss gently to combine the ingredients and set aside.

Prepare the dressing. Using the metal blade, drop the garlic and parsley through the feed tube with the motor running to mince. Add the remaining dressing ingredients to the workbowl and process until well-combined.

Pour enough dressing over the salad to moisten all ingredients. (Reserve any unused dressing for other uses.) Toss gently and refrigerate until ready to serve.

At serving time, garnish with the optional crumbled cheese. Serves 6.

Variation: You can use 1 1/2 cups well-drained Pickled Chiles (p.50), made with red and green peppers, to replace the chiles and/or peppers in the recipe.

Jicama-Orange Salad
Pico de Gallo

The combination of jicama, oranges and chile powder (or in this case sliced red pepper) is a classic Pico de Gallo. "Pico de Gallo" means "beak of the rooster" — so named because a rooster always chops his food before eating.

The Salad:
4 seedless oranges
2 red sweet peppers
1 small jicama

The Dressing:
$1/4$ cup white vinegar
$1/2$ cup safflower oil
1 teaspoon salt
$1/4$ teaspoon white pepper
$1/4$ teaspoon chile powder or paprika
1 clove garlic, peeled and halved
$1/8$ teaspoon sugar
lime wedges for garnish

Use a sharp knife to peel the oranges, then remove the membrane and separate the fruit into sections. Place in a bowl and squeeze any juices from the peel over the sections.

Seed the peppers and slice into 2 x $1/4$ inch strips. Reserve.

Use a sharp knife to remove the outer brown peel from the jicama, then remove the inner fibrous peel as well. Use a 5 or 6mm (thick) slicing disc and the Double Slicing Technique (p.21) to make matchstick strips. (If you don't have this blade, slice by hand into 3 x $1/4$ inch pieces.)

Prepare the dressing by combining all of the dressing ingredients in a screw top jar. Shake vigorously and allow to stand until ready to use — up to several hours.

All of the ingredients can be prepared a few hours ahead of serving, but the salad should be assembled at the last minute. Toss together the oranges, peppers and jicama strips. Arrange on a serving platter. Discard garlic from the dressing and shake to recombine. Lightly coat the salad with dressing and garnish the platter with lime wedges. Serves 6 generously.

Variation: Use your creativity to change this salad. You could add coarsely chopped cucumber, or fruits such as papaya, banana or apple. If you wish, all the vegetables could be cut into small chunks instead of strips for a different "look."

Potato Salad

This salad is equally good served warm or chilled and may be made a day or two in advance. If serving warm, keep the potatoes and vegetables warm after cooking and coat with room temperature dressing.

The Vinaigrette Dressing:
- 1/3 cup fresh parsley sprigs
- 2 cloves garlic, peeled
- 1/2-1 teaspoon sugar
- 2/3 cup safflower oil
- 1/3 cup white wine vinegar
- 1 teaspoon dry mustard
- 1/2 teaspoon salt or to taste
- 1/4 teaspoon white pepper

The Salad:
- 3 hard-cooked eggs
- 6 red potatoes (average size), peeled
- 3 stalks celery, cut in pieces to fit the feed tube
- 4 scallions
- 6 strips bacon, cut in 1 inch pieces
- 1 red bell pepper, roasted and peeled
- 2 chile Poblanos, roasted and peeled, see note
- 1/2 pound fresh spinach leaves, washed and dried

Prepare the dressing. Using the metal blade, drop the garlic and parsley through the feed tube with the motor running to mince. Add the remaining dressing ingredients to the workbowl and process until smooth and well blended. This makes about 1 1/3 cups dressing.

Process the eggs using the French fry disc or the shredding disc. Set aside for garnish. Using the French fry disc or the 3 or 4mm (standard) slicing disc and the Double Slicing Technique (p.21), place the potatoes in the feed tube horizontally and process to make julienne strips. Place the potatoes in a pan with salted water to cover and bring to a boil. Cook about 8 minutes until tender, skimming off foam as necessary. Drain well and reserve.

Meanwhile, use the 3 or 4mm (standard) slicing disc to process the celery. By hand, slice the scallions using all of the white part and about 1 inch of the green.

Saute the bacon until lightly browned, then add the celery and scallions to the skillet. Cook about 1 minute until the onion is soft but not brown, then use a slotted spoon to remove the ba-con and vegetables. (At this point add 1 tablespoon of the bacon fat to the dressing and combine well.)

Discard seeds from pepper and chiles, then slice into thin strips.

At serving time toss the celery and onion with the dressing. Lightly toss together the potatoes, pepper and chile strips. Arrange the spinach leaves on a serving platter or individual salad plates. Mound the potato salad atop the spinach, pour dressing over and garnish with the bacon and hard-cooked eggs. Serves 6.

Note: If chile Poblanos are not available, use 3 roasted and peeled red bell peppers. Do not use green pepper.

Pinto Bean Salad

Most Southwestern households keep cooked beans on hand to make Refried Beans or to season in various ways for dinner accompaniments. Leftover beans are wonderful in salads and are often combined with other vegetables. Canned beans are not a good substitute for home-cooked beans.

The Vinaigrette Dressing:
    1 clove garlic, peeled
    3 tablespoons white wine vinegar
    1/2 teaspoon salt or to taste
    1/4 teaspoon pepper
    1/2 teaspoon dry mustard
    1/2 cup vegetable oil
    1 teaspoon sugar, optional

The Salad:
    3 fresh green chiles, roasted and peeled
        (p.14) or 3 canned chiles, drained
    4 scallions, both green and white parts
    10 cherry tomatoes
    2-3 cups cooked and drained Pinto Beans
        (p.215), chilled
    1 cup cooked green beans, chilled
    1 cup cooked garbanzo beans, chilled
    6 strips bacon, cooked crisp and crumbled
        for garnish
    4 hard-cooked eggs for garnish
    Romaine lettuce leaves
    3-4 ounces crumbled Queso Freso or
        "Enchilada" cheese, optional garnish

Prepare the dressing. Using the metal blade, drop the garlic through the feed tube with the motor running to mince. Add the remaining dressing ingredients to the workbowl and process until well blended. Set aside until ready to use.

By hand, slice the chiles into thin strips about 2 inches long. Slice the scallions thinly and rinse under cold water to remove bitterness. Use the 3 or 4mm (standard) slicing disc to process the tomatoes. Place the chiles, onions, tomatoes, pinto beans, green beans and garbanzo beans in a serving bowl. Toss lightly with the dressing.

Have ready the crumbled bacon. Use the French fry disc to "dice" the hard-cooked eggs. Serve the salad on the lettuce leaves and garnish with the bacon, diced eggs and optional cheese. Serves 8.

Tomato-Melon Salad
Ensalada de Melon

In Texas and California, the selection and variety of fresh melons is quite incredible. The combination of melon and tomato may seem peculiar, but I think you will find it a refreshing taste treat. This salad makes a wonderful accompaniment to any spicy meal.

The Dressing:
    2 shallots, peeled
    4-5 sprigs parsley
    1 tablespoon fresh orange juice
    1 tablespoon red wine vinegar
    7 tablespoons safflower oil
    1/2 teaspoon salt
    1/4 teaspoon black pepper
    1 teaspoon dry mustard

The Salad:
    24 young fresh spinach leaves, washed and
        dried
    1 small or 1/2 medium cantaloupe melon,
        ripe but firm
    1/2 small honeydew melon, ripe but firm
    2 medium tomatoes, cored and quartered
    3-4 slices bacon, cooked crisp and crumbled
        for garnish, optional

Prepare the dressing. Using the metal blade, drop the shallots and parsley through the feed tube with the motor running to mince. Stop machine and add remaining dressing ingredients. Process 5-10 seconds until smooth. Set aside.

Arrange the spinach on each of 6 salad plates. Set aside.

Peel the melons and discard seeds. Cut into sections that will fit horizontally in the feed tube. Use the French fry disc to process into strips. Place in a mixing bowl.

Use the French fry disc to "dice" the tomatoes. Drain in a colander and discard juices and seeds. Add to the melon in the bowl. Toss lightly and divide among the spinach-lined salad plates.

Drizzle the dressing over the salads and top with the crumbled bacon. Serve immediately. Serves 6.

Zucchini Salad
Ensalada de Calabasitas

This is one of my favorite salads — refreshing, festive and in the traditional red, green and white colors. It is a perfect salad for pork or poultry dishes.

The Dressing:
    1 shallot, peeled
    4-5 sprigs parsley
    juice of 1 lemon
    1 tablespoon vinegar
    1/2 teaspoon dry mustard
    3/4 - 1 teaspoon salt to taste
    1/4 teaspoon black pepper
    1/2 cup vegetable oil
    few drops water, if needed

The Salad:
    1 medium jicama
    1 medium zucchini
    1 red Delicious apple
    about 1 tablespoon lemon juice
    1 small apple, optional garnish
    1 small zucchini, optional garnish
    2-3 sprigs parsley, for garnish

Prepare the dressing. Using the metal blade, drop the shallot and parsley through the feed tube with the motor running to mince. Stop machine. Add lemon juice, vinegar, mustard, salt and pepper to workbowl. With the maching running, slowly add the oil through the feed tube. If the dressing seems too thick, add several drops water.

Use a sharp knife to remove both the brown skin and inner fibrous lining of the jicama. Use a 5 or 6mm (thick) slicing disc and the Double Slicing Technique (p.21) to make matchstick jicama strips. Use the same technique to process the zucchini and apple. (If you have a Julienne disc, use instead of the Double Slicing Technique. If you have neither disc, cut by hand into 3 x 1/4 inch slices.) Sprinkle apple with lemon juice.

Combine the jicama, zucchini and apple strips in a bowl. Coat with dressing and toss lightly. Chill about 1 hour. Drain off excess dressing before serving.

If desired, garnish the salad at serving time with julienne strips of apple and zucchini peel. Use a sharp paring knife to cut a few strips about 2 inches long and 1/8 inch wide. Place atop the salad in a spiral design and put parsley sprigs in the center. Serves 6.

Mexican Vegetable Salad
Cazuela de Ensalada

This recipe from the Santa Fe-Albuquerque area typifies New Mexican regional cooking. It is a simple "Mexican style" tossed salad to accompany any main dish.

    1 small head Romaine lettuce, washed and
        dried
    4 large bell peppers
    1 medium onion, peeled
    6 firm tomatoes, cored
    1/2 teaspoon salt
    6 slices bacon
    1 teaspoon red chile powder
    1/2 cup white wine vinegar
    1 ripe avocado
    1/4 cup pine nuts or pumpkin seeds, optional

Use the 6mm slicing disc (or the thickest slicing disc you have) to slice the lettuce. It should be loaded vertically in the feed tube for best slicing. Divide the lettuce among 6 salad plates. Set aside.

The bell peppers have better flavor if roasted and peeled (see p.14 for directions) and also absorb the dressing more readily. When the roasted peppers are cool, remove the seeds and stems. Use a sharp knife to cut them into thin strips about 2 inches long. If you do not roast the peppers, simply cut them into flat pieces and load firmly into the feed tube fitted with the 3 or 4mm (standard) slicing disc. Process to slice. Place the peppers in a large mixing bowl.

Process the onion using the French Fry disc. (It can be processed whole if you have a large feed tube.) Place the onion in a strainer and rinse under cool water to remove any bitter liquid. Add to the peppers.

Process the tomatoes into strips using the French Fry disc. (They can be processed whole if you have a large feed tube.) Add to the peppers and onion. Sprinkle with the salt and toss lightly.

Fry the bacon until crisp, then drain and crumble and reserve. Drain off all but 3 tablespoons fat. Stir the chile powder and vinegar into the hot fat, then pour the mixture over the vegetables. This may be done 8-12 hours in advance.

Peel, pit and cut the avocado into small pieces. Add along with the crumbled bacon to the vegetable mixture and toss gently. Serve immediately on the bed of lettuce. If desired, the salad can be garnished with pine nuts or pumpkin seeds. Serves 6.

Cauliflower Salad
Ensalada de Coliflor

This is an inspiration from a very old cookbook printed in San Antonio in the 1930's called *Fiesta Mexicanas* by Eleanor Ringland. It was compiled by a mother, daughter and grandmother in an attempt to record old family recipes from South Texas. The original recipe was made without chayote squash, but the addition enhances the salad.

Chayote squash is from Costa Rica and, when blanched, tastes somewhat like an English cucumber. The single seed is delicious raw or toasted and is said to be the "cook's bonus." I like to sautee the larger ones in butter and use as a garnish.

The Vinaigrette Dressing:
1 3/4 teaspoons salt
1 teaspoon sugar
1/8 teaspoon pepper
1/3 cup safflower oil
1 1/2 tablespoons tarragon vinegar
1/4 teaspoon dill weed, optional

The Salad:
1 small head cauliflower (to make about
   2 1/2 cups blanched florets)
2 chayote squash or 1 English cucumber
1/3 small yellow onion
1/3 medium green pepper
2 firm medium-size fresh tomatoes
1 ripe firm avocado
Boston lettuce leaves
sliced scallion tops or 2 chayote seeds
   toasted in butter for garnish

Prepare the dressing. Place all ingredients in the workbowl using the metal blade. Process until well-blended. Set aside.

Remove the core from the cauliflower and divide into bite-size florets. Blanch 1 minute in boiling water, then drain and refresh under cool water to stop further cooking.

Peel, seed and rinse the chayote. Slice and saute the seeds in 1-2 teaspoons butter and set aside for garnish. Insert the French Fry disc and stand the chayote vertically in the feed tube. Process to make strips. (If you do not have this disc, cut by hand into strips approximately 1 1/2 x 1/4 inch.) Blanch the strips for 1 minute in boiling water, then refresh under cool water. Set aside. If you are using the cucumber, peel and cut as the chayote, but do not blanch.

Use the metal blade to finely chop the onion and green pepper together. Rinse in a strainer to remove bitter liquid from the onion.

By hand, cut the tomatoes into pieces about the size of your thumbnail. (This process can be shortened by first slicing the tomato with a 5mm or 6mm slicing disc if available. Finish the cutting by hand.)

Place the cauliflower, chayote or cucumber, pepper and onions in a large bowl. Toss lightly with the dressing. Gently fold in the tomato pieces. Refrigerate until serving time. This much can be done a day in advance.

Just prior to serving, peel and pit the avocado and cut into chunks. Line a shallow serving dish with Boston lettuce leaves. Drain off excess dressing from the salad and spoon over the lettuce leaves. Arrange the avocado chunks in the center of the salad. Top with the chayote seeds or sliced scallion tops. Spoon any excess dressing over the avocado. Serves 6-8.

Tomato and Pine Nut Salad
Ensalada con Pignolas

This recipe is from Margarita C de Baca, one of New Mexico's most respected cooks and an authority on their regional food. Her recipes are reprinted with permission from her daughters, who live in Albuquerque, New Mexico. Margarita C de Baca's efforts to preserve her family's Spanish heritage (dating back to Cabasa de Vaca) are reflected in many of the area's regional cookbooks and favorite family home recipes.

This salad is served during the peak of the pigñola season in late October and is a delightfully mild and fresh accompaniment to the picante New Mexican food. Sliced almonds or pumpkin seeds could be substituted for the pine nuts. This filling cannot be prepared in advance for the tomatoes will "weep" liquid. A variation using hard-cooked eggs is found at the end of the recipe and this allows advance preparation.

> 6 firm fresh tomatoes, medium size
> 1 cup pigñolas (pine nuts or pinon nuts)
> 1 bunch celery
> ¼ cup mayonnaise
> ¼ cup sour cream or plain yogurt
> salt and pepper to taste
> 6 leaves Romaine lettuce, washed and dried
> 6 pimiento stuffed olives

Plunge the tomatoes in boiling water, then in ice water. Peel, and scoop out the pulp to leave a shell for the salad. Chop the pulp, then strain and discard juice and seeds. Reserve both shells and strained pulp.

Spread pigñolas in a single layer on a cookie sheet. Place in a preheated 350° oven for 3-4 minutes to roast. Do not brown. Set aside to cool.

Wash the celery without removing stalks from the core by running cold water down the center. (Celery stays crisp much longer if unused portions are left attached to the core.) Remove leaves and reserve for other uses. Insert the 3mm (standard) slicing disc. Cut off a section of celery (about 2 inches) to fit the feed tube. The stalks should fit snugly into the tube. Process to slice. Wash and cut off another section and proceed in the same manner to slice. Refrigerate remaining celery for other uses. Leave sliced celery in workbowl. Add nuts and reserved tomato pulp along with the mayonnaise. Process using pulses to coarsely chop. Stir in sour cream or yogurt and salt and pepper to taste.

Arrange lettuce on individual salad plates. Fill the tomato shells with the salad and place atop the lettuce. Garnish with pimiento stuffed olives. Serves 6.

Variation: Add 3 hardcooked egg yolks to the filling with the mayonnaise and process until smooth. This will enable you to prepare the filling in advance, without the excess moisture problem.

Process egg whites and olives with the julienne or shredding disc and use the combination as a garnish. The taste is quite different, but good.

Cold Rice Salad
Ensalada de Arroz Rajas

If you keep Chile Strips (p.214) or Pickled Chiles (p.50) on hand in your refrigerator or freezer, this salad, which is a favorite among my family and friends, is an excellent way to use them. Otherwise, use the pepper and pimiento combination in the recipe. The entire salad, except for the avocado, can be prepared at least 12 hours ahead.

The Dressing:
1 shallot, finely minced
1 1/2 tablespoons red wine vinegar
3 tablespoons safflower oil
1-2 sprigs fresh minced parsley
1/4 teaspoon salt
fresh ground black pepper to taste
pinch sugar

The Salad:
1 green bell pepper or chile Poblano, roasted and peeled (p.14) or 1 (4 ounce) can mild green chiles
1 red bell pepper, roasted and peeled (p.14) or 1 canned pimiento
2 1/2 cups cooked, cold rice
1/2 cup cooked corn
2 small, ripe acocados
juice of 1/2 lemon

Place all of the dressing ingredients in a screw top jar and shake vigorously to combine.

Remove stems and seeds from roasted peppers and cut into 1 x 1/4 inch strips. In a bowl, combine the chiles or peppers and pimiento, the rice and the corn with the dressing. Adjust seasonings to taste. Cover and refrigerate until ready to serve. (If using prepared Chile Strips or Pickled Chiles, drain and use 1 cup combining as directed for the peppers and chiles.)

At serving time, peel and pit the avocado and cut into small chunks. Sprinkle with lemon juice to retard browning and toss gently with the salad. Serve the salad cold. Serves 4-6.

Variation: Add 1 1/2-2 cups chilled, cooked poultry or seafood to make a refreshing summer entree. Use a double recipe of the dressing.

Pesto Salad
Ensalada de Pesto

Cilantro Pesto or Green Chile Pesto make a delicious salad dressing for these and other cold vegetables.

The Dressing:
1/2 cup Cilantro Pesto (p.53) or Green Chile Pesto (p.52)
1/4 cup vinegar
1/4 cup vegetable oil
juice of 1/2 lemon
salt to taste

Salad Vegetables:
1 large firm tomato, cored or 1 large Delicious apple
lemon juice or vitamin C powder, optional
1 medium zucchini, cut in pieces to fit the feed tube
2 cups cooked spaghetti squash, chilled
1/4 cup seedless raisins for garnish, optional

By hand, or in the food processor fitted with the metal blade, combine all of the dressing ingredients. Set aside.

If using the tomato, cut to fit the feed tube and process using the French fry disc. If using the apple, cut in half and remove the seeds. Then process using the shredding disc. If not using immediately sprinkle the apple with lemon juice or vitamin C powder to retard browning.

Use the shredding disc to process the zucchini. Then combine the tomato or apple, zucchini and spaghetti squash with the dressing in a serving bowl. Garnish with raisins if desired. Serves 4-6.

Christmas Eve Salad
Ensalada Noche Buena

This recipe came from Jorge Schnieder, who opened a magnificent replica of a Spanish hacienda in Houston. There he serves classic Mexican cuisine and Tex-Mex favorites.

The dressing for this salad is somewhat sweet as is the custom to serve with jicama, beets and fruits with cane sugar. If you prefer a more tangy dressing, add a garlic clove or shallot to the dressing ingredients.

The Salad:
1 small jicama
4 fresh beets, cooked until tender or 1 can cooked shoestring beets, drained and chilled
2 oranges
1 fresh or canned mango or 1 fresh papaya
1/3 cup pine nuts
1 tablespoon vegetable oil
lettuce leaves

The Vinaigrette Dressing:
2 tablespoons cider vinegar
2 tablespoons red wine vinegar
3 tablespoons fresh orange juice
1/2 cup safflower oil
1 teaspoon sugar
1/4-1/2 teaspoon salt or to taste
1/8-1/4 teaspoon pure ground red chile powder or cayenne pepper

Peel the jicama being sure to remove both the outer peel and the inner fibrous coating. Use a 3 or 4mm (standard) slicing disc and the Double Slicing Technique (p.21) to make matchstick slices of both the jicama and the beets.

Peel the mango or papaya and cut by hand into strips. Peel the oranges being sure to remove all the white membrane. Section and reserve 3 tablespoons juice for the dressing.

Saute the pine nuts in the oil until lightly browned. Drain on paper towels. Wash and dry the lettuce and use to line a deep platter.

To make the dressing, combine all the ingredients in a screw top jar or in the processor using the metal blade to combine thoroughly.

Arrange the salad atop the lettuce in the following manner: compose the vegetables and fruits in separate rows, sprinkle the pine nuts over the top and serve the dressing separately. Let everyone dress their own salad selection. Serves 3-4.

Avocado Halves
Aguacates a Mitad

Pomegranate seeds are readily available and thus quite popular in the Southwest. Mexican food is so often presented as a combination of red and green colors that I wonder which came first, the national flag or the food combinations! This one is a natural since both avocados and pomegranates are in season at Christmas time. The recipe is from an old book published in San Antonio by a company no longer in existence. The dressing called for was "French," so I have contributed a simple vinaigrette. Avocado halves filled with anything from shrimp and chiles to caviar are very traditional in Texas.

The Dressing:
1/4 cup raspberry vinegar or red wine vinegar
2/3 cup safflower oil
1 teaspoon salt
1/4 teaspoon white pepper
1 clove garlic, peeled

The Salad:
2 pomegranates
3 ripe avocados
juice of 1/2 lemon

Prepare dressing by combining all ingredients in a screw-top jar. Shake vigorously to combine. Let stand for several hours.

To prepare the salad, remove and reserve the seeds from the pomegranate. (Reserve pomegranate fruit for other uses). Cut the unpeeled avocadoes in half and discard the pit. Squeeze the lemon juice over the cut sides to prevent discoloration. Place the avocado halves on a serving platter or individual dishes. Discard the garlic from the dressing and shake to recombine. Drizzle a small amount of dressing over each avocado half. Fill the centers of the avocado with pomegranate seeds. Serve remaining dressing separately. Serves 6.

Variation: Fresh strawberry halves may be substituted for the pomegranate seeds.

Orange Salad
Ensalada de Naranjas

Because growing conditions in the Southwest produce wonderful oranges, Mexican-Americans have adopted this classic Spanish combination of oranges and sweet onions. Fresh pineapple, abundant in the Rio Grande Valley, is a complimentary addition.

The Salad:
4 seedless oranges, peeled and membranes removed
½ fresh pineapple, peeled, cored and halved
1 red onion, peeled and halved if necessary to fit the feed tube
12 Romaine lettuce leaves, washed and dried

The Dressing:
1 clove garlic, peeled
1 tablespoon fresh orange juice
3 tablespoons red or white wine vinegar
½ cup safflower oil
½ teaspoon salt
¼-½ teaspoon red chile powder to taste or ½ teaspoon paprika
⅛ teaspoon dry mustard
6 sprigs fresh mint for garnish

Slice off the ends of the oranges so they lie flat. If your machine has a wide feed tube, slice the oranges and pineapple using a 3 or 4mm (standard) slicing disc. (If the first orange does not slice perfectly, slice the remainder by hand.) If you do not have a wide feed tube, slice the fruits by hand.

Use a 2 or 3mm (thin) slicing disc to process the onion and then place in a strainer and pour hot water over the onions. Rinse immediately in cold water. Chill the lettuce, pineapple, oranges and onion, covered, until ready to use – up to 3 hours.

Prepare the dressing. Using the metal blade, drop the garlic through the feed tube with the motor running to mince. Add remaining dressing ingredients to workbowl and process to blend well. (Note that paprika gives a milder flavor than chile powder.)

To serve the salad, arrange the lettuce leaves on a large serving platter or each of 6 individual plates. Place overlapping slices of pineapple, onion and orange atop the lettuce. Just before serving, pour the dressing over and garnish with the mint sprigs. Serves 6-8.

Mexican Chef's Salad

This recipe from Arizona and California is a natural evolution from the American passion for large and abundant salads. The presentation in a large, fried flour tortilla (Sonora Style) is quite spectacular. Depending upon regional preference, the meat used can be hot or cold, shredded or ground. I give two possibilities here, but many more exist.

The Vinaigrette Dressing:
  1 clove garlic, peeled
  5-6 sprigs fresh parsley
  1/4 cup red wine vinegar
  3/4 cup safflower oil
  1 teaspoon salt
  1/2 teaspoon dry mustard
  1/4 teaspoon ground red chile

The Salad:
  2 (12-16 inch) flour tortillas
  peanut oil for frying, see note
  1/2 head Iceberg lettuce
  1/2 head Romaine lettuce
  2-3 cups cold cooked chicken, turkey or beef
  14 pitted black olives
  4 ounces Longhorn cheddar cheese
  1 avocado, peeled and cut in small chunks
  2 tomatoes, cut in wedges
  1/2 cup sour cream
  1/4 cup heavy cream
  2 green chiles, roasted, peeled and seeded (p.14)
  2 hard-cooked eggs, sliced, optional garnish
  3-4 ounces crumbled Queso Fresco or "Enchilada" cheese, optional garnish

Prepare the dressing. Using the metal blade, drop the garlic through the feed tube with the motor running to mince. Add remaining dressing ingredients to workbowl and process until well blended. This makes about 1 cup dressing.

Prepare the tortillas. Heat about 1 inch peanut oil to 375° in a deep fryer or saucepan just large enough to accomodate the tortillas. Press the tortillas, 1 at a time, into the fryer basket or directly into the pan. Immerse in the oil, holding down with tongs. The edges of the tortilla will turn up slightly to form a shallow shell. Fry about 1 minute until crisp. Drain on paper towels.

Use the thickest slicing disc available to process the Iceberg and Romaine lettuce. (Romaine leaves should first be cut in half, then packed upright in the feed tube.)

Use a 3 or 4mm (standard) slicing disc to coarsely shred the poultry. (Use the metal blade to shred 1 inch chunks of cold beef.)

Use a 3 or 4mm (standard) slicing disc to process the olives. Use the shredding disc to process the cheese.

To assemble the salads, toss the two kinds of lettuce together and line each tortilla shell. Combine the meat or poultry with enough dressing to thoroughly moisten, then mound over the lettuce. Arrange the olives, tomatoes, avocadoes and cheese in rows atop the meat.

Combine the sour cream and heavy cream and dollop in the center of each salad. Garnish with 2 x 1/4 inch strips of green chile, the eggs and the crumbled cheese. Serve additional dressing separately. Serves 2 generously.

Note: An alternate tortilla preparation method is to brush softened tortillas with melted butter. Press into small ovenproof bowls and toast in a 350° oven to make a crisp shell-shape. An alternate presentation is shown in the photograph on p.24 using a Tostado del Rey.

Variation: Saute 3/4 pound ground beef in a 10 inch skillet and drain off the fat. Stir in 1/3 cup Raw Salsa (p.38) or bottled Taco sauce, 3 tablespoons tomato sauce, 1/2 teaspoon ground chile powder and/or cumin, salt and pepper to taste. Use this in place of the shredded poultry or meat. Use half of the dressing for the tomatoes and avocados. Place the warm meat mixture atop the lettuce and top with grated cheese. Surround meat with olives, tomatoes, avocado and chile strips. Garnish with the sour cream mixture. If desired, further garnish with the eggs and/or crumbled cheese.

Paella Salad

Cold rice salads are popular in Southwestern homes and, unfortunately, they seldom appear in restaurants. This is a delicious way to use leftover rice and makes a wonderful light supper or luncheon entree. In addition, it may be made a day in advance.

The Salad:
3-4 threads saffron
¼ cup hot chicken broth
1 large firm tomato, cored
1 cup green peas, cooked crisp-tender and cooled
1 cup artichoke hearts, halved
2 tablespoons diced pimiento, see note
2 cups cold cooked chicken or seafood, cut in bite-sized chunks
3 cups cooked white rice
10-12 sliced black or green olives for garnish

The Vinaigrette Dressing:
3-4 sprigs fresh parsley
1 clove garlic, peeled
3 tablespoons white wine vinegar
2 teaspoons lemon juice
½ cup safflower oil
½-¾ teaspoon salt or to taste
⅛ teaspoon coarse ground black pepper to taste

Soak the saffron in the chicken broth for at least 1 hour. Meanwhile, use the French fry disc to process the tomato into strips. Have ready the peas, artichokes, pimiento, chicken and rice.

Prepare the dressing. Using the metal blade, drop the parsley and garlic through the feed tube with the motor running to mince. Add the vinegar, lemon juice, oil, salt and pepper to the workbowl along with the soaked saffron and chicken broth. Process until well-combined.

Toss the dressing with the rice, chicken and prepare vegetables. Adjust salt and pepper to taste. Chill until ready to serve and garnish with the olives. Serves 8.

Note: When red bell peppers are in season, substitute 1 pepper for the pimientos. Cut into wedges, then slice using a 3mm (standard) slicing disc.

Mixed Meat and Vegetable Salad
Salpicón

The word Salpicón refers to shredded or finely cut meats or poultry often accompanied by a "dash of this or that" and covered with a vinaigrette dressing. Ingredients vary with the season and what is "leftover" and may be arranged in layers or in attractive rows.

If you have Pickled Chiles (p.50) prepared, substitute this for the onion and green chile in the recipe. Both hearts of palm and garbanzo beans are favorite ingredients for cold meat salads and supply the Latin accent inherent in Southwestern cooking. While it is more traditional to shred the meat, I prefer it sliced.

The salad may be made 3-4 hours in advance.

Southwest Vinaigrette Dressing (p.53) using the variation for Mixed Vinaigrette
10-12 fresh spinach leaves, washed and dried
1 pound (approximately) leftover cooked beef or chicken, well chilled
1 red onion, peeled or 1 bunch scallions
10 crisp white mushrooms
4 green chiles or chile Poblanos, roasted and peeled (p.14)
1 cup drained garbanzo beans or 1 can drained hearts of palm

Prepare the Vinaigrette dressing and reserve.

Line a serving platter with the spinach leaves and set aside.

Use a 3 or 4mm (standard) slicing disc to process the chilled beef or poultry. (Stack poultry vertically in feed tube for slicing.) Arrange over the spinach leaves.

Use a 2 or 3mm (thin) slicing disc to process the red onion. (If using scallions, cut into ¼ inch slices by hand and put the white part over the meat, reserving the green tops for garnish.) Place the onions over the meat.

Use a 3 or 4mm (standard) slicing disc to process the mushrooms and place atop the onions.

Cut the chiles into thin strips by hand and place atop the mushrooms. Top with the garbanzo beans or hearts of palm. Slice hearts of palm with a 3 or 4mm (standard) slicing disc.

Coat the salad with the vinaigrette and serve immediately or cover with plastic wrap and refrigerate until ready to serve. Garnish with green scallion tops. Serves 8-10.

*Entree
Salads*

Red Snapper Salad
Ensalada Huachinango

1 1/2 pounds poached and chilled Red
  Snapper, see note
1 yellow onion, peeled and halved
1/2 cup pitted black olives
1 can hearts of palm, drained
1 clove garlic
1 teaspoon salt
1/2 teaspoon fresh ground black pepper
1/2 cup vinegar
1/2 cup safflower oil
1/4 cup olive oil
3 avocados or 6 fresh green chiles, roasted
  and peeled as for stuffed chiles (p.14)
lettuce leaves

Cut or flake the fish into small pieces. Set aside.

Using the 2mm (thin) slicing disc, process the onion and then the olives. Then use the standard slicing disc and stack the hearts of palm vertically in the feed tube, packing tightly. Process to slice. (If the hearts of palm do not fill the feed tube, slice by hand.) Place the fish, onions, olives and hearts of palm in a bowl. Set aside.

Using the metal blade, drop the garlic through the feed tube with the motor running to mince. Stop machine and add salt, pepper, vinegar and both oils. Process 3-4 seconds to combine. Pour the dressing over the fish mixture and toss lightly to combine. Marinate in the refrigerator at lease 3 hours and up to 12 hours.

The salad may be served in peeled, pitted and halved avocados or stuffed into the chiles or simply on a bed of lettuce. Serves 6.

Note: Any firm fleshed fish such as shark or redfish may be used alone or in combination in this recipe. Fresh lump crabmeat is exceptional, albeit expensive.

Red Chile Pasta Salad

Unlike most colored pastas, this bright, unusual and zesty version has a true chile flavor.

The Dressing:
  1 clove garlic, peeled
  4-5 sprigs fresh cilantro or parsley
  1/4 cup white wine vinegar
  3/4-1 teaspoon salt
  1/4 teaspoon cayenne pepper
  1/2 cup salad oil
  2 teaspoons lime juice
  1/2 teaspoon dry mustard

The Salad:
  1/2 recipe Red Chile Pasta (p.220), cooked
    and drained
  1 tablespoon vegetable oil
  1 medium zucchini, cut to fit horizontally in
    the feed tube
  1/3 cup pine nuts or sesame seeds for garnish
  12-14 spinach leaves, cut in strips
  7-8 ounces crumbled Feta or Enchilada
    cheese, see note

Prepare the dressing. Using the metal blade, drop the garlic and cilantro or parsley through the feed tube with the motor running to mince. Add remaining dressing ingredients to workbowl and process to combine. Set aside until ready to use.

Combine the hot pasta with 1/2 tablespoon of the vegetable oil and chill in the refrigerator. Use the shredding disc to process the zucchini and chill.

Saute the pine nuts (if using) in a skillet with 1 tablespoon of the salad dressing and the remaining 1/2 tablespoon oil until lightly browned. Drain on paper towels.

To serve the salad, gently toss together the pasta, zucchini, cheese, spinach and the dressing. Garnish with the sauteed pine nuts or the sesame seeds. Serves 6-8 depending on use.

Note: If you can buy the yellow Enchilada cheese flavored with red chile, it is particularly good in this salad. Omit the cayenne pepper from the dressing.

Jalapeño Chile Pasta Salad

This colorful salad has a delightful combination of flavors and textures. You can regulate the hotness with the choice of cheese and dressing options.

The Dressing:

1 clove garlic, peeled
3-4 sprigs fresh cilantro or parsley
1/4 cup white wine vinegar
3/4-1 teaspoon salt
1/2 teaspoon dry mustard
2 teaspoons fresh lime juice
6 tablespoons safflower oil
1/4 teaspoon white pepper
1/2-1 tablespoon juice from canned Jalapeño chiles, optional

The Salad:

1/2 recipe Jalapeño Pasta (p.221), preferably cut into fettucine, see note
2 tablespoons safflower oil
4 corn tortillas
oil for frying
6 ounces Swiss, Monterey Jack or Jalapeño flavored cheese, chilled
2 firm tomatoes, cored
1 small yellow onion, peeled and halved
1 avocado, peeled and cut in thin slices

Prepare the dressing. Using the metal blade, drop the garlic and cilantro or parsley through the feed tube with the motor running to mince. Add remaining dressing ingredients and process to combine. (Juice from the Jalapeño chiles will make a "hot" dressing.) Set aside until ready to use.

Cook the pasta in boiling salted water for 45-60 seconds. Drain and toss with the safflower oil. Place in a large bowl.

Cut the tortillas into long strips about 1/4 inch wide. Fry, in 6 batches, until nearly crisp, in oil heated to 375°. Drain between paper towels. When the tortilla strips are cool, place atop the pasta. (The strips will soften as other ingredients are added, but preliminary frying keeps them from falling apart.)

Use the shredding disc to process the cheese. (Soft cheeses should be extremely cold, but not frozen.) Add to the bowl with the pasta.

Use the French fry disc to process the tomato into strips. Discard any unprocessed pieces of skin. Strain seeds and juices from tomato and place atop the cheese in the bowl.

Use the shredding disc to process the onion. Place in a strainer and rinse briefly in cool water. Add to the bowl.

Add the avocado to the bowl. Pour the dressing over and toss gently to avoid breaking avocados or tortilla strips. Serve immediately. Serves 6-8 depending on use.

Note: You may substitute a plain egg or spinach-egg fettucine. Cook "al-dente" (firm to the bite) and add 1-2 finely minced Jalapeño or hot green chiles to the dressing.

Variation: Cold sliced cooked chicken, Spanish Chorizo Sausage, beef or seafood is a delicious addition to this salad.

Aspen Village Salad

This is one of those salad recipes that is passed around until the original version is lost. The dressing is typical of Southwest Salads as is the use of tortilla chips in place of croutons. Raw jicama is a welcome addition to the salad.

The Salad:
1 head Romaine lettuce, washed and dried
6 ounces Monterey Jack cheese, well chilled
4 boned and skinned chicken breasts, cooked and cut in bite-sized pieces
1/2 cup pitted black olives
1 small jicama, peeled or canned water chestnuts, optional

The Dressing:
6 scallions
3 ripe tomatoes, cored and quartered
1 (4 ounce) can green chiles, drained and diced
salt to taste
2/3 cup sour cream
1/2 cup mayonnaise
1/4 teaspoon ground cumin

Finishing the Salad:
2 avocados
2 cups tortilla chips, see note
2 tablespoons minced fresh cilantro, optional

Use a 6mm (thick) slicing disc to process the lettuce or cut in coarse pieces by hand. Place in a salad bowl. Use the shredding disc to process the cheese and add to the bowl. Add chicken. Use the 3 or 4mm (standard) slicing disc to process the olives and add to the bowl.

Peel the jicama being sure to remove both the outer skin and the inner fibrous skin. Cut to fit the feed tube and process into small strips with the French fry disc. Add to the bowl and gently toss the salad ingredients. Chill, covered, until ready to serve — up to 2 hours.

Prepare the dressing. Cut all of the crisp green part of the scallions into thin slices. Use the French fry disc to process the tomatoes into small strips. Discard any large pieces of skin and excess liquid. Combine the scallions, tomatoes, chiles and salt to taste. (If you wish, you can use 1 cup bottled Taco sauce in place of the scallions, tomatoes and chiles).

Combine 1 cup of the tomato mixture or Taco sauce with the sour cream, mayonnaise and cumin to use as a dressing. (Reserve any remaining tomato mixture to serve separately with the salad.)

Just before serving, peel and pit the avocados and cut into bite-size pieces. Add to the salad and toss with the dressing. Garnish with tortilla chips and cilantro. Serves 8.

Note: You may use packaged tortilla chips, but a more attractive presentation (albeit more work) is to make your own chips. Cut 6 soft corn tortillas into 3/4 inch strips and then cut again on the diagonal to make pieces about 1 x 3/4 inch. Fry in oil heated to 350° until crisp, then drain on paper towels and lightly salt.

Composed Chicken Salad
Fiambre

This is a traditional Guatemalan dish served on November 1 (All Saints Day) and presents a colorful array of seasonal fruits, vegetables and cooked meat. Variations of this wonderful salad appear in early Texas cookbooks. This one is Latin American in origin and Southwestern in choice of ingredients.

The Dressing:
2 seedless oranges, peeled and sectioned with juices reserved (if necessary, add enough fresh orange juice to make 1/3-1/2 cup)
1 clove garlic, peeled
3-4 sprigs fresh parsley
3 tablespoons tarragon vinegar
1 1/2 teaspoons salt
1/4 teaspoon ground red chile powder or paprika
2/3 cup salad oil
few drops ice water, if needed

The Salad:
1 head Boston lettuce, washed and dried
6 Romaine lettuce leaves, washed and dried
1 bunch scallions
3 cups cooked chicken or turkey
4 hard-cooked eggs, chilled
3 beets, cooked and chilled
orange sections reserved from dressing
2 ripe avocados

Prepare the dressing. Reserve orange sections for the salad and use the juices in the dressing. Using the metal blade, drop the garlic and parsley through the feed tube with the motor running to mince. Add vinegar, salt, chile powder, oil and orange juice to workbowl and process to combine. If the dressing seems too thick, add a few drops of water and process again.

Separate the Boston lettuce into leaves and line a large serving platter. Cut the Romaine leaves in half and pack upright into the feed tube using a 4mm (standard or thick) slicing disc. Process and then arrange the sliced lettuce over the Boston lettuce. Chill.

Trim the scallions to remove 3-4 inches from the tops and the whiskers from the ends. Make a cross cut in each end and then steam over boiling water for 1 minute. Rinse with cold water and place in a plastic bag with 1/4 cup of the dressing. Allow to marinate while proceeding.

Use a 3 or 4mm (standard) slicing disc to coarsely shred the poultry. Remove from workbowl, then use the French fry disc to dice the eggs. Cut the beets by hand into matchstick slices. (All ingredients can be prepared a few hours ahead to this point and chilled separately.)

Peel, pit and slice the avocado just prior to serving. Arrange the vegetables, orange sections and poultry in separate rows atop the lettuce. Drizzle with about half of the dressing. Garnish with the avocados. Pass remaining dressing separately. Serves 6-8.

*Entree
Salads*

Papaya-Shrimp Salad
Ensalada de Papaya

This lovely first course utilizes the native produce of the Southwest and is in the typical colorful and festive spirit of the region. It also makes a marvelous light luncheon entree.

The Vinaigrette Dressing:
1 clove garlic, peeled
2 sprigs parsley
3 tablespoons red wine vinegar
1 tablespoon fresh orange juice
$^2/_3$ cup vegetable oil
1 teaspoon salt
$^1/_4$ teaspoon white pepper
$^1/_8$ teaspoon sugar
1 egg white

The Salad:
$1^1/_2$ pounds medium raw shrimp
5 lemon slices
5 whole black peppercorns
1 bay leaf, broken
1 teaspoon salt
2 ripe firm avocados, see note
2 ripe firm papayas, see note
1 sweet red pepper, roasted and peeled
   (p.14) or $1^1/_2$ tablespoons diced pimiento
1 head Boston Lettuce, washed and dried

Prepare the dressing. Using the metal blade, drop the garlic through the feed tube with the motor running to mince. Add remaining dressing ingredients to the workbowl and process briefly to blend. This makes about 1 cup dressing.

Put the shrimp in a pan with the lemon slices, peppercorns, bay leaf, salt and water to cover. Bring to a boil and boil 1 minute. Rinse the shrimp under cool water to stop the cooking, then peel and devein.

Peel and pit the avocados and cut into $^1/_2$ inch slices. Peel and remove seeds from the papayas and cut into $^1/_2$ inch slices. If using the red pepper, remove stems and seeds and cut into $^1/_4$ x 2 inch strips.

Place the shrimp, avocado, papaya and peppers or pimientos in a large serving bowl. Pour the dressing over and toss very gently to coat. Chill up to 1 hour.

To serve, separate the Boston lettuce into whole leaves. Arrange several leaves on each of 8 salad places. Divide the shrimp mixture among the plates and spoon any extra dressing over the top. Serves 8 as an appetizer, or 6 as a light entreé.

Note: If avocadoes and papayas are very soft, arrange them in rows atop the lettuce rather than tossing with the dressing. Then spoon dressing over the rows. Since some avocados darken quickly, you should slice them just prior to serving. An alternate presentation is shown in the photograph on p.104.

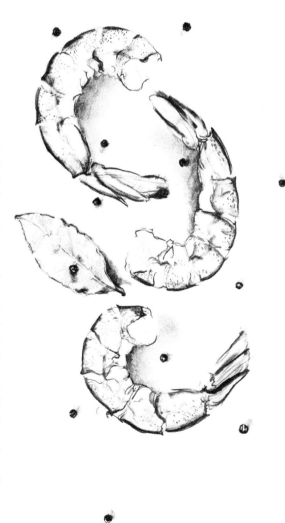

Shrimp Salad with Capers
Ensalada con Camarones

Garnish this salad with fresh tropical fruit slices such as oranges, pineapple, papaya and avocado or with sliced vegetables such as radishes and jicama. Either presentation is beautiful as a colorful and edible garnish surrounding the salad.

A Potato Nest Basket (available at specialty cookware stores) is useful for frying the tortilla "shells." If you don't have this tool, see the note at the end of the recipe for an alternate frying method.

The Salad:
4 corn or flour tortillas
1 1/2 quarts peanut oil for deep frying
3 tablespoons grated Parmesan cheese
1 1/2 pounds medium size raw shrimp
water to cover
5 whole peppercorns
2 tablespoons cider vinegar
1 bay leaf, broken
1 small onion, peeled

The Dressing:
1 clove garlic or 1 shallot, peeled
2 sprigs fresh cilantro or 3 sprigs fresh
   parsley
2 stalks celery, cut in 1 inch pieces
1/2 red bell pepper, cut in several pieces
3 fresh green chiles, roasted and peeled
   (p.14) or 1 (4 ounce) can green chiles,
   drained
1/2 teaspoon ground cumin
1/2-1 teaspoon salt
1 cup mayonnaise, homemade preferred
3 tablespoons large capers
1-2 teaspoons fresh lemon or lime juice to
   taste
sliced fresh fruit or vegetables for garnish

If the tortillas are not soft and fresh, wrap in aluminum foil and place in a 300° oven for a few minutes to soften. Keep covered until ready to fry. Heat the oil in a deep 3 quart saucepan or deep-fryer to 375°. Press the tortillas, one at a time, into a Potato Nest Basket. (The tortilla should press against the sides to form a shallow "bowl" shape.) Immerse the basket in the oil and fry about 1 minute until the tortillas are crisp and lightly browned. Drain on paper towels and sprinkle with some of the Parmesan cheese. Set the "salad bowls" aside.

Place the shrimp, water to cover, peppercorns, vinegar, bay leaf and onion in a medium saucepan. Bring to a boil and boil 1-2 minutes. Rinse the shrimp under cool water to stop cooking, then peel and devein. Remove onion from cooking liquid, quarter and reserve it. Discard cooking liquid or reserve for other uses.

Using the metal blade, drop the garlic and cilantro through the feed tube with the motor running to mince. Add the chiles, bell pepper, celery and reserved onion to the workbowl. Process to coarsely chop. Add the mayonnaise, cumin, salt to taste and 2 tablespoons of the capers. Process briefly to combine.

Lightly toss the shrimp with the mayonnaise mixture. Add lemon or lime juice to taste and toss again.

Fill each tortilla shell with the salad and sprinkle the remaining capers atop. Serve surrounded by the fruit or vegetable slices. Serves 4.

Note: To prepare the tortilla shells without a Potato Nest Basket, heat the oil in a saucepan with a smaller diameter than the tortillas. Press the tortillas, one at a time, into the oil using tongs to keep them immersed. Fry as directed. The tortilla will naturally take a cup or shell shape.

Seafood Salad with Pine Nut Sauce

This is a fresh summer salad using fresh shrimp, crab and vegetables. The classic Spanish Pine Nut Sauce is intentionally light to enhance the delicate flavor of the crabmeat. The vegetables and seafood can be prepared ahead and chilled until you are ready to assemble the salad.

The Salad:

1 pound medium size raw shrimp, or 1 pound scallops
3 quarts water
2 tablespoons lemon juice
1 teaspoon salt
5 black peppercorns
1 pound cooked crabmeat or cooked and diced firm fleshed fish
2 carrots, scraped and cut to fit the feed tube
1/2 pound fresh green beans, cut in 2 1/2 inch pieces
1 bay leaf, broken
1 teaspoon sugar
1 tablespoon lemon juice
3 tablespoons cider vinegar
2 medium zucchini squash
2 medium yellow summer squash

The Sauce:

1 clove garlic, peeled
1/2 cup pine nuts or shelled almonds
3 hard-cooked egg yolks
1 cup heavy cream
1/2 cup sour cream
1/4 teaspoon salt or to taste
1/8 teaspoon white pepper

The Garnishes:

1 head Boston lettuce
2 tablespoons minced parsley
3 hard-cooked egg whites, diced

Have the shrimp and scallops ready. Bring the water, lemon juice, salt and peppercorns to a boil. Add the shellfish and return to a boil. Cook 2-3 minutes until shrimp just turn pink. Drain and rinse under cool water to stop the cooking, then shell and devein shrimp.

Cut the crabmeat or fish into small pieces and reserve.

Use the 2 or 3mm (thin) slicing disc to process the carrots, stacking them horizontally in the feed tube. Then cut by hand into small matchstick slices. Place the carrot slices and beans in a 3 quart saucepan. Cover with water and add the bay leaf, sugar, lemon juice and vinegar. Bring to a boil.

Meanwhile, cut the squash to fit horizontally in the feed tube. Use the 5 or 6mm (thick) slicing disc and the Double Slicing Technique (p.21) to make matchstick slices. (If you don't have this disc, cut by hand into 2 1/2 x 1/4 inch slices.)

When the carrots and beans come to a boil, cook 1 minute. Add the squash and cook 1 minute more. Immediately remove from heat and add 6-8 ice cubes to the pan. Let the vegetables cool in the broth, then drain and reserve.

Prepare the sauce. Using the metal blade, drop the garlic through the feed tube with the motor running to mince. Add the pine nuts and egg yolks to the workbowl and process until smooth. With the machine running, pour the heavy cream through the feed tube and process until thoroughly blended. Stir the mixture into the sour cream and add the salt and pepper. Chill at least 1 hour.

When ready to serve, wash and dry the lettuce and separate into leaves. Use to line a large serving platter. Mound the seafood in the center and surround with rows of the vegetables. Garnish with the parsley and diced egg white. Serve the sauce separately. Serves 6-8.

Chilled Stuffed Chiles
Chile Rellenos Frio

This dish should be prepared with the thick skinned Chile Poblanos because most fresh chile verdes are too thin-skinned to hold the filling well. Some large mild chiles, such as the "Big Jim's" also work well and small bell peppers, although not as attractive, taste good too. See p.202 for more information on Stuffed Chiles.

I have given some options for fillings, but you may use any of your favorite fish, meat or poultry salads with vinaigrette or mayonnaise dressing. The chiles may be prepared 5-6 hours ahead. If preparing at serving time, you may omit the marinade.

Chile Preparation and Marinade:
4 fresh chile Poblanos or thick-skinned chile
    verdes or small bell peppers, roasted and
    peeled (p.14)
3 cups cider vinegar
1 cup oil
1 tablespoon sugar
1 teaspoon salt
$^1/_2$ teaspoon pepper
1 bay leaf, broken
2 cloves garlic, peeled

Filling:
3 sprigs parsley
$1^1/_2$ ounces cream cheese
1 stalk celery, cut in 4-5 pieces
$1^1/_2$ cups cooked chicken, tuna, salmon,
    shrimp or crabmeat
4-5 tablespoons mayonnaise, preferably
    homemade
salt and pepper to taste

Garnishes:
$1^1/_2$ cups sour cream
1 tablespoon minced chives
2 tablespoons large capers
2 tablespoons sliced black olives
thinly sliced onion rings

Remove seeds from chiles, but keep stems intact. Bring the vinegar, oil, sugar, salt, pepper, bay leaf and whole garlic to a boil. Let cool, then pour over the prepared chiles. Refrigerate, covered, until ready to use — up to 6 days.

Place the parsley and cream cheese in the workbowl using the metal blade. Process to mince the parsley. Add the celery and pulse to chop. Add the cooked meat or fish, mayonnaise and salt and pepper to taste. Pulse to chop and mix together. Adjust seasonings to taste.

Drain the chiles and use a knife to increase the slit part way down the side to allow for the filling. Fill each chile with some of the salad mixture.

To serve, arrange the filled chiles on a round platter in a circular fashion. Garnish with sour cream, chives, capers, olives and onion rings. (The onion can be processed using a thin slicing disc, if desired.) Serves 4.

Note: For a different presentation, garnish the chiles with sliced radishes and scallions and Spanish style sauce. (p.43)

Chalupas
Tostados

Chalupas and Tostados are the same dish. The term "tostado" can also mean corn tortilla chips that are crisply fried, but in this case the work refers to a type of salad. "Chalupa compuesta" means "compounded" with assorted fillings and toppings – often beginning with beans. "Chalupa" itself means "little boat" and the first ones made in Xochimilco, Mexico were a fresh masa dough shaped into flattened ovals with turned up edges to resemble a canoe. These deep-fried shells are easy to duplicate (with much less trouble) using oval tart shells. Press the dough into the shells and deep-fry in oil heated to 375° until the tart shells slip away from the dough and the "little boats" become crisp. Drain on paper towels and then use these light and interesting containers for hot or cold seafoods or other salads.

To further confuse the "Chalupa – Tostado" issue, in the Southwest the corn tortilla shells can also be flat, fried crisp and then piled high with an assortment of meats, poultry, lettuce, cheese and sauces – truly a super salad! The toppings can be combinations of hot and cold ingredients and, in California, would be called a Tostado. "Tostado del Roy" (Tostado of the King) is made from Sonora-style 18 inch flour tortillas fried into large shell shapes and make a "royal" presentation.

The following are some of the more popular combinations for Chalupas and Tostados. Most cooks create their own depending on what they have and what they like! See also the following recipe for Chicken Chalupas.

Eat Chalupas like a salad or an open-face sandwich.

The following ingredients in italic should be served warm and all suggested ingredients are listed in order of assembly on the corn tortilla shell.

1. *thin layer Refried Beans (p.215), sauteed Mexican Sausage (p.56),* sour cream, thinly sliced or shredded lettuce, shredded white cheese, chopped tomatoes
2. *Refried Beans, melted Cheddar cheese,* shredded cooked chicken, sliced lettuce, crumbled "Enchilada" cheese, Guacamole (p.49), sour cream, chopped tomatoes
3. *Chicken Stew (p. 56),* Guacamole, sour cream, shredded cheese, chopped tomatoes
4. *Refried Beans, Mexican Sausage,* avocado, sour cream, sliced scallions
5. *grilled beef tips, melted cheese,* sliced Romaine lettuce, chopped tomatoes
6. *Meat in Red Chile (p.165),* Guacamole, shredded lettuce, chopped tomatoes
7. *Refried Beans, Seasoned Meat (p.58),* shredded lettuce, shredded cheese, sour cream, hard-cooked egg slices, black olives

Chicken Chalupas

Many Southwestern recipes use the same combination of ingredients. The presentation then determines the name of the dish. In Chicken Chalupas the tortilla serves as a "plate" for the lightly spiced chicken salad. The combination of chicken, guacamole, cheese, lettuce and tomatoes are also served as flautas (rolled corn tortillas) or as tacos with the filling inside the crisp shell.

The type of chile in the salsa that you select will be the key to how picante your finished salad will taste. One Chalupa looks like it serves one person adequately, but many people manage to eat two or three!

The Salad:

8 corn tortillas
peanut oil for frying
4 ounces Longhorn Cheddar cheese, chilled
1/2 head iceberg or Romaine lettuce
3 whole chicken breasts, split, poached and cooled, boned and skinned
salt and pepper to taste
1 1/2 cups fresh salsa of choice or taco sauce
1/4 cup chopped scallion tops for garnish

The Dressing:

1-2 cloves garlic, peeled
3 ripe avocados, peeled, pitted and cut into chunks
1 small fresh green chile, roasted and peeled (p.14) or 1 tablespoon minced canned green chile
2 tablespoons fresh lemon juice
salt to taste
1 1/2 cups sour cream

Heat about 1 inch oil in a deep skillet or saucepan to 375°. Fry the tortillas until crisp and then drain on paper towels. (If you have a potato nest fryer, the tortillas can be fried in it to produce an attractive curved shell.) Set the shells aside.

Use the shredding disc to process the cheese. Use a 3 or 4mm (standard) slicing disc to process the lettuce. Use the same disc to process the chicken into shreds. Salt and pepper the chicken to taste and combine with 3/4 cup of the fresh salsa or taco sauce. (Reserve remaining salsa for garnish.) Set the prepared salad ingredients aside while making the dressing.

Using the metal blade, drop the garlic through the feed tube with the motor running to mince.

Add the avocado and the chiles, cut into pieces, to the workbowl. Add the lemon juice and pulse 2 or 3 times. Then process until the mixture is smooth. Add salt and the sour cream and process to blend.

To assemble the Chalupas, line each tortilla "plate" or "shell" with some of the sliced lettuce. Divide the chicken salad atop the lettuce. Spoon some guacamole dressing over the top with the shredded cheese. Garnish with the remaining salsa and chopped scallion tops.

All of the ingredients except the guacamole dressing can be prepared a day in advance, but the chalupas should be assembled at serving time and the guacamole made at the last minute to prevent darkening. Serves 8.

Here are two interesting variations for this dish:

1. One variation on this theme is to melt the cheese on the crisp tortilla instead of using it as a topping. Quite often, Refried Beans (p.215), mashed with added shortening or butter will be placed under the cheese as in a Nacho. This is a good way to use up leftover beans.

2. Omit the salsa or taco sauce. Prepare the dressing using only 1/2 cup sour cream. Melt the Cheddar cheese on the crisp tortillas. Put lettuce atop cheese. Warm the shredded chicken in 1/2 cup well seasoned chicken stock and spoon atop the lettuce. Garnish with a mixture of 1 cup sour cream mixed with 1/2 cup heavy cream. Divide 3 chopped tomatoes over the finished Chalupas and crumble "Enchilada cheese" over the entire dish.

VEGETABLES

In the Southwest, vegetables are rarely served alone or unadorned. Instead, as in Oriental cooking, they are often incorporated into the hot entree or cold main dish salad. You will also find them accompanying the meal as Salsa or side dish. If you look in the sections devoted to Accompaniments and to Relishes, Sauces and Fillings, you'll find many more ideas for vegetable dishes.

The following recipes use a selection of vegetables native to and also typical of the Southwest, and most are readily available throughout the rest of the country. Our region is a very big squash area, as these recipes demonstrate. Cabbage, potatoes, chayote, carrots, corn, onions and eggplant are also used extensively, and are often served with indigenous sauces.

The term "quelites" or "quelitas" is used throughout the Southwest to describe a wide variety of greens. Frequently, the greens are spinach or epazote — also called lamb's quarters. These attractive and delicious vegetables add color and taste to any meal.

Top to bottom: Cauliflower Saute, Wild Spinach with Pinto Beans (Quelitas con Frijoles), Vegetable Casserole.

Squash
Calabacitas

2 medium zucchini squash
1 medium yellow Summer squash
1 small yellow onion, peeled
2 Anaheim Poblano chiles or 1 bell
    pepper, roasted and peeled (p.14) or 2
    canned mild green chiles, drained
1 clove garlic, peeled
$^1/_4$ stick (1 ounce) butter
1 cup cooked fresh corn
$^1/_2$ teaspoon salt or to taste

Use the 3mm (standard) slicing disc to process both squashes. Remove and set aside. Use the metal blade to chop the onion. Reserve. By hand, slice the chiles into $^1/_4$ x 1 inch strips.

In a skillet large enough to accomodate all the vegetables, saute the whole garlic and onions in the butter for about 3 minutes until the onion is translucent. Discard the garlic and add the squash, chiles and corn. Cover and simmer about 4-5 minutes until vegetables are crisp-tender. Toss the mixture lightly, season with salt and serve immediately. Serves 6.

Southwest Vegetables with Green Chile Pesto

This is an excellent light vegetable combination to compliment chicken, fish or grilled meats. I fix this when I have leftover cooked spaghetti squash and like it best served with sauteed fish fillets and lime wedges.

3 carrots, scraped and cut to fit the feed tube
1 medium zucchini, cut in pieces to fit the
    feed tube
1 tablespoon butter
2-3 cups cooked spaghetti squash
3 tablespoons Green Chile Pesto (p.52)
2 tablespoons chicken stock
salt to taste

Use the shredding disc to process the carrots. Remove and set aside. Then use the same disc to shred the zucchini.

In a medium skillet, saute the carrots in the butter for 1 minute. Add the zucchini and spaghetti squash. Toss over medium heat for about 1 minute until heated through. Combine the pesto and chicken stock and stir into the hot vegetables. Season to taste with salt. Serve immediately. Serves 6.

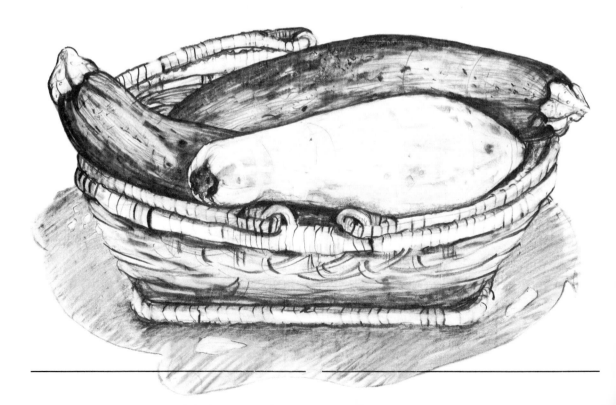

Spaghetti Squash with Spanish Sauce

The yellow spaghetti squash can be as small as an acorn squash or as large as a pumpkin. It's pumpkin-like seeds are delicious toasted and the cooked pulp separates into strands which resemble pasta cooked "al dente." This squash is delicious hot or cold and may be served with many different sauces.

This recipe is a simple preparation of cooked squash covered with Spanish Sauce and topped with grated or shredded cheese. If you wish, you can add 1 medium shredded zucchini which has been lightly sauteed in 1 tablespoon of butter to the squash.

> 1 medium size spaghetti squash
> 1 recipe Spanish Sauce (p.43)
> 3-4 ounces Parmesan or Swiss cheese

Pierce the squash shell in several places, then place directly on the oven rack in a preheated 350° oven. Bake 45 minutes to 1 hour depending on the size of the squash. Turn once during the baking time. The squash is cooked when the shell "gives"when pressed with your finger.

While the squash is cooking, prepare the Spanish Sauce and keep warm. If using Parmesan cheese, have it at room temperature and cut into 5 pieces. Using the metal blade, drop the cheese pieces through the feed tube with the motor running and process until finely grated. If using Swiss cheese, process with the shredding disc using very light pressure.

Remove the squash from the oven and let cool 5 minutes. Then halve lengthwise and, holding the squash with a pot-holder, remove the seeds and strings. Reserve the seeds for toasting or discard them. Run a fork down the squash to remove the spaghetti-like strands. Place about 5 cups of the strands on a lightly buttered platter. Top with the sauce and sprinkle with the cheese. Serve immediately. Serves 8.

Squash with Pesto Sauce

There are endless recipe variations for squash and chiles with cheese because "calabasas" are the most popular Mexican-American vegetable in the Southwest. I particularly like this combination of spaghetti squash and zucchini tossed with a Pesto Sauce.

> 1 medium-large zucchini, cut in pieces to fit the feed tube
> 3 cups cooked spaghetti squash, see note
> 2/3 cups Green Chile Pesto (p.52) or Cilantro Pesto (p.53)
> 1/2 cup cream or sour cream
> 1/3-1/2 cup chicken stock
> salt to taste

Use the shredding disc to process the zucchini, loading it horizontally into the feed tube. Combine in a bowl with the spaghetti squash.

In a medium skillet, combine the Pesto of choice, the cream and chicken stock to thin the mixture. Set over medium heat to warm through. Add the squash mixture and stir over medium heat until hot. Salt to taste and serve immediately. Serves 6.

Note: Spaghetti squash vary in size tremendously and often only large ones can be obtained. Fortunately, the cooked "strands" re-heat well and are good cold in salads. To cook a whole spaghetti squash, pierce the shell in several places and place in a baking dish. Bake 40 minutes to 1 hour at 350°, turning once. The squash is done when the sides are soft. Cool 5 minutes, then cut in half lengthwise. Remove the seeds to dry and toast if desired. Use a fork to scrape the "strands" of squash (resembling spaghetti) from the shell.

Stuffed Squash
Calabasitas Rellenos

The Mexican squash (calabasitas) is almost a cross between a winter and summer squash in taste. My favorite one is about the size of an acorn squash and perfect for stuffing. If you can't find a calabasitas, use the following combination of acorn and zucchini squash to give a similar result.

Toasted chile seeds are a favorite garnish for many salads and vegetable dishes, but this fiery topping is a bit hot for most people. In this recipe I use toasted pumpkin seeds. Note that the recipe doubles easily.

1/4 cup heavy cream
1/2 cup sour cream
2 acorn squash
1 small onion, peeled and halved
1/4 bell pepper
1/2 pound Mexican Sausage (p.56) or spicy bulk pork sausage
1 small zucchini, cut in several pieces
1/2 apple, cored and cut in several pieces
4 crisp corn chips or tostados
1 tablespoon seedless raisins
2 tablespoons hulled and salted pumpkin seeds
salt and pepper to taste
1-2 tablespoons butter
1/8-1/2 teaspoon chile powder or to taste
toasted pumpkin seeds for garnish

Combine the cream and sour cream and let stand 30 minutes. Serve at room temperature.

Wash and halve the squash trimming a thin slice from the bottom portion so it will lay flat. Discard seeds and stringy pulp. Cook the squash, cut side down, in boiling water to cover for about 5 minutes. Drain, scoop out and reserve pulp and leave a 1/4-1/2 inch shell for stuffing. Place the shells in a buttered baking dish.

Using the metal blade, pulse to chop the onion and bell pepper together. Remove and place in a skillet with the sausage meat. Saute until the onions are translucent and the sausage is cooked. Leave in the skillet set off heat.

Use the metal blade to finely chop together the zucchini, apple, corn chips, raisins, pumpkin seeds and squash pulp. Add to the sausage mixture in the skillet and saute 3-4 minutes. Add salt and pepper to taste.

Mound the mixture into the squash shells and dot with the butter. The recipe can be made early in the day to this point and refrigerated. Shortly before serving, preheat the oven to 350°. Cover the stuffed squash and bake 10 minutes (15-20 minutes if it has been refrigerated), then uncover and bake 5 minutes more.

Serve the squash with a dollop of the sour cream mixture and garnish with toasted pumpkin seeds. Serves 4.

Chiles and Onions with Squash
Rajas con Calabasitas

This zesty side dish is a variation of a favorite accompaniment to grilled meats. The thick-skinned chile Poblano is preferred with green bell peppers being the best substitute. A combination of red bell peppers, chile Poblanos, onions and the squash is also flavorful and colorful.

4 chile Poblanos, roasted and peeled (p.14) or green bell peppers, see note
2 red bell peppers, see note
1 large yellow onion, peeled and halved
1 medium zucchini (about 8 inches long)
2 large carrots
2 tablespoons oil
1-2 tablespoons butter
1 tablespoon minced cilantro or parsley
salt to taste
3 ounces "Enchilada" cheese, crumbled

Remove seeds and cut the chiles and peppers into long strips about ½ inch wide. By hand, slice the onion, cut side down, into strips. Use a 3-4mm (standard) slicing disc and the Double Slicing Technique (p.21) to cut the zucchini and carrots into ¼ inch matchstick slices.

Heat the oil and butter in a 10-12 inch skillet. Over low heat, saute the onion until translucent, about 4 minutes. (Do not allow to brown.) Add the chiles, bell peppers and carrots and saute over low heat for 4-5 minutes. Add the zucchini and saute 1-2 minutes until crisp-tender. Add the cilantro and salt to taste. Top with the crumbled cheese and serve immediately. Serves 6-8.

Note: It is optional to roast and peel the bell peppers.

Squash Casserole
Sopa de Calabasas

3 strips bacon, cut in 1 inch pieces
1 onion, peeled and halved
1 bell pepper, stemmed and seeded and quartered
1 clove garlic, peeled
1 pound zucchini squash
2 fresh tomatoes cored and cut in half
3-4 ounces Monterey Jack or Parmesan cheese
½ cup evaporated milk
½ teaspoon salt or to taste
⅛ teaspoon coarse ground black pepper or to taste
pinch sugar

In a skillet large enough to accomodate all the vegetables, fry the bacon pieces until golden brown and crisp. Remove bacon with a slotted spoon and drain. Pour off all but 3 tablespoons drippings and reserve in pan.

Use the 3 or 4mm (standard) slicing disc to process the onion. Leave in workbowl and process the bell pepper using the same disc. Remove the mixture and set aside.

Insert the metal blade and drop the garlic through the feed tube with the motor running to mince. Leave in workbowl and change to French fry disc. Process the squash into strips. (If you do not have this disc, halve the squash horizontally and slice using the thickest disc available. Then cut slices in half by hand to make small chunks). Leave squash in workbowl and use the French fry disc to process the tomatoes into strips. Discard skin. (Or cut tomatoes by hand into 1½-2 inch strips.). Remove the mixture and reserve.

Wipe out workbowl. If you are using Monterey Jack cheese, process using the shredding disc. If using Parmesan cheese, use the metal blade and drop the cheese, cut in 5-6 pieces, through the feed tube with motor running. Process until finely grated.

Saute the onion and pepper in the reserved bacon fat about 3 minutes until the onion is soft. Add the squash, garlic and tomatoes. Cook 3-4 minutes, stirring constantly, until squash is tender but still firm. Add milk, salt, pepper and sugar and toss to coat the vegetables. Reduce heat to low, add cheese and stir until melted. Garnish with reserved bacon and serve immediately. Serves 4-6.

Medley of Southwest Vegetables
Colache

Vegetables vary from state to state, but this colorful combination is typical of the Southwest and makes a lovely accompaniment to almost any main dish.

> 1 yellow onion, peeled and quartered
> 1 pound zucchini (3-4 medium)
> 2 fresh tomatoes, cored, see note
> 1 bell pepper or 2 canned or fresh roasted and peeled (p.14) mild green Anaheim or Poblano chiles
> 1½ cups fresh corn from the cob or thawed frozen corn
> 1 cup fresh or thawed frozen green beans or lima beans
> 2 tablespoons butter, margarine or bacon fat
> ¼-½ cup chicken broth
> ½ teaspoon salt or to taste
> ¼ teaspoon pepper

Use the French fry disc or the 3 or 4mm (standard) slicing disc to process the onion. Use the 3 or 4mm (standard) slicing disc to process the zucchini. Use the same disc to process the bell pepper, if using, first remove stems and seeds and cutting into wedges to fit feed tube. If using chiles, remove stems and seeds and cut by hand into thin strips. Use the French fry disc to process the tomatoes into thin strips discarding any skin left in workbowl and discarding juices. Cut green beans into 1½ inch pieces. Set all vegetables, including corn, aside.

Melt the butter in a skillet large enough to accomodate all the vegetables. Saute the onion, bell pepper and beans for about 3 minutes until the onion is translucent. Stir in the corn, zucchini and ¼ cup of the broth and simmer 1 minute. Stir in the tomatoes and chiles, if using, and simmer just until all vegetables are hot. Add the remaining chicken stock if more liquid is needed. Salt and pepper to taste and serve immediately. Serves 8-10.

Note: When red bell peppers are in season, substitute 1 pepper for the tomatoes. Process like the green bell pepper and add to the skillet with the onion. Proceed as directed.

Cauliflower Saute

Cauliflower with a pureed avocado sauce containing tomatoes, onions and peppers or chiles is a "Southwest-Style" vegetable. I prefer, however, that the vegetables be cut in small pieces. An added advantage to this technique is that the avocado need not be fully ripe.

> 1 head cauliflower
> 6 scallions
> 1 clove garlic, peeled, optional
> ½ bell pepper, stemmed and seeded
> 2 tomatoes, cored
> 2 medium-firm avocados, peeled and seeded
> ¼ stick (1 ounce) butter
> 1 tablespoon vegetable oil
> 1 tablespoon lemon juice
> ½ teaspoon salt or to taste
> ⅛ teaspoon black pepper
> ⅛ teaspoon cayenne pepper

Separate the cauliflower into florets and blanch 1 minute in boiling salted water. Drain and keep warm.

By hand, slice the scallions thinly using both green and white part. Set aside. Using the metal blade, drop the optional garlic through the feed tube with the motor running to mince. Add the bell pepper and pulse to finely chop. Add to the green onions.

By hand, cut the avocados and tomatoes into bite-sized pieces. Set aside.

In a skillet large enough to accomodate all the ingredients, saute the scallions, garlic and pepper mixture in the butter and oil for about 3-5 minutes until soft. Add the cauliflower and avocado, tossing gently. Drizzle the lemon juice over, then season with the salt and both peppers. Stir in the tomatoes. Cook over low heat until the avocado softens and all vegetables are heated through.

The outer portion of the avocado forms a sauce with the tomato juices, butter and lemon. Remove the vegetables with a slotted spoon and spoon butter sauce over all. Serve immediately. Serves 6-8.

Cauliflower with Cheese

Coliflor con Queso

The cheese sauce in this recipe may be used over nearly any vegetable, baked potatoes, omlettes or as a hot dipping sauce for crudites. It's a favorite at my house and one recipe for which most guests enter requests!

1 head cauliflower
1/2 small yellow onion
1 (4 ounce) can mild or hot green chiles, drained
1/4 stick (1 ounce) butter
1 1/2 cups whole milk
3 ounces Monterey Jack cheese, cut in several pieces
3 ounces Cheddar cheese, cut in several pieces
2 tablespoons flour
1/8 teaspoon pure ground chile powder or cayenne pepper to taste
1/8 teaspoon salt or to taste
1 1/2 tablespoons diced pimiento
1 tablespoon minced parsley, optional garnish

Divide the cauliflower into florets, allowing about 4 per serving. Boil in salted water until just tender, then drain and keep warm.

Use the metal blade to mince the onion and chiles together. Saute in the butter for about 3 minutes until the onions are translucent. Set aside.

Bring the milk to a boil in a 1 quart saucepan. Meanwhile, place the cheeses in the workbowl using the metal blade. Pulse to break up the pieces, then process continuously until grated. Add the flour, chile powder and salt. Process to make a paste, then pour the hot milk through the feed tube with the motor running. Process only until smooth, stopping to scrape sides of the workbowl as necessary. Return the mixture to the saucepan and cook over medium heat, stirring constantly, for about 2 minutes until hot and thickened. Stir in the pimiento and chile-onion mixture.

Serve the sauce over the warm cauliflower and garnish with minced parsley, if desired. Serves 5-6.

Wild Spinach with Pinto Beans

Quelitas con Frijoles

The combination of wild spinach and pinto beans is typical of the Southwest, particularly New Mexico. I must admit that I have taken great liberties with the original recipe – coming up with something like a wilted spinach salad. It is one of my favorite green vegetable dishes and wonderful with any meat or poultry.

8 cups (10-12 ounces) tightly packed trimmed fresh spinach leaves
1 red bell pepper, roasted and peeled (p.14) or 2 pimientos, drained
1/2 medium red onion, peeled
4 slices bacon, cut in small pieces
1/3 cup pine nuts or 2 hard-cooked eggs for garnish
1/2 cup vinegar
1/2 teaspoon salt
1 tablespoon granulated sugar
1 cup cooked Pinto Beans (p.215), well-drained

Thoroughly wash and dry the spinach leaves and place in a large mixing bowl. Cut the pepper or pimiento into thin strips and set aside. Use the metal blade to chop the onion medium-fine. Use the French fry disc to dice the hard-cooked eggs if using.

In a small skillet, cook the bacon. Remove with a slotted spoon and drain. Lightly brown the pine nuts in the drippings. Remove with a slotted spoon and set aside for garnish.

Add the vinegar, sugar, salt and chopped onion to the remaining drippings in the skillet. Simmer about 2 minutes and pour over the spinach. Add the Pinto Beans, pepper or pimiento strips and toss to coat with the dressing.

Serve at once garnished with the pine nuts or diced eggs. Serves 6.

Note: All ingredients may be prepared in advance but the salad must be served as soon as the dressing is added.

Spinach Enchiladas
Chalupas de Espinacas

This is my favorite vegetable casserole and is not really a "Chalupa" at all. Taken from an old Southwest cookbook by Eleanor Ringland Winston, this delightful accompaniment to grilled meats or poultry is also a lovely light luncheon entree. The cream softens the tortillas to make a delicate crepe-like texture. Use the thinnest tortilla available.

    20 ounces fresh spinach
    1 cup boiling water
    1 clove garlic, peeled
    3 ounces onion (about 1 small chunk),
        peeled
    1/2 pound sliced mushrooms, optional
    1 tablespoon butter
    1 average slice bread (to make 1/2 cup fresh
        bread crumbs)
    1/2 teaspoon salt or to taste
    1/4 teaspoon black pepper
    1/8 teaspoon nutmeg
    1/8 teaspoon chile powder
    1 egg, beaten
    1 cup heavy cream or evaporated milk
    1 1/2 cups oil for softening tortillas
    12 corn tortillas
    1 1/2 ounces cheese (Meunster, Monterey
        Jack or crumbly "Enchilada Style"
        Farmers cheese), see note

Wash the spinach and remove all the brown pieces. Place in a skillet with about 1 cup boiling water and blanch 1-2 minutes. Drain in a colander and press all liquid from the spinach.

Using the metal blade, drop the garlic, onion and mushrooms through the feed tube with the motor running to mince. Place in a skillet with the butter and saute for a few minutes until the onion is translucent. Meanwhile, tear the bread in pieces and put in the workbowl still using the metal blade. Process to make bread crumbs. Add the spinach, salt, pepper, nutmeg and chile powder. Pulse to combine, then add the egg, onion and mushroom mixture and 3 tablespoons of the cream or evaporated milk. Pulse to combine the mixture.

Heat the oil to 300° in a skillet large enough to accomodate the tortillas. Pass each tortilla through the oil to soften. Drain between paper towels.

Divide the spinach filling among the tortillas. Roll up and place seam side down in a casserole dish large enough to accommodate them. Pour the remaining cream or milk over the tortillas and allow to set covered in the refrigerator at least 2 hours or up to 24 hours. Baste the tortillas with the cream or milk several times during this period.

Let the casserole come to room temperature before baking. Preheat the oven to 350°. If using Meunster or Monterey Jack cheese, process using the metal blade. Otherwise crumble by hand. Spoon the cream over the top of the tortillas and sprinkle with the cheese of choice. Bake 25 minutes. Serves 6.

Note: I prefer a crumbly, non-melting white cheese for this dish, although this is sometimes hard to find. Feta cheese is too salty and dominates the delicate flavor.

Spinach Loaf with Spanish Sauce Torta de Quelitas

When garnished with scallions and a tomato rose, this is a beautiful dish for entertaining. My children, who usually do not eat spinach, love this loaf. The leftovers are also delicious sliced, reheated and served with a poached egg.

20 ounces fresh spinach
4 ounces Parmesan cheese, at room temperature and cut in 6-8 pieces
4 ounces Monterey Jack or Mozzarella cheese, chilled and cut in small pieces
4 ounces cottage cheese
1 egg yolk
2 scallions (white part), cut in several pieces
1½ slices white bread, torn in pieces (to make ¾ cup crumbs)
6 corn tostados, broken (to make ¼ cup crumbs)
3 large eggs
3 tablespoons cream
pinch sugar
1 teaspoon salt
¼ teaspoon white pepper
⅛ teaspoon nutmeg
Quick Ranch Style Salsa (p.41)
1 tomato "rose" for garnish, see note
2 scallions (green part) for garnish, see note

Wash spinach removing any brown parts and tough stems. Drain thoroughly and squeeze dry in a tea towel to remove all moisture. Reserve.

Using the metal blade, drop the Parmesan cheese pieces through the feed tube with the motor running and process until finely grated. (If the cheese is very hard or oily, place directly in workbowl and pulse several times to break up pieces. Then process until finely grated.) Add Monterey Jack cheese to workbowl and pulse until finely minced. Add cottage cheese, egg yolk and white parts of the scallions (save green parts for garnish) and process to combine. Set this mixture aside.

Use the metal blade to process the bread and tostados together to make crumbs. There should be about 1 cup crumbs. Add the spinach in 3-4 batches, pulsing to chop each and reduce volume. (You will need to stop and scrape workbowl several times and remove each batch of spinach before continuing with the next.) During the spinach chopping, add one of the eggs and 1 tablespoon of the cream through the feed tube with the motor running to aid in the chopping process. Add re-maining eggs, cream, sugar, salt, pepper and nutmeg to final spinach batch and process to combine the mixture. Then combine with all of the spinach.

Fold together the cheese and spinach mixtures leaving some streaks of white throughout. Transfer to a buttered 9 x 5 inch loaf pan. Set the pan in a larger pan half-filled with hot water. Add water, if necessary, so it comes halfway up the sides of the loaf pan. Cover the loaf directly with a generously buttered piece of Cut-Rite brand wax paper. (This brand tears less easily.)

Bake for 1¼ hours in a preheated 350° oven removing the wax paper after 1 hour of baking. Remove from oven and cool the loaf in the water bath for 20 minutes.

To serve the loaf, run a knife around the edges of the pan and then invert onto a serving platter to unmold. Garnish with a tomato rose and scallion stems. Serve with warm Quick Ranch Style Salsa. Serves 8.

Note: To prepare the garnishes, use a very sharp knife to peel the tomato. Start at the top and remove the outer peel in one piece by moving the knife around the tomato in a spiral fashion to make a long strip of peel about ½ inch wide. Roll up the strip very tightly and tuck the loose end into the center. (If the peel breaks, simply make two small roses instead of one large one). This is a tomato rose.

To make the "flower" stems, slice the green parts of the scallions into slivers. Arrange these "stems" to extend from the rose in an attractive pattern.

Roasting Corn

Elotes

Summer is the perfect time to cook outdoors in the Southwestern style. Here is a recipe for roasting fresh corn to accompany Grilled Meat (p.160).

 8 ears fresh corn, husks left intact
 water for moistening husks
 1 stick (4 ounces) butter or margarine
 juice from 4 Mexican or 2 all-purpose limes
 $1/2$ teaspoon salt
 $1/8$-1 teaspoon chile powder or to taste

Prepare a medium hot fire (the same as for cooking steaks). I recommend cooking the corn first and keeping it warm while grilling the accompaning meat.

Dampen the husks and, if desired, wrap in foil. Grill for 15-20 minutes, turning to roast both sides.

When ready to serve, remove husks and coat with butter, lime juice, salt and chile powder to taste. Serves 8.

Corn with Chiles

Elote con Chile

My children like corn prepared in this simple and colorful way. It is quite typical throughout the Southwest and, in my opinion, a thoroughly American dish. This recipe is from Fiestas Mexicanas and the Ringland family.

 8 ears of young corn
 $1/4$ stick (1 ounce) butter
 $3/4$-1 cup whole milk
 1 egg, beaten
 1 teaspoon salt
 pinch sugar
 pinch cornstarch
 2 tablespoons diced green pepper or green
  chile
 2 tablespoons diced pimiento

Scrape the corn kernels from the cob and set aside. Continue to scrape to remove the starchy milk from the cob and reserve.

Saute the corn kernels for 3-4 minutes in hot butter, then stir in $3/4$ cup milk and reduce heat to the lowest setting.

Beat the egg with the salt, sugar and cornstarch and stir into the corn mixture. Cook slowly for about 15 minutes, stirring constantly and adding more milk if necessary. Near the end of the cooking time stir in the pepper and pimiento. Serve immediately. Serves 6-8.

Variation: 4 scraped and sliced carrots are delicious cooked with the corn.

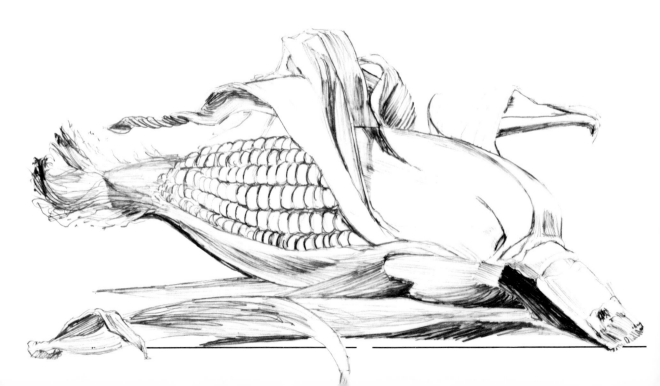

Broccoli Saute with Pine Nuts
Brécoles con Pignolas

This unusual and flavorful combination is well suited to compliment any meat or poultry dish.

     3 cups broccoli florets
     2 tablespoons vegetable oil
     1/3 cup pine nuts or slivered almonds
     1 tablespoon butter
     2 cloves garlic, peeled
     2 tablespoons long grain white rice
     6 tablespoons chicken stock (or more if
        needed)
     2 firm tomatoes, cored
     3 tablespoons seedless raisins
     1 cup artichoke hearts, drained and halved,
        optional
     1/2-3/4 teaspoon salt or to taste
     fresh ground black pepper to taste
     1/8 teaspoon ground chile or cayenne pepper

Use only the broccoli florets and reserve stems for other uses. Heat the oil in a skillet and saute the broccoli and pine nuts for about 1 minute, stirring constantly to prevent nuts from burning. Use a slotted spoon to remove broccoli and nuts and reserve. Add butter to the pan.

Using the metal blade, drop the garlic through the feed tube with the motor running to mince. Add the garlic and rice to the skillet and saute about 2 minutes until the rice is golden. Stir in the stock and simmer about 10 minutes until rice is tender. (Add more stock if needed to cook rice.) Remove the skillet from the heat.

While the rice cooks, process the tomatoes into strips with the French fry disc. Drain off excess liquid and add the tomatoes, broccoli, nuts, raisins and optional artichoke hearts to the skillet, tossing over medium heat just until the vegetables are heated through. Season to taste with salt, pepper and the chile or cayenne pepper. Serve immediately. Serves 6.

Mexican Hominy

Taken from an old South Texas community cookbook, this recipe is like a Southwestern "succotash."

     1 medium onion, peeled and quartered
     8 strips bacon, cut in small dice
     1 (14 1/2 ounce) can Italian plum tomatoes
        including juices
     2 teaspoons chile powder
     1/4 teaspoon salt
     1 1/2 cups fresh or canned white hominy,
        cooked
     1 cup cooked fresh corn
     1 cup cooked fresh or frozen lima beans
     1 (4 ounce) can chopped mild green chiles,
        optional
     4 ounces Monterey Jack or Meunster
        cheese, chilled for garnish, optional

Use the metal blade and pulse several times to coarsely chop the onion. Reserve.

In a medium skillet or saucepan, saute the bacon 2-4 minutes. Then add the onion and continue to cook for about 3 minutes until the onion is translucent. Pour off excess fat, then stir in the tomatoes, salt and chile powder. Break up whole tomatoes with a fork.

Combine the hominy, corn, lima beans and chiles in a 9 x 11 inch baking dish. Stir in the tomato sauce. Bake 30-35 minutes in a preheated 325° oven.

If using the cheese, process using the shredding disc. Sprinkle over the top of the casserole and return to the oven for about 5 minutes to melt the cheese. Serves 6.

Green Beans with Sauce
Ejotes con Salsa

This is a recipe from Fiestas Mexicanas and the Ringland family. The use of pureed potatoes and hard-cooked eggs to make a sauce demonstrates the ever present Spanish influence in what is popularly pegged "Tex-Mex" food.

    1 medium (3-4 ounce) red skinned or new
        potato, peeled and halved
    2 shallots, peeled
    1½ teaspoons butter
    ½ teaspoon salt
    pinch baking powder
    1½ tablespoons vinegar
    1 tablespoon mayonnaise
    ⅛ teaspoon white pepper
    ⅛ teaspoon dry mustard
    4-6 tablespoons heavy cream
    3 hard-cooked eggs, yolks and whites
        separated
    1 pound fresh or frozen green beans
    1 pimiento, diced

Cook the potato in boiling salted water until quite soft. Drain. Using the metal blade, drop the shallots through the feed tube with the motor running to mince. Transfer to a small skillet and saute in the butter about 2 minutes until soft. Insert the metal blade and place the potato, shallot, salt, baking powder, vinegar, mayonnaise, pepper and mustard in the workbowl. Pulse 3-4 times, then add the cream and egg yolks processing continuously until smooth. Leave the mixture in the workbowl while cooking the beans.

Cut the beans in half and cook in salted water to cover until just crisp-tender. Drain and reserve the cooking liquid. Put the potato mixture and ⅓ cup reserved liquid into a sauce pan and set over medium heat. Cook, stirring until the mixture is hot and smooth (add up 3⅓ cup more reserved liquid if sauce seems too thick.) Taste and adjust the seasonings. Keep both sauce and beans warm.

Use the square julienne disc or metal blade to dice the egg white. Place the beans on a warm serving platter, pour the sauce over and garnish with the egg white and diced pimiento. Serve immediately. Serves 4-5.

Vegetable Casserole
Sopa de Verduras

Sopas are one of the main starches of the Mexican-American meal. The word "casserole" is the closest equivalent but does not really explain this "all purpose" term.

    10 corn tortillas
    oil for frying
    1 potato (12 ounces), peeled
    1 medium zucchini or crook neck squash,
        cut in 2½ inch pieces
    3 carrots, peeled and cut to fit the feed tube
    6 ounces Monterey Jack or Meunster
        cheese, chilled
    ½ teaspoon salt or to taste
    3 cups Spanish Style Sauce (p.43)
    ⅓ cup toasted squash or pumpkin seeds for
        garnish, see note
    1½ tablespoons butter
    ½ teaspoon salt
    ½ teaspoon red chile powder
    1 tablespoon fresh minced parsley

Cut the tortillas into long strips about ¼ inch wide. Cut 10-15 of these strips into small pieces to use as garnish. Heat about 1 inch of oil to 375° and fry the tortilla pieces for 20-30 seconds until crisp. Drain on paper towels. Then fry the remaining strips, in 3 batches, until crisp. Drain and set aside.

Use the shredding disc to process the potato and place the shreds in a saucepan with water to cover. Bring to a boil and cook a total of 8 minutes. Drain well.

Use the shredding disc to process the squash and carrots (loaded horizontally in feed tube) separately. Then use the same disc to shred the cheese.

Butter a shallow casserole and layer the vegetables separately with the tortilla strips, sauce and cheese in between each layer. Lightly salt each layer and finish the casserole with cheese on top.

Cover and bake about 20 minutes in a preheated 375° oven. Uncover and bake 5 minutes more.

While the casserole is baking, prepare the garnish. Saute the seeds in butter in a small skillet for about 1 minute. Add the chile powder, ½ teaspoon salt and the parsley and toss together. Garnish the finished casserole with the sauteed seeds and the small tortilla pieces. Serves 8.

Note: To toast seeds, place on a lightly greased baking sheet in a single layer. Bake 5-8 minutes at 375° watching carefully so they don't burn.

SANDWICHES

Southwestern Sandwiches range far afield from the standard bread, butter, mayonnaise and filling concoctions to which many Americans are accustomed. The choice is extensive, and so are the number of shapes and ways of cooking; these sandwiches can be folded or rolled, fried, grilled, or heated in the oven.

Almost everyone knows Crisp Tacos, corn tortillas that are deep-fried and folded, filled with various combinations of meat, seafood or chicken and then garnished. Less familiar are relatively uncommon treats such as Soft Tacos, made with corn or flour tortillas, and served up as énchiladas.

I heartily recommend Puff Tacos from San Antonio, and another native Texan invention, the Breakfast Taco.

Flour tortilla combinations are popular in California and Arizona. The sandwiches called Burros and Burritos are served soft (just heated through) or grilled.

The difference between them is the size of the tortilla — Burros are made with larger tortillas than Burritos. Chimichangas are tightly rolled burros or burritos that are deep-fried.

The turnovers called Quesadillas are traditionally made with fresh Masa Harina, but nowadays both pre-cooked corn and flour tortillas are used.

Flautas — "flutes" — are particularly attractive. I predict that they'll become as popular in the rest of the country as they now are in the Southwest.

For a hearty sandwich, try a Torta. The name might be confusing, since "torta" can signify several quite different preparations, including a paté. As a sandwich, torta means a substantial roll filled with a number of beef or poultry mixtures. Tortas may be served hot or cold.

Depending on the size and filling choice, all Southwestern Sandwiches can be served many ways. You can enjoy them as hors d'oeuvres, with drinks, as snacks at any time, or as appetizers at the beginning of a meal. Arrange several for each serving, and sandwiches become a fine main course for either lunch, dinner or supper.

Clockwise from top left: Flautas, Quesadillas (baked and fried), Texas Hot Salsa, Burritos, Tacos, Chimichangas.

143

Burros, Burritos and Chimichangas

Burros, Burritos and Chimichangas are all rolled sandwiches made from various sizes of flour tortillas. Fillings can be meat, cheese, eggs or sweet fruit fillings used in dessert Chimichangas. The only real difference among the three is the size of the tortilla and the cooking method: Burros and Burritos are served soft or grilled and Chimichangas are fried.

In California and Arizona, where Sonora-style Mexican food and large flour tortillas are common, Burros and Burritos are especially popular. These large tortillas easily enclose fillings to make a truly portable sandwich. In Texas, where 6-8 inch tortillas are popular, the fillings are enclosed by rolling with ends open or folding over like a Quesadilla and are called "tacos" or "breadfast tacos." Since these smaller tortillas do not completely enclose the filling, one needs to master the technique of folding one end and tipping it up to avoid a major disaster and losing the filling!

Chimichangas are simply Burritos that are rolled and folded like a large egg roll and then deep-fried. In Arizona a 16-18 inch flour tortilla is used for this popular dish and in New Mexico and West Texas, Chimichangas are made with 10-12 inch tortillas. As with all tortilla specialties, there are numerous regional variations. Some cooks even grill Chimichangas instead of frying. Jack Laurenzo, of Ninfa's Restaurant in Texas, prefers his "empanada style" which requires an uncooked tortilla dough.

All of the Burros, Burritos and Chimichangas are usually eaten as a sandwich often garnished with fresh salsa, melted cheese, sour cream and/or guacamole. Workers in the fields carried these "sandwiches" for lunch giving rise to the saying that "tortillas are the napkin, plate, fork and spoon" of the Southwest. Today, they are as attractive and appealing as crepes.

One important technique to remember is to soften the tortillas prior to rolling and filling which avoids cracking. You may use any of the softening methods described on p.23. The tortillas may be used in this state or may be then grilled or deep-fried after filling. I have given cooking methods for all three, then, depending upon how you plan to eat the "sandwich," choose one of the filling ideas. It would be impossible to include every cook's version, but these are some of my favorites.

Soft Burros or Burritos:

If you use large (12-18 inch) flour tortillas, you may fold to totally enclose the filling. If you use smaller (6-8 inch) tortillas, either fold over like a Quesadilla (p.146) or roll up like an Enchilada (p.186). The following fillings can be used for either size, but the last two are particularly good for small tortillas rolled like Enchiladas. The ingredients in italic should be served hot.

1. *Refried or Whole Beans (p.215)*, shredded cheese
2. *Shredded or ground Seasoned Meat (p.58)*, shredded cheese and *Beans*
3. *Eggs and fried potatoes*
4. *Eggs and Mexican Sausage (p.56)*
5. *Spicy Meat Hash (p.65)*
6. *Beef Stew (p.164)*
7. Julienne strips of sauteed vegetables such as carrots, zucchini and chayote, Avocado Sauce (p.49)
8. Julienne strips of vegetables, avocado slices, Seasoned Tomato Sauce (p.43) or Spanish Style Sauce (p.43)

Grilled Burros or Burritos:

These are filled and then either rolled or folded to enclose the filling. Grill on both sides in a well-seasoned skillet or griddle. All may be served with Guacamole (p.49), shredded cheese or various cooked Salsas. All of the following filling suggestions in italic should be served hot.

1. *Cooked Beans (p.215),* avocado, *Grilled or shredded meats*
2. *Meat in Red Chile (p.165)*
3. *Shredded cooked chicken,* green chiles, shredded cheese
4. *Cooked Beans,* shredded cheese

Deep-Fried Chimichangas:

Chimichangas can be prepared and filled up to 12 hours ahead, but should be fried just before serving. Use 12 inch flour tortillas spooning the filling into the center. Fold in the sides and roll up tightly to resemble a large egg roll. Secure with toothpicks. Deep-fry, one at a time, in oil heated to 375° for about 1½ minutes turning to brown both sides. Drain on paper towels and serve immediately.

Guacamole (p.49), sour cream, black olives, melted cheese, Green Chile Sauce (p.45), Red Chile Sauce (p.46) or nearly any Salsa of your choice can be served with Chimichangas. Following the filling suggestions, I give a recipe for another savory Chimichanga filling. Be sure to see the Dessert Section for a Sweet Chimichanga.

1. *Meat in Red Chile (p.165)*
2. *Shredded and seasoned beef or pork*
3. *Cooked shredded chicken,* green chiles
4. *Chicken Stew (p.56)*

Savory Chimichanga Filling

1 (3-4 pound) chicken, cut up
water to cover
1 carrot, cut in chunks
4-5 sprigs parsley
2 cloves garlic, peeled
salt and pepper to taste
¹/₂ small onion, peeled
1 medium size, firm tomato
3 ounces Monterey Jack cheese, chilled
¹/₂ cup canned chopped green chiles
6 (12 inch) flour tortillas, softened (p.23)
Salsa or Sauce of choice for garnish

Place the chicken in a heavy pot with water to cover. Add the carrot, parsley, garlic, salt and pepper. Bring to a boil, then lower heat and simmer 30-45 minutes until chicken is tender. Let cool, then remove chicken from stock. Strain the stock and reserve for other uses. Bone and skin the chicken and reserve for filling.

Use the metal blade to mince the onion, then place in a strainer and rinse under cool water to remove bitter liquid. Drain well and reserve. Process the tomato into small strips using the French fry disc. Leave in workbowl and change to the shredding disc to process the cheese. Leave in workbowl and change to a 3 or 4mm (standard) slicing disc to process the chicken into shreds. By hand, stir in the onion and chopped chiles.

Divide the filling among the chimichangas. Roll up and fry as directed. For deep fried Chimichangas see p.145. Serves 6.

Quesadillas

Quesadillas are turnovers even though the term is used loosely to describe many kinds of tortillas with melted cheese. They were originally made with fresh masa, but today are usually made with pre-cooked corn tortillas. Quesadillas made with flour tortillas are becoming more popular as appetizers and snacks, too.

See the recipe for Cheese Crisp in the Appetizer Section for a flat, flour tortilla Quesadilla variation. The flour tortilla versions may be also fried flat on one side and then topped with melted cheese or served soft with the cheese melted inside or atop. As with all Southwestern sandwiches, the fillings are limited only by your imagination!

Quesadillas are often simply filled, then folded over and grilled or baked. (For this type, you can use split Pita breads instead of tortillas if you wish.) Another method, especially popular in New Mexico, is to stack two tortillas with filling in between and then bake the stack. A third method, which uses a Masa Harina dough, is filled, folded like an Empanada and then fried to make a marvelous pastry often called Chilpanzingas.

Most Quesadillas are eaten like a sandwich, but the fried ones can be made smaller and served as an appetizer. Children who grew up in San Antonio during the 1940's and 1950's bought bean and cheese Quesadillas from street vendors or tortilla outlets as an after school snack. Today, my children make their favorite Quesadilla in a microwave oven! Any way you make it, these are a far healthier treat than the standard Coke and cookies.

I give three methods of preparation and suggested filling ideas and/or recipes for each. Use your imagination to come up with more!

Fried Quesadillas:

  2 cups Masa Harina, see note
  1/4 cup stoneground white or yellow
    cornmeal
  1 teaspoon salt
  1 teaspoon baking powder
  2 teaspoons sugar
  1 cup plus 3-4 tablespoons warm water
  filling of choice
  oil for deep-frying

Insert the metal blade and put Masa, cornmeal salt, baking powder and sugar in the workbowl. Pulse several times to combine. With the machine running, pour the water through the feed tube until a ball of dough forms. The amount of water needed will vary somewhat, but the dough should not be overly wet and should mold easily into a ball without breaking apart. Add a small amount of masa or water to achieve this consistency. (The best way to determine the right texture is to pinch off a bit of dough and make 1 tortilla.) Place the dough in a plastic bag and let rest at least 20 minutes.

Pinch off about 12 rounds of dough, each slightly larger than a golf ball. Have ready 2 pieces of plastic wrap and 2 small plates or saucers. (If you have a tortilla press, the following procedure can easily be accomplished in one step.) Place one piece of plastic wrap over a saucer, then a ball of dough, then the second piece of plastic wrap. Place the second saucer over the top and press down. Place the flattened dough, still covered with the plastic wrap, on a work surface. Use a rolling pin (preferably a short, thin one) to roll the dough into a thin circle. Roll, over the wrap, several times in one direction to form an oval, then give the dough a quarter-turn and roll again several times to form a circle. Repeat the procedure until all of the dough is rolled into thin tortillas.

Carefully peel the wrap from the top of the dough and leave the other piece in place. (Always peel the wrap *from* the dough and not the dough from the wrap in order to prevent tearing of the dough.) Place some filling in the center of the tortilla and, holding the plastic wrap, fold the tortilla into a half circle. Carefully peel the remaining piece of wrap from the folded tortilla. Trim ragged edges, then use a fork or pastry wheel to make a crimped border (see p.28).

The Quesadillas can be fried immediately or covered and refrigerated up to 24 hours. They may even be frozen up to 3 months, but should be completely thawed before frying. Refrigerating these pastries at this point helps to ensure good results when frying and also eliminates much last minute preparation.

To fry the Quesadillas, heat 2-3 inches of oil to 360° in a saucepan large enough for deep-frying. Immerse the Quesadillas, one or two at a time, spooning the hot oil over the top rather than attempting to turn them. Fry about 1-1½ minutes until browned and drain on paper towels. Serve immediately. Makes 12 Quesadillas.

Note: Masa Harina is sold nationally by the Quaker Oat-company. If there is a "Molino" or tortilla factory in your area, you can buy and use fresh masa. Fresh masa dough is ready to use immediately and should be stored only a few hours, tightly wrapped in plastic wrap to prevent drying out. The recipe varies from the Masa Harina package instruction. The additional shortening makes it easier to "work" the dough.

Quesadilla Fillings

Grilled or Baked Quesadillas:
soft corn or flour tortillas or split pita breads (any number)
filling of choice
fresh Salsa of choice or taco sauce

Mound the filling of choice over half of each tortilla or split pita bread. Fold over and heat long enough to melt the cheese. These can be placed on a greased cookie sheet and baked in a 375° oven, grilled on both sides on a lightly greased hot griddle, or placed in a microwave oven for about 30 seconds on the High setting. Serve as a sandwich or snack accompanied by your favorite fresh Salsa or taco sauce.

Stacked Quesadillas:
corn or flour tortillas (any number)
melted butter, optional
filling of choice
fresh salsa of choice, or taco sauce, or Ranch-Style Beans (p.216), or Seasoned Tomato Sauce (p.43), optional

Although the tortillas are not usually dipped in oil to soften, the flavor is improved if first brushing them with melted butter. Place the filling of choice between two tortillas (like a sandwich) and bake 10-12 minutes in a preheated 350° oven or until the cheese is melted. Serve plain or with any of the·listed sauces or Ranch-Style Beans as a sauce.

The first list presented here are popular combination fillings for Quesadillas. The second list comprises more elaborate fillings.

1. shredded cheese (Swiss, Cheddar, Monterey Jack or Mexican Goat cheese if available)
2. cooked and mashed Pinto Beans (p.215) with shredded cheese of choice
3. Chile Strips (p.214) with shredded cheese of choice
4. shredded ham and shredded cheese of choice
5. shredded cooked chicken, chopped green chiles and shredded cheese of choice
6. cooked Mexican Sausage (p.56), beans and crumbled Queso Fresco or "Enchilada" cheese

One:

> 2 ounces Longhorn Cheddar, Monterey
> Jack or Mozzarella cheese or a
> combination of the cheeses, cut in
> several pieces
> 1-2 mild or hot canned chiles, cut in 4
> strips
> sour cream of Salsa of choice for garnish

Use the metal blade and pulse several times to grate the cheese. Place about 1 tablespoon cheese and a strip of chile on each of the rolled out tortillas. Fold and crimp and fry as directed. Serve garnished with sour cream or a salsa. Adjust the ingredients to make more Quesadillas. These can be mild or quite hot depending upon the chile that you choose. Yield: filling for 4 Quesadillas.

Two:

> 2 ounces Cheddar, Meunster or Swiss
> cheese, cut in several pieces
> 2-3 tablespoons cooked ham, cut in small
> pieces
> 2 tablespoons chopped green chiles
> 1-2 teaspoons mayonnaise

This is a mild filling, somewhat like a grilled ham and cheese sandwich. The mayonnaise will tone down the chiles, so you may wish to use a hotter chile for a more picante taste.

Use the metal blade and place cheese and ham in the workbowl. Pulse to finely chop. Add the chiles and pulse to combine. Spread the mayonnaise thinly over the rolled out tortillas. Divide the filling among each, then fold, crimp and fry as directed. Adjust the ingredients to make more Quesadillas. Yield: filling for 4 Quesadillas.

Three:

> 12 cooked shrimp (medium size)
> 6 ounces cream cheese or Havarti cheese,
> cut in small pieces
> grated Parmesan cheese
> salsa of choice

Place the shrimp and cheese in the workbowl using the metal blade. Pulse until finely chopped. Divide the filling among 12 rolled out tortillas, then fold, crimp and fry as directed. Garnish with Parmesan cheese and serve with Salsa. Yield: filling for 12 Quesadillas.

Four:

> 6 ounces Monterey Jack cheese, cut in
> small pieces
> 6 scallions, each cut in 3-4 pieces (use
> white part plus 1 inch of the green part)
> 1 small zucchini (about 6 ounces), cut in
> chunks
> 6 tablespoons chopped pimiento

Place the cheese in the workbowl fitted with the metal blade. Pulse until grated. Add the onion, zucchini and pimiento and pulse to combine. Do not overprocess. Divide the filling among 12 rolled out tortillas, then fold, crimp and fry as directed. Note that, unlike the other fillings, this one does not freeze well. Yield: filling for 12 Quesadillas.

Five:

> 2 ounces Parmesan cheese, at room
> temperature and cut into small pieces
> 1 cup sour cream
> 1/3 cup heavy cream
> 4 ounces Swiss or Havarti cheese, cut into
> small pieces
> 8 ounces Monterey Jack cheese, cut into
> small pieces
> 1/4 pound cooked ham, cut into small
> pieces
> 3/4 cup drained Texas Hot Salsa (p.39)

Using the metal blade, drop the Parmesan cheese pieces through the feed tube with the motor running and process until finely grated. Remove and set aside for garnish. Stir together the sour cream and heavy cream and let stand at least 5 minutes at room temperature to thicken.

Place the Swiss and Monterey Jack cheeses and the ham in the workbowl using the metal blade. Pulse to finely chop. Add the Texas Hot Salsa and pulse to incorporate.

Use the ham and cheese mixture to fill 12 rolled out tortillas, then fold, crimp and fry as directed. Sprinkle the hot fried pastries with the Parmesan cheese and serve the sour cream mixture spooned over the top.

These are called Chilpanzingas and the recipe comes from Ninfa's Restaurant in San Antonio. Yield: Filling for 12 entree or 24 appetizer Quesadillas.

Tacos

Tacos are generally known (particularly in California and Arizona) as crisp corn tortilla shells filled with seasoned ground beef, lettuce and tomatoes. The word literally means "snack" or "bite" and is often used to describe small crisp appetizers.

Depending upon regional custom, "taco" may also refer to anything from scrambled eggs wrapped in a flour tortilla to a soft, rolled corn tortilla covered with a Spanish or Green Chile Sauce.

There are many recipes for Soft Tacos in the book such as the variations for Charbroiled Tacos, Northern Tacos and Grilled Beef and Onion Tacos that follow the Grilled Meat recipe in the Meat Section. Many Soft Tacos resemble Enchiladas and may often be described as such.

The following are techniques rather than complete recipes for preparing the most common types of "Tacos." Fillings are a matter of personal preference and I have given you some suggestions.

Crisp Tacos

This is the most familiar preparation. Packaged Taco Shells are readily available, but many are so thin that they collapse with the first bite. You can make your own shells from refrigerated or completely thawed frozen corn tortillas. Heat enough oil to immerse the tortillas to 375° in a deep pan or deep-fryer. Use tongs to dip the tortillas, one at a time, into the oil. Use the tongs to fold the softened tortillas into a shell and hold the shape for a minute or so until the tortillas are fried crisp. Drain on paper towels. (The shells will not be greasy if the oil temperature is kept constant.)

Fill the Tacos with hot or cold chicken, beef or seafood combinations. Diced tomatoes, onions, sour cream, lettuce, Guacamole (p.49) and/or shredded cheese are often added. In many homes the traditional filling of hot potatoes and beef is still used.

Soft Tacos

Disguised as an Enchilada, these are usually corn tortillas prepared and filled like Enchiladas (p.196) and served with Tomato or Green Chile Sauces. Soft Tacos can also be made with 6 inch flour tortillas filled with Beef Stew (p.164) or Grilled Meat (p.160). These are folded rather than rolled and are similar to Burritos except that the tortillas are smaller and the filling is not completely enclosed. Charbroiled Tacos (p.161) or Shephard's Style Tacos (Tacos al Pastor) are made with flour or fresh corn tortillas filled with chunks of grilled skirt steak or cabrito (goat) that has been barbequed over Mesquite wood. Adapted from a northern border specialty, this is the most popular Soft Taco in Texas.

Puff Tacos and Fried Cheese Tacos

Found primarily in San Antonio, Puff Tacos are made from deep-fried fresh corn tortillas. The very fresh tortillas will puff into two layers when fried in hot (375°) oil. During the frying they may be left flat to puff naturally or shaped into the typical Crisp Taco shell. Fill the shells with your favorite combinations of meats, eggs or poultry and use the traditional Crisp Taco garnishes. Flat Puff Tacos are sometimes served with cooked eggs in the slit made between the two layers and covered with Ranch Style Sauce (p.41)

Fried Cheese Tacos are made from fresh corn tortillas filled with cheese and sometimes chiles, then folded and sealed "Empanada Style." They are deep-fried and served like an Empanada (p.82) without any sauce.

If you make corn tortillas for Puff or Fried Cheese Tacos, use packaged Masa Harina and prepare according to package directions adding 1 tablespoon shortening to the dough. Deep-fry in oil heated to 375°. If making a flat Puff Taco, spoon oil over the top of the tortilla to encourage puffing. If shaping into a shell, begin molding with tongs as soon as possible because they will be crisp in a minute or less. Drain the tortillas on paper towels.

Taquitos

These are tightly rolled Tacos similar to Flautas. (See the following recipe for Chicken Flutes.) These "flutes" or Flautas are traditionally made with two corn tortillas, overlapped, filled and then rolled together into a flute shape. Today, most are made with just one tortilla, but rolled in the same way.

Unless the tortillas are soft and fresh, they must be softened by placing in a collander set over simmering water for about 5 minutes or wrapped in plastic wrap and set in a Microwave Oven on the High setting for a few seconds. They are then filled with a small amount of cooked shredded chicken, beef, pork or cheese and chiles, rolled up tightly and secured with toothpicks. Then either grill on a lightly greased griddle or deep-fry in oil heated to 375° until crisp.

Common garnishes are lettuce, tomatoes, Guacamole (p.49), shredded cheese or almost any Salsa. These make great appetizers and may be assembled in advance.

Breakfast Tacos

These are native to Texas where the art of making exceptionally light flour tortillas is still practiced. The popularity is spreading fast though because they make a quick and portable breakfast.

Six inch flour tortillas are filled with such combinations as scrambled eggs and bacon, Spicy Meat Hash (p.57), Mexican Sausage (p.56) and eggs, Seasoned Meat (p.58) and potatoes, or eggs and potatoes. They are then rolled or folded and eaten. In California, these are made with 12 inch tortillas and called a Burrito.

The art of eating Breakfast Tacos and other Soft Tacos must be practiced lest you lose the filling! Pinch one end, tilting it up as you eat from the opposite end.

Other Tacos

As you can see, the term "Taco" can mean a large number of dishes. The most unusual version I've come across was in a Mexican bakery. It consisted of a cake-like Empanada dough rolled around a rich strawberry preserve, then baked, dusted with cinnamon sugar and labeled "Taco."

Chicken Flutes
Flautas

Flauta means "little flutes" and is an apt description for this crispy little rolled chicken taco. Favorite fillings and toppings in Texas and northern Mexico are combinations of chicken, Guacamole, cheese and sour cream. This flauta has it all, including the popular taco "crunch." The chicken filling is mildly flavored. If you wish a more assertive taste, garnish the flautas with your favorite salsa.

The filled flautas may be prepared early in the day and refrigerated, covered, until ready to fry and then served garnished as a finger food. A delicious variation on the theme using shredded pork and a salsa is found at the end of the recipe.

> 12 soft corn tortillas, see note
> 2 cups (approximately) cooked chicken
> warm chicken broth if needed
> 4 ounces Mozzarella or Monterey Jack
>   cheese, chilled
> 1/2 head iceberg lettuce
> 2 tomatoes, diced
> 1-1 1/4 cups sour cream
> 1 small clove garlic, peeled
> 1 ripe avocado
> juice of 1/2 lemon
> 1/4 teaspoon salt or to taste
> 1 1/2 tablespoons canned diced green chiles
> peanut oil for frying

If the tortillas are not soft and fresh, soften by the steaming or Microwave method on p.23. Keep the softened tortillas wrapped until ready to use.

Shred the chicken using a 2 or 3mm (thin or standard) slicing disc. (Moisten with warm chicken broth if it is dry.) Spread 1 heaping tablespoon of shredded chicken across the center of each tortilla. Roll up tightly and secure with one or two toothpicks. Place, seam side down, in a dish. Cover and set aside until ready to fry.

Use the shredding disc to process the cheese. Use the 2 or 3mm (thin or standard) slicing disc to process the lettuce. Place the tomatoes, sour cream, cheese and lettuce in separate dishes and reserve.

Make the guacamole shortly before serving to prevent darkening. Using the metal blade, drop the garlic through the feed tube with the motor running to mince. Peel and quarter the avocado and add to work bowl with the lemon juice, salt and chiles. Process until smooth, then adjust seasoning.

Heat 3 inches of oil in a deep saucepan or deep-fryer to 375°. Use tongs to immerse the flautas, one at a time, in the hot oil and fry 20-30 seconds until crisp. Drain on paper towels.

Remove the toothpicks (I have at times had to resort to pliers) and arrange 3 flautas per serving. Spread with a layer of sour cream, then a layer of guacamole, shredded cheese and a few diced tomatoes. Garnish each plate with the lettuce and serve immediately.

This is a finger food, albeit messy. However, cutting with a fork is practically impossible. Serves 4.

Note: If you can't obtain fresh tortillas, buy the kind in plastic packages in the refrigerated or frozen sections of the grocery store. Completely thaw frozen tortillas and brush off any ice crystals. Do not use canned tortillas.

Variation: Shred about 2 cups of cooked boneless pork using the metal blade and add 2-3 tablespoons beef stock, 1/2 teaspoon chile powder and salt to taste. Use to fill flautas in place of the chicken. Replace the guacamole and sour cream with 1 1/4 cups of Ninfa's Green Salsa (p.42), heated. Garnish with the tomatoes and lettuce as directed.

Tortas

The word "torta" can refer to a little "cake," a loaf or a paté. However, the most common preparation uses fresh or day-old French Rolls or Bolillos (p.227) filled with various beef or poultry mixtures. They are split and some of the center dough removed to form a container to hold the filling, then baked — often with cheese gratinéed atop the filling. Grilled tortas are made by buttering both halves of the split bread and then grilling them on a seasoned griddle or in a heavy skillet. One of the grilled bread halves is then topped with beans, cheese or meats, then covered with the other half and served like a Hero sandwich.

Fillings for Tortas can be nearly anything you wish and may be hot or cold. The following are several suggestions listed in order of assembly. Ingredients in italic should be served warm.

1. *Cooked Beans (p.215), Sauteed Mexican Sausage (p.56), Monterey Jack cheese,* fresh Salsa of choice
2. *Meat in Red Chile (p.165),* sliced avocado, Taco Sauce or Salsa of choice
3. *Chicken Stew (p.56), Monterey Jack cheese,* sliced avocado
4. *Spicy Meat Hash (p.57),* shredded Longhorn Cheddar Cheese, sliced avocado
5. Sliced leftover cooked chicken or beef, Green Chile Sauce (p.45), crumbled "Enchilada" cheese, sour cream

MAIN DISHES

This is an understandably hefty section, containing as it does the many substantial dishes that are the heart of a meal. The recipes here are divided into the categories of Beef & Pork, Poultry, Seafood, and Specialties of the Southwest. However, throughout the book you will find numerous other recipes that can also easily serve as Main Dishes for any meal — breakfast, lunch or dinner. For example, some of the Pasta dishes in the Accompaniment section would be marvelous vegetarian entrees, and many of the Appetizers, Snacks and Sandwiches could easily be a meal. Substantial Soups and Salads are just right for a light supper.

Specialties of the Southwest make wonderful fare, whether for parties or everyday home meals. They include Tamales, Enchiladas, Stuffed Chiles and some unusual quiches. Most of these recipes require specific techniques or methods and thus they are grouped together even though the main ingredient — meat, poultry, seafood or vegetable — may differ.

No Southwestern Main Dish recipe collection would be complete without a version of the dish that everyone has heard of — Chile con Carne! Here is my recipe, with all the garnishes. If you want to be authentic, serve the beans on the side, not in the Chile.

Clockwise from top left: Tamale Pie, Tamales, Sweet Tamales with Lemon-Orange Sauce, Fresh Salsa.

Texas Cornbread

This recipe, along with regional options, appears in one form or another in nearly every local cookbook. I suspect that it is a variation on Tamale Pie.

You can use any fresh table salsa or prepared Mexican style hot tomato sauce, varying hotness according to taste. If you add a few canned Jalapeño chiles to the recipe, you will have Jalapeño Corn Bread.

This cornbread can be served as a hearty hot appetizer that is particularly popular with men. But my favorite presentation is as a brunch entree accompanied by fresh fruit.

1 pound bulk Chorizo Sausage (p.56) or
    pork sausage meat or ground beef
8 ounces Monterey Jack or Longhorn
    Cheddar cheese
1 yellow onion, peeled and quartered
1 bell pepper, seeded and quartered
1 tablespoon butter
3 eggs
1 cup sour cream
1/2 stick (2 ounces) soft butter
1 cup cooked corn kernels (leftover corn cut
    from the cob is ideal)
1 1/4 cups stoneground cornmeal
1/2 cup all purpose flour
1 teaspoon baking soda
1 teaspoon sugar
1 teaspoon baking powder
3/4 cup milk
6 ounces fresh table Salsa of choice or
    prepared Mexican Style hot tomato sauce

Saute the meat in a skillet until juices no longer run pink. Set the skillet aside to use sausage and fat in the cornbread. (You should have about 2 tablespoons fat; if there is more, decrease the butter to compensate.)

Use the shredding disc to process the cheese and set aside. Use the metal blade to chop together the onion and bell pepper. Saute the onion and pepper in the 1 tablespoon butter until the onions are translucent. Set aside off heat.

Place the eggs, sour cream, butter, and corn in the workbowl using the metal blade. Pulse to thoroughly mix and mince the corn. Stir together the dry ingredients and add to workbowl. With the machine running, pour the milk through the feed tube. Immediately stop machine. (The ingredients should be just mixed together.) Remove workbowl

from the base (it will be very full) immediately. Pour 2/3 of the batter into a buttered 11 x 13 rectangular dish or into 2 buttered (8 x 1 1/2 inch) pie pans. Top the batter with a layer of sausage, pepper and onion, salsa and cheese in that order. Top with remaining 1/3 batter.

Bake 40-45 minutes in a preheated 350° oven until just set and the cornbread has a consistency like a quiche. Let rest 10 minutes before cutting into wedges or squares and serve warm. Cut into large pieces for an entree or into small squares for an appetizer. Serves 8 as an entree.

Grilled Steaks with Ninfa's Ranchero Sauce

Grilled meats are one of the specialties of Ninfa's Restaurant. Chicken, shrimp or tender beef cuts are marinated, then char-broiled and served with a Ranch Style Salsa. While nothing quite compares with the flavor of barbequed meat, the sauce is very good on chicken, rib-eye steaks and redfish or red snapper pan-fried in butter and oil.

Marinade:

2 yellow onions, peeled and quartered
1 bell pepper, seeded and quartered
3 cloves garlic, peeled
2 Jalapeño chiles, stems removed (see p.14 for precautions on handling hot chiles)
1 cup water
3 tablespoons soy sauce
$^{1}/_{2}$ cup red wine
$^{1}/_{2}$ cup red wine vinegar
6 (6 ounce) beef tenderloin or rib-eye steaks

Cooking the Meat:

1 recipe Ninfa's Ranch Style Salsa (p.42)
$^{1}/_{2}$ cup peanut oil, for charbroiling or grilling
1 tablespoon *each* butter and oil, for pan-frying

The meat should be marinated for 2-4 hours before cooking. To prepare the marinade, insert the shredding disc and process the onions with light pressure to extract juice and pulp. Leave the pulp in workbowl and discard any whole pieces that remain. Wipe the disc and process the bell pepper in the same way. Change to the metal blade, add the garlic and chiles to the workbowl. With the machine running, pour the water through the feed tube. Transfer to a shallow dish large enough to accomodate the meat and stir in the soy sauce, wine and vinegar. Add the beef and marinate for 2-4 hours, turning several times.

Prepare the Ranch Style Salsa and keep warm.

When ready to cook the meat, drain the steaks. If you plan to char-broil, strain the marinade and add $^{1}/_{2}$ cup peanut oil. Cook the steaks over a charcoal grill to desired degree of doneness, brushing with the marinade several times during cooking.

If you plan to cook the meat indoors, drain the steaks. Pan-fry in the butter and oil over high heat to sear the meat on both sides. Place the meat in a broiler pan and set under a preheated broiler about 4 inches from the heat source to finish cooking to desired degree of doneness. (The approximate cooking time for $^{3}/_{4}$ inch steaks is about 2 minutes per side for searing and about 5 minutes under the broiler.)

Serve immediately with the Ranch Style Salsa. Serves 6.

Pork and Beef

Chile Con Carne

What began as an answer to the problem of spoiling meat has become an American tradition. Most Mexican-American dishes have their roots in Spanish or Mexican customs. However, Chile con Carne is clearly American and some Mexicans consider it an insult to Mexican cuisine. Rather than being offended, Texans boast about such denials and offer them as proof that Chile is a Texas invention.

There are hundreds of varieties with the titles that are as creative as the cooks. "Jailhouse," "Cowboy," "Hot Pants," "Senatorial," "Perdenales River," "Bastard," "Gringo," "Buzzard's Breath," and countless others are names of Chile recipes. Chile contests have become a national fad, though the recipes which contain beans, tomatoes, tomato sauce, green pepper, etc. bear little resemblance to the original dish.

My good friend and food historian, Ella Stumpf (admittedly a romantic), likes to imagine that a Payaya teepee squaw faced with the monotony of another meal, had a moment of inspiration and flung her beef jerky (meat rubbed with the juice of red chile as a preservative) into a pot of boiling water to steam until tender. The result? — Chile con Carne!

The dispute over the most authentic Chile Con Carne is topped only by the "with or without beans" debate. The original recipe was probably close to Mrs. Stumpf's version, including perhaps a few wild onions, garlic, chile peppers and meat. Cumin, a treasured spice kept under lock and key in the kitchen of the Governor's Palace in San Antonio, became a key ingredient. Perhaps that's why cumin is used in so many of the area's regional meat dishes.

During the 1800's, the Military Plaza in San Antonio became known as "La Plaza del Chile con Carne." It was an open market by day, but by dusk the fruit and vegetable stands were replaced by the "peppery and provocative" Chile Queens. Their traditional Chile Stands lasted until the 1940's and are probably responsible for what has been called the "fist-fighting," "festival making" traditions that surround Chile con Carne. A German immigrant, Gebhardt, bottled the first chile powder and thus made an authentic tasting Chile available nationwide.

The Chile Queens prepared Chile con Carne from roasted meats and many Chile experts claim that this is still the best way. All agree that the best quality meat one can afford should be used. The following recipe is a basic one, sometimes dubbed "Reno Red." The addition of tomatoes and beans is optional. The garnishes, while not traditional, add a colorful presentation.

Whatever you call your version, a Chile making party is always a culinary success.

The large quantity of paprika give the "Reno-Red" color to this standard "chile contest" recipe upon which many winning recipes have been patterned. If you can obtain good chile pods, they are worth the effort.

Tomatoes have found their way into most modern chile recipes and you can add or delete them as desired. If you must have beans, cook them separately and serve on the side.

Make the chile early in the day or a day ahead to allow flavors to blend.

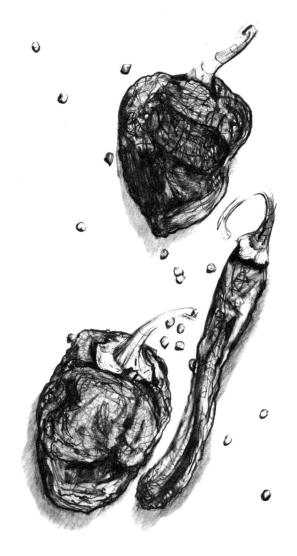

The Chile:

5-6 pounds boneless beef chuck, boneless rump, brisket or sirloin tip pork or bacon fat

6 cloves garlic, peeled

2 large yellow onions, peeled and quartered

3 cups hot water or canned beef stock

1½ cups tomato sauce or 1 (10½ ounce) can Rotel brand tomatoes and green chiles, see note

12 ounces beer

6-8 tablespoons chile powder, see note

3-4 chile Ancho pods, see note

2-3 tablespoons paprika

3-6 tablespoons cumin (use lesser amount if using commercial chile powder containing cumin)

1-2 tablespoons Monosodium Glutamate (MSG), optional

1 tablespoon oregano

1½ tablespoons fresh masa or Masa Harina

3 tablespoons cider vinegar

1-3 diced Jalapeño chiles, optional

1 teaspoon salt or to taste (increase salt if not using MSG)

Garnishes:

12 ounces Longhorn Cheddar cheese, chilled

1 large yellow onion, peeled and halved

2 avocados, peeled, pitted and diced

warmed, cooked Pinto Beans (p.215)

Texas Hot Salsa (p.39)

fresh steamed corn or flour tortillas or warmed Pita breads

Trim and reserve the fat from the beef. Cut the meat into ½ inch cubes. (Some cooks prefer coarsely ground beef which may be done using the metal blade. Process in 4-5 batches in a standard workbowl.)

In a 12-14 inch skillet, fry the beef fat and trimmings to render about 1-2 tablespoons liquid fat. This should take 8-10 minutes. Add enough pork or bacon fat to make 4-5 tablespoons. Discard beef trimmings. Sear the meat on all sides in the fat in the skillet. This should be done over high heat in several batches. As the meat is seared, transfer it to a large stockpot. Pour off all but 2 tablespoons fat from the skillet.

Using the metal blade, drop the garlic through the feed tube with the motor running to mince.

Add 1 onion to the workbowl and pulse to chop. Place in the reserved skillet. Process remaining onion to chop and add to the skillet. (Both onions can be chopped at once in a large workbowl.) Saute the onion and garlic for about 3 minutes until the onion is translucent. Add to the meat in the stockpot and reserve the skillet.

Add 2 cups of the hot water or stock, the tomato sauce or Rotel tomatoes and the beer to the stockpot and bring to a boil. Lower heat and simmer, covered, for 30 minutes.

Meanwhile, place the chile powder, chile pods, paprika, cumin, MSG and oregano in the reserved skillet. (Begin by using the lesser amounts and adjust to taste later.) Stir in the remaining hot water or stock and simmer 15 minutes, stirring often. Add to the stockpot and simmer, covered, over low heat for 1½ hours, stirring occasionally.

During the last 20 minutes of cooking time, remove ½ cup of the liquid from the stockpot and combine with the masa and vinegar. Stir the mixture into the stockpot and continue cooking. Skim off excess fat.

Remove the chile from the heat and allow to stand several hours at room temperature to allow flavors to settle. Then use immediately or refrigerate. When ready to serve, reheat and adjust salt and other seasonings to taste. (If a hotter chile is desired, stir in the Jalapeño chiles.)

Shortly before serving, prepare the garnishes and place each in a separate condiment bowl. Use the shredding disc to process the cheese. Use a 2 or 3mm (standard) slicing disc to process the onion. Rinse under cool water to remove bitterness.

Serve the chile in deep bowls surrounded by garnishes. Serves 10.

Note: Use 3-4 dried chile Ancho or Pasilla pods (or both!) if they are available. Wash carefully, then toast for 2 minutes in a 325° oven. Remove stems and seeds and add to the chile as directed. Use the lesser amount (6 tablespoons) chile powder. After 45 minutes or more of cooking time, the skins of the dried chile pods can easily be removed and discarded. The pulp can then be stirred into the chile mixture. Rotel brand of tomatoes has chiles added. If using, adjust the amount of chile powder and seasonings to taste.

Grilled Meat
Carne Asada

While "carne asada" literally means "roasted meat," the term has become a catch-all for most grilled or roasted meats. The recipe variations for Charbroiled Tacos, Northern Tacos and Grilled Beef and Onion Tacos fall into this category but are Soft Tacos as well.

Skirt steaks are the preferred cut and charcoal or outdoor grilling the preferred cooking method. The steaks may be served whole with a Ranch Style Salsa and an Enchilada, or cut into small pieces and served inside a soft corn or flour tortilla.

Most butchers are familiar with skirt steaks — a flavorful, economical and tender cut from the diaphragm of the steer. The best (but expensive) substitute is beef tenderloin or rib-eye steaks sliced thin across the grain. Flank steak is not a good substitute. The key to good Grilled Meat, in all its varied presentations, is quick cooking over direct heat whether by the grilling, pan-frying or deep-frying method.

Guacamole Salad (p.49), Chile Strips (p.214), a single Enchilada, Grilled Onions (p.214) or Southwest Vegetables are all good accompaniments to Carne Asada.

The following is a basic meat preparation with three cooking methods and variations for presentation.

Meat Preparation:

2-2½ pounds skirt steak, see note
4-6 limes, Mexican or Key preferred
½-1 teaspoon garlic powder
peanut oil for frying
salt and pepper to taste
Ranch Style Salsa (p.41) or Raw Salsa (p.39)

Trim the meat free of all fat and membrane. (The butcher can do this for you.) Do not tenderize. Unless the piece of meat is extremely thin, slice it horizontally to make thin steaks. (Because skirt steaks are quite long, the meat may need to be cut into pieces to fit a small grill.)

Sprinkle the meat on both sides with the lime juice and garlic powder. Do not salt at this time. Let stand about 15 minutes at room temperature.

The meat can be cooked by any of the following methods, but barbeque grilling is the preferred method. The next best is deep-frying which gives a tender and delicious result.

To barbeque, prepare an indoor or outdoor grill by building a hot, direct fire. (Mesquite or hickory wood is a nice addition to the fire.) Using about ¼ cup peanut oil, brush the steaks on both sides. Place directly on the grill and sear about 30-45 seconds on a side until the meat is just done. Season lightly with salt and pepper and serve with the salsa of choice.

To deep-fry, heat about 3 cups peanut oil in a heavy 3 quart saucepan to 400°. Cut the meat into about 4-5 inch pieces. Use tongs to immerse the pieces, one at a time, into the oil. Fry 40-50 seconds until browned on both sides. Drain on paper towels. Season lightly with salt and pepper and serve with the salsa of choice.

To pan-fry, use rib-eye or tenderloin steaks sliced in half horizontally to make thin steaks. Sprinkle with lime juice and garlic powder as directed. Coat the bottom of a heavy skillet with a small amount of oil. Heat to almost smoking, then sear the steaks over high heat about 30 seconds on a side to desired degree of doneness. Season lightly with salt and pepper and serve with salsa of choice.

Serves 4-6.

Note: Mexican-American cooks have an ongoing controversy over the "inside" or "outside" skirt steak — a point I find amusing since the meat is obviously in one piece and each steer has only one diaphragm. My Mexican-American friends insist that one is smaller and more tender. I am unable to solve the mystery, but find that when the steaks are trimmed as described, the results are excellent! If you are pan-frying the meat, tenderloin or rib-eye steaks give the best result.

Grilled Beef and Onion Tacos or Charolitas:

This appetizer from Cuernavaca, Mexico is similar to Tacos al Carbon, but served with grilled scallions instead of Guacamole. Meat and tortilla preparation are the same. This dish makes 8 generous appetizer servings.

> 8 fresh flour or corn tortillas prepared as in
>   Charbroiled Tacos (below)
> Fresh Salsa (p.38)
> 2½ pounds Grilled Meat prepared using
>   the barbeque or deep-fry method
> Grilled Onions (p.214)

Have all of the ingredients ready. Except for the Fresh Salsa preparation, this is essentially a last minute dish.

As soon as the meat is cooked, cut in bite-size pieces and wrap meat and juices in foil to keep warm. Assemble the Tacos by dividing the meat and Grilled Onions among the tortillas. (For an attractive presentation, leave the ends of the scallions sticking out of the tortilla.) Fold over and serve the Salsa on the side.

Charbroiled Tacos or Tacos al Carbon:

This Texas and northern Mexico specialty is similar to the Grilled Meat or Carne Asada Tacos of Southern California. Bite-size chunks of grilled or deep-fried meat are served in a fresh, soft corn or flour tortilla and garnished with Guacamole and Texas Hot Salsa.

> 8 fresh flour or corn tortillas or 4 split Pita
>   breads
> 1 cup basic Guacamole (p.49)
> 2 cups Texas Hot Salsa (p.39), see note
> 4 cups Ranch-Style Beans (p.216)
> 2-2½ pounds Grilled Meat prepared as
>   above using the barbeque or deep-fry
>   method

If the tortillas are not soft and fresh, place on a well-seasoned, ungreased hot griddle for 10-15 seconds on each side to heat and soften. (Do this just prior to cooking and serving the meat and keep wrapped until ready to use.) If using Pita breads, wrap in foil and warm for 10-12 minutes in a preheated 400° oven.

Have ready the Guacamole, Salsa and Beans. As soon as the meat is cooked, cut into bite-size pieces and add salt and pepper to taste. Wrap meat and juices in foil to keep warm.

To assemble the Tacos, spread each warmed tortilla or Pita half with a thin layer of Guacamole. Divide the meat among the tortillas, using a generous amount in each. Fold over and let each person add the Salsa and Beans to his or her plate.

Note: If you wish to serve both a hot and mild sauce, make another recipe of Texas Hot Salsa omitting the hot chiles and substituting bell peppers.

Northern Tacos or Tacos Norteno:

In this variation, the tortillas are filled with the meat, cheese and beans, then folded over and lightly grilled. It is a pleasing combination of taste and texture especially successful if you must use commercial tortillas instead of the homemade variety. (Grilling vastly improves the taste of store bought tortillas.)

> 6 ounces Monterey Jack or Mozzarella
>   cheese
> 8 flour tortillas (commercial or homemade),
>   warmed as in Charbroiled Tacos
> 1 cup Texas Hot Salsa (p.39) or Salsa Cruda
>   (p.38)
> 1 cup Refried Beans (p.215), heated
> 2 pounds skirt steak prepared as directed for
>   Grilled Meat using the barbeque or
>   deep-fry method
> 2 avocados, peeled, pitted and sliced
> 2 fresh tomatoes, sliced

Use the shredding disc to process the cheese and reserve. Have ready all of the remaining ingredients.

To assemble the Tacos, spread each tortilla with a thin layer of Refried Beans. Divide the meat and cheese among the tortillas, then fold in half. Grill on a lightly greased griddle over medium heat until both sides are lightly browned and cheese is melted, 1-2 minutes. Have each guest garnish his or her Taco with avocado, tomato slices and the Salsa as desired.

New Mexican Grilled Meat

New Mexican Carne Asada

I ordered this dish in Albuquerque and, while I prefer steaks unadorned, I found this delicious!

This entree is wonderful served with a Guacamole Salad and Sopaipillas.

New Mexican "Pico de Gallo" Salsa:

8 canned Jalapeño chiles, see note
1 small yellow onion, peeled
1 tablespoon vegetable oil
1/2 tablespoon butter
2 (14 1/2 ounce) cans Italian plum tomatoes including juices
4-5 sprigs parsley or cilantro
3/4 teaspoon salt or to taste

The Meat and Assembly:

6 ounces Monterey Jack cheese, chilled
4 rib-eye or New York strip steaks (each about 3/4 inch thick)
1 1/2 tablespoons vegetable oil

Drain the chiles. (If they are not packed in brine, reserve juices and add to the sauce.) Slice the chiles into thin strips and set aside.

Use the metal blade to chop the onions, then saute in the butter and oil in a 1 quart saucepan until the onion is translucent. Use the metal blade to mash the tomatoes and parsley together, then stir into the onions along with the chiles and salt. Keep warm while preparing the meat.

Use the shredding disc to process the cheese and set aside.

Trim most of the fat from the meat. Place the fat in a large skillet and cook over high heat to render 1 tablespoon liquid fat. Discard solid pieces and add the oil to the skillet. Sear the steaks for 2-3 minutes on a side in the hot oil and fat. The meat juices will run red.

Transfer the steaks to a broiler pan lined with foil (or broil in the skillet if desired). Broil 4-5 inches from the heat source for 3-8 minutes total depending upon degree of doneness desired.

Leave steaks in pan or skillet and mound the warm salsa over each. Top with the shredded cheese and return to the broiler for about 1 minute until the cheese is melted. Serve immediately. Serves 4.

Note: Be sure to read p.14 for precautions in handling hot chiles. If a milder sauce is desired, substitute 2 (4 ounce) cans mild green chiles or 2 minced bell peppers for the Jalapeño chiles and prepare sauce as directed.

Beef and Tortilla Casserole   Chilaquiles

In some places Chilaquiles are called a "sopa" since it is a casserole. The term "sopa" is difficult to define and really has no English equivalent. Variations on this Beef and Tortilla Casserole theme appear from Oklahoma to Southern California and consists of leftover crisp Tostados or tortillas layered with tomatoes, cheese or chiles.

This simple version, especially loved by children, is similar to lasagne because the tortillas are cut and layered like noodles.

10-12 corn tortillas
1 clove garlic, peeled
1 onion, peeled and quartered
1 bell pepper, seeded and quartered or 1 (4 ounce) can mild green chiles, drained
1 pound ground beef
1/2 teaspoon leaf oregano
1/8 teaspoon pepper
1/2-1 teaspoon salt
8 ounces Cheddar or Monterey Jack Cheese, chilled
1 (14 1/2 ounce) can Italian plum tomatoes
1/2 cup tomato sauce
1 cup sour cream or evaporated milk
1 cup cooked Pinto Beans (p.215), optional

Cut each tortilla into 3 strips and set aside.

Using the metal blade, drop the garlic through the feed tube with the motor running to mince. Add onion and pepper or chiles to workbowl and pulse to finely chop.

In a skillet, saute the beef with the onion mixture and oregano until the onions are soft and the meat juices no longer run pink. Drain off excess fat, salt and pepper to taste and set aside.

Use the shredding disc to process the tomatoes, tomato sauce and sour cream until combined.

Butter a 9 x 11 or 9 x 12 casserole dish and layer beginning with the tortilla strips, then sauce, meat and cheese. End with the cheese on top. If you wish, you may add a layer of the pinto beans. The casserole may be made several hours ahead and refrigerated at this point.

Bake 20-30 minutes in a preheated 350° oven until hot. Cut in squares to serve. Serves 6-8.

Variation: You can add a layer of 1 1/2 cups cottage cheese, 2 hard-cooked egg yolks and 1/3 cup cooked and drained spinach. Combine the mixture in the workbowl using the metal and add between the sauce and meat layer. Bake as directed.

Soft Beef Tacos

Tacos may be crisp or soft and made with either flour or corn tortillas. Soft tacos could be mistaken for enchiladas, a confusing state of affairs which causes many Southwesterners visiting neighboring states to exclaim, "This is not a taco!"

Restaurants tend to use canned green chiles, probably grown in New Mexico or California. For best flavor, use the fresh Chile Verde or Poblano Chile if available. Fresh or canned tomatoes, or even tomato sauce can be used. There are even several versions which exclude tomatoes entirely. I have given a choice of two sauces and fillings for the tacos. One is typical of San Antonio, Texas and the other common in New Mexico. The meat filling is intentionally mild.

San Antonio Sauce:
    1 clove garlic, peeled
    1 medium onion, peeled and quartered
    1 tablespoon vegetable oil
    5 fresh tomatoes or 1 (10¼ ounce) can
        tomatoes including juice tomato sauce
    6 ounces tomato paste
    1 cup water
    1 tablespoon sugar
    2 Anaheim or Poblano chiles, roasted and
        peeled (p.14) or 1 (4 ounce) can mild
        green chiles
    1 cup sour cream for garnish

New Mexican Chile Sauce:
    2 pounds fresh green chiles, roasted and
        peeled (p.14) or 2 (7 ounce) cans Ortega
        brand green chiles
    2 cloves garlic, peeled
    2 small yellow onions, peeled and halved
    2-3 tablespoons butter or margarine
    1 (14½) can Italian plum tomatoes
    1½ cups beef or chicken stock

The Tacos:
    8 corn tortillas
    oil for frying
    3 cups cooked ground beef or shredded
        chicken

First make the Sauce of your choice. To make the San Antonio Sauce, use the metal blade and drop the garlic through the feed tube with the motor running to mince. Add the onion to the workbowl and pulse to chop. In a medium saucepan, saute the onion and garlic in the oil about 3 minutes until the onion is translucent.

If using fresh tomatoes, Pulp and Peel (p.21) using the shredding disc. If using canned tomatoes, puree with the metal blade. Add tomatoes to the saucepan and simmer about 5 minutes. Stir in the tomato sauce, water, tomato paste and sugar.

Seed and stem the chiles and cut in small strips. Add to the saucepan and simmer about 10 minutes. Season to taste with salt and pepper. (If the sauce is too thick, it may be thinned with some beef or chicken stock.) The sour cream will be dolloped on the finished Taco.

To make the New Mexican Sauce, stem and seed chiles and cut by hand into thin julienne strips or chop in the processor using the metal blade. Reserve the chiles. Using the metal blade, drop the garlic through the feed tube with the motor running to mince. Leave in workbowl and change to 3mm(standard) slicing disc to process the onion. In a medium saucepan, saute the onion and garlic in the butter about 3 minutes until the onion is translucent. Stir in the chiles, tomatoes and stock. Simmer about 8-10 minutes, stirring to break up tomatoes. Adjust seasonings with salt and pepper to taste.

To make the tacos, the tortillas must first be softened in hot oil. In an 8 or 9 inch skillet, heat about 1 inch oil to 300°. Immerse the tortillas, one at a time, in the oil for a few seconds to soften. They should not be fried crisp. Then dip each tortilla in the sauce of choice. Fill each with about ⅓ cup cooked meat and 1 tablespoon of the sauce. Roll up and place, seam side down, in a baking dish or individual ovenproof dishes allowing 2 tortillas per serving. Cover with foil and bake 8-10 minutes in a pre-heated 350° oven until heated through. To serve, pour some additional hot sauce over the tacos and serve with the sour cream. Serves 4.

Variation: Sliced black olives and scallions are popular garnishes, particularly in Arizona and California. Sprinkle over the finished Tacos.

Note: If making ahead, follow the sauce dipping instructions for Enchiladas made ahead (p.195).

Beef Stew
Carne Guisada

This hearty stew, popular in Texas, is almost always served "family-style" with the filling wrapped "burrito" style in fresh flour tortillas. Warmed split Pita breads or French Rolls (p.227) are equally delicious with Beef Stew. Bowls of fresh Salsa, cubed avocado and Mexican Rice (p.217) or Beans (p.215) often accompany the meal.

    2 pounds boneless beef chuck or pork
       shoulder
    1 tablespoon vegetable oil
    2 cloves garlic, peeled
    1 onion, peeled and quartered
    1 bell pepper, stemmed, seeded and
       quartered or 2 green chiles, canned or
       fresh roasted and peeled (p.14)
    1-2 fresh tomatoes
    2 cups beef stock or water
    2 tablespoons tomato paste
    1/2-3/4 teaspoon salt or to taste
    1-2 teaspoons chile powder
    1 teaspoon cumin (omit if chile powder
       contains cumin)
    1/8 teaspoon black pepper
    6 home-made Flour Tortillas (p.240) or split
       Pita breads or French Rolls (p.227)

Trim the fat, gristle and connective tissue from the meat. In a heavy 3-4 quart stockpot, fry the trimmings until about 2 tablespoons of fat have been rendered. Remove and discard the trimmings. Add oil to fat in pan and reserve. Cut the meat into 1½ inch cubes and set aside.

Using the metal blade, drop the garlic through the feed tube with the motor running to mince. Add the onion and pepper or chiles to the workbowl and pulse until minced. Leave in the workbowl. Change to shredding disc and Pulp and Peel the tomatoes (p.21).

Heat the fat in the stockpot and sear the meat over high heat to brown on all sides. Reduce heat and add the processed vegetables and remaining ingredients except tortillas. Cover and simmer until the meat is tender and the liquid becomes a thick, rich sauce — about 1½-2 hours. If sauce is too thick, thin with additional beef stock or water.

Taste and adjust the seasonings and serve in shallow soup bowls accompanied by warmed tortillas, pita breads or French rolls. The meat filling can be spooned into the accompanying bread. Serves 6.

Green Chile Stew
Guisada de Chile Verde

This stew is similar to the Green Chile Sauce from Rancho Chimaya in New Mexico. As with many stews, this one tastes even better the second day and also freezes well. Serve with hot fresh flour tortillas or French rolls or scoop into the pockets of warmed Pita breads.

    2½ pounds boneless pork shoulder or
       Boston butt, see note
    1/3 cup bacon drippings
    hot water to cover
    2 cloves garlic, peeled
    2 large yellow onions, peeled
    1 teaspoon ground cumin
    2-3 teaspoons oregano
    2-3 teaspoons salt or to taste
    1/2-1 teaspoon coarse ground black pepper
       to taste
    1 (14½ ounce) can Italian plum tomatoes,
       optional
    2 red potatoes, cooked until just tender and
       peeled, optional
    2 (7 ounce) cans mild or hot chiles or 10-12
       fresh green chiles, roasted and peeled
       (p.14)
    flour tortillas, French rolls or Pita breads

Trim excess fat from the meat and cut into 1 inch cubes. Heat the bacon drippings in a heavy kettle and sear the meat on all sides. Leave in kettle and cover with hot water.

Meanwhile, prepare the garlic and onions. Using the metal blade, drop the garlic through the feed tube with the motor running to mince. Leave in workbowl and change to the 3mm(standard) slicing disc to process the onions. Add to the meat in the kettle and add additional water to cover all the ingredients, if necessary.

Bring to a boil, then lower heat to a simmer and skim the surface. Add cumin, oregano, salt, pepper and optional tomatoes. Simmer, covered, for about 1½ hours.

Cut the potatoes into bite-sized chunks. Slice the chiles into thin strips. Add both to the kettle and simmer, uncovered, 15-20 minutes until the liquid has thickened and the potatoes are tender.

Serve the stew with hot tortillas, French rolls or Pita breads. If desired, the stew can be spooned into the tortillas or Pita pockets and used as a "filling." Serves 6.

Note: Beef chuck or a mixture of half beef and half pork can also be used.

Meat in Red Chile

Carne Adobada

Pork and Beef

Adopted from Mexican cuisine, this may be prepared with either beef or pork and is a classic dish throughout the Southwest. It will taste quite different depending on the State you are in because each region has its favorite dried chile. Tomatoes are never used in this dish as they are in many of the other stews.

The classic Carne Adobada calls for sun-dried red chile pods and for a long time I felt that this was one dish in which chile powder could not be substituted. However, when hosting some food experts at one of my favorite restaurants, I found that no one felt the taste or color of the finished dish suffered. In fact, all thought it was outstanding. Thus I have used chile powder in this recipe since good sun-dried chile pods are hard to find in many places. If you wish to use them, see the note at the end of the recipe for preparation.

You may use any pure ground red chile powder, but, in my testing, Gebhart's brand (which has cumin added) was preferred. If using a pure ground chile, you may wish to add 1-2 teaspoons cumin. The real secret of this recipe is in the centuries-old technique of boiling the meat rapidly, then simmering with seasonings until the rich stock has reduced to a flavorful sauce.

Serve with a salad and Mexican Rice. You should also have fresh flour tortillas or halved and warmed pita breads so that the pork may be rolled or stuffed in the pockets if desired. The meat is good, however, alone in its sauce.

1 1/2 pounds fresh pork sirloin or shoulder or beef chuck, trimmed of visible fat with fat and trimmings reserved
3 cloves garlic, peeled
1 cup beef or chicken stock
3 cups water
4-4 1/2 tablespoons Gebhardt's Chile Powder or 8-10 dried chile pods, see note
1 1/2 teaspoons leaf oregano
1/2 teaspoon salt or to taste
1/4 teaspoon black pepper
1 (2-3 inch) piece stick cinnamon or Canela or 1/2 teaspoon ground cinnamon
1/4 teaspoon allspice, optional

You should have 1 1/2 pounds pork after trimming. Cut into 3-4 pieces. Cook the reserved fat and trimmings in a saucepan large enough to accomodate all the meat until about 1 tablespoon drippings are rendered. Discard the trimmings and

add the pork, garlic cloves, stock and water to the pan. Bring to a boil, the reduce heat slightly and boil gently, uncovered, for 1 1/2 - 2 hours.

As the meat cooks, add the chile powder or prepared chile pods, the oregano, salt, pepper, cinnamon and optional allspice. The stock should cook down to a rich, thick sauce. When the meat is tender, remove and cut into bite-sized pieces and return to the sauce. Adjust seasonings to taste and remove cinnamon stick, if using, at the end of the cooking time.

Serve the Carne Adobada as described above. Serves 4.

Note: You may use any available dried chile such as New Mexican Ancho or Pasilla. Toast them on a cookie sheet for 2-3 minutes in a 450° oven, then soak in 1 cup boiling meat stock until the skins loosen. Remove and discard skins, then puree the chiles and the stock using the metal blade. Add as much of this pureed chile pulp as you wish to the simmering meat mixture. Chile pods differ in pulp yield, so quantities are really a matter of personal taste.

Pork and Beef

Meat Strips
Carnitas

Pork that is marinated and/or simmered in Red Chile is a standard Mexican dish adopted by many Southwesterners. In some areas, Carnitas (the pork strips) are often grilled crisp over an outdoor fire or deep-fried and then served sizzling hot with Texas Hot Salsa. This version is slightly different to include an egg batter which allows some of the Red Chile Sauce to cling to the meat. I like to serve these Carnitas with Ninfa's Green Salsa and Texas Hot Salsa.

However you choose to prepare Carnitas, they make an unusually good appetizer or entree. As a main course, serve with Mexican Rice (p.217), Medley of Southwest Vegetables (p.134), and Salsa.

> Red Chile Sauce (p.46)
> Ninfa's Green Salsa (p.42)
> Texas Hot Salsa (p.39)
> 2 pounds pork loin, trimmed of fat
> 4 cloves garlic, peeled and crushed

The Egg Batter:
> 2 tablespoons vegetable oil
> 1 egg
> 1/4 cup plus 2 tablespoons all-purpose flour
> 1/2 cup water

To Cook the Dish:
> 1/2 cup (approximately) peanut oil for frying
> 1/2 cup flour
> 1 teaspoon salt
> 1 teaspoon oregano
> 1/4 teaspoon pepper

Have ready the Red Chile Sauce and both Salsas. Refrigerate Ninfa's Green Salsa and Texas Hot Salsa until ready to serve.

Slice the meat into very thin strips, about 3/4 inch wide and 3 inches long. If your processor is able to slice meat, cut the meat to fit the feed tube and then freeze until firm, but not solid. Process using the 4mm(standard) slicing disc.

Stir the crushed garlic into the Red Chile Sauce and add the pork strips. Marinate at least 12 hours or up to 3 days.

Using the metal blade, process the oil, egg, flour and water for the egg batter. Let rest until ready to fry the Carnitas.

Heat the oil in a deep skillet to 375°.

Combine the flour, salt, oregano and pepper in a shallow dish. Lift the pork from the marinade without draining off the Red Chile Sauce. Dip each strip in the seasoned flour, shake off excess flour and then dip in the egg batter. Fry the strips until browned on both sides. Keep the cooked pork warm while frying all of the strips.

Serve the Carnitas with the 2 Salsas. Serves 5-8 depending on use.

Here are two variations:

1. To barbeque the pork, slice the meat somewhat thicker or cut into 1 inch cubes and thread on skewers. Marinate the meat as directed, then drain well before grilling. Omit the egg batter and grill the meat over hot coals brushing often with the peanut oil. Serve with the Salsas.

2. To deep-fry the meat, do not marinate the meat. Instead, simply deep-fry the strips and then season with salt, pepper and oregano after cooking. Serve with the Red Chile Sauce on the side.

Guarduno's Meat Strips
Guarduno's Carnitas

Dave Guarduno and his family have been in the restaurant business for many years in the Albuquerque-Santa Fe area. This is one of the favorite entrees at his new venture, Guarduno's of Mexico. The Red or Green Chile Sauce must be freshly prepared to ensure success. An alternate serving method follows the recipe as a variation.

2 pounds pork tenderloin
2 bell peppers, stemmed and seeded, see note
1 yellow onion, peeled and halved
1-2 tablespoons peanut oil
4-5 sprigs fresh parsley
1 tablespoon vegetable oil
1 tablespoon butter
2 cups cooked white rice or 4 boiled and sliced potatoes
salt and pepper to taste
1½-2 cups Red (p.46) or Green Chile Sauce (p.45), without meat, heated
1 cup sour cream

Trim the pork and pound with a meat hammer or wooden spoon to tenderize. Slice into thin strips. Cut the pepper into wedges to fit the feed tube. Pack the wedges and bottom of the pepper horizontally into the feed tube using the 3 or 4mm (standard) slicing disc and process. Place the onion cut side down and slice by hand into thin strips. (The idea is to have similar size strips of chiles, onion and pork.)

Coat the bottom of a griddle or saute pan with some of the peanut oil and grill the pork, peppers and onions over high heat until meat is browned on all sides. Add additional oil if necessary.

Meanwhile, use the metal blade to mince the parsley. Melt the butter and oil in a 10-12 inch skillet, then toss in the parsley and rice or potatoes. Season with salt and pepper.

Place the rice or potatoes on a warmed serving plate and spoon the meat mixture over. Top with the Red or Green Chile Sauce and serve the sour cream on the side. Serves 4.

Variation: In Texas, Carnitas may be either beef or pork strips that are grilled or fried and then served in a sizzling hot steak platter accompanied by Guacamole, Texas Hot Salsa and Flour Tortillas. The custom is to scoop meat, onion and pepper strips into flour tortillas and garnish them with Guacamole and Pico de Gallo. Potatoes, rice or Red Chile Sauces are omitted completely.

Pork with Zucchini
Calabacita con Carne de Puerco

Pork and Beef

This dish of pork and vegetables is common throughout the Southwest and should be accompanied by white rice. Served with hot corn or flour tortillas and a platter of fresh seasonal fruits or jicama and sliced oranges, it is a complete meal.

½ yellow onion, peeled
1 yellow summer squash or zucchini
2 cloves garlic, peeled
½ bell pepper, seeded
fat trimmed from pork
2 pounds fresh pork, pounded briefly to tenderize and cut into cubes
water to cover
2 ears fresh corn, cut in 6-8 pieces
1 (10½ ounce) can tomato wedges with juices
1 teaspoon ground cumin
½-1 teaspoon salt or to taste
¼ teaspoon black pepper
small amount beef broth if needed
fresh snipped cilantro or parsley for garnish
cooked white rice (p.217)

Use the 3 or 4 mm (standard) slicing disc to process the onion. Set aside. Use the 4 or 5mm (thicker) slicing disc to process the squash. Set aside.

Wipe workbowl and insert metal blade. With the machine running, drop the garlic through the feed tube to mince. Add pepper to workbowl and pulse to chop.

Heat some of the trimmed pork fat in a large saute pan. Add the pork pieces and brown on all sides. Add the water, onion, garlic, bell pepper and simmer until the pork is tender. Add the corn and juice from the tomatoes. Cover and simmer over low heat about 5-8 minutes. Add the cumin, salt, pepper, sliced squash and tomatoes. Cover and simmer about 3-5 minutes until squash is just tender, but not mushy. Taste and adjust seasonings and add a small amount of beef broth if the mixture seems too thick. Garnish with cilantro or parsley and serve with cooked white rice. Serves 6.

Pork and Beef

Pork Chops in Red Chile

Chuletas de Puerco

Chile Caribe is the blended pulp of red chiles, water and sometimes garlic and other seasonings. It is a Southwest custom to marinate pork overnight in this mixture, then bake the meat in the sauce. Chile Caribe is traditionally made with chile pods and, depending upon the variety, can make a very spicy dish. Because it is unlikely that cooks outside the Southwest can obtain good quality chile pods, I have in this and nearly all Red Sauces in the book recommended the use of dried chile powder. Since chile powder is often hotter and needs "toasting" to remove raw taste, the technique for this classic recipe has been somewhat altered.

All Red Chile Sauces may be toned down by decreasing the amount of chile powder or increasing the amount of tomato sauce or fresh tomato puree. I have chosen to add tomatillos to this traditional recipe because they also tend to neutralize the sauce.

Pork Chops in Red Chile is particularly attractive served with the Medley of Southwest Vegetables (p.134) or sauteed eggplant. It tastes even better made a day ahead to allow the flavors to blend.

> 8 boned loin pork chops (about 2¼ pounds total)
> 4-5 parsley sprigs
> ¼ cup flour
> ½ teaspoon salt
> ¼ teaspoon pepper
> ⅛ teaspoon paprika
> 1½ tablespoons vegetable oil
> coarse ground black pepper
> 1 clove garlic, peeled
> 6 tomatillos or 2 small green tomatoes, cored and halved
> 1½ cups chicken or beef stock
> 2 tablespoons pure ground mild or hot chile powder
> ½-1 cup tomato sauce or to taste
> 1 teaspoon sugar
> sour cream for garnish
> 2 tablespoons sliced scallion tops for garnish

Cut fat and gristle from meat and reserve the trimmings. Pound the meat with a rolling pin to flatten and tenderize. Set aside. Use the metal blade to mince the parsley. Reserve.

In a shallow dish combine the flour, salt, pepper and paprika. Dip each pork cutlet into the mixture shaking off excess coating. (Leave only a fine dusting of flour.)

In a skillet large enough to accomodate the pork, cook the reserved fat and trimmings over medium heat to render about 2 tablespoons of liquid fat. Discard the solid pieces and add the oil to the skillet. Saute the pork on both sides until golden brown and cooked. Sprinkle with a little parsley and some coarse ground pepper as they cook. Remove the meat to a platter and keep warm. Reserve the skillet.

Using the metal blade, drop the garlic and tomatillos or tomatoes through the feed tube with the motor running to mince. Add to the skillet along with ½ cup of the stock and the chile powder. Cook, stirring constantly, over medium heat for 2 minutes. Do not let chile burn.

Stir in remaining stock, tomato sauce, sugar and any remaining parsley. Cook about 2 minutes, then place the meat and any accumulated juices into the sauce and simmer over medium low heat about 3 minutes. Do not allow sauce to boil or baste the cutlets.

Serve the meat surrounded by the sauce and garnish the plate with a dollop of sour cream topped with the scallion tops. Serves 4.

Chicken and Rice

Poultry

Arroz con Pollo

This is a favorite family dish among Southwesterners. It is simple to prepare and is a hit with most children. Arroz con Pollo is a "one-dish-meal" typical of Mexican or Spanish food. It can be made ahead, cooking until the liquid is not quite absorbed, and then refrigerated overnight or frozen up to 3 months. The peas, pimiento and parsley should not be added until the dish is thawed and ready for reheating.

Serve with a Guacamole Salad (p.49) or any fruit salad to complete the meal.

2 strips bacon, cut in pieces
3-4 tablespoons olive oil (approximately)
8 chicken pieces (breast and thigh pieces preferred)
1 clove garlic, peeled
1 yellow onion, peeled and quartered
2 medium size fresh tomatoes or 1 cup canned tomatoes with their juices
2-2 1/2 cups chicken stock
3/4 cup long grain white rice
1 teaspoon salt
1 teaspoon oregano
1/2 - 3/4 teaspoon black pepper
1/2 cup fresh parsley sprigs
1 (3 1/2 ounce) jar pimientos including juice
1 package frozen peas (thawed)

Using the metal blade, pulse to chop the bacon. Saute in a heavy skillet large enough to accommodate all the chicken. Remove the cooked bacon and reserve the skillet with the drippings. Wash the chicken and pat dry. Remove any excess fat from the pieces. Add 2 tablespoons of the olive oil to the skillet and heat. Brown the chicken on all sides over medium heat. Add additional olive oil if necessary. Remove the browned chicken and set aside. (The chicken will finish cooking later).

Pour off excess fat from the skillet, but do not wash. Using the metal blade, drop the garlic through the feed tube with the motor running to mince. Stop machine and add the onion. Pulse to finely mince. Set aside.

If using fresh tomatoes, use the shredding disc to Pulp and Peel (p.21). If using canned tomatoes, chop using the metal blade. Place the tomato pulp and 1/2 cup of the chicken broth in the reserved skillet from the chicken. Cook over medium heat for about 1 minute, scraping up browned bits from the bottom of the skillet. Add onion and garlic and simmer about 3 minutes until the onion is translucent. Add rice, bacon, remaining stock, salt, oregano and pepper. Bring to a boil and add the chicken pieces. Cover and simmer over medium-low heat for about 20-30 minutes or until nearly all the liquid is absorbed. Add additional stock if necessary to prevent sticking to the pan, but do not overcook or stir the rice during cooking.

Meanwhile, use the metal blade to mince the parsley with the pimiento and juices. Taste the chicken and rice and adjust seasonings. Add parsley, pimiento and peas. Cover and simmer 3-4 minutes more.

Serve immediately. Serves 6.

Chicken in Chile Sauce
Molé

This ancient dish is a labor of love reserved for special occasions. An authentic Molé, true to tradition, uses only freshly ground chiles and spices. However, since a fresh supply of the traditional chiles used in this dish (ancho, pasilla, mulato) are not available to most of the country, I have altered the method and ingredients, a liberty I hope my Mexican-American friends will forgive. This is an unusual and delicious dish for entertaining and I urge you to try it. The fresh orange juice lightens the heavier taste of chile powder.

Molé Poblano, which is the national dish of Mexico, was refined by the nuns of Santa Rosa Convent in the 17th century to make an impressive dinner for the Viceroy and visiting Archbishop.

Some feel that Molé, a paste of dried chiles, is the forerunner of our barbeque sauce because it was often used with fish or game cooked over an open fire as well as to cure and preserve beef.

When Ninfa Laurenzo, one of Texas' foremost cooks and restauranteurs, hosted the marriage celebration of her son, a special paste of molé was flown in from Oaxaca, Mexico. This was a unique blend of chile negros (black chiles) with a distinctive taste . . . a bit exotic for most American palates. It is her recipe that I have adapted to available ingredients and taste preferences. The bitter chocolate in the recipe was originally used to produce a darker sauce with a wine-like flavor. Mexican chocolate is quite different from American varieties and is worth obtaining for this dish.

This is an outstanding dish for aficiandos of Mexican food and well worth the effort! Serve with a fresh green salad with grapefruit, orange and avocado and white rice. Begin preparation one day in advance.

5 dried chile pods, see note
1 1/2 cups water
16 pieces chicken or a small turkey, cut up
1 onion, peeled and halved
1 carrot, cut in chunks
1 celery stalk, cut in chunks
1/2 teaspoon white pepper
2 teaspoons salt
1 yellow onion, peeled
1 tablespoon olive oil
3 tablespoons (1 1/2 ounces) butter
2 tablespoons sesame seeds
3 tablespoons pure ground mild chile powder or commercial chile powder, see note
1/2 ounce unsweetened chocolate or Mexican chocolate
1/2 slice stale bread
3-4 crisp tostados
1/4 cup raisins
5 large fresh tomatoes or 1 (10 1/2 ounce) can Italian plum tomatoes
4 whole cloves
1/2 inch piece canela or stick cinnamon
5 peppercorns
2 teaspoons salt
1 teaspoon sugar (if using fresh tomatoes)
1 teaspoon oregano
1/2 cup fresh orange juice, optional

Garnish:

16 pitted black olives, sliced with 3mm (standard) slicing disc
6 hard-cooked eggs, chopped using shredding or square julienne disc
2 cups fresh parsley sprigs, minced with metal blade
1 cup sliced almonds or 3 tablespoons toasted sesame seeds

Begin preparation the day before serving. Prepare the dried chile pods by washing carefully and then spreading them in a single layer on a cookie sheet. Toast in a preheated 350° oven for 1-2 minutes, then turning to toast 1-2 minutes on the other side. (Watch carefully because the chiles burn easily and will be ruined.) This important procedure removes the "raw taste" from the chile. Place the toasted chiles in a small saucepan with 1½ cups water. Simmer over low heat for 20 minutes. Let cool, then remove the chiles and reserve the water. Remove skins and seeds from chiles and, if they are of high quality, return the pulp to the reserved water. (If you are not sure of the quality, discard the cooking water.) Puree the chiles in the water (use some broth if you have discarded the water) in an electric blender. Strain if necessary and set aside.

Place the chicken, halved onion, carrot, celery, salt and pepper to taste in a large pot and cover with water. Bring to a boil, then simmer partially covered for about 1½ hours or until the chicken is tender. Cool in the stock.

Chop the onion using the metal blade. Saute in the butter and oil until soft, then stir in the sesame seeds and chile powder. Cook over medium-low heat, stirring constantly, for 2-3 minutes. (This removes the raw taste from the chile powder.) Watch carefully because the powder burns easily. Remove from heat and set aside.

In a clean workbowl using the metal blade, place the chocolate, bread and tostados. Pulse to begin and then process to fine crumbs. Add the raisins and pulse to coarsely chop. Scrape in the chile powder paste from the skillet. With the machine running, add the chile pulp and liquid through the feed tube. Remove and reserve the mixture.

If using fresh tomatoes, insert the shredding disc to Pulp and Peel (see p.21). If using canned tomatoes, process to mash using the metal blade.

Place the tomatoes and the chile mixture in a 3 quart saucepan. Grind the cloves, cinnamon stick and peppercorns in a spice grinder or Metate and add to the saucepan with the salt, sugar and oregano. Set aside.

Remove cooled chicken from stock. Strain the stock and place in the freezer for 10 minutes to cause the fat to rise to the surface. Skim the fat and add 4 cups of the stock to the saucepan with the chile sauce and tomatoes. Simmer over medium-low heat, stirring occasionally, for 30 minutes.

Taste and adjust salt and pepper. (Note that the sauce will be much more picante the first day. It needs to be assembled with the chicken before the true taste is apparent.) Refrigerate the sauce and chicken, separately, overnight.

About 3-4 hours before serving, remove skin from chicken and arrange the pieces in a large baking dish. Simmer the sauce over medium-low heat for 15 minutes, then stir in the optional orange juice. Pour the sauce over the chicken and let stand, covered with foil, at least an hour until the chicken is at room temperature.

Bake the foil covered dish for 20 minutes in a pre-heated 350° oven. Meanwhile, have ready the olives, chopped eggs and minced parsley in separate condiment dishes.

Uncover the Molé after baking 20 minutes, sprinkle with the almonds or sesame seeds and bake, uncovered, for an additional 5 minutes.

Spoon the Molé onto a serving platter. Serve the garnishes separately and pass any additional sauce.

The sauce freezes well, but loses some of the picante flavor. Serves 8.

Note: Any available dried chile verde (Anaheim) can be used. If a large variety of chile pods are available use 4 each: chile Mulato, chile Pasilla and the wrinkled-skin chile Ancho. Follow the above directions for preparing the dried chiles. If no dried pods are available in your area, increase the chile powder by 2 tablespoons. Commercial Molé powder is often available and is acceptable if combined with some fresh ground chile pods. Use this to replace the chile powder in the recipe.

Poultry

Monterrey Chicken and Rice
Arroz con Pollo Monterrey

This is my version of a classic Southwestern dish of creamy chicken, green chiles and rice. Artichokes, used in both Mexican and Spanish cooking, blend well with the cheese and chiles.

3 cups cooked turkey or chicken, cut in
   bite-size pieces
½ bell pepper, seeded and quartered
4 scallions, sliced
1-2 tablespoons butter
2 tomatoes
½ cup ricotta cheese
3 cups cooked white rice
3 tablespoons flour
2 tablespoons butter
3 ounces cream cheese, cut in 3 pieces
1 clove garlic, peeled
½ teaspoon salt
½ teaspoon white pepper
⅛ teaspoon cayenne pepper
1½ cups chicken stock
1 (4 ounce) can chopped green chiles,
   undrained, see note
1 (14½ ounce) can artichoke hearts,
   drained and halved
½ cup sour cream
3 corn tortillas
oil for frying
3 tablespoons minced parsley for garnish

Have the chicken ready and cut in bite-size pieces.

Use the metal blade and pulse to chop the green pepper and onion. Saute 2-3 minutes in the butter. Set aside off the heat. Use the shredding disc to Pulp and Peel (p.21) the tomatoes. Stir the pepper, onion, tomato pulp and ricotta into the cooked rice and spoon into a generously buttered 6 cup ring mold. Cover with buttered wax paper and place the mold in a larger pan half filled with water. Bake 20-25 minutes in a preheated 350° oven.

Meanwhile, make the sauce. In the workbowl fitted with the metal blade, place the flour, butter, cream cheese, garlic, salt, white and cayenne pepper. Process about 30-40 seconds until well combined. Bring the chicken stock to a boil and pour 1 cup of the hot stock through the feed tube with the motor running. Process until smooth, stopping to scrape the sides of the workbowl as necessary. Transfer the mixture into the remaining hot stock in the pan and cook over medium heat, stirring constantly for about 2 minutes until smooth and

thickened. Gently stir in the chicken, chiles and artichoke hearts and cook over low heat until hot. Stir in the sour cream and keep the mixture warm. Do not allow to boil.

Use a scissors to cut each tortilla into a thin spiral strip. Begin at the outer edge and cut in a circular fashion. Cut each strip into 2-3 inch lengths. Heat about 1 inch of oil to 360° and fry the tortilla pieces, a few at a time, until crisp. Drain on paper towels and set aside.

To serve, unmold the rice onto a round serving platter. Fill the center with the tortilla pieces and sprinkle with minced parsley. Serve a slice of rice with the chicken sauce spooned over the top. Garnish each serving with the tortilla pieces and some parsley. Serves 6.

Note: If chiles are packed in vinegar, discard liquid and rinse chiles. Compensate for the liquid by increasing chicken broth by ¼ cup.

Variation: Omit the artichoke hearts and substitute 2 avocados, peeled, pitted and cut in chunks.

Creamed Chicken with Chiles
Pollo en Crema

This is a favorite Mexican-American dish seldom found in restaurants because of the time involved in preparing the chiles. Most of the recipe can be prepared in advance, however. Roasted and peeled bell peppers are the best substitute for the chile Poblanos.

2 ounces Parmesan cheese, at room
    temperature and cut in 3-4 pieces
4 whole chicken breasts, halved and boned
    with skin left on
3½ tablespoons butter
2 tablespoons oil
1 clove garlic, peeled
1 large yellow onion, peeled and quartered
1 cup chicken stock
2 tablespoons all purpose flour
4 ounces Monterey Jack cheese, cut in 8
    pieces
½ teaspoon salt or to taste
¼ teaspoon white pepper
2 cups milk
4 chile Poblanos or bell peppers, roasted
    and peeled (p.14)
½ cup sour cream
cooked white rice
black olives or sliced radishes for garnish

Using the metal blade, drop the Parmesan pieces through the feed tube with the motor running and process continuously until finely grated. Set aside to use for finishing the dish.

Wash and dry the chicken and remove any excess fat. Saute the chicken in a skillet in 1 tablespoon of the butter and all of the oil. Turn to lightly brown on both sides, then cover and allow to cook about 8 minutes.

Meanwhile, using the metal blade, drop the garlic through the feed tube with the motor running to mince. Add the onion and process to mince. Remove the chicken from the skillet and stir the onion mixture into the drippings. Immediately add the chicken stock, stirring to incorporate pan juices. Simmer 5 minutes, then strain and reserve the stock.

Place the remaining 2 tablespoons butter, the flour, Monterey Jack cheese, salt and pepper in the workbowl fitted with the metal blade. Pulse several times, then run the machine to make a smooth paste. Bring the reserved chicken stock and the milk to a boil and pour 1 cup of the boiling liquid through the feed tube with the machine running.

Stop and scrape sides of the bowl. Process again to make a very smooth texture. Transfer the mixture to the pan with the remaining hot liquid. Stir over medium heat for about 2 minutes until thickened.

Remove seeds and stems from the chiles or peppers and cut into 2 x ¼ inch strips. Saute in about ½ tablespoon butter for 3 minutes. Reserve 4 strips for garnish and place the rest in a buttered baking dish large enough to accommodate the chicken. Arrange the chicken on top of the chiles, cover with foil and bake 15 minutes at 375°.

Meanwhile, use the metal blade to process the sauce with the sour cream for about 10 seconds until blended. Heat through, but do not allow to boil. Pour the sauce over the chicken and top with the reserved grated Parmesan cheese. Bake uncovered for 5 minutes at 375° until the cheese is melted. Garnish the top with the reserved chile strips. Serve with cooked white rice garnished with black olives or sliced radishes. Serves 4-6.

Note: This is a fine "fork-buffet" dish if the chicken is cut into bite-size strips.

Poultry

Chicken with Chile Poblanos

Pollo con Chile Poblanos

The light, low-calorie and moderately thin Texas style sauce that coats the chicken is often served with enchiladas or soft, rolled tacos. This versatile sauce can be made ahead (see note at end of recipe), but the chicken should be sauteed shortly before serving. The dish is especially good accompanied by white rice (p.217).

4 whole chicken breasts, boned, skinned and split
3 tablespoons butter
3 tablespoons vegetable oil
2 cloves garlic, peeled
3 cups chicken stock
2 chile Poblanos or bell peppers, roasted and peeled (p.14)
2 red bell peppers, roasted and peeled (p.14), see note
1 medium onion, peeled and halved
1 tablespoon butter
3 tablespoons cornstarch
1/2 teaspoon salt or to taste
1/4 teaspoon pepper or to taste
2 small fresh tomatoes or 3/4 cup canned tomatoes with juices

Flatten the chicken by pounding with the back of a wooden spoon. Heat 1 1/2 tablespoons each of the butter and oil in a large skillet and saute the chicken, a few pieces at a time, over medium-high heat for 5-7 minutes until golden brown. Add more butter and oil as necessary to cook all of the chicken and add the whole garlic cloves during the last 2 minutes of cooking time. Cover the chicken with foil and keep warm while making the sauce. Do not wash the skillet.

In a 2 quart saucepan, bring the stock to a boil. Pour 1 cup of the hot stock into the skillet. Stir about 1 minute over medium heat to incorporate any browned bits from cooking the chicken. Remove from heat, strain and return the stock to the saucepan. Keep hot.

Discard seeds and stems from the chiles and peppers and cut into thin strips. Use the 3 or 4mm (standard) slicing disc to process the onion. In a medium skillet, saute the onion in the 1 tablespoon butter for about 3 minutes until softened. Remove from heat, add the chiles and peppers and reserve.

Using the metal blade, place the cornstarch, salt and pepper in the workbowl. With the motor running, pour 1 cup of the hot stock through the feed tube. Return the mixture to the saucepan with the remaining stock and cook, stirring, over low heat for about 3 minutes until smooth and thickened slightly. Do not wash the workbowl and change to the shredding disc. Pulp and Peel (p.21) the fresh tomatoes (use the metal blade to puree the canned tomatoes and juices). Add the tomato pulp to the thickened sauce and adjust salt and pepper to taste.

Arrange the chicken on a heated serving platter. Top with the onion and chile mixture and pour the hot sauce over all. Serve immediately accompanied by white rice, if desired. Serves 6.

Note: Although the dish is best made with fresh roasted red bell peppers, you may substitute canned red bell peppers or pimientos. If you wish to prepare the sauce ahead, simply omit deglazing the skillet. Process the stock with the cornstarch and complete the sauce as directed. Saute the garlic with the onion, but do not add the chiles and peppers. Shortly before serving, reheat the sauce, add the chiles and peppers to the onions, saute the chicken and complete the recipe as directed.

Chicken with Green Tomato Sauce

Pollo con Salsa de Fresadilla

The light, lemon flavor of tomatillos makes this sauce distinctive. The sauce is equally good on poached or sauteed fish filets, shellfish or veal. Accompany with hot white rice tossed with peas and diced tomato or other sauteed vegetables.

The Sauce:

1 large mild fresh green chile, roasted and peeled (p.14) or 1 canned green chile
16 medium to large fresh tomatillos or 1 can tomatillos plus 1 fresh green (unripe) tomato
1/2 cup fresh cilantro or parsley sprigs
4 egg yolks
1 stick (4 ounces) very soft butter
1/2-1 teaspoon salt or to taste

The Chicken and Assembly:

2 egg whites
1/3 cup milk
1/4 cup fine bread crumbs
1/2 cup flour
1 teaspoon salt
1/4 teaspoon pepper
1/2 teaspoon paprika
10 boned and skinned chicken breast cutlets, flattened or 5 fish filets (flounder, sole or salmon)
1/4 stick (1 ounce) butter
2-3 tablespoons oil
white rice (p.217)
1 fresh tomato, diced
1 1/2 cups cooked peas
3-4 ounces crumbled white cheese, optional garnish

Stem and seed fresh or canned chiles. Remove husks from tomatillos and wash to remove the sticky residue. Cut in half and place in the workbowl using the metal blade with the chile and green tomato, if using. Process to puree.

Transfer to a saucepan and simmer 3-4 minutes. Return the hot mixture to the workbowl using the metal blade. Add the parsley and, with the machine running, immediately add the egg yolks, soft butter and salt through the feed tube to make a smooth sauce. Set aside.

Beat the egg whites lightly with the milk in a shallow dish. In another shallow dish combine the bread crumbs, flour, salt, pepper and paprika. Dip the cutlets (or fish filets), one at a time in the milk mixture to cover, then in the bread crumb mixture to coat entirely. Shake off excess coating.

Heat the butter and oil in a large skillet until the butter is foamy. Saute the cutlets, a few at a time, in the hot butter and oil turning to lightly brown both sides. (Chicken will take about 6-8 minutes and the fish will take only 3-4 minutes to cook.)

Reheat the sauce, stirring constantly, and do not allow to boil. (For a silken smooth sauce, you may strain it if desired.) Allow two pieces of chicken and one piece of fish per person and serve generously coated with the sauce.

This is excellent served with white rice, adding the diced tomato and cooked peas during the last 5 minutes of cooking time. Garnish with the cheese if desired. Serves 6-8.

Baked Chicken Mexican Style
Pollo Simpático

This recipe from the Junior League in Albuquerque, New Mexico is an easy family dish which typifies Southwestern Style baked chicken.

4 eggs
6 tablespoons Raw Salsa (p.38) or bottled Taco sauce
1 clove garlic, peeled
2 cups fine bread crumbs
¼ teaspoon salt
2 teaspoons chile powder
2 teaspoons ground cumin
½ teaspoon oregano
½ stick (2 ounces) butter or margarine
3-4 whole chicken breasts, halved, boned and skinned
½ head lettuce
6 scallions, sliced
12 cherry tomatoes, quartered
1 cup sour cream
1 ripe avocado, peeled and pitted and cut in chunks
3-4 limes, cut in wedges

Combine the eggs with the Salsa or Taco sauce in a shallow dish. Using the metal blade, drop the garlic through the feed tube with the motor running to mince. Add the breadcrumbs, salt, chile powder, cumin and oregano to the workbowl. Pulse 2 or 3 times to combine. Remove to a shallow dish.

Dip each breast half into the egg mixture, then into the crumb mixture. Dip again into the egg, then into the crumbs, pressing lightly to be sure crumbs adhere.

Melt the butter in a shallow roasting pan large enough to accommodate the chicken in a single layer. Place the chicken in the pan and turn to coat all sides with butter. Bake uncovered for 35 minutes in a pre-heated 375° oven.

Meanwhile, use a 3 or 4mm (standard) slicing disc to process the lettuce. Line a serving platter with the lettuce. Place the green onions, tomatoes, sour cream, avocado and lime wedges in separate condiment dishes. Arrange the chicken atop the lettuce and surround the platter with the condiment dishes. Have each guest garnish the chicken as desired. Serves 5-6.

Tamale Pie

There are many versions of Tamale Pie using corn products. This one is quite simple and is a good family dish. The corn husks add flavor as well as a fun presentation. Whenever you prepare fresh corn on the cob, dry and store the husks for future use. See Tamales (p.185) for more information.

20-24 dried or green corn husks (approximately)
6 fresh green chiles, roasted and peeled (p.14) or 2 (4 ounce) cans whole chiles, drained
4 cups cooked chicken, cut in small pieces
1 cup boiling chicken broth, divided
1 package frozen corn, thawed
1 cup instant Masa Harina
1 (1 pound) can creamed corn
1½ teaspoons baking powder
½ cup melted unsalted butter
6 ounces Havarti or Monterey Jack cheese, chilled
1-1½ teaspoons salt or to taste
Raw Salsa (p.38) or Texas Hot Salsa (p.39)

Thoroughly wash corn husks and soak in hot water for at least 1½ hours. Remove and shake excess water from them. Spray a 10 inch pie pan or springform pan with a non-stick vegetable coating spray and line the pan with the husks arranged so that the pointed ends extend over the sides. Weight down with a bowl while preparing the rest of the pie.

Cut the chiles into strips and combine with the chicken and ½ cup of the broth. Set aside.

Using the metal blade, process the corn for 30-45 seconds. Add the Masa Harina, creamed corn and baking powder. Process to combine. Add the remaining ½ cup hot broth and the melted butter through the feed tube with the motor running.

Pour ⅔ of the batter into the prepared pan. Drain the chicken and chiles and arrange over the crust. Use the shredding disc to process the cheese and place atop the chicken and chiles. Sprinkle with salt and spread the remaining batter over the top.

Make a tent with aluminum foil and cover the pie. Place on a cookie sheet and set in a preheated 350° oven. Immediately lower temperature to 300° and bake for 1 hour and 20 minutes until the pie is set. Remove foil and let cool for 5-8 minutes, then cut into wedges. Serve the pie topped with the salsa of choice. Serves 8.

Paella

Poultry

The word Paella actually refers to the pan and not the recipe. Ingredients and cooking techniques vary regionally, but most contain chicken or shellfish. In this recipe, I give a number of shellfish options to be used according to availability and personal taste.

This is a terrific party dish and much of the preparation may be done in advance (see note at end of recipe).

8 chicken thighs
2 tablespoons vegetable oil
½ stick (2 ounces) butter
1 pound Spanish Chorizo Sausage (p.56)
   or Italian Sausage links
1 pound boneless pork
2 cloves garlic, peeled
1 bell pepper, stemmed, seeded and
   quartered
6 scallions, white part only
1½ cups long grain white rice
1 large tomato
3-4 saffron threads
3 cups chicken stock
1 teaspoon ground cumin
¾ teaspoon salt
¼ teaspoon black pepper or to taste
1 pound large shrimp
1 dozen fresh clams or mussels, if available
1 cup baby lima beans
1 cup fresh or frozen green beans
1 can artichoke hearts, drained and halved

Garnishes:
   ¼ cup parsley sprigs
   3 hard-cooked eggs, diced
   3 tablespoons large capers
   6 scallion tops, sliced
   2 pimientos, cut in strips

In a heavy skillet, saute the chicken in half the oil and butter until browned on all sides. Remove and place in a large baking dish. Slice the sausage into ½ inch pieces and saute in the same skillet until browned and cooked. Add to the baking dish. Tenderize the pork by pounding with a meat mallet or rolling pin, trim off fat and cut meat in cubes. Saute in the same skillet until browned on all sides. Add to baking dish, then cover and bake 15-20 minutes in a preheated 350° oven.

Using the metal blade, drop the garlic through the feed tube with the motor running to mince.

Add bell pepper to workbowl and pulse to chop. By hand, slice the scallion into small pieces and reserve green tops for garnish. In a clean skillet, saute the garlic, pepper, scallion and rice in the remaining butter and oil for 3-4 minutes, stirring often.

Meanwhile, use the shredding disc to Pulp and Peel (p.21) the tomato. Add the pulp, saffron, cumin, salt, pepper and chicken stock to the skillet and simmer, covered for 12-15 minutes until rice is tender.

Prepare the shellfish and vegetables. Peel the shrimp, leaving tails intact. If using clams or mussels, scrub thoroughly and debeard mussels. Place the shellfish atop the rice in the skillet and cook, covered for 6-10 minutes until the shrimp are pink and clam shells open.

Cook the lima beans in salted water until crisp-tender, then add the green beans and artichoke hearts and cook until heated through and crisp-tender. Mince the parsley with the metal blade and reserve for garnish.

When ready to serve, arrange the rice, shellfish and meat mixture on a large platter or paella pan. Gently toss in the vegetables. Garnish with parsley.

Serve the diced eggs, capers, scallion tops and pimientos in separate, small condiment bowls. Serves 8.

Note: The meats and poultry can be sauteed early in the day and baked shortly before serving. The rice mixture can be prepared early in the day, undercooked by 5 minutes to leave some liquid in the pan, and then finished at serving time. Add the shellfish and vegetables while finishing the Paella.

King Ranch Casserole

This is actually a "Sopa Seca," which refers to any dish of layered tortillas, meats, cheese or vegetables. It may be prepared a day ahead, refrigerated and baked just prior to serving. King Ranch Casserole is a South Texas version of Chicken a la King.

The Sauce:

1 cup milk
2 cups chicken stock
1 clove garlic, peeled
¼ stick (1 ounce) butter
¼ teaspoon pure ground chile powder
½ teaspoon salt
¼ teaspoon pepper
dash tabasco sauce
5 tablespoons flour
⅓ cup sour cream

Filling and Assembly:

12 ounces Monterey Jack or Longhorn
    Cheddar cheese, chilled
2 fresh ripe tomatoes, quartered or 1 cup
    chopped canned tomatoes
1 onion, peeled and quartered
2 fresh green Poblano or Anaheim chiles,
    roasted and peeled or 2 medium-hot
    canned green chiles
1 (2 ounce) jar pimientos, drained or 1 fresh
    red bell pepper, seeded
½ pound mushrooms
4 cups cooked turkey or chicken
1 tablespoon butter or more if necessary
16 corn tortillas
oil for softening tortillas

First make the sauce. Heat the milk and stock to a boil in a saucepan. Meanwhile, using the metal blade, drop the garlic through the feed tube with the motor running to mince. Add butter, seasonings and flour to the workbowl and process smooth. With the machine running, pour 1½ cups of the hot liquid through the feed tube. Return the mixture to the saucepan with the remaining hot stock and milk. Cook, stirring constantly, until thickened to the consistency of heavy cream. Stir in the sour cream and set aside off the heat.

Make the filling. Use the shredding disc to process the cheese. If using fresh tomatoes, process into strips with the French fry disc and discard any peel left in workbowl. (If you don't have the shredding disc or are using canned tomatoes, chop coarsely by hand and reserve the juices.)

Using the metal blade, pulse to chop together the onion, chiles and pimiento or bell pepper. Use a 3 or 4mm (standard) slicing disc to "chunk" the chicken or turkey. (If you prefer larger chunks, cut by hand into bite-size pieces.) Slice the mushrooms by hand.

Saute the onion, pimiento or pepper, chiles and mushrooms in 1 or more tablespoons butter until the onions are translucent.

To assemble the casserole, butter a 11 inch gratiné dish or a 9 x 11 inch baking dish. In a skillet or saucepan large enough to accommodate 1 tortilla, heat about ½ inch oil to 325°. Pass the tortillas, one at a time, through the oil to soften and seal. (Do not fry crisp.) Place half of the tortillas in the prepared dish, allowing them to come halfway up the sides.

Put half of the turkey on top of the tortillas, then spoon about ⅓ of the sauce over. Sprinkle with half of the cheese, half of the pepper-onion mixture, all of the tomatoes and some additional sauce. Repeat with the remaining tortillas, sauce, onion-pepper mixture and end with the cheese on top.

Bake 35-40 minutes in a preheated 350° oven until hot and lightly browned on top. The entire casserole may be prepared a day ahead and refrigerated, covered, before baking. Serves 8.

Alternate Presentation: To serve this dish "Chilaquile Style," quarter the tortillas and fry in oil heated to 375° until crisp. Drain on paper towels. Place half of the fried quarters in the prepared dish. Add turkey between each tortilla. Then add tomatoes, half of the sauce, pepper-onion mixture, remaining sauce and end with the cheese on top. Bake in a preheated 500° oven until the cheese melts and the sauce is bubbly. Garnish with thinly sliced Romaine lettuce.

Montezuma Pie

Budin Azteca

In Mexico this dish is known as "Budin Azteca"; in New Mexico it would be called a "Sopa Seca." It is actually a stacked enchilada which appears with different sauces and fillings in every Southwestern state. Whatever the name, it is an attractive and simple to prepare dish that will impress your dinner guests.

Montezuma was famous for his varied and delicious food. His guests, the Conquistadors, responded by stealing his gold, killing his people and going off with his treasured vanilla and chocolate beans. Hopefully, all your guests will leave with is this recipe!

12 ounces Monterey Jack cheese, chilled, see note
4 ounces Mozzarella cheese, chilled, see note
3 cups cooked chicken or turkey
4 Poblano chiles, roasted and peeled (p.14) or 2 (4 ounce) cans green chiles
1-2 Jalapeño chiles, optional
1 medium yellow onion, peeled and quartered
8 sprigs fresh cilantro or parsley
3 tomatoes, cored
1 tablespoon butter
2 tablespoons corn or safflower oil
1/3-1/2 cup chicken stock
1/2 teaspoon salt or to taste
1 cup sour cream
1/2 cup Ricotta cheese
10 corn tortillas
oil for frying tortillas
1 small, fresh Jalapeño or Serrano Chile for garnish

Use the shredding disc to process the Monterey Jack and Mozzarella cheeses together. Set aside.

Use a 3mm (standard) slicing disc to process the chicken to coarsely chop. Set aside.

If using canned chiles, reserve the juice unless packed in vinegar. Using the metal blade, pulse to coarsely chop together the chiles, onion and 4 of the cilantro or parsley sprigs. (Reserve remaining sprigs for garnish.) Set the mixture aside, but do not wash workbowl.

Cut the tomato to fit the feed tube and use the French fry disc to dice. Discard any pieces of skin that cling to the disc or fall in workbowl.

In a skillet, saute the chile mixture in the butter and oil for about 3 minutes until the onion is translucent. Stir in the tomatoes, chicken stock and any reserved juices from the canned chiles. (Use lesser amount of stock if using chile juices.) Add salt to taste. Remove from heat and set aside.

Combine the sour cream and Ricotta cheese and set aside.

Quarter 4 of the tortillas. Heat about 1/4 inch oil to 350° in a medium skillet. Immerse the 6 whole tortillas, one at a time, in the oil for a few seconds until softened, but not crisp. Drain on paper towels. Add additional oil and raise heat to 375°. Then fry the tortilla quarters crisp. Drain on paper towels. Reserve the tortilla quarters for garnish.

To assemble the "pie," butter a 10 inch pie plate or 11-12 inch round quiche pan with a solid bottom. Layer the pie, making 6 layers, in the following manner: tortilla, sour cream mixture, poultry, chile mixture and shredded cheese. Any remaining chile mixture should be placed around the edges of the pan and topped with any remaining sour cream or shredded cheese.

Bake the "pie" in a preheated 350° oven for 20-25 minutes until the cheese is bubbly, but not browned. Wedge the crisp tortilla quarters around the edges of the pan and garnish with the remaining cilantro or parsley sprigs. Place the chile on top of the stack.

Let cool 5-8 minutes, then cut the "pie" into wedges and serve immediately. Serves 6.

Note: If Oaxaca (or Mennonite) cheese is available, use in place of the Monterey Jack and Mozzarella cheeses (use 1 pound). Decrease salt by one-half.

Poultry

Soft Chicken Tacos

This Taco is very much like an Enchilada and is often treated as such. If you prepare it ahead, be sure to follow the advance preparation instructions for Enchiladas on p.195.

This recipe comes from La Fogata Restaurant and is especially good garnished with Guacamole Salad (p.49) and Tostado Chips (p.242).

The Sauce:
2 large fresh tomatoes or 2 whole canned tomatoes, undrained
2 whole pimientos, juices reserved
4 mild canned green chiles or 1 bell pepper, roasted and peeled (p.14)
4 cups well-seasoned chicken stock
1 clove garlic, peeled
1 small yellow onion, peeled and halved
1 tablespoon butter
4 tablespoons cornstarch
1 teaspoon salt or to taste
1/4-1/2 teaspoon coarse ground black pepper or to taste

The Filling and Assembly:
2 whole cooked chicken breasts, split
12 corn tortillas
Guacamole Salad (p.49)
Tostado Chips (p.242)

First make the sauce. Use the shredding disc to Pulp and Peel (p.21) the fresh tomatoes. (If using canned tomatoes, puree with the metal blade.) Remove stems and seeds from the chiles and slice the chiles or bell peppers and pimiento by hand into thin strips. Reserve.

Bring the stock to a boil in a 3 quart saucepan. Meanwhile, using the metal blade, drop the garlic through the feed tube with the motor running to mince. Leave in workbowl and change to the 3 or 4mm (standard) slicing disc to process the onion. In a small skillet, saute the onion and garlic in the butter for about 5 minutes until the onion is translucent.

Place the cornstarch in the workbowl using the metal blade. With the machine running, pour 1 1/2 cups of the boiling stock through the feed tube and process until smooth. Return to the saucepan with the remaining stock. Add the tomato pulp and reserved pimiento juices and cook, stirring constantly, for about 5 minutes until smooth and thickened. Stir in the chile or pepper and pimiento strips and add salt and pepper to taste. Keep warm.

Remove chicken meat from the bone. Insert the 3 or 4mm (standard) slicing disc and place chicken vertically in the feed tube. Process to coarsely shred. (If the chicken is cold, warm in some hot broth and then drain before filling tortillas.)

Soften the tortillas by passing them briefly through about 1/2 inch of oil heated to 300°. (Do not fry crisp.) Drain on paper towels.

Fill each tortilla with some of the chicken and 1 scant tablespoon of the hot sauce. Roll up and place, seam side down, on individual serving plates allowing 2 Tacos per plate. Coat with sauce and serve immediately garnished with Guacamole Salad and Tostado Chips. Serves 6.

Ninfa's Red Snapper

Ninfa's Huachinango

Ninfa Laurenzo is a Mexican-American who grew up along the Texas border. She married an Italian and her cooking style evolved from a blending of the two cuisines. Interestingly, there is a strong Italian influence in much of the cooking of Oaxaca, Mexico and this is where Ninfa shops for many of her special ingredients. Her version of Red Snapper Veracruz begins with a garlic flavored roux and omits the traditional capers.

Fresh red snapper from the Gulf coast areas is quite suitable for poaching or baking. However, in many parts of the country, the fish is either frozen or imported from the West Coast. West Coast snapper is best if sauteed. Thus, unless you are very sure of the origin and freshness of your fish, use the prescribed saute method in the following recipe.

The Sauce:

2 bunches scallions (white part and 1/2 inch green part), cut in pieces
3 cloves garlic, peeled
3 tablespoons butter
2 tablespoons all-purpose flour
2 tablespoons tomato paste
1 (14 1/2 ounce) can Italian plum tomatoes including juices, see note
1 (14 1/2 ounce) can beef broth
1 teaspoon salt or to taste
1/2 teaspoon coarse ground black pepper
1/2-1 teaspoon dried coriander or 4 sprigs fresh cilantro, minced
1/2 cup dry sherry

The Fish Preparation:

2 pounds fresh red snapper fillets
juice of 2 fresh limes
3/4 teaspoon salt
1 egg
5 tablespoons vegetable oil, divided
1/2 cup milk
1/4 teaspoon salt
1/8 teaspoon black pepper
1 cup sifted flour
3 tablespoons butter
6 scallions, cut in slivers for garnish
canned mild Jalapeño chiles, cut in slivers, for garnish

First make the sauce. Place the scallions and garlic in the workbowl using the metal blade. Process to mince, then remove and set aside.

Melt the butter in a medium saucepan until it begins to turn a light brown. Stir in the flour and cook, stirring, over low heat to make a nut colored roux. Add the scallions and cook about 1 minute, stirring constantly. Stir in the tomato paste, then transfer to the workbowl using the metal blade.

In a saucepan, bring the tomatoes and juices to a boil. With the machine running, spoon the hot tomatoes through the feed tube and then pour in the juices. (This combines the roux and liquid into a smooth mixture.) Return the mixture to the saucepan and stir in the beef stock, salt, pepper, coriander and sherry. Simmer about 20 minutes, stirring occasionally, until well-thickened. Let cool and refrigerate until ready to use — up to 24 hours. Reheat to use.

To prepare the fish, wash the fillets, then sprinkle with lime juice and 1/2 teaspoon of the salt. Let stand 5-10 minutes, then pat dry.

Meanwhile, combine the egg, 2 tablespoons of the oil, milk, salt and pepper in a dish large enough to accommodate one piece of fish. Place the flour on wax paper.

Heat about half of the butter and remaining oil in a skillet until sizzling hot. Dip each fillet in the flour, shaking off excess. Then dip in the egg mixture and again in the flour. Saute on both sides, about 6 minutes total cooking time. (Cooking time varies according to thickness of the fish — test the center of the thickest portion — it should separate easily, but still be moist.) Keep the fish warm in a 150° oven until all is cooked. Add more butter and oil as necessary.

Nap each fillet with a small amount of hot sauce in a strip down the center of the fish. Spoon additional sauce around the fish. Garnish each fillet with several strips of scallion and 2-3 thin slivers of the chiles. Serve immediately. Serves 4-6.

Note: When tomatoes are in season, substitute 6 fresh roasted tomatoes (see p.22 for method). Do not peel and use as directed for the canned tomatoes. The sauce will have a deeper color and rich, fresh flavor.

Variation: You may poach the fish in the sauce using a ratio of 1 pound fish to 3 cups sauce. Heat the sauce to a simmer in a skillet or saute pan. Add the fish and cover with sauce. Poach, covered, over low heat for about 10 minutes until the fish is done. Remove from heat and let the skillet stand, covered, for 5 minutes. Carefully remove the fish to a warm platter and keep warm. Boil the sauce for 2-3 minutes, then nap and garnish the fish as above. This will serve 2-3 people.

Red Snapper Veracruz

Huachinango Veracruz

This is a simple, moist and flavorful way to prepare fish. My favorite basic sauce for this recipe is the Spanish Sauce, but you can use any of the red or green cooked Sauces (without meat) in the Salsa section. The dish is good accompanied by boiled potatoes or white rice.

> 2 pounds red snapper fillets, cleaned
> juice of 1 lime
> salt to taste
> 3 cups Spanish Sauce (p.43)
> 1½ tablespoons tomato paste
> 2 canned Jalapeño chiles, drained and cut into thin strips
> ½ cup sliced black olives
> 2 tablespoons capers

Sprinkle the lime juice over the fish, then sprinkle lightly with salt.

Have the Spanish Sauce in a 12-14 inch skillet and stir in the tomato paste. Set the fillets in the sauce, cover and bring to a simmer. Cook over medium-low heat about 15-20 minutes until the thickest portion of the fish is white and separates easily with a fork. Carefully remove fish from sauce and keep warm.

Bring the sauce to a boil and let boil 2-3 minutes. Pour over the fish and garnish with the chile strips, olives and capers. Serve immediately. Serves 4-5.

Vermicelli with Shrimp Sauce

When doing a benefit class for the Albuquerque Junior League, I adapted this recipe from their regional cookbook, *Simply Simpatico*.

> 5 ounces Parmesan cheese, at room temperature and cut into 5-6 pieces
> 2 cloves garlic, peeled
> 1 cup loosely packed fresh parsley sprigs
> 1 large or 2 medium firm to medium-ripe avocados
> 6-8 ounces vermicelli
> 1 pound fresh shrimp, peeled and deveined
> 5 tablespoons lightly salted butter
> ½ teaspoon red pepper flakes
> ¼ cup vermouth
> ¾-1 cup heavy cream

Using the metal blade, drop the cheese through the feed tube with the motor running and process until finely grated. Remove and set aside. Then drop the garlic and parsley through the feed tube with the motor running to mince. Peel and pit the avocadoes and cut, by hand, into bite-size chunks.

Cook the vermicelli in salted water to cover until "al dente" or just tender. Meanwhile, saute the shrimp, garlic and parsley in 2 tablespoons of the butter for about 1 minute. Add the vermouth and continue cooking about 2 minutes until the shrimp are pink and tender. Gently stir in the avocado and pepper flakes, cooking until soft but not mushy. Take off heat, but keep warm.

Drain the vermicelli and toss with the remaining butter, the cheese and cream until the pasta is coated and the cheese is melted. Place the pasta on a serving platter and spoon the hot shrimp mixture over the top. Serve immediately. Serves 4.

Variation: When red bell peppers are in season, add 1 pepper stemmed, seeded and cut into 1½ inch strips. Add to recipe with the avocado and pepper flakes.

Southwestern Fish Stew

Zarauela

Settlers from the Canary Islands came to the Southwestern states in the 1700's and brought with them many culinary traditions including a classic fish stew. The eastern coast of Texas offers an abundance of fresh fish, Mexican chiles are added to make this an unusual and delicious stew with a tangy accent. I prefer to accompany it with Bolillos (French Rolls, p.227) or fresh, homemade flour tortillas (p.240) rather than the usual rice.

The Stew Base:

6 fresh tomatoes or 1½ cans (14 ounce) Italian plum tomatoes

5 Anaheim or Poblano chiles, roasted and peeled (p.14) or 2 (4 ounce) cans mild or hot green chiles, drained

1 red bell pepper, roasted and peeled (p. 14) or 1 small jar pimiento including juice

½ cup fresh parsley sprigs

½ cup fresh cilantro sprigs

4 cloves garlic, peeled

2 red Spanish onions, peeled and quartered

3 tablespoons vegetable oil

1 (14½ ounce) can Italian plum tomatoes

3 tablespoons tomato paste

2-3 saffron threads soaked in 2 tablespoons warm water, optional

1 teaspoon salt or to taste

fresh ground pepper to taste

To Assemble the Dish:

½ cup fresh parsley sprigs

1½ pounds fresh red snapper fillets, skinned, see note

juice of 1 lime

1½ pounds fresh shrimp

24 oysters, shucked or ½ pound fresh scallops

8-10 fresh mussels, cherrystone clams or steamer clams or ½-1 pound fresh or frozen king crab legs in the shell

First make the stew base. It can be made several days ahead and refrigerated or even frozen for longer storage. The soup should be reheated and finished with the fish shortly before serving, though.

If using fresh tomatoes, use the shredding disc to Pulp and Peel (p.21). (If using canned tomatoes, mash with a fork.) Set the tomatoes aside.

Remove the stems and seeds from the chiles and peppers. Place in the workbowl fitted with the metal blade. Add the parsley and cilantro. Pulse to chop, then set aside.

Using the metal blade, drop the garlic through the feed tube with the motor running to mince. Add the onions to the workbowl and process using the pulse until minced.

In a heavy 3-4 quart saucepan, saute the garlic and onion in the vegetable and olive oil about 5 minutes until onions are translucent. Stir in the tomato pulp, chile mixture, tomato paste and canned tomato, breaking up whole pieces of tomato. Stir in the saffron and simmer 15-20 minutes. Add salt and pepper to taste. Keep the mixture warm if finishing the stew immediately.

If necessary, reheat the stew base. Use the metal blade to mince the parsley and set aside for garnish.

Clean the fish fillets and cut into 1-1½ inch chunks. Wash and peel shrimp leaving tails intact. Squeeze lime juice over the fish. Thoroughly clean the shell fish, debearding the mussels if using. Rinse well.

Place half of the stew base in a kettle or stock pot large enough to accommodate all the seafood. Layer remaining sauce and fish, then cover and simmer over medium-high heat for 12-15 minutes until all the fish is cooked.

Remove the fish with a slotted spoon and divide among 4 large soup plates or dishes. Bring the sauce to a boil, stirring constantly. Adjust seasonings. Stir in the parsley and spoon the sauce over the fish. Serve immediately. Serves 4.

Note: Other firm fleshed fish fillets can be used. West Coast Red Snapper is better if lightly sauteed on both sides in 2 tablespoons oil before adding to the sauce. Frozen fish is improved by soaking in milk for about 15 minutes. Thoroughly drain before adding to the sauce.

Shrimp with Rice
Camarones Con Arroz

Shrimp is often plentiful and relatively inexpensive near the Texas Gulf coast. The Mexican style of grilled shrimp wrapped in bacon is a favorite method of preparation. The special flavor imparted by grilling the shrimp, and often an addition of succulant fruits such as fresh pineapple from the Rio Grande Valley, is really only obtained using a barbecue grill. By all means, use this method on an indoor or outdoor grill if possible. I have, however, given an alternative preparation for sauteeing the shrimp indoors on a range-top.

The Tomato Sauce:
6 large ripe tomatoes or 3 cups canned
    Italian plum tomatoes including juice
1 clove garlic, peeled
1 small red onion, peeled and quartered
3 tablespoons butter
$^1/_2$ cup fresh parsley sprigs
pinch sugar
1 teaspoon oregano
$^1/_2$ teaspoon salt or to taste
$^1/_4$ teaspoon pepper

To Finish the Dish:
4 cups cooked Arroz Blanco (p.217)
$^1/_2$ cup chicken stock
1 cup Green Chile Pesto (p.52) or Cilantro
    Pesto (p.53)
2 strips bacon
$^1/_4$ stick (1 ounce) butter
$1^1/_2$ pounds medium or large shrimp,
    shelled and deveined with tails left intact
2 shallots, peeled and minced
1 tablespoon bottled Teriyaki Sauce or to
    taste
1 tablespoon minced parsley (reserved from
    sauce ingredients)
$^1/_4$ teaspoon salt
coarse ground black pepper to taste

First make the sauce. Use the shredding disc to Pulp and Peel (p.21) the fresh tomatoes. (If using canned tomatoes, mash with a fork.) Set aside.

Using the metal blade, drop the garlic through the feed tube with the motor running to mince. Add onion and pulse to chop. In a $2^1/_2$ quart saucepan, saute the onion and garlic in the butter about 5 minutes until the onion is translucent. Meanwhile mince the parsley using the metal blade and set aside 1 tablespoon for use in finishing the dish. Stir the tomato pulp, parsley and seasonings into the onions and simmer 20 minutes. Adjust seasoning and keep warm.

Prepare the rice. Combine the chicken stock and Pesto of choice, then add to the rice during the last 5 minutes of cooking. Stir very gently. Keep rice hot.

In a medium skillet, cook the bacon until crisp, then remove and drain and crumble. Set aside. Add the butter to the drippings in the pan. Add the shrimp, shallots, Teriyaki sauce, parsley, salt and pepper. Cook over medium heat, stirring constantly, for 3-4 minutes until shrimp turn pink.

Serve the shrimp over the rice with crumbled bacon atop. Serve the tomato sauce separately. Serves 4.

Tamales

The dictionary defines a tamale as "a native Mexican food of minced meat and red pepper rolled in cornmeal, wrapped in corn husks and cooked by baking, steaming. . . ." The Aztec Indians called a tamale "food for the gods." The preparation has been referred to as "the fine art of Indian cooking." One thing is certain — Tamale making is an event! It is not a recipe, but an enthusiastic joint effort of food preparation. Aunts, uncles, cousins, friends and household help all meet in the kitchen for the party of the year — a "Tamalada." In many parts of the Southwest, tamale-making, buñuelos and hot chocolate are as much a part of Christmas as Santa Claus.

There is nothing in American cooking that can compare with this tradition. It is a gossip session, coffee klatch and the heart and soul of the holiday season. In the past tamales had no accompaniment — there were the appetizer, main course, side dish AND dessert. The generation gap closed as mothers and daughters shared with their mothers and grandmothers in a loving task.

Homemade tamales bear little resemblance to the dreadful canned imitations. People living in the Southwest, particularly in Southern California and New Mexico and Texas, have a better opportunity to make good tamales because many cities have mills where fresh ground masa may be purchased. The difference between freshly prepared masa and Masa Harina is as striking as the difference between apples and oranges.

Many cooks still purchase the corn, treat it with lime and take the nixtamal to be ground. Obviously, this is impractical and there are good alternatives. You can grind canned hominy or use Masa Harina. Diana Kennedy suggests using Quaker instant grits, an excellent technique adopted by many cooks and caterers.

There are as many varieties of traditional tamales as there are cooks. Large, fat, white tamales from Mexico; tamales with red chile from Texas; sweet tamales with fruit from Arizona; green corn tamales from California — all of these are delicious! Leftover tamales are served "Enchilada-style" with red chile sauce and grated cheese or layered in a version of Tamale Pie.

If you simply cannot obtain corn shucks for tamales, you can use parchment paper or aluminum foil, but neither one will produce quite the same results. Use less with foil or parchment since both are less absorbent than corn shucks. Even if you use the alternative wrappers, try to line the steamer with corn husks for they do contribute to an authentic flavor.

Tamales may be prepared for steaming, then double-wrapped and frozen for several months. This makes preparation of large quantities at one time quite worthwhile.

I have given a Tamale preparation method and several dough options for both the sweet and savory fillings that follow. Serve tamales with a fresh salsa or Red or Green Chile sauce.

Southwestern Specialties

Tamale Preparation

I have often wondered why Tamale recipes are so lengthy and complicated, but in my efforts to simplify them, I soon realized that the key ingredient is the time involved. In keeping with tradition — make Tamales with friends, neighbors or relatives and divide the jobs. One person makes the filling, the other the dough. One spreads the Tamales, the other folds.

I give both a Savory and Sweet Dough recipe with variations to use a number of dough ingredients such as Masa Harina, grits or hominy. If you can purchase fresh masa or treated corn, you can grind your own dough adding only salt, fat and enough water to make a soft dough that spreads easily. This is undoubtedly the best, but not readily available to most of us. Masa Harina is widely used as a substitute, but I find a dough using only Masa Harina to have a distinct aftertaste.

Choose one of the recipes and try some of the fillings that appeal to you. You can freeze Tamales before steaming or afterward provided they are cooled. To reheat after thawing, place in a single layer on a cookie sheet, wrap tightly in foil and bake 10-15 minutes at 350° until heated through. You can also reheat thawed Tamales, 6 at a time, in a Microwave oven on the High setting for about 1 minute.

Tamales are usually eaten without any sauce, but I like to serve them with a Relish Salsa or Seasoned Tomato Sauce (p.43) or Green Chile Sauce (p.45). Leftover Tamales may be served like Enchiladas or Crepes with one of your favorite sauces or a Molé sauce. Garnish these with crumbled "Enchilada" or Queso Fresco cheese.

Tamales are often wrapped with one end left open, then stacked with the open ends up in a deep steamer. If you have such a pot that will accommodate 2-3 dozen Tamales and a lid to keep out moisture, this works well. There is, however, less danger of moisture seeping in if both ends are tied securely or folded. I prefer these methods and the folded wrapping method to make a finished Tamale with an attractive shape.

While not traditional, I serve Sweet Tamales with a thin buttery sauce, much like crepe sauces. Sweet Tamales may be served as a brunch entree or a dessert following a light meal. However, the most traditional Tamale accompaniments are other Tamales! Because of the work and camaraderie involved in the preparation, I heartily recommend this tradition. A Tamale Party with five or six varieties and several sauces makes for a festive occasion. Serve Sangria (p.72) and crisp Jicama with Fresh Limes (p.80), Marinated Vegetables (p.219) or salted pumpkin seeds for appetizers.

Note: You will need about 4 dozen (2½-3 inch) tamales for 8 people.

Fillings

Choose and prepare the fillings a day in advance and refrigerate overnight. All fillings should be cool when using. (See pp.192 and 194 for filling suggestions and recipes.)

The Shucks and Substitute Wrappings

Corn shucks may be cleaned and separated a day ahead, then soaked overnight completely submerged in warm water. They need a minimum of 2 hours soaking time before wrapping and assembly. Any mildewed shucks should be discarded, but imperfect leaves are reserved for lining the steamer and to tear into narrow strips for tying tamales. When you are ready to begin assembly, shake all water from the shucks and cover with a damp towel. Trim ragged edges. If they tear, or you have half-sized shucks, you can fit 2 together using the dough to seal them. The finished shucks should be approximately 6 x 9½ inches.

Corn shucks are by far the most desirable wrappers for tamales and can be purchased in some specialty shops or you can make your own or you can order them by mail. (See mail-order sources on p.283.) In the event that you simply cannot purchase corn shucks, you may use parchment or aluminum foil as wrappers. Both will work, but because they are less porous, the tamales may be drier and less tender without the subtle flavor from the corn shucks.

Parchment should be cut in rectangles about 5½ x 6 inches for a 3½-4 inch tamale and then soaked in warm water for 15 minutes. (Foil is simply cut into the same size rectangles.) Parchment wrappers may be decoratively tied for an interesting, but untraditional presentation. Tamales wrapped in foil should be served unwrapped with an attractive tie for garnish.

Savory tamales may be tied or garnished with strips of scallions which have been steamed 3-4 minutes or long enough to soften. For sweet ones, strips of lemon or orange peel work nicely in combination with string. See the method for preparing the peels at the end of the Sweet Tamale Dough recipe.

The Dough:

Use the Basic recipe (p.190), the Sweet Tamale dough recipe (p.193) or any of the variations and follow the proper instructions. The purpose in mixing the dough is to beat sufficient air into the fat and to grind the corn as finely as possible. The dough should float when placed atop a glass of ice water. If it doesn't, add more melted fat in 1 tablespoon amounts. Process in and retest the dough after each addition. The liquid needs to be added slowly with a few minutes resting time to allow the masa to absorb it all. Grits dough needs more time than those with hominy or masa harina and hominy. The use of lard is traditional and provides the best texture, but you can use margarine or vegetable shortening combined with butter. Because of the water content in margarine, slightly less broth will be needed in the dough. In all cases, first add the minimum amount of liquid and test the dough consistency before adding more. (Before testing, let stand a few minutes to allow liquid absorption). If using Red Chile Sauce in the dough, the amount of liquid needed will be lessened.

The finished dough will feel quite greasy but much of the fat will be absorbed during steaming. A hominy dough will be the consistency of a soft cookie dough and a dough with grits will be quite loose — almost like cooked oatmeal or cream of wheat. Doughs should be made just prior to the assembly and should be covered with plastic wrap or sealed in plastic bags to prevent drying out. If dough is left to stand, it may then need additional liquid.

*Southwestern
Specialties*

Filling and Wrapping

Each tamale wrapper is spread with a heaping tablespoon of dough as directed in the recipes, then 1-2 teaspoons of filling are placed down the center. Spread the dough as thinly as possible. Leave 1½-2½ inches at the top and bottom and ¾-1 inch side margins free of dough. Tamales may be from 2½-3½ inches long and about 3-3½ inches wide (finished size). Fold the sides together, enclosing the filling and making a round shape. The seam margin should be on the outside. If the dough is quite wet, it is helpful to use a silver knife to mold the filling on the wrapper.

Tamales are wrapped in several ways:

1. Rolled with both ends folded up in 3½-4 or 2-2½ inch size tamales. The smaller ones, especially if made with shucks (where Mother Nature controls the size of the wrapper) are easiest to handle by tying both ends as you tie a tube-shaped present. Longer shucks may be tied in the traditional manner, tucking the pointed end inside the bottom one (see illustration).

2. Rolled, pointed end folded up and opposite end left open. In this case the dough and filling are spread slightly longer and a tall steamer is needed. This method is suitable for larger tamales and you can almost double the amounts given for filling and spreading dough in each one.

1 Spreading corn husk with masa dough

2 Spreading filling over the masa leaving a margin of masa dough

3 Rolling top edge over to make round shape

4 Pressing edges together between corn shuck edges to seal tamale

5 Formed and sealed tamale

6 Folding top edge

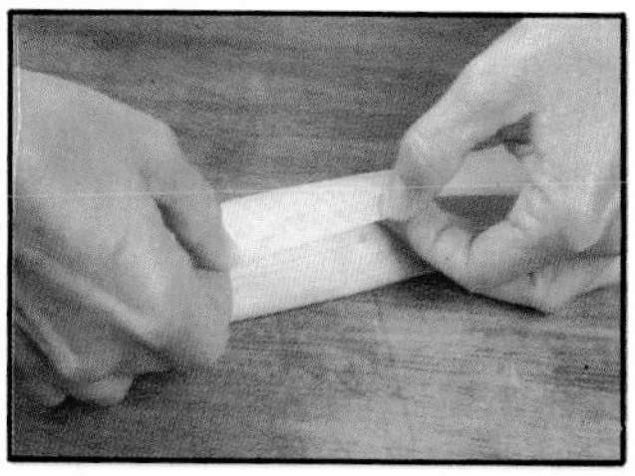

7 Sealing corn husk

8 Procedure for smaller husks, tying both ends

9 Traditional procedure for larger husks; folding pointed end toward center

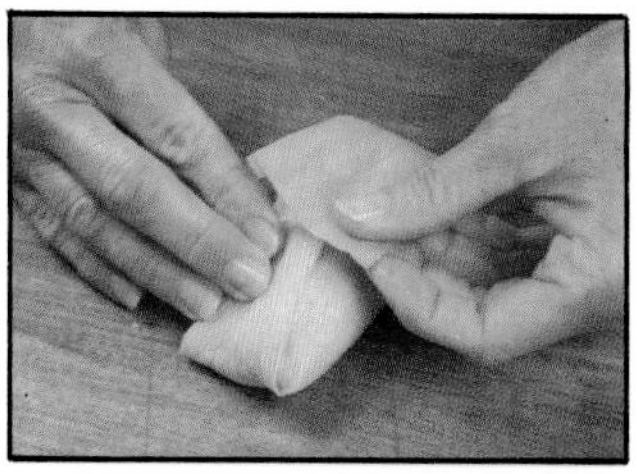

10 Placing straight end over pointed one

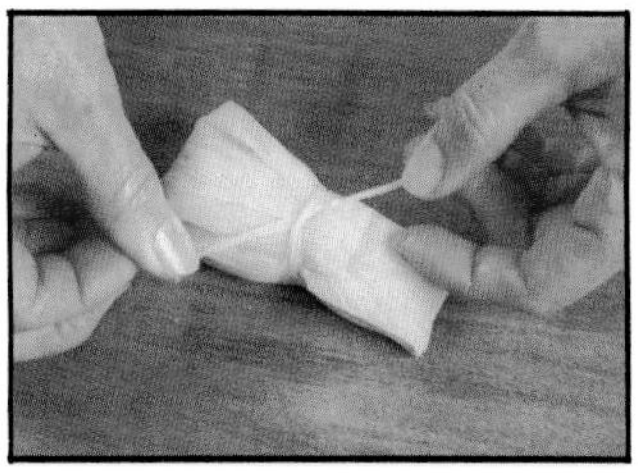

11 Tying with strip of husk in traditional manner

Steaming

Tamales may be stacked upright or layered if using a shallow steamer or wok. The important considerations are:

1. Tie tamales loosely because they need room to swell as they steam.
2. Keep moisture from making direct contact with the dough. (This is harder if one end is left open.)
3. Keep steam from escaping from the container.

Any conventional steamer or wok may be used. If making 4-6 dozen tamales, a turkey roasting pan works quite well. All steamers need a secure and tight-fitting lid. If you have a deep steamer, stand tamales on end in several rows. They should be closely packed, leaving just enough room for the steam to circulate and allow for expansion. In shallow steamers, they can be layered. In all cases, the bottom and sides of the steamer should be lined with several layers of corn shucks before adding the tamales.

Fill the bottom of the steamer with water. As the water boils, it should not reach the tamales. Additional water will be needed, so keep a saucepan of boiling water ready. (It is customary to place a nickel in the water; as long as there is enough water to boil gently, you will hear the nickel.)

Test tamales for doneness by removing one from the top and unwrapping it. The dough should be firm and fall easily from the wrapper. If it doesn't, rewrap and replace in the steamer and cook some more. Cooking time can vary from 1½-3 hours. Foil wrapped tamales cook faster by about 30 minutes and tend to be drier.

To keep cooked tamales warm, remove the steamer from the heat, drain off the water, then recover the pan and let stand about an hour before serving.

Southwestern Specialties

Basic Tamale Dough

This Basic Dough is as close an approximation that I have been able to obtain to the classic dough using fresh ground masa. It has a slightly grainy texture. Many Southwesterners feel that tamales must have red chile added to be "authentic." I prefer to limit the spicy flavors to the fillings, but have given the chile as an optional dough ingredient.

The recipe is followed by three alternate dough types.

> **2 cups (12 ounces) instant grits**
> **1 cup (4½ ounces) masa harina**
> **1 cup (8 ounces) soft lard, see note**
> **1½ teaspoons salt**
> **1 teaspoon baking powder**
> **1½-3 tablespoons pure ground chile powder or up to ⅓ cup Red Chile sauce (p.46), optional**
> **1¾-2 cups room temperature chicken or beef broth**
> **shucks or wrappers of choice**
> **filling of choice**

Have the shucks, fillings and steamer ready before making the dough.

Using the metal blade, process to grind the grits for 2 minutes. Add the masa harina and pulse to combine. Remove and set aside.

Whip the lard until light and fluffy (about 60 seconds) using the metal blade. (You may need to pulse several times and scrape the sides of the workbowl.) Add 1 cup of the grits mixture and process until very smooth and light. Then add the remaining grits mixture, salt, baking powder and optional chile. Process to combine. Then, with the machine running, add the broth very slowly through the feed tube stopping several times. Wait 3-4 minutes between additions to allow the liquid to be absorbed. The finished dough should be the consistency of cooked oatmeal. Test the result by pinching off a small piece of dough and placing in a cup of very cold water. If the dough floats, it has been processed sufficiently with enough fat. (This dough doesn't float as well as the others, but a small piece placed atop the water will float for several seconds.) If the dough does not float, add 1-2 tablespoons melted lard, 1 tablespoon at a time, and process and test again. Let the dough rest about 10 minutes before spreading on the shucks.

Spread about 1 tablespoon or a little more of the dough on the prepared wrapper (preferably corn shucks) as thinly as possible to make a rectangle about 3½ inches long and 3 inches wide. Place 1-2 teaspoons filling down the center of the tamale. (The amount of dough and filling will vary according to the size of the finished tamale and tying method.) Roll and tie as directed in the Assembly Instructions (p.188).

Pack the steamer as directed in the Assembly Instructions and steam for 2-2½ hours. After 2 hours, test one tamale for doneness. The dough should be firm, hold its shape and fall easily from the wrapper.

Serve the tamales in their wrappers if using corn shucks or parchment. (Be sure to advise your guests to remove the wrappers!) If using foil, serve unwrapped with a decorative tie for garnish. Pass a sauce or salsa on the side. Makes 3-3½ dozen.

Note: Lard provides the best result, but you may combine lard and margarine or vegetable shortening or butter if desired.

Tamale Dough using Fresh Ground Masa:

This is the very best dough if you can obtain fresh masa.

2½ pounds *fresh masa* harina (not dried masa harina)
¾ pounds soft lard
2 tablespoons baking powder
1 cup Red Chile sauce (p.46), optional
1-1½ cups beef or chicken or pork broth

Fresh masa does not need to be ground. Simply whip the lard as directed in the recipe, then add the masa and baking powder. Then add the liquid as directed. Steam 2-3 hours.

Tamale Dough using Dried Masa Harina:

Although I feel that this is the least desirable dough, it is commonly used throughout the Southwest.

1 pound (slightly less than 4 cups) masa harina
1 cup (8 ounces) soft lard
2 teaspoons salt
1 tablespoon baking powder or 2 teaspoons baking soda
½ cup Red Chile sauce (p.46), optional
2½-3 cups (approximately) beef or chicken broth

Dried masa does not need to be ground. Whip the lard as directed, then add the dry ingredients. Add liquid as directed and steam 2-3 hours.

Tamale Dough with Hominy:

3 cups (1 pound, 13 ounce can) hominy, drained
1 cup (4½ ounces) masa harina
1 cup (8 ounces) soft lard
1 teaspoon salt
1 teaspoon baking powder
1½-3 tablespoons chile powder, optional
½ cup (or less) hot chicken or beef broth

Grind the hominy very fine using the metal blade. Then add the masa harina and proceed as in the Basic Recipe. Steam 1½-2 hours testing for doneness after 1½-2 hours.

This dough is smoother than the Master Recipe and is somewhat easier to work with. It works quite well for use with parchment or foil, but remember that corn shucks are always preferred.

Southwestern Specialties

Savory Tamale Fillings

This recipe is a basic tamale filling mixture using beef, pork or chicken. Other filling ideas are given at the end. Any Salsa can be used with tamales, but Seasoned Tomato Sauce is especially good with chicken or beef fillings. It is customary to reserve meat stocks to use as liquid in the tamale dough.

Meat Preparation:

2½-3 pounds boneless beef, pork or chicken
2½ quarts water
1 onion, peeled and cut in 6 pieces
1 clove garlic, peeled
1 teaspoon salt
½ teaspoon pepper

To Prepare the Filling:

1 clove garlic, peeled
1 small onion, peeled and quartered
1 bell pepper, stemmed and seeded, optional
1-1½ tablespoons shortening
2 tablespoons chile powder
1 teaspoon salt
1 teaspoon cumin (omit if using commercial or Gebhardt's Chile Powder)
3 tablespoons raisins, optional
1 teaspoon oregano, optional
2-4 ounces canned, chopped green chiles, optional, see note

First, prepare the meat. Trim pork or beef of about half the visible fat. Bring the water to a boil with the onion, garlic, salt and pepper. Add the meat or chicken, cover and let boil gently for about 1½ hours skimming foam from the top several times during the cooking. Remove the meat or chicken from the broth, let cool and then cut into 1 inch chunks. Reserve ¾-1 cup broth for the filling preparation. Using the metal blade, pulse to process the meat or chicken in 2-3 batches until finely ground. Remove and set aside.

Using the metal blade, drop the garlic through the feed tube with the motor running to mince. Add the onion and optional bell pepper and process to mince. Saute the mixture in the shortening until the onion is translucent. Add the reserved meat or chicken, chile powder, salt, cumin, optional raisins, oregano, chiles and enough of the reserved broth to make a moist, but not watery, filling. Let the filling cool completely before using. Makes enough filling for 3½-4 dozen Tamales.

Note: Use either the bell pepper or the canned, chopped chiles but not both. If using the chopped chiles, omit the chile powder. Use the greater amount of shortening if using the bell pepper.

Other Tamale Fillings: All fillings should be cool before using. Allow a total of about 2 cups filling for 3½-4 dozen tamales.

1. Refried Beans (p.215), strips of Monterey Jack, Longhorn Cheddar or Danish Havarti Cheese and Jalapeño chiles.
2. Sauteed bulk Mexican Sausage (p.56) or Chorizo in casings.
3. Boiled shredded beef or pork seasoned to taste with salt, pepper, cumin, chile powder and oregano. (Use the boiling broth as liquid in the tamale dough.)
4. Spicy Meat Hash (p.57)

Sweet Tamale Dough

2 cups (12 ounces) instant grits
$1/4$ cup grated coconut or chopped almonds
$2/3$ cup ($3^1/2$ ounces) masa harina
$1/4$ teaspoon salt
$1/2$ cup sugar
$1/2$ teaspoon baking powder
1 stick (4 ounces) unsalted butter, cut in 4 pieces
$1/2$ cup (4 ounces) lard, cut in 4 pieces
$1^1/2$-$1^3/4$ cups water or complimentary fruit juice
optional ties, see note
shucks or wrappers of choice
filling of choice
lemon orange sauce (p.55) or Guava Sauce (p.54)

Have ready the shucks, filling and steamer.

Using the metal blade, grind the grits with the coconut or almonds for about 2 minutes. Add the masa harina, salt, sugar and baking powder and pulse to combine. Remove and set aside.

Using the metal blade, whip together the butter and lard for 30-45 seconds until light and fluffy. (You may need to scrape the sides of the bowl several times.) Add the grits mixture and process about 20 seconds. With the machine running slowly pour the water or juice through the feed tube until the dough looks like moist oatmeal. (Use the lesser amount of water at first, then let the dough rest for 5-6 minutes before adding the remainder to allow time for absorption of the liquid.) The finished dough should look like loose cooked oatmeal.

Test the consistency of the dough by pinching off a small piece and set atop a glass of ice water. If it floats, the dough has sufficient fat and is well-beaten. If it sinks rapidly, add additional melted lard, 1 tablespoon at a time, processing well and testing after each addition.

Place 1 heaping tablespoon of the dough on the prepared wrappers. Spread to a rectangle about $2^1/2$-$3^1/2$ inches long and 3 inches wide. Place 1-2 teaspoons filling down the center of each tamale. Roll and tie as directed in the Assembly Instructions (p.188).

Steam as directed in the Assembly Instructions for 2-$2^1/2$ hours. After 2 hours, test one tamale for doneness. The dough should be firm, hold its shape and fall easily from the wrapper.

To serve, unwrap the tamales and serve with Lemon-Orange Sauce or Guava Sauce. (If you have used the optional ties, let guests unwrap their own and pass the sauce separately.) Makes 3-$3^1/2$ dozen.

Note: Citrus Peel Ties are an optional tie for Sweet Tamales and make a lovely presentation.

3 oranges
3 lemons
4 cups water
$1/2$ cup sugar

Using a stripper, remove as much of the peel from the fruits as possible in a single strip. You should include a portion of the white membrane of the fruit. Bring the water and sugar to a boil in a medium saucepan and add the fruit peels. Boil for 2 minutes, then let steep off the heat in the liquid for 30 minutes. Cut into 6 inch lengths and use with string as ties for the Sweet Tamales. If the strips tear as you use them, just catch a small strip as you tie the knots.

Southwestern Specialties

Sweet Tamale Fillings

Use about 1¹/₂-2 teaspoons filling per tamale, depending upon the size of the tamale. Each recipe makes enough filling for 3-3¹/₂ dozen Tamales.

1. 2 cups fresh or canned chopped fruit, well drained. Add a light coating of granulated sugar if using unsweetened fruit. (Reserve fruit juices for the dough or a sauce.)
2. 2 cups thickened homemade fruit filling or prepared fruit filling.
3. 2 cups chopped candied fruits (raisins, apricots, dates, pineapple etc.) or chopped candied Mexican fruits (pumpkin, acitron or orange). Mexican fruits should be chopped using the metal blade and are usually moist without the need of additional water. Regular candied fruits should be softened with ¹/₄-¹/₂ cup hot water and ¹/₄ cup sugar after chopping with the metal blade. Press into the liquid and let stand for 30 minutes.
4. Sweet Empanada (Turnover) Fillings (p.84).
5. ³/₄ cup white seedless raisins, plumped for 30 minutes-1 hour in ¹/₂ cup hot water
   ¹/₂ cup grated coconut
   ³/₄ cup chopped nuts (pine nuts, pecans or almonds)
   Drain the raisins and combine with the coconut and nuts.

Enchiladas

Enchiladas are corn tortillas either rolled around fillings or stacked between fillings, coated with a sauce and garnished. Probably no other dish has so many variations of fillings, sauces and garnishes. For example, all regions have a cheese enchilada with a red chile sauce. However the variety of chile pods, chile powder or customary seasonings make each one quite different. The sauce may be made from pure ground chile powder or a combination of chile pods, chile powder and tomato sauce.

The technique for assembling enchiladas is more or less standard whatever the filling or sauce.

1. Prepare the sauce and filling. Have all ingredients ready.
2. Pass tortillas through hot oil to soften and seal them, then press between paper towels.
3. Dip each tortilla in the sauce, letting excess drip into the saucepan. (This is only done if making ahead.)
4. Fill and roll, placing them seam side down in a baking dish. Be sure the edges are coated with sauce. Cover, sealing tightly and set aside or refrigerate until you plan to bake them. This may be done up to 12 hours in advance.
5. Re-heat the sauce and bake enchiladas 10-15 minutes at 350° to heat through. Top with some of the sauce, grated cheese if using, and return to the oven long enough to melt the cheese.
6. Garnish with optional garnishes or crumble white cheese atop and serve.

If you do not plan to prepare enchiladas ahead, you may omit Step 3 which is a bit messy. The point is to keep the tortillas from drying out. If heavily sauced too far in advance, they tend to fall apart or lose their shape.

Tortillas may be softened initially by steaming in a collander. Wrap them in a towel and place over a pan of simmering water for 8-10 minutes. Calories will be saved but some of the flavor will be lost. Step 2, the oil dip process, is to both soften and seal tortillas. Step 3, the sauce dip process, is to keep them from drying out.

Flour tortillas are not suitable for enchiladas though I have friends who use whole wheat flour tortillas which they claim turn out very well.

The recipes that follow are special combinations of Southwestern cooks. Feel free, however, to combine any of the following:

Fillings:
Shredded or ground beef
Chicken
Seafood
Shredded Cheese (Monterey Jack, Swiss, Cheddar, Muenster, Mexican cheeses)
Rice (with or without meat or seafood)
Matchstick slices of vegetables

Sauces:
Red Chile Sauces
Enchilada Sauce
Seasoned Tomato Sauce
Green Chile Sauce

Garnishes:
Melted cheddar or Monterey Jack cheese
Crumbled white cheese
Sour Cream
Olives
Chopped tomatoes
Chunks of avocado
Sliced scallions

Southwestern Specialties

Tex-Mex Enchiladas

There is no doubt that an enchilada sauce made from good quality dried chile pods has a better flavor than one made from chile powder. However, preparation time as well as difficulty in obtaining good chile pods in many parts of the country often make this impractical. Chile powder, either alone or in combination with one or two chile pods, is commonly used throughout the Southwest.

This somewhat heavy and typically "Tex-Mex" sauce uses Gebhardt's Brand of chile powder. It is the use of flour in the sauce preparation that makes it different from other Mexican style Red Chile Sauces. It is the chile Ancho powder with a hint of cumin that also distinguishes "Tex-Mex" from other Mexican enchiladas which use pure ground dried red chile pods. A white, crumbly goat cheese is used in Northern Mexico, but Longhorn cheddar is always used in Texas. I hope my Texas friends will forgive my slight alterations of ingredients.

Many commercial chile powders have added spices and varying amounts of salt, therefore it will be necessary to adjust the seasonings in the sauce to taste. The sauce can be made well ahead and keeps a week in the refrigerator. The assembled enchiladas should be served as quickly as possible after baking, though, because the cheese does not "hold" well. These are most attractive and easiest to serve when prepared in individual baking dishes allowing two enchiladas, per person.

If you wish to have a lighter, though less traditional sauce, use the recipe for Tex-Mex Enchilada sauce.

The Sauce:

1 clove garlic, peeled
3 tablespoons bacon fat
5-6 tablespoons Gebhardt's Chile powder, see note
3 tablespoons flour
1/4-1 1/2 teaspoon salt, or to taste (use more with pure ground chile powder)
4 cups water or beef broth
1 pound cooked ground beef seasoned with 1 teaspoon cumin, optional

Filling and Assembly:

6 ounces Longhorn Cheddar cheese, cut in 4 pieces
6 ounces Swiss cheese, cut in 4 pieces
1 onion, peeled and quartered
8-10 corn tortillas
oil for frying tortillas

Either mince garlic by hand or, using the metal blade, drop the garlic through the feed tube with the motor running to mince. In a 10-12 inch skillet, cook the garlic in the bacon fat for 1-2 minutes. Lower heat and stir in the chile powder watching carefully because it burns easily. Then add the flour, salt and 1/2 cup of the water or broth. Cook over medium-low heat, stirring constantly for 2-3 minutes. This removes the raw taste from the chile powder. Bring the remaining stock to a boil in a saucepan.

Transfer the cooked flour and chile powder mixture to a food processor workbowl using the metal blade. With the machine running, pour 1 1/2 cups of the stock through the feed tube, then transfer the mixture back to the saucepan with remaining stock. Stir over low heat until smooth. Add the ground beef if using. Taste and adjust seasonings. Use the sauce immediately or let cool and refrigerate for later use.

When ready to assemble the enchiladas, reheat the sauce. Put the cheeses in the workbowl using the metal blade. Pulse several times to finely chop. Remove and set aside 1/2 cup for the topping.

Use the metal blade and 5-6 pulses to chop the onion. (If you have a French Fry disc, it will produce an even better result.) Place the onion in a strainer and rinse under cool water to remove bitter taste. Set aside reserving 2-3 tablespoons for garnish.

Heat about 1/2 inch oil to 300° in a skillet large enough to accommodate the tortillas. Pass the tor-

White Cheese Enchiladas with Green Sauce

Enchiladas Queso con Salsa Verde

tillas, one at a time, briefly through the hot oil to soften and seal. Do not fry crisp. Press between paper towels to remove excess oil. Dip each tortilla in the heated sauce, then fill with some of the cheese and onion. Roll up and place, seam side down, in a baking dish just large enough to accommodate them in one layer. Or place 2 enchiladas in each of 4 or 5 individual baking dishes. Cover with foil and bake 10 minutes in a pre-heated 350° oven.

Remove enchiladas and increase oven temperature to 475°. Remove foil and spoon a total of about 1½ cups sauce over the enchiladas, top with the reserved cheese and return to the oven, uncovered, for about 5 minutes or until the cheese is melted.

Serve the enchiladas topped with the reserved raw onion and pass additional sauce separately. Serves 4-5.

Note: You may add 2-3 dried chile pods (Pasilla, Ancho, or Pisado) to the sauce using only 4 tablespoons chile powder, *or* if good dried red chile pods are available, you can substitute all pods (18-24) in this recipe. Wash them thoroughly and toast for 2-3 minutes in a 350° oven. Remove stems and seeds, then cover with 2 cups of boiling water. Simmer for 20 minutes to steam off the skins. Discard skins and process the chile pulp and its water with the metal blade. This 2 cups of water replaces half the water or stock in the recipe. Add cooked flour, garlic and fat to this chile pulp and proceed as above.

See section on dried chiles (p.15) and Red Chile Sauce (p.46) for more information.

As early as 1542, the New Mexican Indians and their Mexican neighbors learned to make cheese from sheep and goat's milk. This soft cheese, similar to Ricotta, is still being made by many Southwesterners. This is great served with a fruit salad.

> **8 corn tortillas**
> **peanut oil for frying,**
> **3 ounces Parmesan cheese, at room temperature and cut in small pieces**
> **6 ounces Mozzarella cheese, chilled**
> **1½ cups Ricotta cheese**
> **2 egg yolks**
> **¼ stick (1 ounce) melted butter**
> **2½ cups Green Salsa (p.40)**

Soften the tortillas by passing them, one at a time, through about 1 inch of peanut oil heated to 325°. Press between paper towels to remove excess oil and reserve.

Using the metal blade, drop the Parmesan cheese pieces through the feed tube with the motor running and process until grated. Set aside 1 tablespoon and leave remainder in workbowl. Insert the shredding disc and process the Mozzarella cheese. Set aside 2 tablespoons and add this to the reserved Parmesan cheese. Leave remainder in workbowl.

Insert the metal blade again, twisting to move cheese away as you place it securely on the stem. Pulse to combine the cheeses, then add the Ricotta cheese and egg yolks. Process until smooth and well-combined.

To assemble the enchiladas, divide the cheese filling among the tortillas. Roll up tightly and place, seam side down, in a baking dish just large enough to hold them. Brush with melted butter. (The enchiladas may be frozen at this point. Thaw to room temperature before baking.)

Bake uncovered for 10 minutes in a preheated 350° oven until the tops of the tortillas are crisp. Cover with Salsa and sprinkle with the reserved cheese. Cover lightly with aluminum foil making sure it does not touch the tortillas or the sauce. Bake an additional 10-12 minutes until the sauce is heated and the cheese melted.

Variation: Add 2 cloves minced garlic and ¼ cup cooked, drained and chopped spinach to the cheese filling.

Green Chicken Enchiladas
Enchiladas Verdes

Tomatillos make a delightful and refreshing sauce for chicken or fish. The canned variety may be used, but the juices should be discarded. I usually combine canned tomatillos with one fresh green tomato to give a fresher taste.

The Filling:
2 whole chicken breasts, halved, see note
2 cloves garlic, peeled
1/2 carrot, cut in pieces
1 yellow onion, peeled and halved
1 bay leaf, broken
several sprigs fresh parsley
2 cups sour cream
1/2 cup heavy cream or half and half cream
6 ounces Swiss or Monterey Jack cheese, chilled

The Sauce and Assembly:
3 pounds fresh tomatillos or 2 cups canned tomatillos
1 clove garlic, peeled
3-4 chile Serranos, stems removed (remove seeds for a milder sauce)
1 teaspoon sugar
salt and pepper to taste
1/2-3/4 cup chicken broth (reserved from poaching chicken)
3 ounces Quseo Fresco or crumbly "Enchilada" cheese, crumbled, optional garnish

First, prepare the filling. Place the chicken in a saucepan with water to cover. Add the garlic cloves, carrot, 1/2 of the onion (reserve other half for garnish), bay leaf and parsley. Bring to a boil, then reduce heat and simmer, covered, for about 30 minutes until the chicken is tender. Let cool in the broth, then remove meat from skin and bones. Drain meat and shred using a 3 or 4mm (standard) slicing disc. Keep the chicken covered to prevent drying out. Strain and reserve the stock.

Combine the sour cream and cream and let stand 30 minutes at room temperature to thicken.

Use the shredding disc to process the cheese and reserve.

Slice the remaining 1/2 onion with a 3mm (standard) slicing disc. Rinse with cold water. Set aside 12 slices to use as a garnish and use the rest to season the stock.

Combine the shredded chicken with half of the cheese (reserving other half for topping the en-chiladas) and 1/2 cup of the sour cream mixture. Set aside while preparing the tortillas.

Heat about 1 inch of oil to 300° in a skillet large enough to accommodate 1 tortilla. Pass the tortillas, one at a time, through the oil to soften and seal. Press between paper towels to remove excess oil.

Divide the filling among the tortillas. Roll up and place, seam side down, in a buttered casserole or individual ovenproof casseroles that will each accommodate 2 tortillas. Keep covered while making the sauce.

Remove husks from fresh tomatillos and wash off any sticky residue. Using the metal blade, drop the garlic through the feed tube with the motor running to mince. Add the fresh or canned tomatillos and the chiles. Pulse several times, then run machine to puree. Place the mixture in a saucepan and bring to a boil. Stir in the sugar, salt, pepper and the chicken broth. Keep hot.

Bake the tortillas, covered, in a preheated 400° oven for 10 minutes until heated through. Cover with the sauce and top with the reserved shredded cheese. Return to the oven and bake, uncovered, for 5-8 minutes to melt the cheese.

Garnish the enchiladas with the reserved onion slices and the optional crumbled cheese. Serve immediately with the remaining sour cream mixture (at room temperature). Serves 6.

Note: Leftover cooked chicken can be used. It should be warmed in chicken stock to restore moisture.

Variation: All of the shredded cheese may be sprinkled atop the casserole before baking instead of using in the filling.

Swiss Seafood Enchiladas
Enchiladas Suizas Mariscos

Enchiladas with sour cream sauces are prepared in nearly every Southwestern state and recipes vary to use different cheeses and sauces. Quite often the sauce will contain pureed spinach and the following version is exceptionally good with shrimp or crab. They are equally good, however, without the seafood.

You can fill the enchiladas and prepare the sauce 8-12 hours in advance. Reheat the sauce and add the sour cream just prior to serving.

The Enchiladas:
- 1/2 small onion
- 1/2 tablespoon butter
- 3 ounces Monterey Jack cheese, cut in several pieces and chilled
- 1/3 cup Ricotta cheese
- 8 ounces softened cream cheese
- 1 (7 ounce) package frozen crabmeat, thawed or 1/2 pound cooked shrimp, peeled and deveined
- 12 (6 inch) corn tortillas
- oil for softening tortillas
- 3 tablespoons grated Parmesan cheese for garnish

The Sauce:
- 1 cup milk
- 1 1/4 cups chicken stock
- 2 cloves garlic, unpeeled
- 1/2 stick (2 ounces) butter
- 1/4 cup flour
- 1/4-1/2 teaspoon salt or to taste
- dash tabasco sauce
- 1/8 teaspoon white pepper
- dash paprika
- 10 ounces fresh spinach or 1 (10 ounce) package frozen spinach, cooked, squeezed and pureed, optional
- 1/2 cup sour cream

To make the filling, first chop the onion using the metal blade. Saute in the butter until the onion is very soft. Set aside off heat.

Place the Monterey Jack cheese in the workbowl using the metal blade. Process to grate the cheese. Add the Ricotta and cream cheese and process until smooth and creamy. Add the seafood and sauteed onion and pulse just until incorporated. Reserve the filling.

Soften the tortillas by passing them, one at a time, through about 1 inch of oil heated to 300° for a few seconds until they are softened. Press between paper towels to remove excess oil.

Divide the filling among the tortillas, roll up and place seam side down in a lightly buttered baking dish or individual ovenproof casseroles that hold 2 enchiladas each. Cover with foil. Refrigerate if not baking immediately.

To make the sauce, first bring the milk and chicken stock to a boil. Meanwhile, place the unpeeled garlic in a lightly greased skillet over medium heat and cook 5-8 minutes until soft and "toasted." Remove garlic peel and place the pulp in the workbowl using the metal blade. Add the butter, flour, salt, tabasco, paprika and pepper and process until pureed into a paste. With the machine running, pour 1 cup of the hot milk mixture through the feed tube. Scrape sides of workbowl and add the optional spinach. Process to combine, then add the mixture to the remaining hot milk mixture in the saucepan. Cook, stirring, over medium heat until thickened. Adjust seasonings to taste. If serving immediately, add the sour cream and keep warm and do not allow to boil. If preparing sauce ahead, reheat at serving time and stir in the sour cream.

When ready to serve, bake the enchiladas, covered, for 12-15 minutes in a preheated 375° oven until hot. Coat with warm sauce and sprinkle with the Parmesan cheese. Increase oven temperature to 450° and bake the enchiladas for 5 minutes more. Serve immediately. Serves 6.

Southwestern Specialties

Sante Fe Enchiladas

This is a classic Southwestern cheese enchilada. The fried egg on top (worth trying) is a West Texas and New Mexico tradition — perhaps the forerunner of stacked pancakes with a fried egg. Eggs are supposed to temper the very hot New Mexican chiles and purists would not tone down the sauce with tomato paste or flour. The cheese filling is usually Cheddar, but with due respect to my New Mexican friends, I prefer a combination of Cheddar, Monterey Jack and Ricotta.

Sometimes the tortillas are stacked with the egg on top. My own version (which follows this recipe as a variation) is to prepare a small, crisp and puffy tortilla with Masa Harina. You could, of course, fry prepared corn tortillas until crisp, but the fresh masa cakes (called gorditas) are significantly better.

There is an interesting Southwest saying that the "sauce should put the soul pleasantly on fire." Gebhart's Chile Powder produces quite a mild "fire," but the added cumin makes the sauce more "Tex-Mex." Use less chile powder or more tomato puree to reduce hotness. If you wish to be truly "authentic," prepare a dried red chile paste (see p. 15), and use in place of the chile powder.

These enchiladas may be served for breakfast, lunch or dinner and are thus a versatile addition to your cooking repertoire. Any extra sauce can be refrigerated for one week or frozen for longer storage.

The Sauce:
- 3 cups water
- 3 cups chicken stock
- 2 cloves garlic, peeled
- 1/4 cup pure ground chile powder or Gebhardt's Chile Powder
- 1 tablespoon pork or bacon fat, see note
- 6 ounces tomato paste
- 1/2 teaspoon oregano
- 2 teaspoons salt

Filling and Topping:
- 1/2 head iceberg lettuce
- 12 ounces Ricotta cheese
- 1 yellow onion, peeled and quartered
- 12 ounces Monterey Jack or Longhorn Cheddar cheese
- 12 commercial corn tortillas
- oil for softening tortillas
- 6 eggs, poached or fried
- sour cream for garnish

To make the sauce, place the water and stock in a saucepan and bring to a boil. Meanwhile, insert the metal blade and drop the garlic through the feed tube with the motor running to mince. Set aside.

In a 2 quart saucepan, combine the chile powder, pork fat and 3-4 tablespoons of the hot stock. Stir 3-5 minutes over medium heat to remove the raw taste from the chile powder. Stir in the tomato paste, oregano, salt and garlic. Slowly stir in the remaining water and stock, combining well. Simmer over medium-low heat for 20 minutes, then adjust seasonings to taste. The sauce may be refrigerated for 3-4 days or frozen up to 4 months.

Insert a 3 or 4mm (standard or thick) slicing disc. Cut the lettuce into wedges to fit the feed tube and slice. Set aside for garnish.

Insert the metal blade and place the Ricotta cheese and onion in the workbowl. Pulse to chop and combine. Leave in workbowl and change to shredding disc to process the Monterey Jack or Cheddar cheese. Set aside about 1/4 cup of the shredded cheese, then combine the onion, Ricotta and remaining shredded cheese with a fork. (If you do this ahead, process onion separately, rinse with cold water and then combine with the cheeses.)

Soften the tortillas by briefly passing them through oil heated to 300°. Press between paper towels to remove excess oil. Fill each tortilla with about 2/3 cup of the cheese and onion mixture, then roll up and place seam side down in a lightly buttered baking dish (or individual ovenproof dishes that hold 2 tortillas each). Spoon on enough sauce to cover tortillas. Bake, covered, about 15 minutes in a preheated 350° oven. Uncover and sprinkle with the reserved shredded cheese. Return to oven for about 5 minutes or until the cheese is melted.

Cover with additional warm sauce and top with a fried or poached egg. Place 1 egg over 2 tortillas. Garnish with shredded lettuce and sour cream. Serves 6.

Note: Ask the butcher for pork back fat and melt it down. This rendered fat adds a very good flavor to the sauce.

Tortillas or Gorditas

sauce from previous recipe
filling and topping from previous recipe
1 cup masa harina
$\frac{1}{2}$ teaspoon salt
$\frac{1}{2}$ teaspoon baking soda
2 tablespoons flour
1 cup plus 2 tablespoons warm water
oil for frying

Make the sauce and prepare the filling and toppings as above.

To make the tortillas, place the masa, salt, baking soda and flour in the workbowl using the metal blade. With the machine running, pour the warm water through the feed tube until a ball of dough forms. The ball should be neither wet nor dry and crumbly. Add a bit more masa or water to obtain the right consistency. Place the dough in a plastic bag and let rest 20 minutes.

Pinch off 6 rounds of dough about the size of a golf ball and use your hands to flatten each into a $2\frac{1}{2}$ inch circle about $\frac{1}{4}$ inch thick. Keep unused portions of dough covered so it will not dry out. If there is extra masa mixture, refrigerate for other uses.

Heat about 2 inches of oil in a deep saucepan to 365°. Fry the tortillas, spooning hot oil over the top to encourage puffing, until golden brown. This should take less than a minute if oil is at proper temperature. Drain on paper towels, then use a sharp knife to split each in half horizontally.

To assemble, place the thicker portion of each split tortilla on a large cookie sheet. Fill each with about $\frac{1}{3}$ cup of the filling, then put the top on each tortilla and sprinkle with reserved shredded cheese. Bake 15-20 minutes in a preheated 300° oven to melt the cheese.

To serve, cover each enchilada with $\frac{1}{3}$ cup sauce and top with a poached or fried egg. Garnish with the lettuce and pass additional sauce separately. Yield: 6 Gorditas

Green Chile Enchiladas
Chile Verde Enchiladas

Southwestern Specialties

This is a typical New Mexican enchilada with a cheese sauce. The local love for pure green chile is evident in many recipes and the tomato is quite often omitted in New Mexico. In nearly all other Southwestern states, however, tomatoes find their way into fillings and sauces.

1 (7 ounce) can mild green chiles, drained or
   5-6 fresh green chiles, roasted, peeled and
   seeded (p.14)
$\frac{1}{2}$ medium yellow onion
$\frac{1}{4}$ stick (1 ounce) butter
$1\frac{1}{2}$ cups milk
4 ounces Cheddar cheese, cut in small pieces
3 tablespoons flour
$\frac{1}{4}$ teaspoons salt or to taste
$\frac{1}{8}$ teaspoon cayenne pepper
1 cup sour cream
12 corn tortillas
oil for frying
$1\frac{1}{2}$ cups cooked chopped turkey or chicken
minced scallions or parsley, optional garnish

Use the metal blade to coarsely chop together the chiles and onion. Saute in the butter about 3 minutes until the onion is translucent. Set off heat.

Bring the milk to a boil in a $2\frac{1}{2}$ quart saucepan. Meanwhile, use the metal blade and pulse to coarsely chop the cheese. Add the flour and $\frac{1}{4}$ cup of the hot milk. Process to make a paste. With the machine running, pour remaining hot milk through the feed tube. Stop several times to scrape sides of workbowl, then process until smooth. Return the mixture to the saucepan and stir over medium heat for about 1 minute until smooth and thickened. Add salt and pepper. The sauce may be done in advance to this point. Reheat when ready to serve and stir in the sour cream. Keep warm, but do not allow to boil.

To assemble the Enchiladas, heat about $\frac{1}{2}$ inch oil to 300° in a skillet large enough to accommodate the tortillas. Pass the tortillas, one at a time, through the oil to soften and seal. Do not fry crisp. Press between paper towels to drain.

Fill each tortilla with about $1\frac{1}{2}$ tablespoons each of chicken, chile and onion mixture, then roll up and place seam side down in a baking dish large enough to accommodate all 12. Cover and bake about 10 minutes in a preheated 350° oven. Uncover, coat with sauce and bake an additional 8 minutes. Serve immediately garnished with minced scallions or parsley if desired. Serves 6.

Southwestern Specialties

Stuffed Chiles

A homemade Chile Relleno is one of the most attractive and delicious dishes that you can prepare. Most restaurants serve a very poor imitation. Unfortunately, the preparation can be most frustrating. The batter is very light and messy and it is difficult to dip and fry a large chile filled with meat or cheese. An added burden on the cook is that the Chile Rellenos are best when served within 15-20 minutes after preparation.

Fresh chile Poblanos are traditional and preferred because their thick flesh accepts the filling without tearing. Canned green chiles are often too thin-fleshed to stuff. Chile growers and manufacturers are constantly trying to improve on a thick, fleshy green chile without sacrificing picante flavor. Incidentally, New Mexicans use a chile Verde and Californians use the California green chile for Chile Rellenos even though fresh Poblano chiles are available. Fresh chiles, with stems intact, also make a more attractive presentation than the canned variety.

The good news is that innovative cooks in the Southwest have devised creative ways to either bake the dish as a casserole (p.206) or use a "croquette" method (p.204), both of which are much easier and adaptable for canned chiles. The traditional filling has been beef or Spicy Meat Hash (p.57), but almost any seafood, poultry or cheese is delicious.

Invite a few friends to help and try one of the methods at least once. You will find that they are worth the effort!

Traditional Stuffed Chiles
Chile Rellenos

If you are looking for a quick and easy recipe, this is not the one! It is, however, one of the most delicious classic dishes in Mexican cooking. Restaurants usually make a poor imitation for they often resort to using frozen products. Chile Rellenos require fresh thick-fleshed chiles, time and careful preparation to guarantee the best result. You can use good quality fire-roasted canned chiles if fresh are simply not available and I have given an alternate preparation for this at the end of the recipe.

The sauce may be prepared ahead as well as the roasting and peeling of the chiles. Many fillings can also be prepared in advance. The actual assembly, the batter and the frying must be done just prior to serving.

In some Southwestern states as well as in Mexico, chile Poblanos are used, but in other areas large chile Verdes such as "Big Jim" are popular. Fillings are usually meat or cheese, but others are typical depending upon regional preferences. The following recipe is primarily the method of preparation. At the end of the recipe, I give a number of filling choices and you may use your own creation of meat and/or cheese combinations. Fillings are often quite picante because the chiles are mild to medium-hot. Feel free to combine fillings or invent your own.

The Tomato Sauce:

6 ripe tomatoes (about 2¹/₂-3 pounds), roasted and peeled (p.22) or 1 (14¹/₂ ounce) can Italian plum tomatoes
2 cloves garlic, peeled
3 tablespoons vegetable oil
2 tablespoons red wine vinegar
2 tablespoons minced parsley
1¹/₂ teaspoons minced cilantro
¹/₂ teaspoon salt or to taste
¹/₂ teaspoon pepper
pinch sugar
¹/₄ cup tomato juice, optional

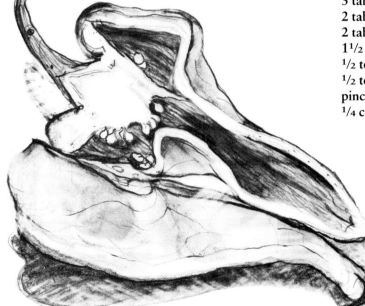

The Chiles and Assembly:

> 6-8 fresh chile Poblanos or large chile
>   Verdes such as "Big Jim," roasted and
>   peeled (p.14)
> filling of choice (see end of recipe)
> 1 cup sour cream
> 1/2 cup heavy cream
> 2 eggs, separated
> 1-2 tablespoons flour, see note
> 1/8 teaspoon salt
> salt and pepper to taste
> peanut oil for deep frying
> minced chives or sliced scallion tops for
>   garnish

First make the tomato sauce. It can be reheated at serving time or served at room temperature.

Core the roasted and peeled tomatoes, if using fresh. Place fresh or canned tomatoes in workbowl using the metal blade and process until smooth. Remove and set aside.

Using the metal blade, drop the garlic through the feed tube with the motor running to mince. In a medium saucepan, saute the garlic in the oil for about 1 minute, then stir in the remaining sauce ingredients using the optional tomato juice if the mixture lacks good color. Simmer 4-5 minutes, then use immediately or let cool and refrigerate until ready to use. Bring to room temperature or reheat at serving time. If the sauce seems too thick, thin with a little water.

Carefully make a small slit down the length of each chile to allow for the filling. Keep the stem intact and gently remove the seeds without breaking the chile. (I find scissors more useful than a knife for this job.) Stuff with the filling of choice and, if necessary to enclose the stuffing in the chile, overlap the slit edges and secure with a toothpick.

Combine the sour cream and heavy cream and allow to stand about 30 minutes at room temperature.

Beat the egg yolks with the flour until very thick. Beat the whites with the 1/8 teaspoon salt to stiff peaks, then fold the whites into the yolks. This is the batter.

Heat about 3 inches of peanut oil in a deep saucepan or deep-fryer to 375-400°. Spoon 2 heaping tablespoons of the batter, in the shape of the stuffed chile but slightly larger, into the oil. Use tongs or two spoons to place a stuffed chile in the center of the batter. Use the tongs to support the chile upright and spoon about 2 more tablespoons batter over the top to cover the chile completely. Immediately spoon hot oil over the top of the chile and batter to seal. Fry 2-2 1/2 minutes to brown both sides, turning once during the frying. Remove from oil and salt and pepper lightly. Keep warm while repeating the procedure to fry all of the chiles.

To serve, cover a platter with some of the tomato sauce and arrange the chiles atop the sauce in a circular fashion with stems pointing outward. Top with a dollop of the sour cream mixture and a few chives or scallions. Pass additional sauce. Serves 6-8.

Note: The amount of flour in the batter varies from "cook to cook." Use a lesser amount for a thinner, crispy coating.

Variation for canned chiles: Use only the best quality, preferably "fire-roasted" chiles. (Remember, canned chiles use a smaller amount of filling.) Spread flat on a work surface and remove seeds. Place about 1 tablespoon of the desired filling in the center of each, then wrap the chile around the filling to enclose completely. Secure with a toothpick, then fry and serve as directed.

Fillings:

1. Sliced cheese (Havarti, Monterey Jack, Meunster, Longhorn Chedder or a combination), allowing 1 1/2-2 ounces per fresh chile depending on size. Shred cheese for use in canned chiles.
2. Sliced avocado sprinkled with lemon juice and salt, allowing about 3 slices per fresh chile.
3. Cooked halved shrimp combined with cheese or avocado, allowing a scant 1/4 cup per each fresh chile.
4. One pound well-seasoned ground pork, cooked and drained and combined with 2 tablespoons raisins that have been plumped in 1/2 cup hot water (drain before adding), 2 tablespoons chopped pecans or pine nuts, 1 tablespoon dry bread crumbs and 1/2-1 teaspoon salt to taste. Allow a scant 1/4 cup filling per each fresh chile.

Southwestern Specialties

Chile Croquettes C. De Baca Style
Rellenos Croquetta

This recipe is from one of New Mexico's finest cooks. Her daughters tell me that the "croquette" method was her way of coping with the difficult task of Chile Relleno preparation using thin-skinned New Mexican chiles. The method is further simplified with a food processor.

The Chile-Meat Mixture:
2 pounds beef chuck or shoulder, trimmed of fat and gristle
1 teaspoon salt
4-5 sprigs parsley
1 bay leaf, broken
1 small piece carrot
6 fresh chile Verdes, roasted and peeled (p.14) or 2 (4 ounce) cans mild or hot green chiles, drained
1 egg
1 (14½ ounce) can Italian plum tomatoes, drained and juices reserved
¼ teaspoon pepper
½ teaspoon salt
⅓ cup seedless raisins or finely chopped pine nuts or pecans, optional

The Tomato Sauce:
1 small onion, peeled
3 tablespoons (1½ ounces) unsalted butter
reserved juice from the tomatoes
2 cups broth from cooking the meat
1 teaspoon celery salt
½ teaspoon oregano
¼ teaspoon pepper or to taste
pinch sugar
3 tablespoons tomato paste

The Batter and Frying:
1 cup sour cream
⅓ cup heavy cream
4 eggs, separated
1-2 tablespoons flour
⅛ teaspoon salt
peanut oil for deep frying

The meat and chile mixture may be made ahead and refrigerated. Cut the meat into 3 or 4 pieces and place in a 4 quart saucepan. Add the salt, parsley, bay leaf, carrot and water to cover. Bring to a boil and cook, partially covered for 30-40 minutes, turning occasionally. Skim the surface foam several times. Remove the meat and let cool. Strain and reserve 2 cups of broth for the tomato sauce. Cut the completely cooled meat into 1 inch chunks and place half in the workbowl using the metal blade. Pulse to chop, then remove and repeat with the other half. Leave in workbowl and add the chiles, egg, salt, pepper, optional raisins and tomatoes. Process to combine well, then add the reserved chopped meat and pulse to combine the entire mixture. Set aside until ready to use.

Prepare the sauce. Use the metal blade to chop the onion, then saute in the butter in a 2 quart saucepan until the onion is limp. Stir in the reserved juice from the tomatoes, 2 cups reserved beef broth, celery salt, oregano, pepper, sugar and tomato paste and bring to a boil. Lower heat and simmer about 15 minutes.

Combine the sour cream and cream and let stand 30 minutes at room temperature.

When ready to prepare the Chile Rellenos, make the batter. Beat the egg yolks with the flour (use a lesser amount for a thin crispy coating) until very thick. Beat the egg whites with the salt to stiff peaks. Fold the whites into the yolks.

Form the meat mixture into 16 oval patties, each about 3-4 inches long. Heat enough oil to 375° to deep-fry the croquettes. Spoon 2 heaping tablespoons of the batter, in the shape of the croquette but slightly larger, into the oil. Use tongs or two spoons to place a croquette in the center of the batter. Use the tongs to support the croquette and spoon about 2 more tablespoons batter over the top to cover the croquette completely. Immediately spoon hot oil over the top of the batter to seal. Fry 2-2½ minutes to brown both sides, turning once during frying. Remove from oil, drain on paper towels and keep warm while frying all of the croquettes.

Serve the croquettes with the warm tomato sauce and garnish with the cream mixture. Allow 2 croquettes per person. Serves 8.

Variation: For a different taste, mix together ¼ cup sugar, ¼ teaspoon each of ground cloves and cinnamon, ½ cup raisins and ¼ cup vinegar. Use in place of the plain raisins or nuts. Proceed as directed.

Souffled Stuffed Chiles
Souffled Chile Rellenos

Although this is not a traditional method of preparation, it is my favorite way to serve this classic to guests. It may be either a first course at dinner or an entree at lunch or brunch. Good quality canned chiles may be used in place of fresh, but the presentation will not be quite as attractive.

The Tomato Sauce:
6 ripe tomatoes (2½-3 pounds), roasted and peeled (p.22), or 1 (14½ ounce) can Italian plum tomatoes
2 cloves garlic, peeled
4 tablespoons vegetable oil
2 tablespoons red wine vinegar
2 tablespoons minced parsley
1½ teaspoons minced cilantro
½ teaspoon salt or to taste
½ teaspoon pepper
pinch sugar
¼ cup tomato juice, optional

Chiles and Souffle Mixture:
6 chile Poblanos or large chile Verdes, roasted and peeled (p.14) or 6 whole canned chiles, drained, see note
1 cup milk
6 ounces Monterey Jack or Swiss or Longhorn Cheddar cheese, chilled
1½ ounces (3 tablespoons) butter
½-¾ teaspoon salt
1½ tablespoons flour
4 eggs, separated
¼ cup minced ham or diced shrimp

The tomato sauce can be made ahead. Core the fresh roasted and peeled tomatoes. Place fresh or canned tomatoes in the workbowl using the metal blade and process to puree. Set aside.

Using the metal blade, drop the garlic through the feed tube with the motor running to mince. In a medium saucepan, saute the garlic in the oil for about 1 minute, then stir in the remaining sauce ingredients using the tomato juice if the sauce lacks good color. Simmer 4-5 minutes. Serve warm or at room temperature.

If using fresh chiles, make a slit ⅔ of the way down the chile and carefully remove the seeds but leave stems intact. Lightly butter a 10 inch pie plate and arrange the chiles in a circular fashion with stems pointing out. If chiles are very large, you may need to use two 7-8 inch pie plates. Set aside.

Bring the milk to a simmer in a 1 quart saucepan. Meanwhile, use the shredding disc to process the cheese. Remove and set aside 2 tablespoons of the cheese. Leave remainder in workbowl and change to metal blade, twisting into place. Add the butter and flour and process to a paste. With the machine running, pour the hot milk through the feed tube, stopping to scrape sides of workbowl as necessary. Process until smooth. Transfer back to the saucepan and cook over low heat for 3-4 minutes, stirring constantly. Add salt to taste.

Using the metal blade, process the egg yolks until lightly beaten. Remove the hot sauce from the heat, let cool slightly, then blend in the egg yolks.

Use an electric mixer to beat the egg whites to stiff peaks. Fold the cheese sauce, ham or shrimp into the egg whites and mound the mixture into the chiles. Bake 30-45 minutes in a preheated 375° oven until puffed and browned.

Serve immediately with the tomato sauce. Serves 6.

Note: If using canned chiles that are not whole or intact, open flat and line individual ramekins. Spoon souffle mixture over and bake 20-25 minutes at 375°.

Baked Stuffed Chiles

Chile Rellenos al Horno

Cooks have wrestled with Chiles Rellenos for years and, without the fresh chile Poblano, this can be a trying dish to prepare. I think that the many baked versions must have originated in New Mexico where the native chiles used to have a very thin flesh and chile Poblanos were not available. These thin-fleshed chiles are difficult to stuff and fry in the classic manner. Chile growers now produce thicker-fleshed chile Verdes that are suitable for Chile Rellenos, but the simplified baked versions remain popular.

If you cannot obtain large fresh green chiles, use good quality thick-fleshed canned chiles. Make a slit down the side and spread them flat. Line the baking dish, then spoon the filling over instead of trying to stuff them. Bell peppers should be used only in desperation.

The following recipe gives both the customary meat version and an optional cheese version.

The Chile Preparation:
> 1 recipe meat or cheese filling (recipes follow)
> 10-12 fresh green chiles, roasted and peeled (p.14) or canned whole green chiles, drained

The Batter:
> 4 eggs, separated
> 1 tablespoon flour
> pinch salt
> paprika or chile powder

The Sauce:
> 1 large fresh tomato
> 3 sprigs fresh parsley
> 2 cloves garlic, peeled
> 2 tablespoons vegetable oil
> 1 tablespoon vinegar
> 1 (14 1/2 ounce) can Italian Plum tomatoes including juices
> 1/2 cup beef or chicken stock
> 2 tablespoons tomato paste
> 1/2 teaspoon oregano
> 1/2 teaspoon salt or to taste
> 1/2 teaspoon sugar
> 1/4 teaspoon white pepper
> 1/8 teaspoon ground cloves, optional

The Garnish:
> 1 cup sour cream
> 1/2 cup heavy cream

Stir together the sour cream and heavy cream and let stand 30 minutes at room temperature. Set aside for garnish.

Have ready the filling of choice. Generously butter two 9 inch pie plates. Remove seeds from chiles and leave stem intact if using fresh chiles. Make a slit half-way down one side of each fresh chile to allow for the filling. (Lay canned chiles flat in the prepared pan.) Stuff fresh chiles with the filling and arrange in a circle, stems pointing outward, in the prepared pans. (Place filling atop canned chiles.) Set aside.

Beat the egg yolks with the flour until very thick. In a separate bowl, use an electric mixer to beat the egg whites and salt to stiff peaks. Fold the whites into the yolks and mound this batter over the chiles. Leave stems uncovered for a nice presentation. Sprinkle with paprika or chile powder and bake 20-25 minutes in a preheated 325° oven until the batter is lightly browned on top.

While the chiles are baking, prepare the tomato sauce. Use the shredding disc to Pulp and Peel the tomato (p.21) and remove from workbowl.

In the same workbowl using the metal blade, drop the parsley and garlic through the feed tube with the motor running to mince. In a medium saucepan, saute the garlic and parsley in the oil for 1 minute, then stir in the tomato pulp, vinegar, canned tomatoes, stock, tomato paste, oregano, salt, sugar, pepper and cloves. Simmer 15 minutes and adjust seasonings to taste.

To serve the chiles, spoon some of the sauce into each of 6-8 shallow dishes. Cut the baked chiles into wedges and place each atop the sauce. Top with a dollop of the sour cream mixture and serve any remaining sauce separately. Serves 6-8.

Meat Filling:

- 1/2 small onion
- 1/2 pound ground pork
- 1/2 pound ground beef
- 2 tablespoons shortening or vegetable oil
- 1 fresh tomato, cored
- 2 tablespoons cider vinegar
- 1/4 teaspoon ground cloves
- 1/4 teaspoon ground cinnamon
- 1/4 teaspoon salt or to taste
- 1/8 teaspoon black pepper
- 1 piece candied acitron or candied pineapple, diced
- 2 tablespoons chopped almonds or pecans
- 2 tablespoons seedless raisins

Use the metal blade to mince the onion. In a medium skillet, saute the onion, pork and beef in the shortening until the meat is cooked. Meanwhile, use the shredding disc to Pulp and Peel the tomato (p.21). Drain cooked meat of excess fat and stir in the tomato pulp, vinegar, cloves, cinnamon, salt and pepper. Simmer about 5 minutes, stirring often. Add acitron, nuts and raisins. Taste and adjust salt and pepper. Use as directed to stuff the chiles.

Cheese Filling:

- 1 medium yellow onion, peeled and quartered, optional
- 1 1/2 tablespoons butter, optional
- 6 ounces Cheddar cheese, chilled
- 6 ounces Monterey Jack or Swiss cheese, chilled
- 4 ounces Ricotta cheese

If using the onion, mince with the metal blade. Saute in the butter for about 3 minutes until translucent. Set off heat.

Use the shredding disc to process the Cheddar and Monterey Jack cheeses together. Combine with the Ricotta cheese and sauteed onions. Use as directed to stuff the chiles.

Variation: 1 1/2 cups diced ham could be added to the cheese filling ingredients.

Sweet Stuffed Chiles

Chile Rellenos Dulce

Sweet meat fillings for Empanadas and Rellenos are quite typical. In the recipe for stuffed Chiles C. de Baca Style, I have given a variation for a slightly sweet version.

This recipe is from *Simply Simpatico,* a regional Junior League cookbook. Unusual because it is served with a sugar syrup, this one could become one of your favorites! Although sweet, it is not really a dessert and is most often served as an appetizer or part of a buffet.

The Chile Mixture:

2¹/₂ pounds lean beef, cut in cubes without trimming fat

water to cover

1 cup seedless raisins

³/₄ cups sugar

2 teaspoons cinnamon

¹/₄ teaspoon ground cloves

¹/₄ teaspoon black pepper

1 cup pine nuts, pecans or almonds

2 cups chopped mild green chile, canned or fresh roasted and peeled (p.14)

1 egg

The Syrup:

1 cup granulated sugar

1 cup brown sugar

¹/₂ cup water

¹/₄ teaspoon cinnamon

The Batter and Frying:

³/₄ cup flour

3 eggs, separated

1 teaspoon flour

¹/₄ teaspoon salt

oil for deep-frying

Place the meat in a saucepan and cover with water. Simmer, covered, about 1 hour until tender. Drain, then process in 2 or 3 batches using the metal blade until coarsely ground. Remove and place the mixture in a large bowl. In the same workbowl with the metal blade, process the raisins, sugar, cinnamon, cloves, pepper, nuts, chile and egg until well blended. Add 1 cup of the ground meat and process to combine. By hand, stir the mixture into the remaining meat in the bowl and mix well.

The syrup can be made just before or during the frying of the Chile Rellenos. Place the granulated sugar in a 2 quart saucepan. Set over medium heat and cook until the sugar melts and caramelizes. Watch carefully because it burns easily once it melts. When the sugar turns amber, immediately remove from heat and stir in the brown sugar and water. The mixture will bubble furiously. Stir in the cinnamon and keep the syrup warm over low heat until ready to use.

Form the meat mixture into 2 inch oval croquettes. Spread the flour on a shallow plate and roll each croquette in flour to coat lightly. Beat the egg yolks with the 1 teaspoon flour until very thick. In a clean bowl, beat the whites with the salt to stiff peaks. Fold the whites into the yolks. Heat 3 inches of oil in a deep pan or deep-fryer to 375°. Dip each croquette into the egg batter and fry, 1 or 2 at a time, in the hot oil for 30-45 seconds until golden brown. Drain on paper towels and keep warm until all are fried.

Serve immediately drizzled with the warm syrup. Makes 20 croquettes.

Quiche with Cheese and Chiles
Chile con Queso Quiche

Corn tortillas make a quick and easy pastry shell that forms its own crisp, decorative edge. For the most attractive results, use a fluted quiche pan with a removable bottom. My children delight in preparing this dish because it looks quite professional and everyone likes it.

6 corn tortillas
1/4 stick (1 ounce) butter
2 tablespoons oil
6 ounces Monterey Jack cheese, well chilled
6 ounces Mozzarella cheese, well chilled
1 medium tomato, cored
1/2 medium yellow onion, peeled and halved
1 (4 ounce) can mild or hot green chiles,
    drained and seeded
3 eggs, separated
1 cup milk or half and half cream
1/4 teaspoon salt
coarse ground black pepper to taste
1/4 cup chopped spinach, all moisture
    removed, optional

Spray an 8 x 1 1/2 inch quiche pan (preferably one with a removable bottom) with a nonstick vegetable spray. In a skillet large enough to accomodate the tortillas, heat the butter and oil to 300°. Pass the tortillas, one as a time, through the hot oil. Turn to coat both sides until tortillas are flexible, but do not fry crisp. Press between paper towels to remove excess oil. Line the prepared pan with the softened tortillas to make a crust. Place the first one in the center, then the others around the edges, overlapping and allowing the rounded portion to come above the rim of the pan. They will take the curve of the pan easily and form a natural fluted edge. Set the quiche shell aside. Reserve the frypan and any remaining butter and oil mixture for sauteeing chiles and onions.

Use the shredding disc and process both cheeses. Set aside.

Quarter the tomato and process with the French fry disc to make small strips. Set aside. Then change to the metal blade and place the onion and chiles in the workbowl. Pulse to chop.

In the pan used to soften the tortillas, saute the onion and chiles for 3-4 minutes. Stir in the tomatoes and cook 1 minute. Set off heat.

Insert the metal blade and place egg yolks in the workbowl. With the machine running, pour the milk, salt and pepper through the feed tube until well blended. Process in the spinach, if using.

Add the tomatoes, cheese and onion mixture to the workbowl and pulse 1-2 times to combine. Leave in workbowl.

Use an electric mixer to beat the egg whites to stiff peaks. Add the beaten whites to the workbowl and pulse 2-3 times to incorporate. Fold in any uncombined whites with a spatula as you remove the mixture from the workbowl.

Immediately pour the mixture into the prepared shell (If you allow it to sit in the bowl, some may leak down the center) and place the quiche on a cookie sheet in a pre-heated 375° oven. Bake 35-40 minutes until soft-set. Do not overbake for it will firm up after removal from the oven. Let stand 5 minutes before slicing. Serves 6-8.

Zucchini Quiche
Pastel de Calabasitas

"Calabaza" actually means pumpkin, but seems to be an all-inclusive term for the many varieties of unusual pumpkin squash in the Southwest — including a small one much like a sweet zucchini. I've never seen this one outside of San Antonio, but it is one of the most delicious squash I've ever encountered. Fortunately, zucchini is a good substitute.

Using tortillas is a popular way to make a simple "crust" and even with the traditional technique of passing through oil to soften, the fat content is less than ⅓ of a pastry crust. In addition, most health experts agree that a corn tortilla is better for you than white flour.

The quiche may be served with a salad and accompanied by any of the Relish Salsas.

1 medium-large zucchini
8 ounces Monterey Jack cheese, chilled
1 medium yellow onion, peeled and
    quartered
2 tablespoons oil
¼ stick (1 ounce) butter
6-7 corn tortillas
1 cup Ricotta or cottage cheese
3 large eggs
2-3 sprigs fresh parsley
¾ cup milk
1½ tablespoons diced pimiento
¼-½ teaspoon salt or to taste
pinch cayenne pepper
Guacamole (p.49) or Salsa of choice

Use an 8 or 9 inch quiche pan, preferably one with a removable bottom. Spray with a non-stick coating and place on a cookie sheet. Set aside.

Cut the zucchini into long pieces that fit horizontally in the feed tube. Process using the shredding disc. Remove and set aside. Then process the cheese using the same disc. Set aside.

Using the metal blade, pulse to chop the onion. Set aside.

Heat the butter and oil to about 300° in a skillet large enough to accommodate the tortillas. Pass each tortilla, one at a time, through the hot oil turning to soften both sides. The object is to soften and seal the tortilla — not fry it crisp. The tortilla should "sizzle" when it hits the butter and oil and may even puff up a bit, but it should not be crisp. Reduce the temperature of the oil if necessary. As each tortilla is softened, press it between paper towels to remove any excess oil, then press into the prepared quiche pan. Place the first one in the center, then the others around the edges overlapping and allowing the rounded edge to come above the rim of the pan. They will take the curve of the pan easily and form a natural fluted edge.

Use the same skillet with remaining butter and oil to saute the onion for about 3 minutes until translucent. Add more oil if necessary. Set aside off heat.

Use the metal blade to process the Ricotta cheese, eggs and parsley until smooth. Then, with the machine running, add the milk through the feed tube. Pulse in the pimiento, sauteed onion and the salt and cayenne papper.

Place the shredded zucchini and Monterey Jack cheese in an even layer in the prepared "crust" and pour the liquid over. Set the pan on a baking sheet in case some liquid leaks out during baking.

Bake about 40 minutes in a preheated 350° oven until "soft set." Allow quiche to stand 5 minutes before slicing. Serve with a salad and your favorite Salsa or Guacamole. Serves 8.

Cheese and Chile Pie
Chile con Queso Pie

This dish consists of stacked corn tortillas with layers of cheese, sauce, chiles and sometimes poultry. There are endless variations including Montezuma Pie. If you are using bell peppers, choose hot chiles to accompany them or the dish may seem a bit bland.

The sauce and cheese and chile preparation may be done ahead, but the tortillas should be prepared and the dish assembled just prior to baking.

> 12 ounces Monterey Jack cheese, chilled
> 4 ounces Mozzarella cheese, chilled
> 1 medium onion, peeled and quartered
> 1 (4 ounce) can mild or hot green chiles
> 1 tablespoon butter
> 2 tablespoons corn or safflower oil
> 3 chile Poblanos or bell peppers, roasted and peeled (p.14)
> 3 tomatoes, cored and quartered or 1 (10$\frac{1}{2}$ ounce) can tomatoes with their juices
> $\frac{1}{2}$-1 teaspoon salt or to taste
> $\frac{1}{3}$ cup cream or milk
> 6 corn tortillas
> peanut oil for softening tortillas
> 8 ounces softened cream cheese

Garnish:

> 3 corn tortillas, quartered and fried crisp in peanut oil
> chopped tomatoes
> thinly sliced lettuce
> 6 sprigs fresh cilantro or parsley

Use the shredding disc to process the Monterey Jack and Mozzarella cheeses. Combine the cheeses and set aside.

Using the metal blade, pulse to chop together the onion and canned chiles. In a 10-12 inch skillet, saute the onion and chile in the butter and oil until the onions are soft. Meanwhile, stem and seed the fresh roasted chiles or peppers and cut into narrow strips. Add to the skillet and continue cooking for about 1 minute.

Use the French fry disc to dice the fresh tomatoes discarding any large pieces of skin. Gently stir the fresh or canned tomatoes and their juices into the mixture in the skillet. Stir to break up canned tomatoes. Remove from heat and stir in the salt and cream. Set aside.

Heat about 1 inch of peanut oil in a skillet large enough to accomodate the tortillas to about 350°. Immerse the tortillas, one at a time, into the oil for a few seconds to soften. Do not fry crisp. Press between layers of paper towels to remove excess oil.

To assemble the pie, butter a 10-12 inch pie plate or quiche pan. Spread each tortilla with about $\frac{1}{6}$ of the cream cheese. Then make layers in the prepared pan beginning with a tortilla, some of the vegetable mixture, then some of the shredded cheese. Repeat with the remaining ingredients to make 6 layers, pressing each down as it is completed. Spoon any remaining vegetables around the edges of the stack and top with any remaining cheese.

Bake 20-25 minutes in a preheated 350° oven until the cheese is melted and lightly browned. Wedge the fried tortilla quarters into the excess melted cheese and vegetables. Arrange tomatoes and cilantro sprigs atop pie. Let stand 5 minutes, then slice into wedges.

Garnish each individual plate with some of the sliced lettuce. Serve immediately. Serves 6.

ACCOMPANIMENTS

All the dishes here are traditional accompaniments to Main Dishes — either served alongside the entree or as a separate course before it. Beans, rice and corn are staples in Southwestern cooking, and at least one seems to accompany every meal. Unfortunately, many people assume that the basic "Tex-Mex" plate of Tacos, Enchiladas, beans and rice *is* Southwestern cuisine. While the combination does exist, it certainly is not representative.

Bean Dishes serve not only as the main starch in a meal, but they are often used as part of a filling for Tacos or Burritos. Rice, either plain or spicy, complements many Main Dishes, and the Pasta Dishes fall into the *Sopa Seca* category. (*Sopa Seca* doesn't really mean "dry soup"; the term indicates a casserole-like dish). Vegetable and fruit accompaniments typify the colorful and healthful style of eating that is Southwestern cooking.

It is true that Relish Salsas are also accompaniments, but for ease of reference they are placed in another section. (See Relishes, Sauces and Fillings.) Frequently a Grilled Meat entree is also served with a single Enchilada and you will find these under Specialties of the Southwest. Breads, especially Tortillas, are a standard part of most meals, too. Serve Accompaniments as you wish; Southwestern meals are not limited to set menus, but instead give the cook the opportunity to use creativity and imagination.

From top to bottom: Pinto Beans, Mexican Rice, Red Chile Pasta, Chile Strips (Rajas).

Grilled Onions
Cebollas al Carbon

Grilled onions often accompany meat dishes. A classic example is the grilled skirt steak entree called Charolitas (p.161). The grilled onions are placed in a flour tortilla along with the steaks, then folded over and served as a taco.

Though not beautiful to look at, Cebollas Al Carbon are delicious! This recipe is from a fine San Antonio restaurant called La Fogata, but the dish originated in Cuernavaca, New Mexico. See the variation for a preparation using yellow onions.

> 1 bunch scallions
> peanut oil for brushing
> 1 tablespoon liquid smoke, optional for indoor cooking
> 2 fresh limes, cut in wedges (Mexican or key limes preferred)

Trim the onions and remove any "whiskers" or bruised portions. The best method of cooking is to grill over hot coals. Brush the onions with the oil, then place directly on the grill. Cook, turning, to brown both sides. They should be crunchy and the white parts translucent. (If cooking indoors, brush the onions with a combination of the oil and the liquid smoke and broil in the oven.)

Serve the onions with lime wedges. Serves 2.

Variation: Yellow onions, sliced thickly, may be grilled as above or pan-fried. To pan-fry, saute the thick sliced onions in equal amounts of butter and oil for about 5 minutes until golden brown. Then place under a pre-heated broiler about 3 inches from the heat source. Broil a few seconds, watching carefully, to get a "charred look."

Chile Strips
Rajas

This sauteed chile and onion relish is a favorite accompaniment to grilled meats. The thick-skinned Chile Poblano is preferred over the thinner-skinned Chile Verdes. If these are not available, bell peppers are the best substitute despite their less distinctive flavor. A combination of red bell peppers and green peppers or chiles are both flavorful and colorful.

This basic recipe can be served in a tortilla to make Quesadillas con Rajas or can be combined with zucchini, red bell peppers and green beans for a substantial vegetable dish or addition to omelettes and fritattas.

> 6 large chile Poblanos or bell peppers, roasted and peeled (p.14)
> 1 large yellow onion, peeled and halved through the core, see note
> 2 tablespoons oil
> 1-2 tablespoons butter
> salt to taste

Remove seeds and stems from chiles and peppers. Cut into thin strips each about 2 x ½ inches. Place the onion halves, cut side down, on a flat surface and cut into similar size strips. (They will straighten out as they cook.) Saute the onions in the butter and oil in a 10-12 inch skillet for about 3 minutes until softened but not brown. Add the chiles and peppers and saute over low heat for 4-5 minutes. Salt to taste and serve immediately. Serves 4.

Note: The onions may be cooked a few hours ahead. The chiles and peppers can also be sliced ahead, but should not be cooked until ready to serve.

Pinto Beans

Frijoles

Beans, prepared in a number of ingenious ways have kept many Southwesterners well nourished during lean, impoverished years. Fresh pinto beans, mashed, refried, stewed, or simply simmered with salt pork are a standard accompaniment to many Mexican-American meals. The broth is rich and delicious and often served as a sauce over Enchiladas, Quesadillas or other snacks. Well seasoned beans, used whole, are frequently used to fill corn or flour tortillas.

Throughout the book, there are many recipes calling for "beans" and the following is a standard recipe for cooking pinto beans. At the end are variations and techniques for baking, refrying or using as a sauce. The only important rule is to cook the beans properly.

Buy the freshest beans possible and keep the following points in mind:
1. Do not soak beans overnight.
2. Add only boiling water to the beans while cooking.
3. Add salt last to prevent toughening of the bean skins.
4. Cook the beans covered.

> 2 cloves garlic, peeled
> 1 small yellow onion, peeled
> 2 strips thick slab bacon or 3-4 pieces salt pork
> 1½ cups pinto beans, see note
> 8-10 cups boiling water
> ½ teaspoon coarse ground black pepper
> 1-2 teaspoons salt to taste
> 1 cup fresh or canned tomatoes, pureed, optional
> 2 green chiles, roasted and peeled (p.14), and chopped, optional

Using the metal blade, drop the garlic through the feed tube with the motor running to mince. Add onion and bacon or salt pork to the workbowl and pulse to finely chop. Place the beans in a heavy 3 quart kettle and cover with 8 cups of boiling water. Add the onion mixture and pepper. Simmer, covered, over medium heat for 2½-3½ hours until the beans are tender. (Cooking time varies according to the freshness of the beans.) Add additional boiling water as needed during cooking to ensure an ample broth. When the beans are tender, stir in the salt and optional tomato puree or chiles and let cool. Store in the refrigerator. Makes about 4½ cups of beans.

Refried Beans or Mashed Beans:

> about 3 cups cooked Pinto Beans with their liquid
> 1 small fresh tomato
> 2-3 tablespoons pork or bacon fat or butter or 1 pound cooked bulk Mexican Sausage (p.56) with drippings reserved
> salsa of choice for garnish
> shredded cheese for garnish
> sliced avocado for garnish
> tostados (p.242) for garnish

Place the beans and liquid, the tomato and the fat or drippings from the sausage in the workbowl using the metal blade. Process to mash to desired consistency. (The beans need not be thoroughly mashed especially if they will be baked.) Heat the mixture in a skillet and serve hot. If using the sausage, add the cooked meat to the skillet while heating the beans.

Baked Beans:

> about 3 cups Refried Beans or 2½-3 cups plain cooked Pinto Beans with 2-3 tablespoons fat or evaporated milk to taste
> 4-6 ounces shredded Longhorn Cheddar or Monterey Jack cheese

You can bake Refried Beans by folding in most of the shredded cheese, placing the mixture in a casserole and sprinkling the remaining cheese atop. You can bake plain cooked Pinto Beans in the same way as long as you add about 2-3 tablespoons additional fat or evaporated milk. Bake either one 20-25 minutes in a preheated 350° until heated through. (You may also prepare plain cooked Pinto Beans by using the metal blade to coarsely process the beans with a tomato, some cooked Mexican Sausage and a few sprigs of cilantro. Bake as directed and then top the casserole with some shredded cheese.) All Baked Beans can be garnished as in Refried Beans.

Beans with Salsa:

> desired amount of plain cooked Pinto Beans with liquid
> salsa of choice or diced green chiles
> snipped fresh cilantro, optional

Heat the beans, without mashing, then add Salsa or chiles and cilantro to taste.

Ranch Style Beans
Frijoles a la Charra

Beans, rice and corn are basic staples in Southwestern cooking and at least one seems to accompany nearly every meal. Unfortunately, many people assume that the basic "Tex-Mex" plate of Tacos, Enchiladas, beans and rice *is* Southwest cuisine. While the combination exists, it is not representative.

Frijoles a la Charra or Ranchero Beans, as they are sometimes called, have long been popular among Texas home cooks. They are also termed "Cowboy Beans," though I doubt that any Texas cowboy ever prepared them this way. Because the dish contains a good deal of broth, it can be served as a soup accompanied by lime wedges and tortillas. It is also excellent served with beef or pork entrees.

This recipe comes from the San Antonio restaurant La Fogota, by way of one of my friends. She enjoyed the beans enough to return time after time until she was permitted to enter the kitchen to watch the preparation. The secrets are adding only *hot* water and salting the dish at the end.

If you add the beer, the dish becomes Frijoles Barracho or "Drunken Beans."

> 2¹/₂ cups pinto beans, rinsed in cold water
> 12 cups hot water
> ¹/₂ pound lean bacon
> 1 green chile, roasted and peeled (p.14), see note
> ¹/₄ cup fresh cilantro leaves
> 3 fresh tomatoes, peeled
> 1 bunch scallions, trimmed and sliced
> 2-3 teaspoons salt
> ¹/₂ cup beer, optional
> 3 limes, cut in wedges

Place the beans and 8 cups of the water in a heavy 4 quart kettle or saucepan. Bring to a boil, then reduce heat and simmer, partially covered, for 2¹/₂-3 hours. Skim the top occasionally and add additional hot water (up to 4 cups) as necessary to make a "broth." (The beans should never dry out.)

Meanwhile, prepare the remaining ingredients. Cut the bacon into quarters and chop coarsely using the metal blade. Fry crisp in a medium skillet. Drain bacon and reserve 1 tablespoon drippings. Using the metal blade, pulse to mince together the chile and cilantro. Use the French fry disc to process the tomatoes into strips.

When the beans are cooked, add the bacon, drippings, chile, cilantro, scallions and tomatoes. Cook, covered, about 30 minutes over low heat until the beans are tender. Add more hot water if necessary. (There should be as much broth as in a bean soup.) Add salt to taste, stir in the optional beer and heat through. Serve in deep bowls garnished with the lime wedges.

The beans can be made 3-4 days ahead and gently reheated. Do not add salt or beer until ready to serve. Serves 8-10 depending on use.

Note: Use Anaheim, Poblano or Jalapeño chiles depending on "hotness" desired.

White Rice

Arroz Blanco

White rice is often preferred to accompany many chicken dishes. I have also given some optional additions for the basic rice mixture. They should be tossed in gently during the last 5 minutes of cooking time.

2 cloves garlic, peeled
1 onion, peeled and quartered
1½ cups regular long grain, white rice
2-3 tablespoons oil
3 cups hot chicken stock
½-¾ teaspoons salt dependent on saltiness
    of chicken stock
¼ teaspoon white pepper

Optional Additions:
½ cup fresh parsley or cilantro, minced
½ cup chopped chives
1 cup cooked hominy
1 cup cooked corn
½ cup sauteed pine nuts or shelled
    pumpkin seeds
½ cup Green Chile Pesto (p.52) mixed with
    ½ cup cream or chicken stock

Using the metal blade, drop the garlic through the feed tube with the motor running to mince. Add onion to workbowl and pulse to chop. In a 2 or 3 quart saucepan, saute the garlic, onion and rice in the oil for about 2 minutes, stirring constantly. Do not brown. Stir in the hot chicken stock, salt and pepper. Bring to a boil, then reduce heat and simmer, covered and undisturbed, for about 15 minutes. Uncover and check, without stirring, to see if rice is tender. Add additional stock if the rice seem too dry. Add whatever optional additions you want depending upon what will be served with the rice. Cook 3-4 minutes more until rice is tender. Serve immediately. Makes 5½ to 6 cups and serves 8.

Mexican Rice

Arroz Mejicana

In this typical Southwestern accompaniment, the rice is first sauteed to bring out full flavor and keep the grains separated. The vegetables may be varied according to personal taste and leftover Mexican Rice can be used in such dishes as Chicken Soup on p.101.

2 cloves garlic, peeled
1 small onion, peeled and quartered
1½ cups long grain white rice
3-4 tablespoons bacon fat or oil
1 medium-small bell pepper or mild green
    chile, roasted and peeled (p.14)
½ carrot, cut in 1 inch chunks
3 cups chicken stock
2-3 saffron threads, optional
1 tablespoon tomato paste, optional
1 large tomato
½ teaspoon salt
⅛-¼ teaspoon pepper to taste
½-⅔ cup cooked fresh or frozen green peas
1 tablespoon minced parsley for garnish,
    optional

Using the metal blade, drop the garlic through the feed tube with the motor running to mince. Add onion to workbowl and pulse to chop. In a large skillet saute the garlic, onion and rice in the oil for about 3 minutes, stirring constantly until rice is lightly browned. Take skillet off heat.

Seed and stem the pepper or chile and place, along with the carrot, in the workbowl using the metal blade. Pulse to coarsely chop. Add to the skillet along with 1 cup of the stock. Simmer 4-5 minutes. Meanwhile, bring the remaining stock, optional saffron and tomato paste to a boil in a 2-3 quart saucepan.

Use the shredding disc to Pulp and Peel (p.21) the tomato. Add the pulp and boiling stock mixture to the skillet. Bring to a boil, then reduce heat and simmer, covered, for 15-20 minutes. Uncover, add the peas and additional stock if the rice seems dry. Do not stir the rice. Cook, uncovered, for about 5 minutes more until the rice is tender. Add salt and pepper to taste. Fluff gently with a fork just before serving. Garnish with minced parsley if desired. Serves 6-8.

El Mirador Rice

Arroz El Mirador

This rice preparation is excellent served with many dishes, but is especially good with El Mirador Mexican Soup (p.98).

> 3/4 cup rice
> hot water to cover
> 1 tablespoon fresh lemon juice
> 1 clove garlic, peeled
> 2 medium tomatoes, peeled and quartered
> 2 medium bell peppers, quartered and seeded
> 2 tablespoons vegetable oil
> 1 cup chicken stock or 3 chicken bouillon cubes dissolved in 1 cup boiling water
> 1 teaspoon ground cumin
> 1/4 teaspoon salt
> fresh ground pepper to taste

Place the rice in a bowl with hot water to cover and stir in lemon juice. Let soak 5 minutes, then drain in a colander.

Meanwhile, using the metal blade, drop the garlic through the feed tube with the motor running to mince. Add the tomatoes and peppers to the workbowl and pulse to coarsely chop.

Heat the oil in a 14 inch skillet. Add the rice and saute about 5 minutes over medium-low heat until golden. Stir in the tomatoes and peppers and simmer about 5 minutes over medium-low heat. Add the remaining ingredients and simmer, covered, for 15 minutes. Do not lift lid or stir rice during cooking time.

To serve, lightly fluff rice with a fork. Serves 4-8 depending on use.

Baked Rice with Cheese

Arizona Arroz con Queso

An old college chum sent me this recipe when she knew I was writing a book on Southwestern food.

> 1 (4 ounce) can mild or hot green chiles, drained
> 5 ounces Monterey Jack cheese, chilled
> 3 cups hot cooked long-grain white rice
> 1/2 cup sour cream
> 1 cup cooked corn (fresh or canned) or 1 cup cream style corn
> 1/2 cup whole or evaporated milk
> 1/2 teaspoon salt
> 1/2 teaspoon paprika

Use the metal blade to chop the chiles. Leave in workbowl and insert the shredding disc. Process the cheese using light pressure. Remove 3 tablespoons of the cheese and reserve. By hand, combine the remaining cheese and chiles with the rice, sour cream, corn, milk, salt and paprika. Spoon into a buttered 1 quart casserole and top with the reserved cheese. Bake 25-30 minutes in a preheated 350° oven until heated through. Serve immediately. Serves 6.

Variation: Try this using leftover Mexican Rice (p.217) in place of the white rice. Or, replace the corn with 1 cup of cooked hominy. Both are delicious.

Marinated Vegetables
Escabeche

Blanched vegetables cooked in water, vinegar and seasonings make a standard accompaniment or appetizer in Southwest cuisine. The typical "Tex-Mex" combination is simply carrots, Jalapeño chiles and onions. Tourists get a "warm" welcome when eating these Texas carrots!

Vegetables can be varied according to preference and availability and the finished dish can be refrigerated in the liquid for several weeks. They can also be packed decoratively into sterilized jars to make a colorful and tangy Christmas gift. Serve them plain, with a salad dressing of choice, or as a garnish for Enchiladas or New Mexican Grilled Meat (p.162).

2 chile Poblanos or green bell peppers, roasted and peeled (p.14)
2 red bell peppers, roasted and peeled (p.14), optional
1 pound carrots, peeled and cut to fit the feed tube
2 yellow onions, peeled
2 chayote, peeled, optional
1 small jicama, peeled, optional
1 pound fresh green beans, cut in 2 inch lengths
1 head cauliflower, separated into florets
4 or more cups water
1 1/2 cups cider vinegar
1/4 cup safflower oil
2 teaspoons salt
1 tablespoon sugar
1 teaspoon oregano
1 bay leaf, broken
1 tablespoon lemon juice
2 cloves garlic, peeled
4 sprigs parsley

Stem and seed the chiles and peppers and cut into thin strips about 1/4 x 1 1/2 inches. Process the carrots using a 2 or 3mm (thin or standard) slicing disc. Then, by hand, cut each slice in half or thirds to make "sticks." Use a 3 or 4mm (standard) slicing disc to process the onions.

If using the chayote or jicama, use 5 or 6mm (thick) slicing disc and the Double Slicing Technique (p.21) to make matchstick strips. (If you don't have this disc, use the thickest disc available to slice the vegetables, then cut by hand into matchstick strips.) Blanch the chayote or jicama for 1 minute in boiling water, then drain.

Layer all the vegetables including beans and cauliflower in a stockpot large enough to accommodate them. Cover with 4 cups water. Add the vinegar, oil, salt, sugar, oregano and bay leaf. Bring to a boil and cook 1 1/2 minutes. Remove from heat and let cool in the liquid, then add the lemon juice, whole garlic and parsley sprigs.

Refrigerate the vegetables and liquid in glass containers up to 4 weeks. For a decorative touch, pack the vegetables into sterilized jars making alternate horizontal and vertical rows of like vegetables. Drain before serving. Serves 8-10 depending on use.

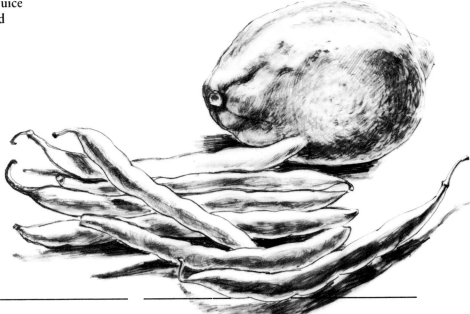

Red Chile Pasta

This egg pasta dough may be rolled by hand or processed through a pasta machine. The bright red-orange color and mild chile taste is a pleasant surprise. Since both eggs and flour temper chiles, the very hot New Mexican chiles or hot chile powder is recommended in the recipe. Be sure to see the recipe for Jalapeño Chile Pasta on the next page. See also the Red Chile Pasta Salad on p.118.

If using a pasta extruding machine or processor attachment, follow the dough formula included in the machine directions, but replace 3 tablespoons flour with chile powder for every 2¼-2½ cups flour used.

The Dough:
3-4 tablespoons pure ground hot red chile powder, see note
2¼-2½ cups unbleached flour
1½ teaspoons salt
1 teaspoon cumin, see note
½-1 teaspoon garlic powder, see note
3 large eggs
1 tablespoon vegetable oil

The Sauce:
2 tablespoons unsalted butter
½ cup cilantro leaves, minced
½ cup sour cream
1 cup crumbled Enchilada cheese or ⅔ cup fresh grated Parmesan cheese

Place the chile powder on a cookie sheet and set in a 250° oven for about 8-10 minutes to "toast." Watch carefully to prevent burning the powder.

Use the metal blade to combine the flour, chile powder, salt, cumin and garlic powder. With the machine running, add the eggs and oil through the feed tube and process until a ball of dough forms around the blades. (It may be necessary to add some additional flour if the dough is sticky or a few droplets of water if a ball does not form and the dough crumbles. Knead the dough by running the machine about 60 seconds. Remove dough from workbowl, cover with plastic wrap and let stand at room temperature for about 20 minutes.

Divide the dough into thirds and flatten each into an oval about ¼ inch thick. Dust each oval with flour and pass through a pasta machine with the rollers at the widest setting. Fold the dough in thirds (like a business letter) and give the dough a quarter turn. Dust again with flour and repeat the rolling, folding and turning 4 times. You will have a rectangular strip of pasta the width of the rollers. (You may use a rolling pin to roll by hand. Fold and turn as directed.)

Lightly flour the dough again and decrease the width of the rollers. Pass the pasta through the rollers again a few times using a thinner setting each time. You will have a long thin strip of dough. (Roll by hand as thin as possible.) Hang the dough over a broom stick or chair back for 10-15 minutes to dry.

When the dough feels dry, but still flexible, cut into desired shapes using the pasta machine or by hand. (Some suggested shapes are fettucine, spaghetti or vermicelli.) You may hang the pasta to dry completely before cooking or you may drop it immediately into lightly salted boiling water. Fresh pasta cooks in about 35-60 seconds depending upon the thickness. Immediately drain the pasta.

To make the sauce, place the butter in a large pan to melt. Toss the hot pasta with the butter and toss in the cilantro and sour cream. Toss to heat through, but do not allow to boil. Serve immediately topped with crumbled Enchilada cheese or grated Parmesan cheese. Yield: 1 pound, 2 ounces dough and serves 8.

Note: If using a commercial chile powder with added spices, such as Gebhardt's, do not use garlic or cumin. If using red chile pods, I recommend that they be stemmed, seeded and toasted on a cookie sheet in a 250° oven for 8-10 minutes. When they are dry and crisp, grind into a powder using a coffee grinder. Use 2 pods per 1 tablespoon powder.

Red Chile Fettucine may be served with any meat or cheese sauce or Cilantro Pesto (p.53) thinned with ½-¾ cup cream or sour cream to make a medium-thin sauce.

Jalapeño Chile Pasta

The flour and egg tames the fiery Jalapeño to a light, picante flavor in this green-flecked pasta. Fresh chiles are more flavorful than canned ones.

You will use slightly more flour with this variation because of the moisture from the fresh chiles and cilantro. You can increase the hotness by replacing one egg with an equal volume of juice from canned Jalapeño chiles

8 fresh Jalapeño chiles, seeded and stemmed or 12 fresh Serrano chiles, seeded and stemmed (see precautions on handling hot chiles on p.14)
several sprigs fresh cilantro or parsley for color
3 large eggs
2¹/₂ cups unbleached flour
1¹/₂ teaspoons salt
1 tablespoon vegetable oil

Do not scrape veins from the chiles. Using the metal blade, drop the chiles and cilantro through the feed tube with the motor running to mince. Add one of the eggs and process to aid the mincing of the chiles. Add all of the remaining ingredients and process as directed in the recipe for Red Chile Pasta. The same sauce can be used.

Note: If you are using a pasta extruding machine or attachment for Jalapeño Pasta, follow directions and formula for making a vegetable pasta.

Chile Pesto Pasta

Green chiles and pine nuts are harvested in the fall in New Mexico. During the season, a fresh salsa of chile and garlic is used to season nearly everything from eggs to grilled meats. When combined with pine nuts or pumpkin seeds, it makes a marvelous pesto sauce for rice or pastas such as the traditional vermicelli.

1 cup Green Chile Pesto (p.52)
8 ounces vermicelli or fettucine
¹/₂-1 cup heavy cream or sour cream
¹/₄-¹/₂ teaspoon salt or to taste

Have the Green Chile Pesto at room temperature.

When ready to cook the pasta, bring salted water to a boil and cook the pasta until just tender (al dente). Drain well and return to pan. Combine the pesto with ¹/₂ cup of the cream and pour over the hot pasta. Stir gently over medium low heat to coat, then add enough additional cream to make a smooth sauce.(Do not allow to boil at any time after adding the cream.) Salt to taste and serve immediately. Serves 4.

Vermicelli Soup with Pesto

Pesto Sopa de Fideo

This pasta dish is like a thick soup and makes a wonderful first course or accompaniment to meat or poultry. I often add a cup of shredded carrot, zucchini, cooked spaghetti squash or sliced artichoke hearts for an interesting difference. If you use the vegetables, toss in at the last minute and use an additional 1/4 cup cream and 1/4 cup Pesto.

> 3-4 tablespoons oil
> 5 ounces vermicelli, broken
> water to cover
> 3/4 cup Green Chile Pesto (p.52)
> 1/4 cup cream or milk
> 1/2 cup diced pimiento, including juices
> 1 cup chicken stock
> salt and pepper to taste

Heat the oil in a 10-12 inch skillet and saute the vermicelli to brown lightly. Stir to prevent burning. Add enough water to cover the pasta, then simmer, covered, for about 8 minutes until pasta is tender. Drain off all liquid.

Combine the Pesto with the cream, pimiento and 1/2 cup of the stock. Stir remaining stock into the pasta, then stir in the Pesto mixture. Toss over low heat just long enough to heat through. Add salt and pepper to taste and serve immediately. Serves 4.

Vermicelli Soup

Sopa de Fideo

This is an example of how misleading the term "sopa" can be. Vermicelli Soup is really a hearty pasta accompaniment and not a liquid soup. This particular version is a classic in the Southwest and usually served alone, often as a first course.

> 2 cloves garlic, peeled
> 1 bunch scallions, white part only
> 2 green chiles, canned or fresh roasted and peeled (p.14)
> 1 pimiento, including juice
> 3 tablespoons vegetable or olive oil
> 5 ounces vermicelli, broken
> 1 (14 1/2 ounce) can Italian plum tomatoes, including juices
> 2 1/2 cups chicken stock
> 4 ounces Monterey Jack or Parmesan cheese, cut in 5 pieces

Using the metal blade, drop the garlic through the feed tube with the motor running to mince. Leave in workbowl and change to the 2 or 3mm (thin) slicing disc. Process the white part of the scallions. By hand, cut the chiles and pimiento into thin strips.

Heat the oil in a 2-3 quart saucepan and lightly brown the vermicelli over medium-low heat, stirring constantly to prevent burning. Add the garlic and scallions and saute lightly. Immediately add the tomatoes, chicken stock, chiles and pimiento. Simmer about 8 minutes or until the pasta is tender and most of the liquid is absorbed.

Meanwhile use the shredding disc to process the Monterey Jack cheese. Using the metal blade, drop the Parmesan cheese through the feed tube with the motor running and process to finely grate. Serve the cheese of choice sprinkled atop the cooked pasta. Serves 4.

Fresh Fruit Platter

An attractive platter of seasonal tropical fruits is the perfect accompaniment to any buffet table or any Main Dish. Papayas, pineapples and mangos are available in most areas, but you may use any colorful arrangement that appeals to you.

> **5 fresh papayas, peeled, halved and seeded**
> **2 pints fresh blueberries, washed and stemmed**
> **1 ripe pineapple, peeled, cored and halved**
> **3 fresh or canned mangos, drained**
> **4 kiwi fruit, peeled and sliced**
> **2 pints fresh strawberries, washed**
> **fresh mint sprigs**

Fill the cavities in the papaya halves with the blueberries. Use a 4mm (standard) slicing disc to process the pineapple. Peel, seed and quarter the fresh mangos. Arrange all fruits decoratively on a large serving platter. Garnish with fresh mint sprigs if available. Serves 12.

BREADS & PASTRIES

Corn and flour tortillas are not the only Southwestern breads adopted from Mexican cooking. Mexican bakeries are found in only a few Southwestern cities, but the breads and pastries are still made in the traditional manner in these bakeries. Neighborhood families will rely on the bakery and tend not to make the breads at home. Mexican-American bakery owners, often third generation, bake just as their fathers and grandfathers did, turning out a copious assortment of sweet breads, empanadas, pastries, cookies and jellyroll cakes. Many are seasoned and spiced with cinnamon, chocolate, anise and/or dried fruits. In the past, the traditional fat used was lard, but today most bakeries use butter or a combination of butter and shortening.

The influence of French cooking manifests itself in various interesting puff pastries such as Cuernos (croissants), Huesos (bones), turnovers and Orejas (ears or palmiers). Not all pastries are French nor are they all sweet. There are Spanish fritters and fried breads which may be eaten unadorned or with a number of sweet or savory fillings.

Many bakeries share the same space with a cafe and the custom is to take a tray and choose your favorites, then retire to the cafe area for pan dulce (sweet bread) with coffee or chocolate.

This section includes recipes for a variety of sweet breads and flour tortillas. (Since corn tortillas are most difficult to make successfully at home, I suggest you purchase fresh ones if you can or buy high-quality frozen or refrigerated corn tortillas.) Also see the appetizer section for Empanadas, a pastry, and the Meat Section for Texas Cornbread which is served as an entree or appetizer. Many of the cookies in the Dessert Section are also found in Mexican bakeries.

The following recipes barely touch the surface of the variety found in good Mexican bakeries — this could almost be a book in itself!

Upper right corner: American Indian Bread and French Rolls (Bolillos). Center, in basket: Egg Bread and Cream Puffs. Bottom right: Bread of the Dead.

Yeast Breads

All of the following yeast breads use a food processor method for mixing and kneading the dough. If you make yeast bread by hand, see p.22 for the Hand Method.

All yeast bread recipes may be doubled if you have a large capacity food processor (such as a Cuisinart DLC-7). If the total amount of flour is under 4 cups, use the metal blade. If you are doubling the recipe (and have more than 4 cups flour), use the plastic dough blade standard with the machine.

Bread flour, which is made by Pillsbury and Gold Medal is recommended in all recipes. Bread flour is also found in health food stores. If you must use all-purpose flour, the amounts may vary slightly.

American Indian Bread
Zuni Bread

This is an American Indian bread with a delicious flavor. Because the cornmeal has little or no gluten, it is not a light and high rising loaf. However it keeps well and makes excellent toast or sandwiches.

> 1½ tablespoons active dry yeast
> 2 tablespoons molasses
> 1¼ cups warm water (105-115°)
> 2 tablespoons vegetable oil
> ¾ cup whole wheat flour
> 1½ cups white bread flour (or more if needed)
> 1 teaspoon salt
> 1 cup stone ground yellow or white cornmeal

Dissolve the yeast and molasses in the warm water. Allow to stand for 5-8 minutes until a thick, foamy layer forms on top. Stir in the oil.

Using the plastic dough blade (or metal blade if your machine has no dough blade), place the whole wheat flour, bread flour and salt in the workbowl. With the machine running, quickly pour the yeast mixture through the feed tube. Process until smooth. You may need to scrape the sides of the workbowl several times.

Add the cornmeal and process until a soft mass of dough gathers together and begins to clean the sides of the workbowl. (The dough should be soft and even slightly sticky, but if it is extremely sticky, add the remaining bread flour, up to ½ cup more, a little at a time.) Process about 30 seconds to knead. Place the dough in an oiled bowl, cover lightly with plastic wrap and let rise in a warm place for 1½-2 hours until doubled in size.

Punch down and divide the dough in half. Shape into one large or two smaller loaves and place the large loaf in a lightly greased 9 x 5 pan. Place the smaller loaves in 3 x 5 pans. Cover lightly with plastic wrap that has been sprayed with a nonstick coating such as Pam. Let rise in a warm place until light, springy and nearly doubled in size. This may take up to 2 hours since the bread is slow-rising.

Bake in the center of a preheated 375° oven 25-30 minutes for the large loaf and about 20 minutes for the smaller loaves. The bread is done when browned and the loaf sounds hollow when tapped on the bottom. Remove from pan and let cool on a rack at least 10 minutes before slicing. Yield: 2 loaves.

French Bread and Rolls

Bolillos

When the French came to Mexico and what is now part of the Southwestern United States, they taught the local people how to make delicate pastries and hearty breads. Many authentic Mexican bakeries in San Antonio and Southern California carry on these traditions.

Although it is not necessary to have a food processor to make the bread, it does make short work of an otherwise arduous task. The dough can be shaped into a single loaf or rolls. The rolls are often split and filled with meat or poultry or some of the same fillings used in Tacos, Chalupas or Chimichangas.

> 1 package active dry yeast
> 1 teaspoon sugar
> ¼ cup warm water (105-115°)
> 3-3¼ cups white bread flour
> 1 teaspoon salt
> 1 cup water, at room temperature
> ¼ stick (1 ounce) melted butter, optional glaze
> 1 egg white beaten with 2 tablespoons water and a pinch of cornstarch, optional glaze

Dissolve the yeast and sugar in the warm water. Let stand for 5-8 minutes until a thick layer forms on top.

Insert the dough blade (or metal blade if you have no dough blade) and place 3 cups of the flour and salt in the workbowl. Pulse several times to combine. Remove the cover and add the yeast mixture and half of the water. Pulse several times, then pour remaining water through the feed tube, continuing to pulse until the liquid is absorbed. Run the machine continuously until the dough forms a mass and begins to clean the sides of the workbowl. (The dough should be soft, but if it feels sticky, add remaining flour, 2 tablespoons at a time, to the right consistency.) Process 20-30 seconds to knead. Place the dough in an oiled bowl, cover with lightly buttered plastic wrap and let rise in a warm place for 2 hours.

Punch the dough down, then stretch and pull it to collapse all air bubbles. To shape into a loaf, roll the dough into a rectangle about 8 x 12 inches. Roll up from the long side to form a wide loaf and taper the ends by pinching and tucking under. Place, seam side down, on a buttered baking sheet. To make rolls, stretch the dough into a long roll about 3 inches wide and cut into 10-12 pieces. Shape into oval rolls and taper both ends. Place on a buttered baking sheet allowing 2 inches in between.

Use a serrated knife to make a lenghwise slash down the center of the loaf or rolls to give the characteristic shape. Cover loosely with buttered plastic wrap and let rise in a warm place for about 1 hour or until doubled in size.

If you desire a soft crust, lightly brush the unbaked bread with melted butter. If you wish a crisp crust, brush lightly with the egg white mixture. Bake the bread or rolls in the center of a preheated 450° oven 25 minutes for a loaf and about 20 minutes for the rolls. (The bread is done when it is browned and sounds hollow when tapped on the bottom.) Remove from baking sheets and let cool on a rack. Because the bread has no shortening, it should either be used on the day of baking or frozen for later use. Yield: 1 loaf or 10-12 rolls.

Pumpkin Rolls
Molettes de Calabaza

These rolls come from Margarita C. de Baca, daughter of the second governor of New Mexico and descendant of Cabeza de Vaca. Her family's recipes have been adopted and adapted throughout the state and have preserved many Spanish traditions.

The delicious variation for Pumpkin Raisin Bread (Pan de Calabaza) is filled with a walnut mixture, baked as a loaf and glazed with a powdered sugar topping. It makes a wonderful breakfast or teatime treat.

> 1 tablespoon plus 1 teaspoon dry yeast
> 1 teaspoon sugar
> $^1/_3$ cup warm water (105-115°)
> 3-3$^1/_4$ cups white bread flour
> $^1/_2$ cup sugar
> 1 teaspoon salt
> 1 teaspoon pumpkin pie spice
> $^1/_2$ teaspoon cinnamon
> $^1/_2$ teaspoon nutmeg
> 2 tablespoons vegetable oil
> 1 cup mashed pumpkin or other squash, at room temperature
> $^1/_2$ cup raisins or currants
> 1 egg white beaten with $^1/_2$ cup milk for glaze
> $^1/_2$ cup light brown sugar

Dissolve the yeast and sugar in the warm water. Set aside for about 5 minutes until a thick layer of foam forms on top of the liquid.

Insert the dough blade (or metal blade if your machine has no dough blade). Place about 2$^1/_2$ cups flour, $^1/_2$ cup sugar and the spices in the workbowl. Pulse several times to combine the ingredients.

Add the yeast mixture, oil and pumpkin and run the machine to make a smoothly combined dough. You will need to scrape the sides of the bowl several times. Add an additional $^1/_2$ cup flour and the raisins and run the machine until the dough forms a soft ball that rotates around the blades and cleans the sides of the bowl. If this does not occur, add the remaining flour and process. (If you are using a metal blade in your processor, do not add raisins to the machine. Instead, knead them in by hand into the finished dough.) Place the ball of dough in a greased bowl, turning to grease the top. Cover and let rise about 1$^1/_2$-2 hours until doubled in bulk. This is a slow rising dough.

Punch the dough down and pinch off rounds slightly larger than a pingpong ball. Place in buttered muffin tins. Cover loosely with plastic wrap that has been sprayed with a nonstick coating such as Pam. Let rise again until light and spongy and nearly doubled — 1$^1/_2$ to 2 hours. Gently brush the rolls with the egg white and milk combination. Use your thumb to make an indentation in the top of each roll and dot with 1 teaspoon of the brown sugar. Bake the rolls about 20 minutes in a preheated 350° oven until golden brown. Remove from pans and let cool on a rack. Yield: 16 rolls.

Pumpkin Raisin Bread or Pan de Calabaza:

> 1 recipe dough made as directed above
> $^1/_2$ cup raisins or currants
> $^1/_2$ cup brown sugar
> $^1/_3$ cup walnuts
> 2 tablespoons butter
> 1 cup powdered sugar
> $^1/_2$ teaspoon vanilla
> small amount warmed orange juice or water

Make the dough as directed in the master recipe and, by hand, knead in the raisins. Let rise as directed in master recipe.

While the dough is rising, make the filling. Use the metal blade to process the brown sugar, nuts and butter to a smooth paste. Punch down the risen dough and roll on a lightly floured surface to a 9 x 12 rectangle. Spread the filling over the dough leaving a 1 inch border. Roll up from the short end, pinching the ends and seam to seal. Place, seam side down, in a greased 9 x 5 loaf pan. Cover lightly with plastic wrap which has been sprayed with a non-stick coating such as Pam and let rise in a warm place until light and spongy — about 1$^1/_2$ hours.

Bake the bread for 30-35 minutes in a preheated 375° oven until browned and the loaf sounds hollow when tapped on the bottom. Remove from pan and let cool on a rack.

While the loaf is cooling, prepare the glaze. Place the powdered sugar in the workbowl using the metal blade. With the machine running, add the vanilla and enough warm juice or water through the feed tube to make a smooth glaze of drizzling consistency. Drizzle the glaze over the cooled loaf. Yield: 1 loaf.

Cream Puffs

Mi Tierra, a bakery and cafe in San Antonio, makes this unusual roll filled with custard and topped with icing and nuts. The dough is the same as for Egg Bread in the following recipe. The custard can be made ahead and should be chilled before using.

The Custard:
1¹/₂ cups whole milk
¹/₂ package unflavored gelatin
¹/₃ cup sugar
1 tablespoon cornstarch
2 eggs plus 1 egg yolk
¹/₂ teaspoon vanilla

The Dough:
1 tablespoon active dry yeast
1 tablespoon sugar
¹/₄ cup warm water (105-115°)
3²/₃ cups white bread flour
1 teaspoon salt
¹/₃ cup sugar
2 tablespoons shortening
5 large eggs

The Topping:
4 cups powdered sugar
2 tablespoons softened unsalted butter
boiling water
1 teaspoon vanilla
1 large egg white
2 cups sliced almonds or chopped pecans

Prepare the custard. Bring the milk to a boil and take off heat. Meanwhile process the gelatin, sugar, whole eggs, egg yolk and cornstarch with the metal blade. With the machine running, pour 1 cup of the hot milk through the feed tube. Transfer the mixture back to the saucepan with the remaining milk and cook over medium heat, stirring constantly, for about 3 minutes until thickened. Do not allow to boil. Stir in the vanilla, let cool and then refrigerate about 4 hours until set.

To make the dough, dissolve the yeast and 1 tablespoon sugar in the warm water. Let stand 5-8 minutes until a thick layer of foam forms on top.

Insert the dough blade (or metal blade if your machine has no dough blade) and place 3 cups of the bread flour, the salt, sugar and shortening in the workbowl. Pulse once to combine, then remove cover and add the yeast mixture and 2 of the eggs. Pulse several times, then stop the machine

and add the remaining eggs through the feed tube. Process about 15 seconds only until the dough is well-mixed — do not overmix. (You may need to scrape sides of workbowl several times to assure even mixing.) Add the remaining bread flour and process just until the dough forms a loose, soft and elastic mass that just begins to clean the sides of the bowl — do not knead in the machine or the dough will be tough. Although the dough is sticky, it should be firm enough to shape easily with buttered hands.

Butter a work surface and the top of the dough. Shape into a 4 x 6 inch rectangle about 1¹/₂ inches thick, then use a sharp buttered knife to cut the dough into 16 squares. Loosely cover with plastic wrap and let rise in a warm place for 1-1¹/₂ hours.

Remove and separate the dough squares taking care not to pull or stretch the pieces. Place on a smooth, flat and unfloured surface. To shape the dough, make a circle using the middle finger and thumb of your left hand and resting the heel of your hand on the work surface. Place one piece of dough against the palm of your hand and within the circle made by your fingers. Roll the dough counter-clockwise firmly and rapidly into a circle taking care not to push down on the top. Repeat to use all of the dough and place the rolls, 2 inches apart, on a lightly greased cookie sheet. Let rise in a warm place for 1-1¹/₂ hours until doubled in bulk.

Bake the rolls for 12-15 minutes in a preheated 350° oven until lightly browned. Remove rolls to a rack to cool completely before filling and icing.

While the rolls are cooling, make the topping. Use the metal blade to process the powdered sugar and butter until smooth. Add the vanilla and a small amount of boiling water through the feed tube — just enough to make a stiff icing. Process in the egg white and enough additional boiling water to make a soft icing. Keep warm over hot water until read to use.

To assemble, make a small slit in each roll and remove about 1¹/₂ tablespoons dough. Place the chilled custard in a pastry bag with a plain tip and pipe about 1¹/₂ tablespoons into each roll. Spoon the icing over the top and press the nuts into the icing to cover completely.

Although the rolls and filling can be made ahead, they should be served soon after assembling. Yield: 16 rolls.

Egg Bread
Pan de Huevos

This egg bread dough has far less shortening than most, which makes it light and high-rising, but also gives it a tendency to dry out quickly. My recipe increases the shortening slightly to keep the bread moist for a longer period. The dough is shaped into rolls and decorated with a vanilla, chocolate or lemon sugar topping etched into a shell or "concha" design. Leftover Egg Bread is used to make a spicy cookie called Rocks (p.263).

The Dough:
    1 tablespoon active dry yeast
    1 tablespoon sugar
    1/4 cup warm water (105-115°)
    3²/3 cups white bread flour
    1 teaspoon salt
    1/3 cup sugar
    2 tablespoons shortening
    5 large eggs

Sugar Topping:
    1 tablespoon lemon peel (yellow part only)
    1¹/2 tablespoons granulated sugar
    1¹/2 tablespoons all-purpose flour
    1/4 cup unsalted butter
    1/4 cup shortening
    1 cup powdered sugar
    1 cup all-purpose flour
    1 teaspoon vanilla
    1 tablespoon cocoa
    1/8 teaspoon cinnamon

Dissolve the yeast and 1 tablespoon sugar in the warm water. Let stand 5-8 minutes until a thick layer of foam forms on the top.

Insert the dough blade (or metal blade if your machine has no dough blade) and place 3 cups of the bread flour, the salt, sugar and shortening in the workbowl. Pulse once to combine. Remove cover and add the yeast mixture and 2 of the eggs. Pulse several times, then stop machine and add the remaining eggs through the feed tube. Process only about 15 seconds until the dough is well-mixed. Do not overmix. You may need to scrape sides of the workbowl several times. Add the remaining bread flour and process just until the dough forms a loose, soft and elastic mass that begins to clean the sides of the bowl. Do not knead in the machine or the dough will be tough. It should be slightly sticky, but firm enough to shape easily with buttered hands.

Butter a work surface and the top of the dough. Shape into a 4 x 6 inch rectangle about 1¹/2 inches thick, then use a sharp buttered knife to cut the dough into 16 squares for medium rolls (smaller for petite rolls). Cover lightly with plastic wrap and let rise in a warm place for 1-1¹/2 hours.

Remove and separate the dough squares taking care not to pull or stretch the dough. Place on a smooth, flat and unfloured surface. To shape the dough, make a circle using the middle finger and thumb of your left hand and resting the heel of your hand on the work surface. Place one piece of dough resting against the palm of your hand and within the circle made by your fingers. Roll the dough counter-clockwise firmly and rapidly into a circle taking care not to push down on the top. (This method is a bakers trick well worth acquiring since it results in perfectly round circles which bake up quite light and puffy.) Place the rolls 2 inches apart on a lightly greased cookie sheet, repeating to use all of the dough. Set aside.

Use the metal blade to process the lemon peel, granulated sugar and 1¹/2 tablespoons flour until the peel is finely minced. Remove and set aside.

Use the metal blade to process the butter, shortening, powdered sugar, 1 cup flour and vanilla until smooth. Remove from the workbowl and divide into three parts. Leave one part plain and shape into a log. Use the metal blade to process together another one third with the lemon peel mixture. Remove from workbowl and shape into a log. Place the remaining one third in the workbowl with the cocoa and cinnamon processing to combine. Remove and shape into a log. Chill the three different flavors of sugar topping until ready to use.

Pinch off about 2 tablespoons of one of the topping "logs" and flatten between your palms into a disc. Flatten one of the rolls and place the disc on top of the roll. (It should completely cover the top.) Use a sharp knife to make a shell design (concha) or criss-cross in the topping. Repeat to use all of the rolls and toppings. Let rise in a warm place about 1-1¹/2 hours until doubled in bulk.

Bake 12-15 minutes in a pre-heated 350° oven until lightly browned. Cool on a rack for a few minutes. These are best served fresh from the oven. Leftovers are delicious toasted or may be ground into crumbs to make "Rocks." Yield: 16 medium or 24 petite rolls.

Variation: Semitas

These large, delicate egg rolls are made with the same dough and preparation but without the sugar topping. Simply add 1 tablespoon anise seed to the dough mixture and bake as directed. All traditional Semitas (anise flavored breads or shortbreads) have a small hole in the center of each roll to impede rising and make a flat, more unleavened bread and you may do this if you wish. Mexican Americans are strong on these traditions.

1 Buttering work surface

2 Transferring dough to work surface

3 Buttering top of dough

4 Patting into 4 x 6″ rectangle

5 Cutting into 24 equal sections

6 Pushing dough square together

7 Placing a piece of dough on the surface resting against the palm of your hand and within the circle made by your fingers

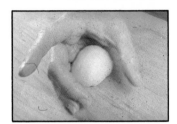

8 Rolling dough rapidly counter-clockwise

9 Finished round of dough

10 Flattening disc of sugar topping

11 Cutting shell design atop of finished rolls

Bread of the Dead
Pan de Meurtos

This sweet bread is traditionally made for a holiday similar to Halloween. The crosses (actually skeleton bones) can be made from the yeast dough, but I prefer to make them with a sugar cookie dough traditional with many Pan Dulce. This soft, rich bread has a high sugar and shortening content and is thus a relatively slow rising dough. Serve it warm with hot chocolate or coffee.

The Dough:
    1 package active dry yeast
    1 teaspoon sugar
    1 cup warm milk (105-115°)
    3 cups (approximately) white bread flour
    1/4 cup sugar
    1 teaspoon salt
    1/4 cup shortening or butter at room
        temperature
    1 whole egg plus 1 egg yolk
    1 egg yolk beaten with 1 tablespoon milk
        for glaze

Sugar Cookie Topping:
    1/2 cup light brown sugar, lightly packed
    1/2 teaspoon cinnamon
    1/2 teaspoon nutmeg
    1/3 cup shortening
    2/3 cup all-purpose flour
    powdered sugar for rolling out

Dissolve the yeast and 1 teaspoon sugar in the warm milk. Set aside for 5-8 minutes until a thick layer of foam forms on top.

Insert the dough blade (or metal blade if your machine has no dough blade) and place 2 1/4 cups of the bread flour, the sugar, salt and shortening in the workbowl. Pulse to combine and cut in the shortening. Add the egg, yolk and yeast mixture through the feed tube, pulsing as you pour in the liquid. Process continuously to make a batter, stopping several times to scrape sides of workbowl. Add enough remaining flour, processing, until a soft ball of dough just begins to clean sides of the workbowl. Do not process more than 20-30 seconds after adding the final amount of flour. Place the dough in a lightly buttered bowl, cover and let rise in a warm place for 45 minutes to 1 hour.

Turn the dough onto a lightly floured surface and divide into three pieces. Roll each into a 12 inch log. (The dough is quite soft and not very elastic, but is workable.) Braid the three logs together and place the braid on a lightly greased cookie sheet. Cover with buttered plastic wrap and let rise again until light but not doubled, about 1 hour.

Meanwhile, make the topping. Insert the metal blade and place the brown sugar, cinnamon, nutmeg and shortening in the workbowl. Process until creamy, then pulse in the flour to combine. Place the topping dough on a surface dusted with powdered sugar and roll out to 1/8-1/4 inch thick. Cut out 8 "bones" to make 4 crosses. Brush the bread dough with the beaten egg yolk mixture and affix the crosses on top.

Bake 25-30 minutes in a preheated 375° oven. Serve warm. Yield: 1 braided loaf.

Any leftover cookie topping dough may be shaped into balls, flattened slightly and baked 12-15 minutes at 350° for sugar cookies.

Note: Because bread flour in doughs rises dramatically in the oven, the second rising need not be as long and the dough need not double in bulk.

Three Kings Bread
Rosca de Los Reyes

In Mexico, Christmas is celebrated with "posadas" which are parades through the streets representing Mary and Joseph asking for lodging and being turned away. For nine days before Christmas children parade through different neighborhoods each night and the people throw gifts such as oranges, peanuts and candy to the marchers.

In most of the Mexican provinces it is still customary to bake Rosca de los Reyes to celebrate Twelfth Night. The fruit-filled yeast bread is baked in a ring and garnished with "jewels" of candied fruit and nuts to signify the Three Kings. A tiny clay or porcelain doll is hidden inside the loaf before baking. On January sixth (Twelfth Night), children leave their shoes outside the door to be filled with toys by the Three Magi.

If you don't have a clay ornament, you can use any small decorative ornament or candy as your hidden treasure. Wedge it into the dough after baking, then cover the opening with icing. The one who finds the doll is supposed to give the "El Dia da la Candelaria" on Candlemas Day on February 2. In our house we always have a Christmas piñata, and the one who finds the doll gets the first "whack."

The Bread:
    1 tablespoon plus 1 teaspoon active dry
        yeast
    1 teaspoon sugar
    3/4 cup warm water (105-115°)
    zest of 1/2 an orange, colored part only
    zest of 1 lemon, colored part only
    1/4 cup sugar
    3-3 1/2 cups white bread flour
    1 teaspoon salt
    2 tablespoons non-fat dry milk powder
    3/4 stick (3 ounces) unsalted margarine or
        vegetable shortening, cut in 6 pieces
    1/4 stick (1 ounce) butter, cut in 3 pieces
    2 large eggs
    1/4 cup raisins or currants
    1/4 cup coarsely chopped walnuts
    1/4 cup assorted candied fruits
    1-2 tablespoons melted butter

The Glaze and Garnish:
    1 1/2 cups powdered sugar
    3 tablespoons heavy cream
    1/2 teaspoon vanilla
    hot water
    tiny doll or other ornament
    whole walnuts or pecans
    assorted candied fruits

Dissolve the yeast and 1 teaspoon sugar in the warm water. Let stand 5-9 minutes until a thick layer of foam coats the top.

Insert the metal blade and place the orange and lemon zest as well as the 1/4 cup sugar in the workbowl. Process until zest is finely minced. Add 2 1/2 cups of the bread flour, the salt, dry milk powder, margarine and butter. Pulse until the shortening is cut into the flour evenly. Change to the plastic dough blade (or continue with metal blade if your machine has no dough blade) and add the eggs and half of the yeast mixture. Pulse once or twice to incorporate the liquid. Pulse in the remaining yeast mixture, then run the machine for 15-20 seconds. The batter will be loose. Scrape sides of workbowl and then process briefly to be sure all the ingredients are incorporated. Do not overprocess or the dough will be tough. Add enough additional flour and process just to make a soft dough that will begin to clean the sides of the bowl. Dough will not form a ball. Scatter the raisins, nuts and candied fruits over the dough and sprinkle with the remaining flour. Pulse 2-3 times to combine.

Place the dough in a lightly buttered board, cover with plastic wrap and let rise 1 1/2-2 hours.

Divide the dough in half and on a lightly floured surface, shape each into a 12-14 inch rope. Join the ends together to make 2 rings. Place on lightly greased baking sheets. (Incorporate as little extra flour as possible while shaping the dough.) Cover lightly with plastic wrap and let rise again in a warm place for about 1 hour until light and spongy. Brush with the melted butter and bake about 20 minutes in a pre-heated 400° oven. Remove from baking sheets and let cool on a rack.

Meanwhile, insert the metal blade and process the powdered sugar, heavy cream and vanilla until smooth. Add just enough hot water to make a pourable icing. When the bread is cool, make an opening to hide the tiny doll, then glaze the loaves and decorate with the nuts and candied fruit. Yield: 2 loaves.

Sopaipillas
Pillows

Sopaipilla means "pillow" and is an apt description for this light and puffy fried dough that is traditionally served with honey as a dinner roll (much like traditional bread and butter). In Arizona, Sopaipillas are sometimes filled with fruit and served as dessert. In other areas they are sprinkled with powdered sugar and served with honey or whipped cream as a pastry. I have even seen yeast doughs for Sopaipillas, though they are uncommon. Again, Sopaipillas show the variety and creativity of Southwest cooking — anything goes, limited only by your imagination. Master the basic techniques and you can easily present a great meal!

Sopaipilla dough is similar to that for flour tortillas, but is rolled and folded to ensure even puffing when fried. The most important technique is to spoon the hot oil over the pastry while frying.

New Mexican Indians make a similar bread called Navaho Fry Bread (p.236) which also puffs up dramatically. To impede this puffing they poke a hole in the middle of the dough. Navaho Fry Bread is often stuffed with a variety of savory fillings, but can also be served plain or sugared and called a Buñuelo — confusing, but delicious! Perhaps this is the original doughnut.

A most interesting Sopaipilla variation is found in La Poblanita, a Mexican bakery in San Antonio. It is an unusual pastry called Pastel de Polve or "powder pastry" made from a Sopaipilla dough that is rolled and folded three times with a light dusting of flour between the folds. The pastry is filled with preserves or fresh fruit, baked in a hot oven to result in a tender and flaky sweet that resembles a crumbly puff pastry without the layers of butter.

This is a basic recipe and technique for making the Sopaipillas.

> 2 cups all-purpose flour
> 1½ teaspoons salt
> 1½ teaspoons baking powder
> 2 tablespoons shortening
> ¾ cup very hot water
> oil for deep frying
> powdered sugar
> honey, optional

Place the flour, salt, baking powder and shortening in a mixing bowl. Use your fingers or a pastry blender to thoroughly combine and evenly distribute the shortening. Add the hot water and stir with a fork until the mixture forms a dough. (If the dough is too dry to mold or knead, add a bit more water. If it seems wet, add 1-2 tablespoons flour.) Knead a couple of times, then place in a plastic bag to rest for 20 minutes.

Lightly flour a work surface and roll the dough into a rectangle about ¼ inch thick. (If the dough seems too elastic to roll easily, cover and let it rest a few minutes, then roll again.) Fold the dough in half and let rest a few minutes, then roll again to a ¼ inch thick rectangle. (This can be done in a pasta machine using the thickest setting. Pass through two times.)

Heat 3 inches of oil in a 3 quart saucepan or deep-fryer to 350-360°. Cut the dough into approximately 3 x 4 inch rectangles. Fry, one or two at a time, spooning hot oil over the top to encourage even puffing. Drain on paper towels and dust with powdered sugar (omit powdered sugar if using savory filling). The Sopaipillas may be served plain, with honey or with any of the following sauces or fillings. Sopaipillas are filled after frying by making a slit in each and spooning in the filling. Yield: 16 Sopaipillas.

Sweet Cream Sauce:

This is my version of a sour cream sauce studded with nuts and raisins from Ninfa's Restaurant in San Antonio.

> ¼ cup seedless raisins
> 2 ounces warmed Kahlua
> 1½ cups heavy cream, chilled
> 2 tablespoons powdered sugar
> ¼ teaspoons cinnamon, optional
> ½ cup chopped pecans or walnuts
> ½ teaspoon vanilla (Mexican preferred)

Soak the raisins in the Kahlua for 15 minutes. Insert the metal blade and pour the cream through the feed tube with the machine running and process until thickened. Add powdered sugar and cinnamon and process until thickened and combined. (Watch closely for the cream can turn to butter.) Fold together the cream, raisins and liquid, nuts and the vanilla. Spoon the sauce over warm Sopaipillas. Yield: about 3 cups.

Savory Fillings:

You can use the following savory fillings for Sopaipillas, or, for sweet fillings, the apple recipe that follows, Mincemeat (p.58), or any of your favorite fruit fillings.

1. Spicy Meat Hash (p.57)
2. Chicken Stew (p.56)
3. Seasoned Meat (p.58)

Apple Filling:

Make the Sopaipillas larger (about 10 instead of 16) and fill with the following.

> 4 apples, peeled and quartered
> juice of 1 lemon
> ½ cup sugar
> 3 tablespoons butter
> pinch cinnamon
> 2 tablespoons cornstarch
> ¼ cup apple juice
> whipped cream or ice cream, optional

Sprinkle the apples with half of the lemon juice. Place 2 of the quartered apples in the work bowl using the metal blade and pulse until chopped into thumbnail size pieces. Remove and repeat with the remaining apples.

Place the chopped apples, sugar and butter in a small saucepan and simmer until soft. Stir in the remaining lemon juice and cinnamon. Dissolve the cornstarch in the apple juice, then stir into the saucepan. Cook, stiring, until thickened.

Fill the Sopaipillas as directed and top each with whipped cream or ice cream, if desired.

Navaho Fry Bread

This Albuquerque-Sante Fe specialty has become most popular throughout the Southwest. The old Mexican philosophy in which "houses are for sleeping — food is prepared outdoors" is well demonstrated in the original preparation of this dish. Since, in the old days, the breads were always cooked outdoors. Despite the national trend towards low calorie foods, Fry Bread enjoys enormous popularity and, surprisingly, the completed dish still contains fewer calories than an American hamburger!

The dough is similar to a flour tortilla without the fat. The traditional hole punched in the center is necessary for the dough puffs dramatically. After making as many fry breads as you need from the recipe, the remaining dough can be rolled a bit thinner and fried in the same way to make Buñuelos (p.237).

My favorite filling is Meat in Red Chile (p.165), but in case your time is limited, a shortened version of this is included at the end of the recipe.

> **2 cups all purpose flour**
> **1 tablespoon shortening**
> **3 teaspoons baking powder (reduce to ½ teaspoon in high altitudes)**
> **1 teaspoon salt**
> **¾ cup very hot water**
> **oil for frying**

Combine the flour, shortening, baking powder and salt in a mixing bowl. Add the hot water, stirring in with a fork. The dough should come together in a ball firm enough to roll out. (If it seems too wet, add 1-2 tablespoons additional flour). Place in a plastic bag and let rest at least 45 minutes at room temperature.

This dough is rolled and shaped in the same way as flour tortillas, but is slightly more elastic. Pinch rounds of dough about the size of a golf ball. Dip each one in flour to coat all sides. Roll several times in one direction, then turn one quarter turn and roll several times to make a 2 inch circle. The clean surface need not be dusted with flour unless the dough sticks. (The dough "feel" varies with different brands of flour and is dependent upon the humidity of the room). After working with the dough a few times, you will develop the proper "feel." This is quite similar to the dough for flour tortillas, fried Empanadas, Sopaipillas and Buñuelos so if you master one, you master them all.

After rolling all the 2 inch circles, roll the dough again in the same manner to obtain very thin circles about 7 inches in diameter. Try to roll the dough only about two times in each direction so that it will not be overworked. Let the circles rest 2-3 minutes, then poke a hole in the center of each.

Heat about 2 inches of oil in a deep pan large enough to accommodate the circles to 375-380°. Fry the circles, one at a time, until browned and crisp. They cook very quickly if the oil is at the proper temperature. Drain on paper towels and top with one of the following fillings, Meat in Red Chile, or nearly anything that appeals to you. Makes about 12 breads.

Meat Filling:

> **2 cups cold cooked pork or beef, cut in chunks**
> **½ cup beef stock**
> **1 tablespoon chile powder**
> **3 tablespoons tomato sauce, approximately shredded Iceburg or Romaine lettuce chopped tomatoes chopped avocado**

Place the meat in the workbowl fitted with the metal blade. Pulse several times to coarsely chop. Put the chopped meat in a skillet and stir in the beef stock and chile powder. Add enough tomato sauce to coat the meat. Simmer 5-8 minutes over medium-low heat to blend the flavors.

Meanwhile, prepare the garnishes. Lettuce should be sliced with the 3mm (standard) slicing disc. (Romaine should be placed vertically in the feed tube.) Cut the avocado by hand into pieces about the size of your thumb. Tomatoes should be chopped by hand if quite ripe. Otherwise they can be processed using a French Fry disc and draining off excess liquid.

Use the filling to stuff the fry breads. The amounts of filling can easily be varied to suit your own needs.

Bean and Cheese Filling:

> **1½ cups warm Refried Beans (p.215)**
> **6 ounces grated Cheddar or Swiss cheese**
> **4 green chiles, roasted and peeled (p.14), cut into strips and lightly salted**

Spoon the beans on the warm fried breads. Top with the cheese and chile strips.

Buñuelos
Fritters

If you have ever watched Mexican women making Buñuelos by hand, you will instantly have a new appreciation for the cook's skill. Often described as "just another pancake," Buñuelos are usually a very thin flour tortilla dough which is fried rather than cooked on a griddle. There are two varieties — one with eggs and one without. You will notice a similarity in this dough and the ones for Sopaipillas, flour tortillas and Indian Fry Bread. I have even seen some very old recipes using part corn meal with the finished "buñuelo" sprinkled with sugar. I have given two recipes in this book for Buñeulos. The first is a simple dough like flour tortillas and the other a specialty of a well-known Mexican American cook, Ninfa Laurenzo, which has anise and eggs added.

The recipe is simple. The skill comes in getting the soft, elastic dough into a thin circle without toughening, tearing or worse yet — sticking to everything! Mexican women seem to inherit this art, but it is helpful to have a thin rolling pin (a 10-12 inch piece of a broom handle does quite nicely). Preliminary shaping is also important. Buñuelos keep well, airtight, for about a week.

Popular year round in the Southwest and sometimes served with ice cream, Buñuelos are, however, a traditional Christmas Eve confection served with foaming mugs of hot chocolate. It is not unusual to find raisins added to the sugar syrup and one of my northern Mexican-American friends uses the syrup from canned guavas to replace half the sugar and water in the syrup ingredients (see note).

You can make a "quick" Buñuelo by frying commercial flour tortillas (see recipe for Sun Baskets or Cinnamon Crisps on p.242). When quartered, these make an easy and terrific edible decoration for ice creams or sherbets.

The Dough:
    2½ cups all purpose flour
    1 teaspoon baking powder
    ½ teaspoon salt
    1 tablespoon sugar
    2 tablespoons lard or shortening
    1 cup (approximately) boiling water
    oil for deep-frying
    cinnamon sugar or powdered sugar

The Syrup:
    1 stick cinnamon (preferably Canela)
    1 cup brown sugar
    2½ cups water, see note
    ½ cups seedless raisins, optional

Place the flour, baking powder, salt, sugar and lard in a mixing bowl. Stir with a fork to evenly distribute the ingredients. Stir the boiling water into the dough with a fork, then turn onto a lightly floured work surface. Knead about 1 minute to make a smooth ball of dough, then cover with plastic wrap and let rest about 1 hour.

Pinch off 15-16 rounds of dough, each about the size of a golf ball. If the dough sticks to your hands, work in a bit more flour when rolling and flour your hands when shaping. Using your thumbs, flatten each ball into a thick, fat cake and place on a lightly floured work surface. This is the preliminary shaping.

When ready to fry, heat about 3 inches of oil to 375°. Also make the syrup by bringing all syrup ingredients except optional raisins to a boil, stirring to dissolve sugar. Then boil gently, undisturbed, to 260° on a candy thermometer or until syrup begins to spin a fine thread when dropped from a wooden spoon. This takes 12-15 minutes. Stir the raisins into the thickened syrup. Remove cinnamon stick before serving.

While the syrup is cooking, dip each dough cake in flour to coat both sides. Then roll with a thin rolling pin using several decisive strokes in one direction. Give the dough a one-quarter turn and roll again in the opposite direction to make a thin circle. This takes a bit of practice, but lopsided circles are better than overworked dough. Try to roll as thin as possible, then drop the Buñuelos, one at a time, into the hot oil. Fry, turning once, until crisp and golden. This takes less than a minute. Drain on paper towels and sprinkle with cinnamon sugar or powered sugar.

These may be served immediately drizzled with the hot syrup. Or they can be stacked and wrapped in plastic wrap for up to a week. Reheat syrup when ready to serve. Makes 15-16 Buñuelos.

Note: You may substitute 1 cup heavy syrup from canned mangos or guavas. Reduce sugar to ⅔ cup and water to 2 cups.

Ninfa's Buñuelos
Ninfa's Fritters

There are as many variations of Buñuelos as there are cooks. Some have eggs, some milk and some cinnamon. This one, flavored with anise, is the favorite of the owner of a wonderful Texas restaurant chain, Ninfa's. Note the two lovely presentations at the end of the recipe.

The Syrup:
1 tablespoon anise seed
1 cup packed dark brown sugar
3 cups water
1 cinnamon stick, broken

The Dough:
1/2 tablespoon anise seed
1/2 cup water
2 cups all purpose flour
1 1/2 teaspoons baking powder
1/4 teaspoon salt
1 egg, lightly beaten
oil for frying
cinnamon sugar

First, make the syrup. Boil the anise seed, brown sugar, water and cinnamon stick until thick and syrupy (220° on a candy thermometer). Let cool, then strain and set aside.

Make the dough. Place the anise seed and water in a small saucepan. Bring to a boil, then remove from heat. In a mixing bowl, combine the flour, baking powder and salt. Add the hot anise water with the seeds and the egg. Mix with a fork, then knead thoroughly with your hands to make a smooth dough. Place the dough in a plastic bag and let rest at room temperature at least 30 minutes or up to 2 hours.

Pinch off balls of dough about the size of a golf ball. Dip each one in flour, then flatten with your hands to a 2-3 inch circle. Place one circle on a clean, dry surface. Use a rolling pin to make thin circles. The best method is to roll several times in one direction, turn the dough a quarter-turn and then roll firmly in the same direction. If the dough sticks, dip again in flour, shaking off excess. The object is to make circles with as few rolls as possible to avoid overworking the dough. Until you are adept at this, it is better to have lopsided circles than overworked perfect ones. Repeat the process to roll out all the buñuelos. Allow them to rest while you heat the oil for frying.

To fry, heat at least 2 inches of oil in a deep saucepan large enough to accommodate the buñuelos to 375°. Shake off any excess flour, then fry one at a time. Turn carefully with tongs to brown both sides. Do not spoon oil over the top of the frying buñuelos or the dough will puff outrageously. When crisp and brown, drain on a paper towel and dust lightly with cinnamon sugar while still hot. Repeat to fry all the buñuelos. If smaller buñuelos are desired, simply make the dough balls smaller. Roll out and fry as directed above.

Before serving, drizzle with the warmed sugar syrup. Serve this dessert warm. Makes about 12.

Here are two of my favorite presentations for Buñuelos:

1. Serve the Buñuelos with a scoop of Vanilla Ice (p.246) or your favorite ice cream. Drizzle with the anise sugar syrup and garnish with a single slice of tropical fruit (papaya, mango, pomegranate seeds or pineapple).

2. After rolling the dough, cut each circle in half. Use tongs when frying to turn up both edges to produce a half-cone shape. Dust with powdered sugar. Then place curled Buñuelo in a sherbet dish with a scoop of Vanilla Ice or Mexican Chocolate Ice (p.247) and drizzle with the anise sugar syrup.

Spanish Fritters
Churros

This popular light and crispy Spanish pastry is often sold by street vendors in the border towns from Texas to California. My search for the recipe began when one of my restaurant friends showed me an old tin contraption that resembled an oversized cooky gun which was used to squeeze out the churro dough. I have since encountered recipes varying from "cream puff dough" to "just another Buñuelo." After much experimentation, this is the formula that I found most satisfactory.

The Cinnamon Sugar:
   1 cup granulated sugar
   2 teaspoons cinnamon

The Dough and Preparation:
   1 cup water
   1/4 stick (1 ounce) butter
   2 tablespoons vegetable shortening
   1 tablespoon sugar
   1/2 teaspoon salt
   1/2 cup white cornmeal
   1/2 cup all purpose flour
   2 large eggs
   peanut oil for deep frying

Combine the sugar and cinnamon in a shallow bowl and reserve.

In a 3 quart saucepan bring the water, butter, shortening, sugar and salt to a rolling boil. Remove from heat and stir in the cornmeal and flour all at once. Return to low heat and stir vigorously with a wooden spoon until a ball of dough forms. Remove from heat and place the warm dough in the work bowl using the metal blade. Add the eggs and process about 20 seconds until smooth and shiny.

Meanwhile, heat 3 inches of oil in a deep heavy skillet or deep fryer to 375°. Transfer the dough to a pastry bag fitted with a #5 star tip. Pipe 8-10 inch strips of dough into the hot oil and fry on both sides until browned and crisp. Drain on paper towels and dredge in the cinnamon sugar. Be sure the oil remains at a constant temperature for even cooking. Yield: about 12.

Here are two variations on churros:

1. Add 1/2 teaspoon anise oil to the batter with the flour and cornmeal.

2. Add 2 tablespoons unsweetened cocoa and 2 tablespoons additional sugar with the eggs. Dredge in the cinnamon sugar or dust with plain powdered sugar.

Tortillas

Corn and flour tortillas, often called the "knife, fork, plate and napkin" of the Southwest are an integral part of the majority of dishes from the Southwest. Tortillas have been called the bread of Mexican food, but they are actually far more versatile. They serve as scoop, croutons, pasta, thickening for soups and sauces and, when broken up, as a base for casserole dishes.

Homemade corn tortillas, prepared with fresh ground masa and shaped by hand are a rare and delicious treat. Unfortunately, it is next to impossible for home cooks to duplicate a tortilla made from fresh ground nixtamal. Attempts to do so with Masa Harina can be both frustrating and disappointing. Fresh masa is made from nixtamal, which requires a lengthy process of boiling dry white field corn with lime. After washing the nixtamal, it is then wet ground (usually by machine) into fresh masa from which corn tortillas are made. The dry grinding process that produces cornmeal is quite different and cannot produce a good corn tortilla. Therefore, I recommend that packaged, commercial tortillas be used for all the recipes in this book that call for cooked tortillas. Despite being machine made, they are quite good and many brands made locally in Mexican-American neighborhoods are indeed fresh and of excellent quality. The best ones for Enchiladas are thin and pliable. Good quality corn tortillas will probably puff and could be separated into two layers when fried. Frozen ones are the next best choice. Canned corn tortillas are dreadful and should be avoided. Brand names differ in all areas, so it may take a bit of searching to find what's available.

Salted corn chips under varying names are not good substitutes for tostados and I urge you to prepare your own from corn tortillas (see tostados on p.242)

Flour tortillas are usually slightly larger than standard corn tortillas. There are also 12 inch Burrito size and 18 inch Sonora-style flour tortillas. Flour tortillas are now widely available, but the homemade ones are significantly better and well worth the effort. It does take some practice to produce tender tortillas. A tortilla press is not used; these delicate discs are rolled by hand. The packaged ones are especially good if buttered, then reheated by grilling or toasting.

Both corn and flour tortillas freeze well and fresh ones will keep 4-5 days refrigerated. The best bet is to find some Southwestern friends to keep you in good supply!

Flour Tortillas

Tortillas Trigo

A homemade fresh flour tortilla can compete with your Grandmother's prize biscuits. It is an art that is "passed down" and especially highly respected in Southwest Texas and New Mexico. If you have ever watched Mexican women mix and roll out flour tortillas or read some of the simple recipes, you would never suspect the skill and art involved. They produce light, thin and delicate tortillas with apparant ease while many dedicated American cooks struggle to produce even a mediocre result.

There seem to be several secrets: fresh flour, good quality shortening, a thin, short rolling pin (often a sawed-off broom handle) and a two-step process of shaping, rolling and resting the dough. I have been told that accurate measurements are essential, but this seems almost unbelievable after watching Mexican-Americans do this almost intuitively with their hands. A greater amount of shortening produces a softer, lighter tortilla but an excess of shortening or a heavy hand may produce a greasy or cracked result.

While frozen tortillas are acceptable (though not nearly as tender or tasty) and split Pita bread is a good substitute in some dishes, a freshly made flour tortilla really has no equal. There is an old Indian saying: "After tasting flour tortillas, the children cry for them as a man craves good whiskey."

Use vegetable or animal fat in this recipe. Butter or margarine will not produce the desired result.

> **2 cups all-purpose flour**
> **1½ teaspoons salt**
> **1½ teaspoons baking powder**
> **4-5 tablespoons vegetable shortening or lard, softened**
> **¾ cup very hot water, approximately**

Use a blending fork or your hands to combine the flour, salt, baking powder and shortening in a mixing bowl. Be sure the shortening is evenly distributed. (You could use a food processor, but there is a risk of overprocessing.) Using a blending fork, blend in enough hot water to make a moderately soft dough that is like a stiff biscuit dough. Using your hands, gently knead the dough for 10-15 seconds. If the dough seems too wet to knead, work in 1-2 tablespoons additional flour. Cover the dough with oiled plastic wrap and let rest in a warm place for 20 minutes.

Pinch off golf ball size rounds of dough and place in a plastic bag. Let rest 20 minutes or up to 3 hours at room temperature.

When you are ready to roll out the tortillas, begin heating a well-seasoned cast iron skillet or griddle. (Non-stick electric fry-pans and crepemakers can be used provided they maintain a high enough heat, but the tortillas are not as tender.) The pan should be heated to 425-450° (a drop of water will sizzle on the pan). This is a "pancake type" operation in that you are rolling out and cooking at the same time.

Dip each ball of dough in flour to lightly coat. Use your thumbs to gently stretch each into 2-2½ inch circle. (This preliminary stretching helps eliminate the common problem of dough shrinkage while rolling.) Use a marble or metal work surface to prevent sticking and roll the circles, one at a time, using a thin rolling pin. Roll with several short, confident strokes into an oval. Give the dough a quarter turn and roll again to obtain a thin circle. (Your first tries will probably produce a lopsided circle, but this is better than overworking the dough.) The ideal tortilla is very thin, but thicker ones are just as tasty.

Carefully lift the rolled tortilla and immediately place on the preheated pan or griddle. Cook 30-45 seconds until little bubbles appear on the surface. Use a spatula to flip the tortilla and cook just a few seconds on the other side. Do not push down the air bubbles or the tortilla will be tough and greasy. Repeat to use all of the dough balls. As the tortillas are finished, stack them and then wrap in a towel or foil to keep warm and soft.

Tortillas can be frozen and reheated. Freeze in a stack with a sheet of waxed paper between each tortilla. Overwrap the entire stack with foil or freezer paper. To use frozen tortillas, thaw first and reheat on a hot griddle or skillet for a few seconds on a side.

If you are lucky enough to be able to buy good fresh tortillas (from a restaurant for example), they can be used fresh or frozen and reheated as directed above.

Tortillas were traditionally served spread with meat drippings. The custom today is to use butter and salt. Makes 12-14 tortillas.

1 Mixing fat into the flour

2 Finished texture

3 Incorporating warm water into fat and flour

4 Completed dough ball ready to be covered and set aside

5 Pinching off section of dough

6 Shaping round of dough

7 Pinching to close seam

8 Preliminary shaping into 3-3½″ circle

9 Rolling into an oval

10 Rolling into a circle after a quarter turn

Sun Baskets or Cinnamon Crisps

Sun Baskets are made from prepared flour tortillas. They are fried, then dredged in cinnamon sugar to make a crisp, sweet pastry. When the tortilla is quartered before frying, the result is a "cookie" that is a grand garnish for Ices, Granitas or Sherbets. When shaped into a "sun-basket," they become the double container for the same desserts. Packaged flour tortillas make wonderful "sun-baskets."

> 1 cup granulated sugar
> 2 teaspoons cinnamon or 1 (1 inch) piece canela
> 6-8 packaged flour tortillas (7-8 inch size)
> oil for deep-frying

Combine the sugar and cinnamon on a shallow plate. (If you use canela, first grind it in a spice or coffee grinder.) Set aside.

To make a "sun-basket container," use scissors to cut the tortillas into the shape of a sun (see illustration, P.24). If you wish to make "cinnamon crisps" to wedge into Ices or Granitas as a cookie, cut each tortilla into quarters.

Heat about 3 inches of oil to 360° in a deep saucepan or deep-fryer. (If you are making "sun-baskets," use a pan with a diameter 1-1½ inches smaller than the tortillas for ease in shaping the basket.)

To make "sun-baskets," use tongs to push the tortillas, one at a time, into the oil. Take care that it does not stick to the bottom of the pan. Turn the tortilla as soon as it takes shape (this takes only seconds) and crisp on the other side for a few seconds. Try not to let the tortilla brown. Drain on paper towels and dredge in the cinnamon sugar while still warm.

If you are making "cinnamon crisps," fry the tortilla quarters, 3-4 at a time, for a few seconds until crisp. Drain and dredge in the cinnamon sugar while still warm.

To use the "sun-baskets," place on a small dessert dish and fill with a scoop of Ice, Sherbet or Granita (see Dessert Section) and garnish as desired. The quartered "cinnamon crisps" can be wedged into the Ices or Granitas for a stunning presentation. Yield: 6-8 sun baskets or 24-32 "cookies."

Tostados or Tostaditos
Corn Chips

Tostados or Tostaditos are the "potato chip" of the Southwest and fresh ones are infinitely better than any packaged variety. Corn tortillas have only 25-35 calories each and are a very healthy product — even the Pritikin diet approves! When quartered and fried in hot oil, very little fat is absorbed (3-5 calories per chip) and you can control the amount of added salt.

Tostados have a variety of uses: a marvelous snack chip for dipping into any Salsa, a base for Nachos (p.94) or a terrific garnish for dishes such as Marinated Fish (p.81), Pinto Beans (p.215) and all manner of salads. Leftover or broken chips can be used for Beef and Tortilla Casserole (p.162) or to pep up scrambled eggs. Many recipes throughout this book use Tostados. The following is a method; make as many as you wish.

> stale corn tortillas, quartered
> vegetable oil for frying
> salt to taste

Heat about 3 inches of oil to 375-400°. Fry 4 or 5 tortilla quarters at a time for about 45 seconds or until crisp. Drain on paper towels and add salt to taste. Store in airtight containers.

Southwest Cornbread

I think that all cornbread recipes using corn kernels or creamed corn are descendants of the Tamale Pies so prevalent throughout the Southwest.

This New Mexican dish is usually made with hot green chiles, but canned mild chiles are quite acceptable. It is a good way to use leftover corn and makes an excellent accompaniment to any main dish, especially soups and Chile con Carne.

> 2 cups cooked corn cut from the cob
>   (including the milky residue from the cob)
> 3 mild or hot green chiles (about one 3½-4
>   ounce can)
> ¼ medium size yellow onion, peeled
> ½ cup yellow cornmeal
> 2 eggs
> 1 teaspoon salt
> 1 teaspoon baking powder
> 1 tablespoon sugar
> 3 tablespoons all-purpose flour
> ¼ cup corn oil
> 1½ cups buttermilk

Use the metal blade to coarsely grind the corn kernels. Add the onion and chiles to the work bowl and pulse until coarsely chopped. Add the cornmeal, eggs, salt, baking powder, sugar, flour and oil to the workbowl. With the machine running, pour the buttermilk through the feed tube. Pour immediately into a buttered 9 or 10 inch pie pan.

Bake 1-1¼ hours in a preheated 350° oven. Serve warm. Serves 8-10.

Variation: Fold 4 ounces (1 cup) shredded or grated cheese into the finished batter. Bake as directed.

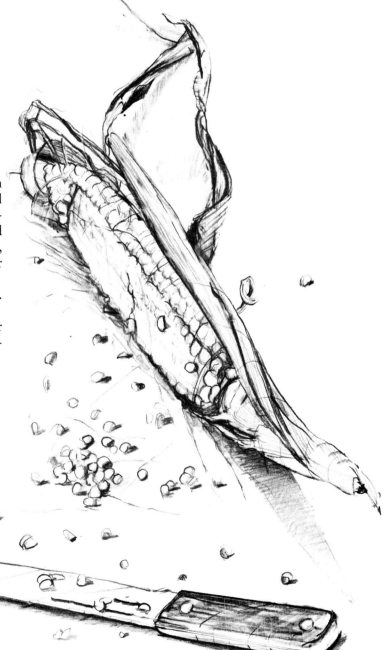

DESSERTS

Desserts in the Southwest are more than just the finale of a meal; they serve a salutary purpose. The sweetness present in a dessert has a tempering and neutralizing effect on the tongue, disarming the aftermath of hot chiles and spicy foods. It goes without saying that Southwestern desserts are colorful and delicious!

Any of the Ices, Granitas or Freezes provides a perfect light sweet course after a filling meal. You'll find techniques here to make them quickly and easily. Most of them are perfect for enthusiastic dessert lovers of all ages, though a few — those with a lacing of alcohol — are for adults only. I serve them at dinner parties, as convivial toppers to the meal.

If you want a sweet morsel to go along with the iced confections, we have a panoply of cookies. They are good snacks at any time, too. The egg custard desserts are customary endings to Mexican meals.

I have also included an array of candies. They traditionally fill the celebratory piñatas, hollow papier-mâché forms usually made to resemble animals. Blind-folded children whack at a suspended piñata with sticks, until it breaks open and rewards the little ones with a shower of candies. However, there is no need to wait for a piñata party to enjoy these candies.

In addition, I give you a marvelous cake roll, delightful crepes, a very different sweet Chimichanga, and a fruit and cheese platter that goes with any meal.

Clockwise from top center: Citrus Fruit Ice, Mango Ice, Green Lemon Sherbet with Mexican Wedding Cookies, Sugar Cookies, Mexican Chocolate Crinkles, Mexican Wedding Cookies, Anise Sugar Cookies, Coffee Granita in Sun Basket, Watermelon-Raspberry Ice.

Frozen Desserts

Ices, Granitas and Sherbets

Mexican-Americans love a variety of ice creams and sherbets. One reason, I'm sure, is that the smooth and creamy texture is a perfect ending to a spicy meal. Another is the ready availability of ripe, seasonal fruits.

I have never been patient enough to fool with a large capacity ice cream freezer and find that most reasonably priced counter models are inefficient or break down easily. Since I'm always searching for a better and easier way to prepare good food from "scratch," I turned to my food processor for help. After much experimentation, I was delighted to find that I could make nearly "instant" Ices, Granitas and Sherbets simply by freezing whole fruit pieces or a milk-sugar mixture. Shortly before serving, they can be processed, in one short step, to a perfect consistency. This technique has now been a favorite of mine and my students for years. I find the light texture and sweetness preferable to sugary commercial ices and sherbets. Since the sugar content is quite low in most, the crystals are larger and the melting time more rapid than "bought" ice creams. The addition of unflavored gelatin helps to retard the melting time.

In experimenting with different fruit and juice combinations, I find that watermelon, used alone or in combination with other fruits, gives an excellent texture to a sherbet or ice. Since watermelon is not always available, I have developed a method using frozen sweetened milk in conjunction with the frozen fruits. Fruit juice can also be used to make an ice or sherbet.

These recipes for Ices, Granitas and Sherbets presented here are my favorites, but you can develop your own variations with different combinations of fruits. Amounts given are for standard size food processors. Double quantities can be made in large capacity machines.

Vanilla Ice
Granita de Vanilla

If you can obtain Mexican vanilla, be sure to use it in this creamy dessert. Otherwise, use the best quality pure vanilla extract that you can find.

  2 cups whole milk
  1 1/2 packages unflavored gelatin
  1/3 cup cold water
  1 cup granulated sugar
  2 teaspoons vanilla, preferably Mexican
  1 (13 ounce) can evaporated milk
  2 cups plus 6 tablespoons half and half or heavy cream
  2-3 tablespoons additional milk or cream, if needed

Bring the whole milk to a boil. Soften the gelatin in the cold water, then stir into the boiling milk until dissolved. Keep hot.

Place the sugar and vanilla in the workbowl using the metal blade. With the machine running, pour 1 1/2 cups of the hot milk mixture through the feed tube and process until the sugar is dissolved. Pour into a large bowl and stir in the remaining milk, the evaporated milk and the cream. Pour into 3 divided ice cube trays or a large shallow freezer container. Freeze at least 24 hours or up to 3 days.

At serving time or up to 3 hours ahead, remove one ice cube tray from freezer and run a knife around the edges of the "cubes" to loosen. (If using a single freezer container, use a knife to remove 1/3 of the mixture and cut into 1 1/2 inch cubes.) Place the "cubes" in the workbowl using the metal blade. Pulse 15-20 times until the mixture is chopped and has a "snowy" texture. Run machine continuously until the mixture swirls around the blade and begins to look like ice cream. (This will take a minute or longer and you may need to add a small amount of additional milk or cream to hasten the process. Take care to add as little as necessary or the ice will become runny.)

One tray of "cubes" will serve 2-3 people. Process the remaining, one tray at a time, to serve more.

Serve immediately or return the finished ice to the freezer for up to 3 hours. Serve topped with Kahlua or your favorite liqueur. Serves 8-10.

Variation: Pulse 1 1/2 cups coarsely chopped Mexican Praline into the finished ice. (Be sure to use firm, not chewy pralines.)

Mexican Chocolate Ice
Granita de Chocolate

When Cortes found Montezuma II, he was astonished by the vast array of food that people prepared for each meal. He was most impressed by a delicious chocolate beverage flavored with an unusual ingredient made from an orchid. The Mayans had used chocolate in Mexico for centuries and enjoyed steaming, frothy mugs of the rich beverage sweetened with honey. In mountainous areas, this drink was chilled with snow. Cortes was so taken with the result that he found time to stop by the local market, as he fled from Mexico, to take home some of the treasured chocolate beans and vanilla pods.

This granita has a light chocolate taste with a delicate hint of cinnamon. Use Mexican chocolate if you can.

    3 cups whole milk
    6 ounces Mexican chocolate or 4 ounces
        semi-sweet chocolate plus 1/4 teaspoon
        cinnamon
    1/2 cup granulated sugar
    1 package unflavored gelatin
    1/4 cup cold water
    1 cup half and half or heavy cream
    1 1/2 teaspoons vanilla, preferably Mexican
    1-2 tablespoons additional cream if needed

Bring the whole milk to a boil, then reduce heat and keep hot.

Cut the chocolate into 6-8 pieces. Using the metal blade, drop the chocolate pieces through the feed tube with the motor running to chop. Process until finely ground. Add the sugar and cinnamon, if using, and process until the mixture is evenly and finely ground. Leave in workbowl.

With the machine running, pour 1 cup of the hot milk through the feed tube and process until the chocolate is melted. Reserve.

Soften the gelatin in the cold water, then stir into the remaining 2 cups hot milk until dissolved. Stir together the hot milk, the chocolate mixture, the vanilla and the half and half or cream.

Pour the mixture into 2 divided ice cube trays or a large shallow freezer container. Freeze at least 24 hours or up to 3 days.

At serving time or up to 3 hours ahead, remove one ice cube tray from freezer and run a knife around the edges of the "cubes" to loosen. (If using a single freezer container, use a knife to remove half of the mixture and cut into 1 1/2 inch cubes. Return remaining mixture to freezer.) Place the cubes

in the workbowl using the metal blade. Pulse 15-20 times until the mixture is finely chopped and begins to look like "chocolate snow." Then run the machine continuously for a minute or more until the mixture swirls around the blade and begins to look like ice cream. (It may be necessary to add 1-2 tablespoons additional milk or cream to hasten this process.) Stop to scrape sides of workbowl as necessary.

This much granita serves 3-4 people. If you wish to serve more, process the remaining cubes in the same manner. (The entire amount may be processed at one time in a large capacity processor providing you chop half of the mixture before adding the remainder.)

Serve immediately or return to freezer for up to 3 hours. Serves 6-8.

Kahlua-Coffee Freeze

This very adult dessert is like a thick, heavenly coffee milkshake. Serve it in your prettiest glassware, with Mexican Nut Cookies (p.261), for an elegant finish to any meal.

**1 cup excellent quality coffee ice cream
3 cups excellent quality vanilla ice cream
1/3 cup Amaretto liqueur
1/3 cup Kahlua
1/4 cup heavy cream, optional**

Using the metal blade, drop spoonfuls of the ice creams through the feed tube with the motor running until smooth. You may need to scrape the sides of the workbowl several times. Add the liqueurs, processing to combine. If the mixture seems too thick, stir in the optional cream.

Serve immediately or freeze for several hours. You may need to stir the drink, if frozen, to restore the smooth texture. The liqueurs, however, prevent it from freezing solid.

Use a straw, spoon or both. Serves 6.

Coffee Granita
Granita de Café

Coffee gelatin or "granitas" are a popular dessert in Southwest Texas. Granitas are by definition low in sugar, have large crystals and are "stirred" rather than churned in an ice cream freezer. This one-step food processor method produces a smooth and delicious ice or granita which is much lighter than rich ice cream. It refreezes well and, when served with chocolate curls in a cinnamon-sugared Sun Basket, tastes like frozen Cappuccino. Coffee Granita has long been a favorite dessert among my family and friends.

**1 envelope unflavored gelatin
1/2 cup cold water
1 1/2 teaspoons vanilla
3 cups very hot coffee
3/4 cup sugar
3-4 tablespoons Kahlua
1 cup heavy cream, well chilled
2 tablespoons powdered sugar
chocolate curls
Sun Baskets (p.242), optional presentation**

Soften the gelatin in the cold water and vanilla, then dissolve in the hot coffee. Stir in the sugar until dissolved. Let cool, then pour into two divided ice cube trays. Freeze at least 12 hours or overnight.

Remove one ice cube tray from the freezer and run a knife around the edges for easy removal. Process half the cubes using the metal blade and pulsing until the mixture looks like shaved ice or fine "snow." Add the remaining chunks and process in the same manner. Then run the machine continuously to make an ice cream-like texture. With the motor running, add the Kahlua through the feed tube. Remove the granita from the workbowl and replace in the freezer. Process the mixture in the second ice cube tray in the same manner and refreeze while making the whipped cream.

In a clean workbowl fitted with the metal blade, pour the chilled cream through the feed tube with the motor running. Process a few seconds or up to a minute until thickened. (Watch carefully for the cream can quickly turn to butter.) Pulse in the powdered sugar just until blended.

To serve the granita, spoon into sherbet dishes or into Sun Baskets and garnish with the whipped cream and chocolate curls. Serves 6.

Note: The granita may be made and refrozen up to 3 days. After that it becomes quite icy.

Watermelon-Raspberry Ice
Granita de Sandiá

This technique for making sherbet eliminates the usual two-step procedure of processing before and then again after freezing. The result is a smooth and creamy dessert. For best texture the ice should be served within 30 minutes of processing since, due to a low sugar content, the mixture will freeze quite hard. If you wish to make a sweeter ice, add ½ cup granulated sugar to the watermelon cubes during processing.

> **4 cups watermelon cubes, seeded and cut in 1 inch cubes**
> **⅓ package (10 ounce package) frozen sweetened raspberries or strawberries**
> **⅓ cup heavy cream or unflavored yogurt**
> **½ cup miniature chocolate chips, optional**

Place the watermelon cubes in plastic bags and freeze solid. Remove from the freezer 5 minutes before ready to make the ice. Cut the frozen berries into 2 inch chunks.

Using the metal blade, place half of the watermelon cubes in the workbowl and pulse until the cubes are finely chopped and resemble shaved ice. Add the remaining cubes and all of the berry cubes. Add the cream and process until the ice is smooth and creamy, stopping several times to scrape sides of workbowl.

Store in freezer and serve within 30 minutes. Just before serving, stir in the optional chocolate chips to resemble watermelon "seeds." Serves 5-6.

Papaya Ice

This light and delicate fruit ice is lovely served in sherbet glasses with a mint sprig, or quartered and crisply fried flour tortillas triangles dipped in cinnamon, or with a slice of fresh fruit and served in a Mexican Sun Basket (p.242). Be sure to begin the recipe at least 24 hours ahead.

Milk-Sugar Mixture:
> **2 cups whole milk**
> **⅓ cup granulated sugar**
> **1 teaspoon gelatin**
> **½ teaspoon vanilla**

Fruit Mixture:
> **1 ripe papaya**
> **¼ cup sugar**
> **3 peeled fresh orange slices (if needed)**
> **2-3 tablespoons fresh orange juice or cream (if needed)**

Bring the milk to a boil. Meanwhile, place the sugar and gelatin in the workbowl using the metal blade. With the machine running, pour 1 cup of the boiling milk and then the vanilla through the feed tube. By hand, stir in the remaining milk and pour the mixture into an ice cube tray. Freeze at least 24 hours or until quite solid.

Peel, seed and cut the ripe papaya into chunks about the size of ice cubes. Sprinkle with ¼ cup sugar. If the fruit is not fully ripe, add the orange slices. Place the mixture in plastic bags, seal and freeze at least 12 hours until solid.

Run a knife around the edge of the milk-sugar cubes and remove ⅓ (5-6 cubes) from the tray. (Re-freeze the remainder for use in another batch of fruit ice). Separate the papaya chunks, but do not let either the fruit or milk-sugar cubes thaw. Place both mixtures in the processor fitted with the metal blade and pulse until very finely chopped and looks like "snow." Then run the machine continuously, pulsing if the mixture masses together, until an ice cream-like texture is achieved. Stop the machine and scrape sides of workbowl several times. Depending upon the moisture content of the fruit, it is often necessary to add 2-3 tablespoons of orange juice or cream (I prefer some of each) to make a creamy texture.

This can be served at once or refrozen for 3-4 hours. After that, it becomes quite hard. Serves 3-4.

Mango Ice

Fresh mangos are very difficult to obtain and even more difficult to core. For these reasons frozen or canned mangos are better. This delicious "ice" is simple to prepare and is especially attractive served "Mexican Style" in Sun Baskets (p.242). Be sure to begin preparation 24 hours in advance.

Milk-Sugar Mixture:
2 cups whole milk
1/3 cup granulated sugar
1 teaspoon gelatin

Fruit Mixture:
2 1/2 cups fresh mango chunks or 1/2 can mangos including juice (about the size of ice cubes)
2-3 tablespoons lime juice or cream

Bring the milk to a boil. Meanwhile place the sugar and gelatin in the workbowl fitted with the metal blade. With the machine running, pour 1 cup of the boiling milk through the feed tube. By hand, combine with the remaining milk and pour the mixture into an ice cube tray. Freeze at least 24 hours or until quite solid.

Place the mangos and their juice into plastic bags. Seal and freeze until solid — at least 12 hours.

When ready to process the ice, have ready both frozen mixtures as well as the processor fitted with the metal blade. Use a sharp knife to cut the frozen mango into blocks about the size of ice cubes. Place in workbowl. Run a knife around the edge of the milk-sugar cubes and remove 1/3 (5-6 cubes) from the tray. (Re-freeze the remainder for use in another batch of fruit ice.) Add the cubes to the workbowl and pulse until the mixture is very finely chopped and looks like a snow cone. Then run the machine continuously, pulsing if the mixture masses together, until an ice cream-like texture is achieved. Depending upon the moisture content of the fruit, it may be necessary to add 2-3 tablespoons lime juice or cream and scrape the sides of the workbowl to achieve a creamy texture.

The ice may be served immediately in the Sun Baskets or in sherbet glasses garnished with mint sprigs and a single fresh fruit slice. The "ice" may also be refrozen up to 3-4 hours before serving. Serves 4.

Pina Colada Freeze

This is an icy dessert version of the popular Pina Colada cocktail. The sweetness of the drink lends itself well to a refreshing dessert. If you wish to omit the alcohol, use 1 teaspoon rum extract instead of the Triple-sec and rum.

1 cup fresh very ripe pineapple, crushed or 1 cup canned crushed pineapple
1/2 cup coconut milk or coconut cream
1/2 cup fresh squeezed orange juice
1/2 ounce light rum
1/2 ounce Triple-sec
2-3 tablespoons heavy cream if needed
1/2 cup sweetened coconut for garnish
1 tablespoon butter

Begin preparation at least 24 hours in advance. If you are using fresh pineapple, it may be crushed by using the metal blade. Stir together the pineapple, coconut milk, orange juice, rum and Triple-sec. Pour into a divided ice cube tray and freeze solid for about 24 hours.

Just prior to serving or up to 4 hours in advance, finish the dessert. Run a knife around the edges of the "cubes" and place in the workbowl using the metal blade. Pulse the machine until the mixture is finely chopped, then run continuously to make a smooth, ice cream-like texture. It is usually necessary to add 2-3 tablespoons heavy cream to achieve the desired consistency.

Spoon into dessert bowls and freeze until serving time.

In a small skillet, saute the coconut in the butter until golden. Let cool and use to garnish the dessert. Serves 3-4.

Green Lemon Sherbet

Sorbete de Limón Verde

Make this when you have fresh mint in your garden. Southwesterners from New Mexico share the Mexican love for wild mint (yerba buena) in both sweet and savory dishes. This recipe is adapted from the Ringland's *Fiestas Mexicanas*. I like the icy fresh taste following a picante meal.

    2 cups water
    1 cup sugar
    1½ cups fresh mint leaves
    ½ envelope unflavored gelatin
    ⅓ cup cold water
    ⅓ cup fresh lemon or lime juice or a few
        drops more if necessary
    ⅓ pinch salt
    1 tablespoon green creme de menthe
    1 fresh mint for garnish

Boil the water, sugar and mint leaves together for 2 minutes. Then allow to "steep" until cool. Strain and reserve liquid.

Soften the gelatin in cold water, then add 1 cup of the "mint water" and heat gently, stirring to dissolve gelatin.

Combine dissolved gelatin mixture, remaining mint water, ⅓ cup lemon juice, salt and creme de menthe. Freeze in two divided ice cube trays at least 12 hours or overnight.

When frozen solid, remove from freezer and run a knife around the edges of the cubes to loosen. Transfer the cubes, one tray at a time, to the work bowl using the metal blade. Pulse until the cubes are finely chopped, then run machine continuously until you have a smooth, ice cream-like texture. It may be necessary to add a few drops lemon juice as the mixture is processing. Serve immediately garnished with fresh mint or re-freeze up to 3-4 hours. Serves 6-8.

Citrus Fruit Ice

This ice is very attractive served in fresh orange or lemon shells and garnished with a sprig of mint.

    zest of 2 lemons or 1 orange (colored part
        only)
    1¼ cups sugar
    1½ cups water
    1 envelope unflavored gelatin
    ⅓ cup cold water
    ¾ cup fresh lemon or orange juice
    1 cup evaporated milk
    ½ cup heavy cream or half and half cream
    3 tablespoons additional lemon or orange
        juice if needed

Use the metal blade to process the citrus zest with the sugar until finely minced. Bring the zest, sugar and water to a boil and allow to boil 3-4 minutes to make a syrup.

Soften the gelatin in cold water, then dissolve in the hot sugar syrup. Add the fruit juice and let the mixture cool. Stir in the milk and cream and pour into two divided ice cube trays. Freeze 8-12 hours or until very solid.

When ready to serve the ice or up to 4 hours ahead, remove trays from the freezer and run a knife around the edges of the "cubes" to loosen. Do not allow to thaw. Place all of the cubes in the workbowl using the metal blade. Pulse until the mixture is finely chopped and resembles shaved ice. Then run the machine continuously to make a texture similar to soft-serve ice cream. You may neeed to add a small amount of juice during the final processing if the cubes have been frozen extremely hard.

Serve immediately or refreeze up to 4 hours. Serves 6.

Egg Custard Desserts

Mild and egg custards such as Flans, meringue or flavored gelatin desserts are reflections of the Spanish influence in Mexican-American food. Many old Southwestern cookbooks feature desserts using uncooked egg white meringues, usually served with a custard sauce but sometimes filled with a combination of candied fruits and nuts. Whipped cream was rarely used in these old desserts.

Almendrado is a popular uncooked meringue and gelatin dessert in California, Arizona and parts of New Mexico. It is nearly always colored red and green (the colors in the Mexican flag) and served with a rich "creme anglaise" or custard sauce. Because I am not fond of artificial food color, I have taken great liberties with these classic Almendrado recipes by flavoring the sauce with raspberry jam and creme de menthe to add both taste and color. The Chocolate Almondrado on p. 257 has a baked meringue and an Italian meringue is used in the Coconut Almondrado on p. 258. I hope that you are as happy with the results as I am.

Sweet Rice Pudding
Pudin de Arroz Dulce

This sweet dessert will bring back childhood memories for many people. I prefer to make a plain pudding and serve it accompanied by small bowls of plumped raisins, coarsely chopped guava and seasonal tropical fruits.

3 cups whole milk
1 cinnamon stick
1/2 cup long grain rice
1 cup water
1/4 teaspoon salt
1/4-1/3 cup sugar (the greater amount makes a sweeter pudding)
1 teaspoon Mexican vanilla or 2 teaspoons pure vanilla extract
1/2 cup half and half or heavy cream
1 egg, separated (optional to make a lighter pudding)

Garnishes:
1/2 cup white seedless raisins plumped in 1/4 cup wine or Kahlua
6 canned or fresh guavas, coarsely chopped
chopped tropical fruits such as papaya or pineapple

Heat the milk and cinnamon stick in a 2 quart saucepan until bubbles form around the edge and nearly comes to a boil. Remove the scalded milk from the heat. At the same time, bring the rice and water to a boil in a 3 quart saucepan. Lower heat and stir in the salt. Simmer for 5-8 minutes until the liquid is nearly all absorbed.

Stir the scalded milk and the sugar into the rice mixture and simmer 20 minutes, stirring occasionally. Skim any residue that comes to the surface. Remove from heat, stir in vanilla and discard cinnamon stick.

Place the mixture in a 1 1/2 quart baking dish and bake, uncovered, for 30-35 minutes in a preheated 300° oven. The mixture should be "slushy" and the rice tender. Stir in the cream. (If using the egg, beat about 1/2 cup of the hot rice mixture into the beaten egg yolk, then stir back into the remaining mixture.) Bake the pudding an additional 5-10 minutes until creamy in texture.

Beat the optional egg white to stiff peaks and fold into the rice pudding. Let cool, then cover and refrigerate until serving time — up to 8 hours.

Serve the pudding accompanied by the garnishes in separate condiment dishes. Serves 8.

Caramel Custard

Flan

Depending upon custom and region, flans can be rich and heavy or light and custardy. Many old recipes call for a milk and egg custard to be baked separately from the sugar syrup. The denser Tex-Mex Flan (p.254) has more eggs and sugar and is often made with condensed milk.

I prefer the lighter Spanish-style flan. It can be made with either whole eggs or with yolks and whites beaten separately, then folded together. The addition of chocolate or coconut often improves the consistency. However you make it, a flan should be mixed together very lightly for the finest of textures.

The following recipe is simple to prepare and has a hint of orange flavor. A variation is given at the end.

> 1 cup sugar
> $^{1}/_{2}$ cup water
> 4 cups whole milk or 1 can evaporated milk
>   and enough whole milk to make 3$^{1}/_{2}$ cups
> 1-2 teaspoons fresh orange peel, orange
>   part only
> $^{1}/_{2}$ cup sugar
> 6 large eggs
> 1 teaspoon vanilla

In a small saucepan, combine 1 cup sugar and $^{1}/_{2}$ cup water and bring to a boil, stirring to dissolve the sugar. Dip a brush in ice water and use to wash down any sugar crystals clinging to the pan. Let boil, undisturbed, until it caramelizes. As soon as the sugar syrup turns an amber color, stir and take off heat. Pour immediately into a 9 x 5 loaf pan or an 8 cup ring mold, tilting pan to coat the bottom and sides with the caramel. Set aside while making the custard.

If using whole milk only, bring to a boil and simmer 12-15 minutes to reduce to 3$^{1}/_{2}$ cups. If using a mixture of evaporated and whole milk, simply bring to a boil. Meanwhile, use the metal blade to process the sugar and orange peel until the peel is grated. Add eggs and vanilla to workbowl and pulse 3-4 times to "beat" the eggs. With the machine running, add 1 cup of the hot milk through the feed tube. Stop the machine and whisk the egg-milk mixture into the remaining milk in the pan. Pour into the caramel lined pan or mold and place in a larger pan half-filled with water. Bake the flan for 1 hour and 15 minutes in a pre-heated 350° oven until a knife inserted off-center comes out clean and the custard is set.

Let cool, then chill at least 1$^{1}/_{2}$ hours before unmolding. Unmold onto a deep serving platter allowing the caramelized sauce to run over the custard. Slice to serve and include some sauce in each serving. Serves 8-10.

Variation: You can add $^{1}/_{4}$ teaspoon cinnamon (or $^{1}/_{2}$ teaspoon ground canela) to the custard with the vanilla. You can also sprinkle $^{1}/_{2}$ cup thinly sliced almonds over the caramel in the mold, adding quickly before the syrup has hardened. Proceed with the recipe as above.

Mexican Chocolate Flan with Kahlua Syrup

This is an interesting variation of the classic Flan. When the ground chocolate rises to the top with the egg whites, a light crust is formed.

1 cup sugar
1/2 cup water
2-3 tablespoons Kahlua
1 3/4 cups whole milk
3 ounces Mexican chocolate or 2 ounces
    semi-sweet chocolate plus 1/8 teaspoon
    cinnamon
1-2 teaspoons orange peel, colored part only
1/2 cup sugar
6 large eggs, separated
13 ounces evaporated milk
1 teaspoon vanilla

In a 2 quart saucepan, bring the sugar and the water to a boil, stirring constantly to dissolve sugar. Use a brush dipped in ice water to wash down any sugar crystals clinging to sides of the pan. Continue to boil, undisturbed, until it turns a rich amber color. As soon as the mixture "caramelizes," stir and remove from heat. Pour in the Kahlua, 1 tablespoon at a time. The syrup will boil up furiously. Pour immediately into a 9 x 5 loaf pan or an 8 cup ring mold. Tilt pan to coat bottom and sides evenly with the caramelized syrup. Let cool 5 minutes at least.

Bring the milk to a boil in a 2 or 3 quart saucepan, then simmer 10 minutes over medium heat. Remove from heat. Meanwhile, insert the metal blade and drop the chocolate pieces through the feed tube with the motor running. Process until finely ground, then add the orange peel and 1/2 cup sugar. Process until well blended and the peel is finely minced. Add the egg yolks, evaporated milk and vanilla and pulse until just combined. Stir the mixture into the milk and set aside.

In a large bowl of an electric mixer, beat the egg whites to stiff peaks. Fold the milk mixture into the egg whites, then pour the custard into the prepared pan.

Set the pan in a larger pan half-filled with water and bake 1 hour and 20 minutes in a pre-heated 350° oven until a knife inserted off-center comes out clean and the custard is set. Let cool, then chill at least 1 hour before unmolding.

To serve the Flan, unmold onto a deep serving platter allowing the caramel sauce to run down the custard. Serve a slice of Flan and some sauce to each person. Serves 8-10.

Tex-Mex Flan

Mexican flans are more dense and heavy than the lighter Spanish style version. Sweetened condensed milk is nearly always used in place of the old-fashioned and time consuming reduction of milk and sugar.

This flan is simple to prepare and may be made several days in advance.

1/2 cup sugar
3 tablespoons water
3 large eggs
3 egg yolks
1 (14 ounce) can sweetened condensed milk
1/2 teaspoon almond extract
1 teaspoon vanilla, preferably Mexican
1 cup whole milk

In a small saucepan, melt and caramelize the sugar with the water over high heat. Do not stir. As the sugar melts, wash down any undissolved crystals with a brush dipped in ice water. As soon as the sugar is amber colored and bubbly, stir and remove from heat. Immediately pour into a 4-5 cup ring mold, tilting to coat all sides with syrup. Let cool 10 minutes while preparing the custard.

In the workbowl using the metal blade, process the eggs, yolks, condensed milk, almond and vanilla extract 3-4 seconds until just mixed. With the machine running, pour the whole milk through the feed tube. Stop machine and immediately pour the mixture into the prepared mold. Set the mold in a larger shallow pan half-filled with hot water and bake 55-60 minutes in a pre-heated 325° oven. Let cool at room temperature, then refrigerate at least 2 hours. At serving time, unmold onto a deep serving platter allowing caramel syrup to run down over the flan. Cut into serving pieces, each with some of the syrup spooned over. Serves 8.

Floating Island Custards
Nantillas

Milk and/or egg custards and flans are favorite Mexican-American desserts and the origin of this food custom is found in Spanish cooking. Their popularity may be explained because dairy products tend to neutralize hot chiles.

Some of these sweets are quite similar to the French "floating island" except that the egg whites are not poached, but rather beaten stiff and folded into the hot custard. These are often garnished with chopped nuts, raisins or cherries.

The following caramel custard recipe was given to me by the daughters of Margarita C. de Baca from New Mexico. I have chosen to poach the meringue in the milk, as the custard is quite delicious as is. You can make a plain custard by simply omitting the sugar caramelization step and adding the sugar to the custard.

My grandmother used to fix a similar dessert, but she baked the meringues until dry and floated them atop the caramel custard.

The food processor method is helpful in producing a smooth texture.

> **2 cups whole milk**
> **1 cinnamon stick**
> **2 egg whites**
> **1/8 teaspoon salt**
> **2 tablespoons powdered sugar**
> **1 teaspoon cornstarch**
> **1/2 cup heavy cream or half and half cream**
> **3 egg yolks**
> **1/3 cup granulated sugar**
> **1 teaspoon vanilla**

Bring the milk and cinnamon stick to a boil, then reduce to a simmer.

Beat the egg whites with the salt until almost soft peaks. Gradually beat in the powdered sugar until soft peaks form. Mound the egg whites by spoonfuls in a cone shape and place atop the simmering milk. Cook about 5 minutes over medium-low heat. Remove the poached meringues with a slotted spoon and reserve. Strain the milk and keep hot.

Dissolve the cornstarch in the cream, then stir into the hot milk. Beat the 3 egg yolks using the metal blade. Then, with the machine running, pour 1 cup of the hot milk through the feed tube. Set aside.

In a medium saucepan, caramelize the sugar over medium heat. As it begins to turn amber, stir and add 1/2 cup of the remaining hot milk. (It will boil up furiously.) Add a little more hot milk, then return the mixture to the remaining hot milk in the pan. Stir in the egg yolk mixture and cook over medium heat, stirring constantly, until thickened. Do not allow the custard to boil. Stir in the vanilla and cool the custard over a bowl of ice cubes, stirring several times. (If the texture seems a bit grainy, you can process with the metal blade to smooth it out.)

When the custard is cool, float the meringues atop and chill until serving time. This is best if served within 3-4 hours of preparation. Serves 4.

Almond Dessert
Almendrado

This light dessert of meringue and gelatin is very popular in Arizona and parts of Southern California. The dessert is often colored with a red and green food coloring to represent the Mexican flag, however I have chosen to use a raspberry puree and flavor the sauce with creme de menthe.

The Meringue:
1 envelope unflavored gelatin
1/3 cup cold water
1 tablespoon arrowroot
1 cup water
3/4 cup sugar, divided
6 egg whites
1/2 teaspoon vanilla
3/4 teaspoon almond extract
2 tablespoons raspberry preserves
1 cup skinned, sliced almonds, lightly toasted
fresh raspberries or strawberries, optional garnish

The Custard Sauce:
2 cups milk or half and half
6 egg yolks
1/4 cup sugar
2 teaspoons arrowroot
1/2 teaspoon almond extract
2 tablespoons green Creme de Menthe, Amaretto liqueur, or Hazelnut liqueur

In a 2-cup measure, sprinkle gelatin over cold water to soften and let stand without stirring for 3-5 minutes.

Meanwhile, stirring constantly, bring arrowroot and water to a boil and then stir into softened gelatin. Add 1/4 cup sugar, stirring to combine. Chill for about 45 minutes to 1 hour or until it begins to thicken. The consistency will be slightly thicker than unbeaten egg whites.

Meanwhile prepare and chill the custard sauce. Bring milk or half and half to a boil in a 2 1/2-3 quart saucepan. Insert the metal blade and place egg yolks, sugar, arrowroot and almond extract into the workbowl. Process until well blended. With the machine running, pour 1 cup of the hot milk through the feed tube. Stop the machine and scrape sides of workbowl, then return the mixture to the hot milk in the pan. Set over medium-low heat and cook, stirring constantly, 3-4 minutes until the custard coats a spoon and is almost as thick as crepe batter. Do not allow to boil. Add liqueur of your choice and remove from heat, let cool and then chill until serving time.

Using an electric mixer, beat the egg whites in a separate bowl until stiff peaks are formed. Add vanilla and almond extract and slowly pour in the remaining 1/2 cup sugar, beating constantly until stiff and glossy.

Remove gelatin mixture from the refrigerator. Using the same beaters, beat the gelatin about 2 minutes or until white and foamy.

Gently but thoroughly combine egg white and gelatin mixtures. Separate and set aside approximately 1/3 of the mixture. Mix 2 spoonfuls of this with raspberry preserves and then fold the raspberry mixture into the remaining reserved 1/3 portion of the egg whites.

Line a loaf pan with wax paper lightly sprayed with Pam. Form a collar that extends 2 inches above the pan.

Spread 1/3 of the white mixture in a 9 x 5 x 3 inch pyrex loaf pan. Sprinkle with about 1/3 of the almonds. Put raspberry portion next and sprinkle with another 1/3 of the almonds. Mound remaining white portion on top and chill at least 4 hours.

When thoroughly chilled, unmold on an oblong serving platter. Sprinkle with remaining toasted almonds. Garnish the platter with fresh raspberries or strawberries, if desired.

Chocolate Almond Dessert

Chocolate Almendrado

This is an Almendrado variation made with Mexican chocolate. When served with the creme de menthe flavored custard sauce, the taste is reminiscent of "Grasshopper Pie."

The Custard Sauce:

    1 quart whole milk or 2 cups milk and 2
        cups half and half cream
    8 egg yolks
    1 tablespoon cornstarch
    1/2 cup granulated sugar
    1 teaspoon vanilla (Mexican if available)
    2-3 tablespoons green creme de menthe,
        optional

The Meringue and Assembly:

    1 cup thinly sliced almonds
    8 squares Mexican chocolate, broken into
        8-10 pieces
    2 1/2 tablespoons water
    3 tablespoons sugar
    8 egg whites, at room temperature
    1 teaspoon cornstarch
    pinch salt
    1/3 cup granulated sugar

The custard sauce can be made a day ahead and refrigerated. Bring the milk to a boil in a 2 1/2-3 quart saucepan. Using the metal blade, process the egg yolks with the sugar, cornstarch and vanilla until blended. With the machine running, pour 1 cup of the hot milk through the feed tube. Stop machine and scrape sides of workbowl. Then return the mixture to the remaining hot milk in the pan. Cook 3-4 minutes over medium-low heat, stirring constantly, until custard coats a spoon and is almost as thick as crepe batter. Stir in creme de menthe. Do not allow to boil. Remove from heat and let cool. Chill.

The meringue should be made shortly before serving for best results. Spread the almonds in a single layer on a cookie sheet and "toast" in a preheated 350° oven for about 8-10 minutes until lightly browned. Let nuts cool.

Using the metal blade, drop the chocolate pieces through the feed tube with the motor running and process to make a fine powder. Leave in workbowl. Bring the water and sugar to a boil in a small saucepan. Then pour the hot mixture through the feed tube with the motor running to melt the chocolate. Leave in workbowl.

Use a large bowl and an electric mixer to beat the egg whites, cornstarch and salt to soft peaks. Gradually add the sugar until stiff peaks form. The meringue should be shiny and moist. Add about 1/2 cup of the meringue to the workbowl and pulse 2-3 times to lighten the chocolate mixture. Then, by hand, fold the chocolate into the remaining meringue.

Spray a 9 x 5 loaf pan with a non-stick vegetable spray such as Pam. Spoon 1/3 of the meringue in an even layer in the loaf pan, then sprinkle with 1/3 of the almonds. Repeat to make three layers with the almonds on top. Bake 35 minutes in a preheated 350° oven. The meringue will rise but remain moist.

To serve, spoon some of the custard sauce into individual shallow dessert bowls and place a slice of the meringue atop the custard. Pass additional custard sauce. Serves 8.

Coconut Almond Dessert
Coconut Almendrado

This Almendrado variation is a little more work than the preceeding recipes, but has the distinct advantage of being a total "make-ahead." It features a lovely presentation that is guaranteed to please coconut lovers.

The Custard Sauce:
1 cup coconut milk
3 cups whole milk
8 egg yolks
1/2 cup sugar
2 teaspoons cornstarch
1 teaspoon vanilla

The Raspberry Sauce:
1 (10 ounce) package frozen raspberries, thawed
2 tablespoons raspberry preserves
1 tablespoon kirsch

The Meringue:
1/4 cup cold water
1 package unflavored gelatin
1/4 cup boiling water
1/3 cup sugar
8 egg whites, at room temperature
2 teaspoons cornstarch
2/3 cup sugar
1/3 cup water
1 1/4 cups grated coconut

The Assembly:
1/2 cup grated coconut
1/2 cup thinly sliced almonds
1 1/2 cups heavy cream, chilled
1 tablespoon powdered sugar

Both the custard sauce and the raspberry sauce can be prepared a day or two ahead and refrigerated. To make the custard sauce, bring the coconut milk and whole milk to a boil in a 2 1/2-3 quart saucepan. Insert the metal blade and place egg yolks, sugar, cornstarch and vanilla in the workbowl. Process until well blended. With the machine running, pour 1 cup of the hot milk mixture through the feed tube. Stop machine and scrape sides of workbowl, then return the mixture to the hot milk in the pan. Set over medium-low heat and cook, stirring constantly, 3-4 minutes until the custard coats a spoon and is almost as thick as crepe batter. Do not allow to boil. Remove from heat, let cool and then chill until serving time.

To make the raspberry sauce, use the metal blade to process the raspberries, preserves and kirsch until smooth. Chill until serving time.

The meringue should be made 12-24 hours ahead of serving. In a shallow bowl, soften the gelatin in the cold water. Then stir in the boiling water and 1/3 cup sugar to dissolve the gelatin completely. Chill 15-30 minutes until the consistency of unbeaten egg white.

Use the large bowl of an electric mixer to beat the egg whites and cornstarch to stiff peaks. Meanwhile, bring the 2/3 cup sugar and the 1/3 cup water to a boil in a small saucepan. Let boil about 3 minutes to make a syrup. With mixer at high speed, pour the hot syrup into the beaten egg whites in a thin, steady stream. Continue to beat until the meringue is stiff and shiny. Use the same beater to beat the thickened gelatin until frothy (resembling stiffly beaten egg whites), then fold the gelatin and coconut into the beaten egg whites. Spray a 9 x 5 loaf pan with a non-stick vegetable coating such as Pam and spoon the meringue into the pan. Chill at least 4 hours or up to 12 hours until firm.

At least 2 hours before serving the dessert, toast the almonds and coconut on a cookie sheet in a pre-heated 350° oven for about 5 minutes until lightly browned. Watch carefully for coconut burns easily. Set aside to cool. Run a knife around the edge of the meringue in the loaf pan and invert the dessert onto a serving platter. Place the meringue in the freezer while preparing the whipped cream.

Using the metal blade, pour the chilled cream through the feed tube with the motor running and process about 15 seconds until very thick. Add the powdered sugar and process about 3 seconds to combine. Use about 2/3 of the whipped cream to frost the meringue, then spoon the remainder into a pastry bag and and pipe a decorative edge around the Almendrado. Garnish the top and/or sides of the dessert with the toasted coconut and almonds. Place the finished dessert in the freezer for 2-3 hours.

To serve the Almendrado, spoon some of the custard sauce into individual dessert bowls, top with a slice of the meringue, then spoon a ribbon of raspberry sauce over the dessert. Serves 8.

Cookies

"Reposterias" is a general "catch-all" name for a wide variety of sugar cookies baked for special occasions. Among these are Wedding Cookies, Baptism Cookies and Christmas Cookies — all with different names depending on the State or region of origin. They can be coated with cinnamon, powdered sugar, ground chocolate or colorful coarse sugars. Food color is often used to tint the dough yellow, pink or "chocolate" and the dough can be shaped into many different combinations.

I have selected several typical cookie doughs, making substitutions for the traditional lard in most instances. Using all butter changes the texture in many cases and often necessitates chilling the dough before shaping or rolling. The general rule for most cookie baking is to use an equal weight of flour and fat with varying amounts of sugar. If in doubt as to the texture, test one cookie before baking the whole batch. If the dough spreads as a result of overprocessing or casual measuring, simply chill it for 30 minutes to an hour. All of the cookie doughs may be made up to a week before baking. Store in the refrigerator, then bring stiff, chilled doughs to room temperature before shaping and baking.

The following recipes are representative of traditional cookies, though the names may be in some dispute.

Sugar Cookies
Reposterias

Reposterias are always made with lard and results in a soft, tender cookie. Using all butter changes this texture, therefore I prefer the combination of cream cheese and butter or margarine. The cookies are usually rolled in colored granulated sugar.

> 10 ounces cream cheese, room temperature and cut in several pieces
> 1 stick (4 ounces) butter or margarine, cut in several pieces
> 2 cups all-purpose flour
> 2/3 cup granulated sugar or 1 cup powdered sugar
> 1 teaspoon vanilla
> 1/4 teaspoon cinnamon or nutmeg, optional
> colored granulated sugar or plain sugar, see note

Insert the metal blade and place the cream cheese, butter, flour, sugar, vanilla and cinnamon or nutmeg in the workbowl. Pulse several times to combine, then run the machine just until the dough forms a ball.

Shape into 3 1/2-4 dozen small balls, then flatten slightly and place 3/4 inch apart on lightly greased baking sheets. Bake about 12 minutes in a preheated 350° oven. (Cookies should not brown.) Because this is a delicate cookie, remove carefully from baking sheets with a spatula. While still warm, place in the bowl of plain sugar and gently coat all sides. Yield: 3 1/2-4 dozen.

Note: If using colored sugar, roll the unbaked cookies in the colored sugar. Omit rolling in sugar after baking.

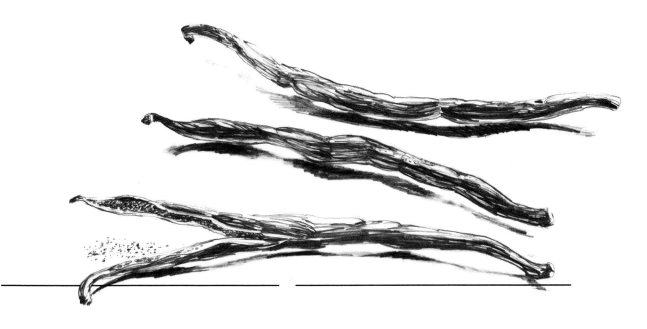

Powder Cakes
Polvorones

Similar to the Mexican Wedding Cookie, traditional recipes call for toasting the flour to result in a very crumbly cookie that is nearly impossible to keep in one piece. I use untoasted flour and bake the cookie longer at a reduced temperature. The result is similar with much less trouble. If nuts are added, they should be finely ground. This is my favorite version of a typical cookie found in Mexican-American bakeries in South Texas.

Chocolate-Cinnamon Coating:
  $1/2$ ounce semi-sweet chocolate
  $1/2$ teaspoon cinnamon
  1 cup granulated sugar

Cookie Dough:
  $1/2$ cup almonds or pecans, optional
  $1^1/4$ stick (5 ounces) unsalted margarine
  $1/2$ cup Crisco or lard
  $1/2$ cup powdered sugar
  1 teaspoon vanilla
  $1/2$ teaspoon cinnamon or nutmeg
  2 cups self-rising flour

First make the coating. Using the metal blade, drop the chocolate through the feed tube with the motor running to finely grate. Add the cinnamon and sugar and process to combine. Place in a shallow bowl.

If you are using nuts, process to grind finely using the metal blade and leave in workbowl. Add the margarine, shortening, powdered sugar, vanilla and cinnamon or nutmeg. Process until light and creamy. Add the flour and pulse until incorporated.

In Mexican-American bakeries you would shape the dough with buttered hands into walnut sized balls, then flatten to make a cookie about $1/2$ inch thick and the diameter of a fifty cent piece. If you prefer, you can drop the balls into cake flour for easier handling or even press through a pastry bag as the dough is moderately soft. Place on a lightly greased cookie sheet.

Bake 20-25 minutes in a pre-heated 300° oven. Let cool on sheet about 1 minute, then carefully transfer to the bowl of chocolate sugar and coat on all sides. Yield: 2 dozen.

Mexican Wedding Cookies

There are many recipes and different names for this popular Mexican shortbread. They can be called Reposterias, Polvorones or Bride's cookies. The traditional recipes use lard, but I prefer this delicate cookie made with unsalted butter only. They are crisp and rich — excellent with fruit ices. Two methods are given since the technique varies with the kind of nuts used.

  $3/4$ cup pecans or skinned almonds
  2 sticks (8 ounces) unsalted butter, cut in
    8-10 pieces
  1 cup powdered sugar
  $1/2$ teaspoon vanilla
  1 cup plus 2 tablespoons cake flour
  1 cup self-rising flour
  several drops hot water if necessary
  powdered sugar for dredging, see note

If using almonds, use the metal blade to finely chop the nuts. Leave in workbowl and, with machine running, drop the butter pieces through the feed tube and process until creamed. Stop the machine and add the sugar and vanilla, then process to combine. Add both flours processing briefly just until flour is incorporated. If the dough is quite stiff, add several drops hot water and process in.

If using pecans, place the nuts and the cake flour in the workbowl using the metal blade. Pulse until the nuts are coarsely chopped. Remove and set aside. Process, using the metal blade, to cream the butter, sugar and vanilla. Add the self-rising flour and reserved nut-flour mixture and pulse 2-3 times to incorporate. Do not overmix. If the dough is quite stiff, process in several drops hot water.

Shape about 1-$1^1/2$ tablespoons dough into a ball, flatten slightly and place on cookie sheet that has been sprayed with a nonstick coating such as Pam. Allow 1 inch between cookies.

Bake 12-15 minutes in a preheated 350° oven. Cool 5 minutes, then carefully remove from the cookie sheets and dredge in powdered sugar. The cookies are delicate and the easiest method for dredging is to put the sugar in a small bowl, add a cookie and spoon sugar over. Remove the sugared cookie with a spatula and let cool on a rack. Yield: 25 cookies.

Note: The flavor of the powdered sugar is improved by storing with a vanilla bean in it.

Mexican Nut Cookies

I am quite sure that this is an American recipe and developed by the many Mexican-Americans who preserve numerous traditions in Texas bakeries. It is similar to the Mexican Wedding Cookie, but has a much lighter and crisper texture. I must have used 100 pounds of flour and powdered sugar trying to duplicate the recipe which seems to be a well-guarded secret. Neiman-Marcus makes a similar cookie and is equally delicious.

Like many good recipes, this is surprisingly simple. Once I was able to reproduce it, I had trouble understanding why I ever had any problems with it!

- $^2/_3$ cup pecans
- $^1/_2$ pound (2 cups) powdered sugar
- 1 stick (4 ounces) unsalted butter, softened and cut in several pieces
- $^3/_4$ cup Crisco or other soft vegetable shortening
- 1 teaspoon vanilla
- $^1/_2$ pound (2$^1/_2$ cups) cake flour
- $^1/_4$ teaspoon salt
- additional powdered sugar

Use the metal blade and pulse to chop the pecans with $^1/_2$ cup of the powdered sugar. Set aside.

Using the metal blade, drop pieces of butter and shortening through the feed tube with the motor running. Add the vanilla and process until light and creamy.

Add remaining powdered sugar to workbowl and process until the mixture is smooth. Add the flour and salt and process briefly just to combine. Use a spatula to stir in the nuts by hand.

Form dough into $^3/_4$ inch balls and place 1 inch apart on two lightly buttered cookie sheets.

Bake 12-15 minutes in a preheated 350° oven. Cookies should not be browned. Cool on a rack, then sift a very light coating of powdered sugar over each cookie. Yield: 4$^1/_2$ dozen cookies.

Mexican Chocolate Crinkles

This delicious variation on a traditional Mexican cookie contains Mexican chocolate, but a combination of regular semi-sweet chocolate and cinnamon produces a similar result. If you can't get Mexican Chocolate, try rolling the cookies in cinnamon sugar before baking.

- 2 cups all purpose bleached flour
- 2 teaspoons baking powder
- $^1/_4$ teaspoon salt
- 6 ounces Mexican chocolate or 4 ounces semi-sweet chocolate plus $^1/_4$ teaspoon cinnamon
- 1 cup granulated sugar
- $^1/_3$ cup warmed corn oil
- 4 medium or 3 large eggs
- 2 teaspoons vanilla
- 1 cup finely chopped nuts or shredded coconut, optional
- powdered sugar for dredging

In workbowl fitted with the metal blade, process the flour, baking powder and salt for about 3 seconds to combine. Remove and set aside.

In same workbowl, place the chocolate and pulse several times to break up the pieces. Then add the sugar and process until the chocolate is grated to a fine powder. With the machine running, add the warm oil through the feed tube. Then add the eggs and vanilla. Process about 10 seconds until smooth. Add the flour mixture and nuts or coconut if using. Pulse just until the flour is incorporated. Chill the dough at least 2 hours.

Drop dough by teaspoonfuls into powdered sugar, coating all sides. Shape into balls and place 2 inches apart of lightly greased baking sheets. Bake 12-15 minutes in a preheated 350°. Cool on brown paper or paper towels. Yield: 5 dozen cookies.

Anise Sugar Cookies
Biscochitos

This New Mexican sugar cookie is traditionally made with lard and shaped like a Fleur de Lis. I prefer the combination of cream cheese, butter and unsalted margarine to make a better handling dough. Because it can easily be rolled without chilling, Biscochitos are perfect for cookie cutters and junior cooks. Since the basic cookie is not overly sweet, it lends itself well to all the sugar sprinkles, icings and coatings for Christmas cookies. I suggest cinnamon sugar and a simple powdered sugar icing — add sliced almonds, raisins, candied fruits, "red hots" or colored sugar to your heart's delight. My children love to ice the "Christmas Trees" and decorate with colored candied fruits.

The Cookies:
3/4 cup granulated sugar, see note
5 ounces cream cheese, cut in several pieces
1/2 stick (2 ounces) butter, cut in several pieces, see note
1 1/4 sticks (5 ounces) unsalted margarine, cut in several pieces
1 1/2-2 teaspoons anise seed
3 tablespoons sweet sherry or wine
1 egg
3 cups self-rising flour
1/4 teaspoon salt
1 cup powdered sugar for work surface
1/2 cup cake flour for work surface
1/2 cup granulated sugar mixed with 2 teaspoons cinnamon, optional
1 egg white beaten with 2 teaspoons water for glaze, optional

Optional Icing:
2 cups powdered sugar
1/2 egg white
1/2 teaspoon vanilla
small amount hot water

Process the sugar, cream cheese, butter, margarine, anise seed, sherry and egg using the metal blade until the mixture is well blended. Add the flour and salt and pulse only until the flour is incorporated. Let the dough rest, uncovered, for about 20 minutes.

Combine the powdered sugar and cake flour and use as needed for your work surface. Roll the dough to about 1/8-1/4 inch thick and cut into shapes with cookie cutters dipped in the flour-sugar mixture. If not using the icing, brush the cookies with the egg white mixture and then sprinkle with cinnamon sugar. If you plan to ice the cookies, bake plain. Place the cookies on lightly greased baking sheets and bake about 12 minutes in a preheated 375° oven. The cookies will be only slightly brown. Let cool on a rack and ice if desired.

To make the icing, use the metal blade to combine the powdered sugar, egg white and vanilla. With the machine running, pour enough hot water through the feed tube to make a pourable icing. Spread or drizzle icing over cookies and decorate with candied fruits, nuts, raisins or other other decorations if desired. Yield: about 3 1/2 dozen cookies.

Note: You may increase the sugar to 1 1/4 cups for a sweeter cookie. You may also increase the butter content to replace up to 8 tablespoons of the margarine. The resulting dough will have to be chilled before rolling and results in a richer cookie.

Rocks

Piedras

This is my favorite cookie and, with all due respect to all bakeries, I like the homemade ones better. Often the bakery versions are too floury for my taste, though they do look more like "rocks" than mine. The flavor is terrific, especially if you can get candied pumpkin or sweet potato. Dates will supply a similar texture as would candied pineapple that has been softened in ¼ cup hot water.

This is the way that Mexican-American bakeries use up the stale Egg Bread. A similar cookie recipe called "Cake Crumb Hermits" is in the 1918 edition of *The Boston Cooking School Cookbook*.

> 3 ounces candied acitron
> 3 ounces candied pumpkin or sweet potato
> ½ cup coconut
> ½ cup coarsely chopped pecans
> ½ cup shortening
> ½ cup granulated sugar
> ½ teaspoon baking soda
> 1 egg
> 1 teaspoon vanilla
> 1 cup ground Egg Bread (p.230) or 1¼
>   cups cake crumbs
> ½ teaspoon allspice
> ½ teaspoon cinnamon
> 1¼ cups all-purpose flour
> ⅓ cup seedless raisins
> white powdered sugar icing

Using the metal blade, process the acitron, candied pumpkin, coconut and pecans until chopped. Remove and set aside.

Using the metal blade, cream together the shortening, sugar and baking soda. Add the egg and vanilla through the feed tube with the motor running until blended. Add the ground Egg Bread, allspice, cinnamon and chopped candied fruit mixture to the workbowl and pulse to combine. Add the flour to the workbowl and pulse just enough to combine. Stir in the raisins by hand.

Chill the dough at least 2 hours. Then shape into ovals, each about half the size of an egg. Bake on lightly greased cookie sheets for 12-15 minutes in a pre-heated 375° oven. Let cool on racks and then frost with a powdered sugar icing. Yield: 2 dozen.

Candies

Colorful paper mache replicas of folk figures and animals hang from the ceiling in many Mexican markets. More than decoration, they are waiting to be filled with candies to supply a seemingly endless source of fun and gaiety. These Piñatas are popular at birthdays, comunions, Christmas and holidays.

Sweets (dulce) are very popular in Mexico and many areas of the Southwest where Mexican customs are preserved. I am particularly intrigued by the Piñatas and my children never seem to tire of the mad scramble for candies as they burst from the shattered dolls. Like most parents, I try to limit their desserts and, as a result, they look for any excuse to satisfy a sweet tooth. The year we moved to San Antonio they saw their first River Boat parade during Fiesta week and were so overcome by the profuse shower of candies along the river banks that they both fell in the river!

I'm not sure whether the custom of eating sweets is preserved because sugar tends to neutralize hot chiles or because of the fun loving, spontaneous personality of the culture. I *am* sure that the colorful Piñata parties will be embraced by the rest of the country.

The candies in this section are traditional and suitable for Piñatas. Their yields may be doubled by individually wrapping small pieces for stuffing into the Piñatas.

Burnt Milk Candy

Leche Quemada

This is a Mexican burnt sugar candy similar to what is often called "Patience Candy" in the states. Recipes vary, some calling many hours of simmering of the sugar and milk to make a thick, fudge-like confection. This method is quicker and easier.

3 cups sugar
1 cup whole milk
1 stick (4 ounces) butter or margarine
1½ cups chopped pecans

In a heavy 3-4 quart saucepan, bring 2 cups of the sugar, the milk and butter to a boil stirring to dissolve sugar. Reduce heat to a simmer.

Meanwhile, caramelize the remaining 1 cup sugar in a heavy saucepan over medium heat. As soon as it melts and turns amber, stir and remove from heat and add to the simmering milk mixture. The mixture will foam up furiously.

Return to medium heat and cook, stirring occasionally, to 250-260° on a candy thermometer (hard ball). Note that just before this stage is reached, the bubbles will become quite large.

Take off heat and let cool, undisturbed, 5-8 minutes. Then set the pan in a larger pan of cold water and beat with a wooden spoon until the fudge thickens and begins to lose its gloss. Immediately pour into a very lightly buttered 9 x 9 pan. Sprinkle the nuts evenly over the top and press into the candy. Let cool, then cut into 1½ inch squares. Yield: 36 squares.

Tex-Mex Pralines

These soft and chewy pralines are like the ones found so often in Texas.

The fire that sometimes burns your lips is not soothed by water, but is neutralized by sugar. That is why sweet pecan and caramel candies are found in nearly every Mexican restaurant.

1 cup packed brown sugar
2 cups granulated sugar
¾ cup evaporated milk or buttermilk
2 tablespoons light corn syrup
1 teaspon baking soda
1 stick (4 ounces) butter, softened
1 teaspoon vanilla (preferably Mexican)
2 cups pecan halves

In a 3-4 quart saucepan, bring the brown sugar, 1 cup of the granulated sugar, the milk, corn syrup and baking soda to a boil. Stir to dissolve the sugar, then allow the mixture to boil gently, undisturbed.

Meanwhile, melt and caramelize the remaining 1 cup granulated sugar in a heavy skillet over medium-high heat. When the sugar turns amber, stir and immediately remove from heat and pour into the boiling brown sugar mixture. (The mixture will foam furiously which is why a large saucepan is necessary.)

Boil the candy, undisturbed, for about 15 minutes until it reaches a soft-ball or 240° on a candy thermometer. Remove from heat and let cool 10 minutes, then beat vigorously adding the butter and vanilla. When the candy thickens and looks glossy, quickly beat in the pecans and drop by spoonfuls onto buttered wax paper. Work rapidly because the candy will become firm quickly. Let cool until completely set, then wrap each in plastic wrap and store at room temperature. Yield: 24 candies.

Note: If you beat the candy too long and it becomes dull or sugary, re-heat it with several tablespoons hot water. Then drop onto wax paper as directed.

Coconut Fudge

Pecan Candy
Nogada

Coconut candies are often colored red and green to symbolize the Mexican flag or bright pink, yellow and green to use for Piñatas. They are often made with sweetened condensed milk to shorten preparation time. Here is the traditional method; add food coloring if desired.

> 2 cups granulated sugar
> 1 cup heavy cream or half and half
> ¾ cup grated coconut (preferably fresh)

Bring the sugar and cream to a boil, stirring to dissolve the sugar. Then cook, undisturbed, over medium heat to 240° on a candy thermometer (soft ball). This should take 10-15 minutes.

Remove from heat and beat in the coconut. Continue beating until the mixture thickens. Drop onto wax paper and let cool completely. Yield: 16 candies.

This is a sugary pecan candy quite common in the Southwest. It is delicious crushed and folded into vanilla ice cream. If you can't obtain the piloncillo cones, try one of the other candy recipes.

> 2 cones piloncillo, broken up
> 1 stick whole cinnamon
> 1 cup water
> 2 tablespoons unsalted butter
> 1 pound pecans

Bring the piloncillo, cinnamon and water to a boil stirring to dissolve the piloncillo. Boil gently to 235-240° on a candy thermometer (soft ball). Remove cinnamon stick and immediately stir in the butter. Let cool 5-8 minutes, then beat with a wooden spoon until the mixture begins to thicken. Stir in the pecans, then immediately drop by teaspoonfuls onto waxed paper. Let cool until set. Yield: 5 dozen.

Mexican Chocolate Roll

Cajeta Crepe

This festive dessert comes from author and chef, Diane Lucas. My adaptation is made with cinnamon flavored chocolate and is remarkably light. The cake is equally good filled with plain sweetened Kahlua whipped cream or the typically Mexican raisin-nut combination.

> 1/2 cup dark seedless raisins, optional
> 1/2 cup chopped pecans, optional
> 1/4 cup heated Kahlua
> 8 large eggs, separated
> 1/2 cup granulated sugar
> 9 ounces Mexican chocolate or 8 ounces German sweet chocolate plus 1/4 teaspoon cinnamon
> 1 ounce unsweetened chocolate, see note
> 1/4 cup boiling water
> pinch salt
> pinch cornstarch
> 2 cups heavy cream, chilled
> 1/3 cup powdered sugar
> additional powdered sugar for garnish
> unsweetened cocoa for garnish

Soak the raisins and nuts in the warm Kahlua for at least 2 hours.

To make the cake, use an electric mixer to beat the egg yolks with the granulated sugar until very thick. Set aside.

Break the chocolate into 8 pieces. Using the metal blade, drop the chocolate through the feed tube with the motor running and process to grind finely. With the machine running, pour the boiling water through the feed tube to melt the chocolate. Cool the chocolate by placing the workbowl in the freezer for about 10 minutes. Do not solidify.

Meanwhile, butter an 11 x 17 inch jelly roll pan and line with buttered "Cut-Rite" brand wax paper having the paper overlap the edges of the pan. (Cut-Rite brand is the least likely to tear.)

Return workbowl to the machine base, taking care to secure the metal blade. Add the beaten egg yolk mixture and pulse once or twice to combine. Leave in work bowl.

Using a clean electric mixer bowl and beaters, beat the egg whites, salt and cornstarch to stiff peaks. Pulse several spoonfuls of the egg whites into the chocolate mixture to lighten, then fold in the remainder by hand.

Spread the batter in the prepared pan and bake 10 minutes in a preheated 350° oven. Lower temperature to 325° and bake an additional 10-15 minutes until the cake is firm, but not dry or browned. Remove from oven and cover immediately with a cool, slightly dampened towel. Refrigerate at least 1 hour.

Meanwhile, make the filling. Process the chilled cream a few seconds until thickened. Then add the powdered sugar and process about 15 seconds or until very thick. (Watch carefully for the cream can separate and turn to butter.) Remove about 1/2 cup of the whipped cream and place in a pastry bag fitted with a star tip and reserve to garnish the dessert. Drain the raisins and nuts and fold into the remaining cream.

To assemble the cake roll, remove the cloth from the cake, dust lightly with cocoa and invert onto a piece of waxed paper placed on a work surface. (Use the overlapping edges of waxed paper in the pan to loosen the cake.) Peel off the waxed paper and dust the cake lightly with cocoa.

Spread the Kahlua flavored cream over the cake, leaving about 1 1/2 inches on the long sides free of filling. Roll up from the long side, using the wax paper as an aide. Transfer, using the wax paper to lift, and place seam side down on a serving platter.

Decorate the cake roll with rosettes of whipped cream and dust the entire surface with additional powdered sugar and cocoa. Chill until ready to serve. Serves 12-14.

Note: Mexican chocolate brands vary as to amount of cane sugar. If using La Fonda or La Popular, S.A. brands, you will need to add the unsweetened chocolate to the recipe.

Caramel Crepes

This caramel sauced dessert has become very popular in many Mexican-American restaurants. Various kinds of cheeses, combined with raisins and brown sugar, are traditional "sweets." The dessert may also be served plain, without the filling. Note the variation using a fresh fruit filling.

The Crepe Batter:
    4 eggs
    3/4 cup water
    1 teaspoon vanilla, preferably Mexican
    3 tablespoons melted butter
    1 1/2 cups all purpose flour
    3/4 cup milk

The Filling:
    1/3 cup raisins
    1/3 cup chopped pecans or almonds
    1/2 cup warm apple juice
    1 tablespoon sugar
    3-4 strips orange peel, colored part only
    1/4 stick (1 ounce) butter
    3 1/2 ounces cream cheese, cut in 3-4 pieces

The Sauce:
    2 cups Caramel Sauce (p.55), see note
    1 ounce Kahlua
    1 ounce Triple-sec

Use the metal blade to blend together the eggs, water, vanilla and melted butter. Add the flour to the workbowl. With the machine running, pour the milk through the feed tube and process until the batter is smooth. Let stand about 30 minutes, then prepare 12 (7 inch) crepes. The crepes may be used immediataely or refrigerated or frozen for later use.

To make the filling, first soak the raisins and nuts in the apple juice for 30 minutes to 1 hour. Meanwhile, place the sugar and orange peel in the workbowl using the metal blade. Process to mince the orange peel, then add the butter and cream cheese and process until smooth and creamy. Drain the raisins and nuts and stir by hand into the cheese mixture.

Spread a thin layer of filling over each crepe, then roll up and place seam side down in a single layer in a buttered baking dish. Bake, covered, for 8-10 minutes in a preheated 450° oven.

Meanwhile make the sauce. Place the Caramel Sauce, Kahlua and Triple-sec in a saucepan and heat, stirring constantly.

Allow two crepes per person and serve with the hot sauce. Serves 6-8.

Note: If using commercial Cajeta which is very thick, thin with cream or evaporated milk to the consistency of crepe batter.

Variation: You may use 1/2 cup fresh diced pineapple, orange, mango or papaya in place of the raisin and nut mixture in the filling. Process by pulsing into the cream cheese mixture until just combined. Proceed as directed.

*Other
Desserts*

Sweet Chimichangas

It seems that there are both sweet and savory versions in many tortilla specialties and Chimichangas are no exception. You can use prepared 12 inch flour tortillas. You can also use the sweet fillings for Empandas (p.82) or any fruit filling of your choice.

The techniques for rolling, folding and frying are the same as for savory Chimichangas (p.145). The finished pastry can be topped with powdered sugar or cinnamon sugar and served with whipped cream or ice cream.

The Filling:
4 tart apples, peeled, cored and cut into
  bite-size chunks
3 tablespoons (1½ ounces) butter
juice of 1 lemon
2 teaspoons cornstarch
pinch ground cinnamon

The Tortilla Preparation:
6 (12 inch) flour tortillas, warmed, see note
1 egg white
2 teaspoons cold water
peanut oil for frying
powdered sugar

In a saucepan, saute the apples in the butter for 3-4 minutes until softened. Add the remaining filling ingredients and cook, stirring, until the mixture is thickened and the apples are tender. Let cool.

Keep the warmed tortillas wrapped so that they stay soft. Beat the egg white with the water. Spoon about ⅓ cup filling into each tortilla, then brush the exposed surfaces with the egg white mixture. Fold both sides toward the center, then roll up tightly and securely and set seam side down. Allow the filled and rolled tortillas to stand long enough for the egg white to dry.

In a deep saucepan, heat enough oil to deep-fry the chimichangas to 375°. Fry, one at a time, for about 1½ minutes turning to brown both sides. Drain on paper towels and sprinkle immediately with powdered sugar. Serve warm. Serves 6.

Note: The tortillas can be warmed in a microwave oven for about 30 seconds on the High setting or wrapped in a tea towel and set in a collander over simmering water for about 5 minutes.

Tropical Fruits with Cheese   Fruitas con Queso

As an alternative to a tropical fruit ice, fresh fruits with cheese accompanied by Cuban biscuits or Bremner wafers makes a delicious Northern Mexican dessert. You can use any assortment of fresh or canned fruits. Canned guava's, drained of their syrup, accompanied by fresh papaya, pineapples and mangos are my favorite. Canned mangos, drained and cut into bite-sized slices, are equally acceptable. Cream cheese or any of the French goat cheese are a good substitute for the Mexican white cheeses.

Leftover flour tortillas make a terrific quick "cracker" if brushed lightly with butter, quartered and toasted at 375° until crisp and lightly browned.

1 fresh pineapple
2-3 fresh papayas
3 fresh or 1 can mangos, drained
1 can guavas or strips of guava paste
2 pounds cream cheese or assorted soft and
  creamy goat cheeses
toasted tortillas, Mexican biscuits or
  Bremer wafers

Remove the leafy stem and bottom portion from the pineapple, then remove core. Reserve the leafy top for garnish. Fit the processor with a 5mm (thick) slicing disc. (If you do not have a thick slicing disc, slice the pineapple by hand for a thin disc may shred the pieces.) Cut the fruit into sections that will fit the feed tube and process to slice. Drain the slices reserving the syrup for other uses. Set aside.

Peel the papaya and remove the seeds. Slice by hand into bite-sized slices. Then slice the mangos and guavas in the same manner. Reserve the juices for other uses such as a delicious syrup over ice cream.

Place the pineapple top in the center of a large serving platter. Arrange the fruits and cheese on the platter and serve the crackers separately in a basket. Serves 8-10.

GLOSSARY

The Spanish language is very easy to pronounce, once you understand a few certain principles. Every letter in every Spanish word is pronounced fully and clearly, with two exceptions. The letter "H" is never sounded before a,e,i,o,u; the letter "U" followed by "q" or "g", and before "e" or "i" is also silent. For example — "qu" is pronounced "K", before "e" or "i"; gu is hard (as in got or get) before "e" and "i".

Two other rules to note are: Words ending in a consonant, except "n" or "s", are stressed on the last syllable; and words ending in a vowel and "n" or "s" are stressed on the next to the last syllable.

There are five vowels in the Spanish language and are pronounced as follows:

"A" as in father (Avoid a long "A" as in hay)

"E" as in memory

"I" as in machine

"O" as in north

"U" as in moon (never as in you) The "Y" alone means "and" and sounds like the "I" in machine

The consonants in English and Spanish are pronounced basically the same, but there are some differences:

CA, CO, CU, and QU—pronounced as a "K" (there is no "K" in Spanish)

CE, CI and Z—pronounced as a "S"

GA, GO, GU—as in gun

GI, GI and J—a throaty "H"

H—always silent

R—a vibrating, rolled "R" made by vibrating the tongue on the palate just above the teeth

RR—a stronger, vibrating trill

LL—like the "Y"

N—something like the sound in canyon

A

Achiote
a-chi-o-te
(ah-chee-oh-teh)
red paste seasoning from annatto seed, used in rice to produce a yellow color

Acitrón
a-ci-tron
(ah-cee-thrón)
candied cactus

Aguacate
a-gua-ca-te
(ah-wa-kah-teh)
avocado

Ajo
a-jo
(ah-ho)
garlic

Ajon-Joil
a-jon-jo-il
(a-hon-ho-eel)
sesame seeds

Albanil
Al-ban-il
(al-ban-eel)
Red sauce from Mexico

Albondigas
al-bon-di-gas
(al-bon-dee-gahs)
meat balls, poached in simmering water; usually served with a soup

Al horno
al hor-no
(al-or-no)
baked

Almendra
al-men-dra
(al-men-thra)
made with almonds

Almendrado
al-men-dra-do
(al-men-thra-tho)
a dessert made with almonds and egg whites

Almuerzo
al-muer-zo
(al-mooer-soh)
equivalent to brunch

Aloe Vera
(ahlo veh-ra)
succulent plant which heals cuts and burns

Al Pastor Asada
al pas-tor a-sada
(al pahs-tor ah-sa-tha)
meat that is impaled on a stick, then roasted over direct fire; (Shepherd's style)

Anaheim
ana-heim
(ana-hí-m)
mild, California chile, 6-8″ long, thick flesh

Ancho
an-cho
(ahn-cho)
"wide"; refers to dried chile

Añejo
a-ñe-jo
(ah-nyeh-ho)
aged; also crumbly dry cheese, quite salty; used for enchiladas

Annatto
ann-a-tto
(an-ah-toh)
seeds of the Achiote

Anticuchos
an-ti-cu-chos
(ahn-tee-coo-chos)
marinated beef chunks grilled on a stick

Antojitos
an-to-ji-tos
(ahn-toh-hee-tohs)
appetizers

Árbol
ár-bol
(ár-bol)
very hot dried chile, slimmer and longer than jalapeños, can also refer to any hot chile powder

Arroz
a-rroz
(ah-rrohs)
rice

Arroz con Leche
con le-che
(con leh-che)
rice pudding

Arroz con Pollo
con po-llo
(con poh-yo)
classic chicken and rice dish

Asadero
a-sa-de-ro
(ah-sah-de-ro)
a braided cheese similar in taste and consistency to Oaxaca, and Chihauhau

Atole
a-to-te
(ah-tóh-leh)
a gruel made from corn or flour, sometimes blue corn

Azafrán
a-za-frán
(ah-sah-fráhn)
saffron

B

Bahamian
ba-ha-mi-an
(bah-hā-me-an)
hot New Mexican chile

Barbacoa
bar-ba-co-a
(bahr-bah-coh-ah)
barbequed; in Texas it refers to a dish made from a cow's head, cooked in the ground surrounded by coals. "Barbacoa Tacos" are a weekend regional dish

Bebidas
be-bi-das
(beh-bee-thas)
drinks

Berenjena
ber-en-jen-a
(ber-en-hen-ah)
eggplant

Big Jim
(New Mexico)
mild, New Mexican long green chile, thick fleshed

Blanco
blan-co
(blan-coh)
white

Biznaga
biz-na-ga
(Bes-nah-gah)
candied cactus; like acitrón

Bolillo
bol-i-llo
(bol-ee-yoh)
french style roll

Borracho
bo-rra-cho
(boh-rah-cho)
with beer or liquor, "drunken"

Budín
bu-din
(boo-théen)
"pudding"; often used to describe a dish with stacked enchiladas

Buñuelos
bu-ñue-los
(boon-yuel-ohs)
fried, round pastries

Burro
bur-ro
(boo-roh)

Burrito
burr-i-to
(boo-ree-toh)
soft, 14-18″ flour tortilla, filled and rolled in a certain way. (In Texas, Breakfast or egg Burritos are called "Breakfast Tacos")

C

Cabrito
ca-bri-to
(kah-bree-toh)
young goat

Al horno
al hor-no
(al or-no)
baked

Al pastor
al pas-tor
(al pahs-tor)
roasted Shepherd's style sometimes over mesquite

Cacahuates
ca-ca-hua-tes
(kah-kah-wah-tes)
spicy hot peanuts

Cajeta
ca-je-ta
(kah-heh-tah)
thick caramel sauce or fruit butter

Calabacita
ca-la-ba-ci-ta
(kah-lah-bah-see-tah)
summer squash

Calabaza
ca-la-ba-za
(kah-lah-bah-sah)
pumpkin (not the orange jack-o-lantern well known in the States, but many other varieties)

Caldillo
cal-di-llo
(Kahl-dee-yoh)
a stew from West Texas and New Mexico of meat, potatoes; called "poor man's stew"

Caldo
cal-do
(cal-doh)
broth or soup

California Chile
long, bright green chile, often called Anaheim

Camarones
ca-ma-ro-nes
(kah-mah-ron-es)
shrimp

Camote
ca-mo-te
(kah-moh-teh)
sweet potato

Campechana
cam-pe-cha-na
(kahm-peh-cha-nah)
round flaky pastries with shiny tops

Cañela
ca-ne-la
(kah-neh-lah)
cinnamon bark

Capsaicin
cap-sai-cin
(cap-sĩ-seen)
the hot volatile oil found in veins of chiles

Capirotada
ca-pi-ro-ta-da
(kah-pee-roh-tah-tha)
a sweet Mexican bread pudding, usually made with a cinnamon sugar syrup, cheese, raisins, or other fruits. Sometimes with an egg batter topping.

Carne
car-ne
(car-neh)
meat

Carne Adovada
a-do-va-da
(ah-tho-vah-tha)

Adobada
a-do-ba-da
(ah-tho-bah-tha)
meat or pork cooked in red chile (or marinated in red chile)

Carne Asada
a-sa-da
(ah-sah-tha)
grilled meats

Carne Seca
se-ca
(seh-kah)
beek jerky

Carnitas
car-ni-tas
(car-nee-tahs)
little strips of browned or fried pork

Cascabel
cas-ca-bel
(kahs-kah-bel)
dried red chile, medium to hot, smooth skin

Cascavel
cas-ca-vel
(kahs-kah-vel)

Cayenne
hot chile grown in New Mexico

Cazuela
ca-zuela
(kah-swel-la)
refers to a shallow pot or earthenware clay pot in which stews are made. Can refer to beef stew

Cebolla
ce-bo-lla
(seh-boh-yah) — onion

  al la Parilla
  a la pa-ri-lla
  (pah-ree-ya) — broiled

  al carbón
  al car-bón
  (cahr-bón) — grilled

Cervesa
cer-ve-sa
(sehr-veh-sah) — beer

Ceviche
ce-vi-che
(seh-vee-cheh)
"Acapulco Style" — raw fish marinated in lime juice and usually combined with fresh salsa

Chalupa
cha-lu-pa
(cha-lu-pah) — a round corn tortilla, fried crisp. In Mexico, the edges were curled up (hence the name "little boat")

Champurado
cham-pu-ra-do
(chahm-poo-rah-tho) — Mexican chocolate gruel popular in New Mexico

Charro
cha-rro
(chah-rroh) — ranch style or "cowboy"

Chata
cha-ta
(chah-tah) — flat

Chayote
cha-yo-te
(shy-yo-teh) — a crisp light green vegetable; often called a vegetable pear

Chicharrones
chi-cha-rron-es
(chee-cha-ron-es) — fried pork skins (fat from under the skin of hogs or beef)

Chicos
chi-cos
(cheé-cos) — dried corn kernels

Chihuahua
chi-hua-hua
(chee-wah-wah) — white, creamy Mennonite cheese, with excellent melting quality

Chilaquilas
chi-la-qui-las
(chee-lah-key-las) — literally "broken-up old sombrero" and a name given to any concoction that used pieces of old, fried corn tortillas from scrambled eggs to baked casseroles.

Chile
chi-le
(chee-leh) — usually refers to the chile pepper; though in Texas it can mean "with meat sauce"

Chile Caribe
ca-ri-be
(kah-ree-beh) — red chile paste; blended chile pulp, garlic and water

Chile Gravy — a gravy made with chile powder

Chile con Queso
con que-so
(con keh-so) — classic Southwestern combination of cheese, chiles, onions, and sometimes tomatoes or red chile

Chile Powder — commercially a blend of chile ancho powder, cumin, garlic and salt. In some areas (generally Southwest and Southern California) you can obtain pure ground chile powder from many different kinds of chile.

Chile Rellenos
chi-le Re-lle-nos
(chee-leh reh-yeh-nos) — Poblano chiles stuffed with meat, deep fried in egg batter, and served with a tomato sauce. In some areas green chiles are used.

Chile Ristras
ris-tras
(rees-tras) — strings of drying or dried red chiles

Chile Sauce — in Texas, usually a meat sauce; in Arizona and New Mexico, refers to a red or green chile sauce

Chimichanga
chi-mi-chan-ga
(chee-mee-chan-gah)
Chimichango
chi-mi-chon-go
(chee-mee-chan-goh) — large flour tortillas, folded "Burrito style" and deep fried. Topped with cheese, guacamole or sauces

Chimichurri
chi-mi-churr-i
(chee-mee-chur-ee) — a sauce of fresh and dried chiles, usually served with meats

Chipotle Chile
chi-pot-le
(chee-pot-le) — dried hot chile with smoky flavor

Chongas
chon-gas
(chon-gahs) — "little knots," sweet pudding, squares made with rennet, sugar and milk; popular in California

Chorizo
cho-ri-zo
(cho-ree-soh) — Mexican sausage seasoned with red chile, oregano, vinegar, garlic and sometimes cumin. Spanish chorizo is quite different in taste and texture.

Chuleta
chu-le-ta
(chu-leh-tah) — chop or cutlet

Cilantro
ci-lan-tro
(see-lan-troh)
leaf of the coriander, commonly used in Southwest cooking

Colorado
co-lo-ra-do
(koh-loh-ra-tho)
refers to a red sauce made from dried red chile; can mean red chile powder (pure ground)

Comal
co-mal
(koh-mahl)
earthenware or metal plate used for cooking corn and flour tortillas; flat griddle

Comida
co-mi-da
(co-mee-tha)
main meal, eaten mid-day; often full eight courses

Comino
co-mi-no
(koh-mee-noh)
cumin, popular spice

Compuesta
com-pues-ta
(com-pes-tah)
mixed or combinations; often on chalupas or tostados beginning with a layer of beans

Concha
con-cha
(kohn-cha)
means shell; name given to a sweet sugar topped roll

Con Chile
con chi-le
(con chee-leh)
in Texas, with meat sauce in New Mexico, green or red chile sauce

Coriander
a round pale yellow or brown seed from the coriander plant

Cuarasmeñ
cuar-as-meñ
(kooahr-as-mehn)
another name for the jalapeño chile

Cuban Biscuits
hexagon shaped biscuits often served with cheese and guava fruit

Cuerno
cuer-no
(coo-er-noh)
a French croissant, made in Mexican bakeries, usually with lard and butter

D

de ajo
de a-jo
(de ah-ho)
with garlic

de la fauna
de la fau-na
(de la fahow-nah)
entree

Dulce
dul-ce
(dóol-seh)
sweet

Dulce Blanco
dul-ce blan-co
(dóol-seh blan-coh)
coconut candy

Dulce de Nueces
dul-ce de nue-ces
(dóol-seh de noo-eh-sehs)
nut brittle

Dulce do Piloncillo
dulce de pi-lon-ci-llo
(dóol-seh de pee-lon-see-yo)
Mexican pralines

E

Ejote
e-jo-te
(eh-ho-teh)
green bean

Elote
e-lo-te
(eh-loh-teh)
roasting ears of corn

Empanada
em-pan-a-da
(em-pahn-ah-tha)
fried or baked turnover with pastry or flour tortilla shell. Can have meat, fowl or sweet fillings.

Enchiladas
en-chi-la-das
(en-chee-lah-thahs)
rolled or stacked corn tortillas, with Chile con Carne

Enchiladas Chatas
cha-tas
(chah-tahs)
flat enchiladas with masa and cheese; fried

Enchilada "cheese"
white crumbly cheese, labeled "enchilada cheese"; a farmers cheese, does not melt

Enchilada Sauce
usually a red chile sauce or sauce made from fresh green chiles

Enchurito
en-chur-i-to
(en-chewr-ee-toh)
like a Chimichanga or deep fried burrito

Ensalada
en-sa-la-da
(en-sa-la-thah)
salad

Entomatadas
en-to-ma-ta-das
(en-toh-ma-tha-thas)
corn tortilla, filled then folded or rolled, grilled and served with a mild tomato sauce

Entrada
en-tra-da
(en-tra-tha)
cooked vegetable, a fish course of the comida

Epazote
e-pa-zo-te
(eh-pah-soh-teh)
Mexican herb used in beans

Escabeche
es-ca-be-che
(es-cah-beh-cheh)
pickled or marinated in vinegar, often with chiles

Española
es-pañ-o-la
(es-pahn-yo-lah)
cayenne hot New Mexican chile

Espinaca
es-pin-a-cas
(es-peen-ah-kas)
spinach

Etomote
e-tom-ote
(eh-tohm-oh-teh)
tomato

F

Fajitas
fa-ji-tas
(fah-hee-tas)
grilled or boiled skirt steaks

Farmer's Cheese
Fresco Cheese
often called Queso Fresco; made with rennet or a native berry; acid cheese which crumbles easily and is used as topping or filling for enchiladas. It does melt, unlike anejo which is similar

Fideo
fi-de-o
(fee-de-o)
fine vermicelli

Flan
flan
(flahn)
light custard dessert with a caramel syrup

Flaquito
fla-qui-to
(fla-key-toh)
a tightly rolled crisp taco made with corn tortilla; like a Flauta, thinner than taquitas

Flauta
flau-ta
(fl-ow-ta)
means "flute" and refers to the shape of a crisp, rolled corn tortilla filled with chicken

Fresadilla
fres-a-di-lla
(fres-ah-dee-ya)
same as a tomatillo

Fried Cheese Taco
a quesadilla with fresh masa, folded empanada style and filled with cheese, deep fried

Fried Ice Cream
popular in Mexican American restaurants; scoops of ice cream usually rolled in crushed cereal or bread crumbs and honey and refrozen. Fried for a few seconds before served.

Frijoles
fri-jo-les
(free-hô-less)
beans, usually refers to pinto beans

Frijoles Refritos
re-fri-tos
(reh-free-tohs)
beans fried well

Frito
fri-to
(free-tô)
fried

Fundido
fun-di-do
(fuhn-dee-tho)
melted cheese; literally "forged"

G

Gallina
ga-lli-na
(gah-yee-nah)
hen or fowl

Garbanzo
gar-ban-zo
(gahr-bahn-so)
chick peas

Gordita
gor-di-ta
(gor-thee-tah)
fried, small round masa cake, usually filled with shredded meat

Grande
gran-de
(grahn-theh)
large

Guacamole
gua-ca-mo-le
(wah-kah-mo-le)
avocado salad, butter or concoction

Guajalote
gua-ja-lo-te
(wah-hah-lô-teh)
Guajolote
gua-jo-lo-te
(wah-hô-lô-teh)
Mexican turkey (Spanish word is "pavo" as early settlers were convinced it was a peacock)

Guajillo Chile (dried)
gua-ji-llo
(wa-hee-yo)
smooth-skinned dried chile, very hot

Guava
gua-va
(wah-vah)
sweet red fruit; pungent tropical fruit

Guëro
guë-ro
(wooeh-roh)
small hot chile, not easily available in the Southwest

Guisado
gui-sa-do
(gee-sah-tho)
stewed meat or fowl with green peppers, onions and tomatoes

Guiso
gui-so
(gee-soh)
meat stew, most commonly with beef tips

H

Haba
ha-ba
(ah-bah)
fava or haba bean

Harina
ha-ri-na
(ah-ree-nah)
white flour

Helado
he-la-do
(eh-la-tho)
ice cream or frozen

Helote
he-lo-te
(eh-lô-teh)
green corn

Hojas
ho-jas
(oh-has)
sometimes used to describe corn husks

Hongo
hon-go
(on-goh)
mushroom

Huachinango
hua-chin-an-go
(wah-cheen-ahn-go)
red snapper

  a la Veracruz
a la Ver-a-cruz
(a la Ver-ah-croos)
with tomatoes, capers and jalapeño chiles

Huesos
hue-sos
(weh-sos)
literally means bones, a flaky twisted pastry that looks like a bone

Huevos
hue-vos
(weh-vôs)
eggs

Huevos Rancheros
ran-cher-os
(rahn-cher-os)
eggs (any style) with a soft corn tortilla and salsa, or in some areas with flour tortillas

Huitlacoche
huit-la-co-che
(weet-la-coh-che)
a fungus from corn used in Mexican cooking, but not in the Southwest

I

Indian Fry Bread
a New Mexican flat bread that is fried and topped with beans, cheese, chiles, and lettuce

J

Jalapeño Chile (fresh)
ja-la-peñ-o
(ha-la-pain-yoh)
shiny, fat, small, dark green chile about 2½ inches by 1 inch. Hot.

Jalapeño Jelly
a sweet, hot jelly made from ground bell and jalapeño peppers.

Jalapeño Relish
a hot relish made with jalapeños (usually fresh, not roasted or peeled), tomatoes and onions; also known as "Pico de Gallo".

Jamonsillo
ja-mon-si-llo
(ha-mon-see-yo)
sweet sauce like Cajeta

Japonés
ja-pon-és
(ha-pon-és)
very hot, small dried chile (Serrano fresh)

Jícama
jí-ca-ma
(hé-kah-mah)
large, root tuber with thick brown skin ranging from the size of a grapefruit to a small pumpkin. Tastes like the combination of an apple and large water chestnut.

Jitomate
ji-to-ma-te
(he-toh-mah-teh)
tomato

L

Leche
le-che
(leh-cheh)
milk

Leche Quemada
que-ma-da
(keh-ma-tha)
usually a fudge-like candy, made from boiling sugar and milk 5 or more hours. Topped with nuts. Can also refer to a thick, sweet caramel pudding.

Lechuga
le-chu-ga
(leh-chu-gah)
lettuce

Lengua
len-gua
(len-gwah)
tongue

Limón
li-món
(lee-món)
lime or small lemon

Longhorn Cheese
a type of yellow chedder used in both northern Mexico and Texas for Enchiladas and cheese dishes

M

Machaca
ma-cha-ca
(mah-cha-kah) — shredded boiled meat

Machacado
ma-cha-ca-do
(mah-cha-ca-tho) — scrambled eggs with dried beef

Maiz
maiz
(mah-ees) — corn

Mango
man-go
(mahn-goh) — an oblong, yellow-orange tropical fruit available canned, sometimes fresh

Mano
ma-no
(mah-noh) — a stone "rolling pin" used with a metate for grinding corn

Mantecado
man-te-ca-do
(mahn-teh-cah-tho) — made with lard

Manzanilla
man-zan-i-lla
(mahn-sahn-nee-ya) — herb used for tea

Manzano (chile) fresh
man-zan-o
(mahn-sahn-o) — similar to jalapeño (yellow-green) but milder

Mariscos
ma-ris-cos
(mah-rees-cos) — seafood

Marquesote
mar-que-so-te
(mar-keh-soh-teh) — cake

Masa
ma-sa
(mah-sah) — fresh ground moist dough of nixtamal (dried corn which has been soaked in limewater and then cooked); perishable

Masa Harina
Ma-sa Ha-ri-na
(mah-sah ah-ree-nah) — Dehydrated corn flour, commercially packaged, usually contains some flour, only water is needed to make tortillas

Masa (Trigo)
ma-sa tri-go
(mah-sah tree-go) — commercial mix made of flour, shortening, and salt for flour tortillas

Mazapanes
ma-za-pan-es
(mah-sah-pahn-es) — marzipan

Melón
me-lón
(meh-lón) — melon

Membrillo
mem-bri-llo
(mehm-bree-yoh) — quince

Menudo
me-nu-do
(meh-new-dôh) — classic tripe soup seasoned with cumin and lime (a legendary cure for a hangover)

Merienda
me-ri-en-da
(meh-ree-en-da) — mini meal or snack eaten in the late afternoon

Mesquite
mes-qui-te
(mehs-key-teh) — the wood used for outdoor cooking throughout Northern Mexico

Metate
me-ta-te
(meh-tah-teh) — inclined rough stone for grinding corn

Migas
mi-gas
(mee-gahs) — crumbs

Molcajete
mol-ca-je-te
(mohl-kah-heh-teh) — mortar and pestle

Molé
mo-lé
(moh-leh) — refers to a "sauce" made with chile (perhaps an early barbeque sauce); can also be the classic red chile and chocolate sauce; sometimes refers to a powder which is a blend of seasonings in classic molé sauce

Molettes
mol-et-tes
(mohl-eht-tes) — sweet rolls, usually with anise

Molé Verde
mo-le ver-de
(moh-leh vehr-deh) — a mixed green sauce which can have chiles, greens, lettuce and squash seeds

Molido
mo-li-do
(moh-lee-tho) — West Texas or California term for pure ground red chile powder

Molino-Nixtamal
(moh-lee-noh nees-tah-máhl) — tortilla factory

Monterey (style)
Mon-ter-ey
(mon-teh-ray) — usually with sour cream

Morsillo
mor-si-llo
(mohr-see-yo) — blood pudding with nuts and raisins

Mulato
mu-la-to
(moo-lah-toh) — wide, wrinkled-skin dried chile, darker than Ancho

N

Nachos
na-chos
(nah-chos)

corn tostados topped with beans, cheese and topped with a jalapeño

Nachos Rancheros
ran-cher-os
(rahn-cher-os)

tostados with melted cheese, jalapeño, beans, grilled meat, sour cream, and guacamole

Nantillas
nan-ti-llas
(nahn-tee-yas)

a milk custard with beaten, uncooked egg whites folded into the custard or floated atop

Naranja
na-ran-ja
(nah-rahn-hah)

orange

Nata
na-ta
(nah-tah)

the material that collects on top of boiled milk, cooled and used on tortillas or chile rellenos

Negro
ne-gro
(neh-gro)

black; often used to describe dark, dried chiles

Nixtamal
nix-ta-mal
(nees-tah-máhl)

wet, hulled corn grains ready to grind to be used as "masa" for fresh corn tortillas

Nogada
no-ga-da
(noh-gah-tha)

Mexican nut and praline candy made from piloncillo cones

Nopal
no-pal
(noh-pahl)

the joint of the cactus; "prickly pear"

Nopalitos
no-pal-i-tos
(noh-pahl-ee-tohs)

chopped cactus shoots, often added to eggs or salads

O

Oaxaca (cheese)
oa-xa-ca
(wah-ha-kah)

a high fat cheese with a delicious acid taste; made in a similar way as Mozzarella; melts well, stringy and elastic

Oaxaca (Quesillo)
que-si-llo
(keh-see-yo)

(same as above)

Olla
o-lla
(o-ya)

round earthenware pot used for stews

Orejones
o-re-jon-es
(o-reh-hôn-es)

dried fruits

Orégano
o-re-ga-no
(ô-réh-ga-no)

wild marjoram

Orejas
o-re-jas
(o-reh-has)

"ears"; refers to a Mexican pastry like the French palmiers

Ostiones
os-tion-es
(os-teeon-es)

oysters

P

Pan
pan
(pahn)

bread

Panaderia
pa-na-de-ri-a
(pah-na-deh-ree-a)

bakery

Pan de Huevo
pan de hue-vo
(pahn de weh-vo)

egg bread (sometimes sugar topped)

Pan Dulce
pan dul-ce
(pahn dóol-seh)

sweet breads

Panela
pa-ne-la
(pah-ne-la)

used with fruit; soft, like cream cheese

Panocha
pa-no-cha
(pah-noh-cha)

usually refers to sprouted wheat flour used to make an Indian pudding (New Mexico); can sometimes refer (Arizona) to the brown sugar cones like piloncillo

Panuchos
pa-nu-chos
(pah-new-chos)

a quesadilla from Yucatan

Papas
pa-pas
(pah-pas)

potatoes

Pasilla
pa-si-lla
(pah-see-ya)

wrinkled skin; can refer to several dried chiles, chile powder (see chile chart)

Pastel
pas-tel
(pahs-tel)

pastry or pie

Pastel de Polvo
pas-tel de pol-vo
(pahs-tel de pol-vo)

Mexican flaky pastry

Pastelitos
pas-tel-i-tos
(pahs-tel-ee-tohs)

fruit tarts

Pastitas de Frijol
(pahs-tee-tahs de free-hôl)

bean patties

Pepita
pe-pi-ta
(peh-pee-tah)

seeds, usually pumpkin

Pequín
pe-quín
(peh-keén)

hot dried red chile

Perejil
pe-re-jil
(peh-reh-heel)

parsley

Petín
pe-tín
(pe-teen)

hot dried red chile

Pescado
pes-ca-do
(pehs-kah-tho)

fish

Pib, Pibil
pib, pib-il
(peeb, peeb-eel)

usually means barbequed

Picadillo
pi-ca-di-llo
(pee-kah-dee-yoh)

ground or shredded meat and potato mixture, similar to "hash" used for fillings and stuffings

Picante
pi-can-te
(pee-cahn-teh)

hot or spicy; sharply seasoned

Pilón
pi-lón
(pee-lóhn)

"something extra"; a free bag of pastries, given when one makes a large purchase; similar to "Baker's Dozen"

Piloncillo
pi-lon-ci-llo
(pee-lohn-see-yoh)

sugar cane

Piña
pi-ña
(pee-nyah)

pineapple

Piñata
pi-ña-ta
(pee-nyah-tah)

paper mache replicas of animals or other objects, filled with candies to be broken with a stick on festive occasions

Pinole
pi-no-le
(pee-noh-leh)

sweet thick drink made with cornmeal, sugar and cinnamon

Piñón
piñ-ón
(peen-yóhn)

pine nuts

Piñon Dulce
pin-on dul-ce
(peen-yóhn doól-seh)

nut brittle made with pinons

Piñon Nuts
(Pignolas)
pig-no-las
(peen-yoh-las)

small white nut grown in Arizona and New Mexico

Pipian
pi-pian
(pee-peeahn)

sauce of ground nuts, seeds or spices

Pisado
pi-sa-do
(pee-sah-tho)

dried chile, like the ancho

Plátano
plá-ta-no
(plá-tah-no)

banana

Platillo Fuerte
pla-ti-llo fuer-te
(pla-tee-yoh fuer-teh)

main course; "heavy plate"

Plaza
pla-za
(plah-sah)

central square, market

Poblano
po-bla-no
(poh-blah-noh)
(Fresh)

mild to medium hot dark green chile

Pollo
po-llo
(poh-yo)

chicken (not a hen)

Polvorones
pol-vo-ron-es
(pohl-voh-rohn-es)

"powder cakes"; a shortbread type cookie traditionally made with toasted flour, though not presently

Pomegranate
po-me-gran-a-te
(po-meh-gran-ah-teh)

a red fruit with edible seeds

Posole
po-so-le
(poh-soh-leh)

New Mexican holiday soup made with pork, hominy and pigs feet; served with red chile

Postre
pos-tre
(pohs-treh)

dessert

Puerco
puer-co
(pooehr-coh)

pork

Pulque
pul-que
(pool-keh)

fermented sap from a century plant, used like alcohol

Q

Quelitas
que-li-tas
(keh-lee-tahs)

"greens"; usually means the wild spinach in New Mexico

Quemada
que-ma-da
(keh-mah-tha)

burnt sugar candy

Quesadillas
que-sa-di-llas
(kehs-ah-dee-yahs)
a flat tortilla (corn or flour) with melted cheese (Arizona) or folded tortillas with cheese, chiles or beans, grilled or fried or baked; can also refer to raw masa which is filled like an empanada

Queso
que-so
(keh-so)
cheese

Queso Flameado
fla-mea-do
(flahm-eah-tho)
grilled cheese served in flour tortillas

Queso Fresco
fres-co
(frehs-coh)
native goat cheese made with rennet; more crumbly than cream cheese; salty, like feta

Queso Fundido
fun-di-do
(foon-dee-tho)
"forged" or melted cheese served with flour tortillas or tostados

R

Rajas
ra-jas
(rah-has)
strips of roasted, peeled chiles, sometimes with onions

Ranchero
ran-che-ro
(rahn-cheh-ro)
"country" style; cowboy style

Refritos
re-fri-tos
(reh-free-tôs)
refried

Relampagos
re-lam-pa-gos
(reh-lahm-pah-gos)
cookies

Relleno
re-lle-no
(reh-yeh-no)
stuffed

Reposterias
re-pos-ter-i-as
(reh-pos-ter-ee-yas)
sugar cookies

Requesones
re-que-son-es
(reh-keh-sohn-es)
whey cheese

Revolcada
re-vol-ca-da
(reh-vol-kah-dah)
a chocolate covered "semita," like a shortbread

Rio Grande
rí-o gran-de
(ree-oh grahn-deh)
(fresh)
a mild, New Mexican chile

Rojo
ro-jo
(roh-hoh)
red

Ropa Vieja
ro-pa vie-ja
(roh-pah vee-eh-ha)
a stew

Rosca
ros-ca
(ros-kah)
ring shaped cookie; popcorn ball

S

Sabroso
sa-bros-o
(sah-bros-oh)
tasty, delicious

Saffrón
saf-frón
(sahf-fróhn)
see Azafron

Salpicón
sal-pi-cón
(sahl-pee-cóhn)
shredded boiled meat or fish served in a cold vinaigrette usually with vegetables

Salsa
sal-sa
(sal-sah)
sauce

Salsa Cruda
sal-sa cru-da
(sal-sah cru-tha)
uncooked sauce (meaning not boiled)

Salsa Picante
sal-sa pi-can-te
(sal-sah pee-cahn-teh)
a very hot sauce, usually cooked (red or green)

Santaca
san-ta-ca
(sahn-tah-cah)
(Japanese)
very hot chile, #9 New Mexican

Seca
se-ca
(seh-ka)
dry

Semita
se-mi-ta
(seh-mee-tah)
an anise flavored pan de huevo or shortbread with nuts

Serrano
se-rra-no
(seh-rahn-o)
smallest green chile, very hot

Simpático
sim-pa-ti-co
(seem-pah-tee-coh)
agreeable, pleasant

Sonora Omelette
so-no-ra
(sohn-no-ra)
with sliced avocado, cheese and red chile sauce

Sonora Style
so-no-ra
(sohn-no-ra)
as in the State of Sonora (regional cooking style and ingredients)

Sopa
so-pa
(soh-pah)

soup with vegetables and meats; quite substantial; sometimes like a casserole or bread pudding

Sopaipilla
so-pai-pi-lla
(soh-pa-pee-ya)

puffed, fried bread; may be a yeast bread, though more commonly flour tortilla dough rolled, folded once and fried. Often stuffed with fillings and served with melted cheese or sauce. Some are sweet

Sopa Seca
so-pa se-ca
(soh-pah seh-kah)

an accompaniment, usually a starch dish like beans or rice

Sopes
so-pes
(soh-pehs)

a round, grilled tortilla, filled with various meats and beans

Sorbete
sor-be-te
(sor-beh-teh)

sherbet

Suizas
sui-zas
(swee-sahs)

"Swiss" style, meaning with dairy products and always sour cream. "Enchiladas Suizas" is enchiladas with sour cream in the sauce.

T

Tabasco
ta-bas-co
(tah-bas-coh)

hot chile

Taco
ta-co
(tah-koh)

"snack"; in most states a crisp, folded corn tortilla but can be corn or flour, soft or rolled or folded; breakfast tacos are usually flour (soft) filled with eggs, potatoes and meats (Texas)

Taco Grande
ta-co gran-de
(tah-koh grahn-deh)

large crisp corn or flour tortillas topped with meat or chicken; sometimes folded and grilled crisp and garnished with guacamole or red or green chile

Taco Sauce

green or red "salsa," usually cooked

Tacos al Carbón
ta-co al car-bón
(tah-koh al car-bóhn)

northern Mexico and Texas taco; a fresh flour tortilla filled with chunks of grilled skirt steaks; sometimes grilled

Tacos al Pastor
ta-co al pas-tor
(tah-koh al pahs-tor)

same dish as Tacos al Carbon, with corn tortillas (shepherd's style)

Taguito
ta-qui-to
(tah-kee-tõh)

rolled corn tortilla, about the size of a cigar

Tamal
ta-mal
(tah-mal)
Tamales
ta-ma-les
(tah-mah-lehs)

fresh masa, rolled in a corn husk, filled with sweet or savory fillings and steamed

Tamale Pie

similar to the ingredients in tamales, only made like a shepherd's pie, using the masa as a top and bottom crust; Spanish Omelettes (New Mexico); little pancakes

Tamalina
ta-ma-lin-a
(tah-mah-leen-ah)

a Texas term for fresh masa dough

Tampiqueña
tam-pi-queñ-a
(tahm-pee-kán-ya)
(carne a la)

tenderloin beef in "the style of tampiqueña"; grilled, served with rajas and an enchilada

Tapatias
ta-pa-ti-as
(tah-pah-tee-as)

flat fried corn tortillas, topped with beans, lettuce, tomatoes; West Texas term for something like a chalupa or tostado, sometimes soft tortilla

Tejolote
te-jo-lo-te
(teh-ho-lo-teh)

pestle for the molcajete

Tequila
te-qui-la
(teh-kee-lah)

alcohol made from maguey cactus plant

Ternera
ter-ner-a
(tehr-nehr-ah)

veal

Teswin
tes-win
(tehs-ween)

an Arizona drink made with white corn

Tomate
to-ma-te
(toh-ma-teh)

tomato

Tomate Verde
to-ma-te ver-de
(toh-ma-teh vehr-deh)

tomatillo

Tomatillo
to-ma-ti-llo
(toh-ma-tee-yo)

small husk-covered green tomato with a lemony flavor

Torrija
torr-i-ja
(tor-ee-ha)

French toast

Torta
tor-ta
(tor-tah)

"little cake"; sandwich made with bolillos; omelette (New Mexico); or flat cake of corn masa

Tortilla
tor-ti-lla
(tor-tee-yah)

corn or flour flat bread, from 7-18 inches

Tortilla Press

wood or iron "hinged press" to make perfect round corn tortillas

Tortillera
tor-ti-ller-a
(tor-tee-yer-ah)

woman who makes tortillas

Tostaditos
tos-ta-di-tos
(tohs-tah-thee-tos)

crisp fried corn tortilla chips

Tostado
tos-ta-do
(tohs-táh-tho)

flat, fried tortillas with meats, lettuce, tomatoes, beans piled on top with different garnishes; large flour tortilla, crisped, topped with melted cheese (also called a quesadilla)

Tostado "Del Rey"
del rey
(del ray)

large Sonora style tortilla fried and shaped to look like a crown filled with beef and trimmings

Totopos
to-to-pos
(toh-toh-pohs)

in Arizona, can be a crisp tortilla (usually flour) filled with chicken, lettuce, tomatoes (like a chalupa); like a "Mexican Chef Salad"; sometimes interchangeable with tostados

Trigo
tri-go
(tree-goh)

wheat

V

Verde
ver-de
(vehr-deh)

green

Verduras
ver-dur-as
(vehr-dhur-as)

vegetables

Vinagrete
vin-a-gre-te
(veen-ah-greh-teh)

oil and vinegar dressing

Y

Yerba Buena
yer-ba buen-a
(ee-air-bah booen-ah)

wild mint

MAIL ORDER SOURCES

California

El Nopalito #1
560 Santa Fe Drive
Encinitas, CA 92024

Don Juan Foods, Inc.
1715 Crows Landing Road
Modesto, CA 95351

Monterrey Food Products
3939 Brooklyn Avenue
Los Angeles, CA 90063

Colorado

Valdez Farms Natural Foods
P.O. Box 75
La Jara, CO 81140

Johnnie's Market
2030 Larimer Street
Denver, CO 80205

Illinois

La Preferida
91 South Water Market
Chicago, IL 60608

Minnesota

Morgan's Mexican-Lebanese Foods
736 South Robert Street
St. Paul, MN 55107

New Mexico

Tia Mia
P.O. Box 685
Sunland Park, NM 88063

Specialty Foods
Box 1269
San Juan Pueblo, NM 87566

New York

Moneo & Son, Inc.
Casa Moneo
210 West 14th Street
New York, NY 10011

Oklahoma

Nayphe's International
7519 North May Avenue
Oklahoma City, OK 73116

Texas

Horticulture Enterprises
P.O. Box 340082
Dallas, TX 75234

San Antonio Spice Company
P.O. Box 28125
San Antonio, TX 78228

Lazy Susan, Inc.
P.O. Box 10438
San Antonio, TX 78210

INDEX

D

E

F

INDEX

M

N

O

P

T

W

Z

V